Environmental Policy in India

This book systematically introduces historical trajectories and dynamics of environmental policy and governance in India.

Following the features of environmental policy in India as outlined in Chapter 1, subsequent chapters explore domestic and international factors that shape environmental policy in the country. The chapters examine the interplay between governmental and non-governmental actors, and the influence of social mobilisation and institutions on environmental policy and governance. Analysing various policy trajectories, the chapters identify and explore five central environmental policy subsystems: forests, water, climate, energy and city development. The authors drill down into the social, economic, political and ecological dimensions of each system, shedding light on why striking a balance between national economic growth and environmental sustainability is so challenging.

Drawing on political science theories of policy processes and related theoretical concepts, this innovative edited volume will be of great interest to students and scholars of environmental policy and politics and South Asian studies more broadly.

Natalia Ciecierska-Holmes is developing her PhD project focusing on gender and climate change adaptation in India. She graduated from the Euromaster programme with a degree in European Studies and Politics from the University of Bath, the Humboldt University Berlin and the Freie University Berlin. She has a background in linguistics, languages and politics and has developed a strong interest in environmental politics and governance in India.

Kirsten Jörgensen is a Senior Lecturer at the Department of Political and Social Sciences, Freie Universität Berlin. She received her PhD in 1996 at Freie Universität Berlin. Her primary fields of interest include comparative environmental politics, European and Indian environmental and climate policy as well as the role of subnational governance. She was coordinator of the Indian-European Multi-level Climate Governance Research Network.

Lana Laura Ollier is a PhD student at the ETH Zürich and works for the Institute for Advanced Sustainability Studies (IASS) in Potsdam. She graduated with a degree in Environmental Policy and Regulation from the London School of Economics and Political Science, and has a broad background in environmental politics, economics and law.

D. Raghunandan is the Director of the Centre for Technology & Development at the Society for Economic & Social Studies and the President of All India People's Science Network (AIPSN). He also volunteers with the Delhi Science Forum where he contributes to research and campaigns in the areas of Environment, Climate Change & Water Resources, Aerospace and Disarmament & Strategic Affairs. He currently leads the AIPSN campaign on climate change, conducts research and modelling exercises, and has published extensively in India and abroad with a focus on India's climate policy and international negotiations.

Routledge Studies in Environmental Policy

Environmental Policy and the Pursuit of Sustainability
Chelsea Schelly and Aparajita Banerjee

Green Keynesianism and the Global Financial Crisis
Kyla Tienhaara

Governing Shale Gas
Development, Citizen Participation and Decision Making in the US, Canada, Australia and Europe
Edited by John Whitton, Matthew Cotton, Ioan M. Charnley-Parry, Kathy Brasier

The Politics of Aquaculture
Sustainability Interdependence, Territory and Regulation in Fish Farming
Caitríona Carter

Strategic Designs for Climate Policy Instrumentation
Governance at the Crossroads
Gjalt Huppes

The Right to Nature
Social Movements, Environmental Justice and Neoliberal Natures
Edited by Elia Apostolopoulou and Jose A. Cortes-Vazquez

Guanxi and Local Green Development in China
The Role of Entrepreneurs and Local Leaders
Chunhong Sheng

Environmental Policy in India
Edited by Natalia Ciecierska-Holmes, Kirsten Jörgensen, Lana Laura Ollier and D. Raghunandan

For more information about this series, please visit: https://www.routledge.com/Routledge-Studies-in-Environmental-Policy/book-series/RSEP

Environmental Policy in India

Edited by Natalia Ciecierska-Holmes,
Kirsten Jörgensen, Lana Laura Ollier
and D. Raghunandan

First published 2020
by Routledge
2 Park Square, Milton Park, Abingdon, Oxon OX14 4RN

and by Routledge
52 Vanderbilt Avenue, New York, NY 10017

Routledge is an imprint of the Taylor & Francis Group, an informa business

© 2020 selection and editorial matter, Natalia Ciecierska-Holmes, Kirsten Jörgensen, Lana Laura Ollier and D. Raghunandan; individual chapters, the contributors

The right of Natalia Ciecierska-Holmes, Kirsten Jörgensen, Lana Laura Ollier and D. Raghunandan to be identified as the authors of the editorial material, and of the authors for their individual chapters, has been asserted in accordance with sections 77 and 78 of the Copyright, Designs and Patents Act 1988.

All rights reserved. No part of this book may be reprinted or reproduced or utilised in any form or by any electronic, mechanical, or other means, now known or hereafter invented, including photocopying and recording, or in any information storage or retrieval system, without permission in writing from the publishers.

Trademark notice: Product or corporate names may be trademarks or registered trademarks, and are used only for identification and explanation without intent to infringe.

British Library Cataloguing-in-Publication Data
A catalogue record for this book is available from the British Library

Library of Congress Cataloging-in-Publication Data
Names: Ciecierska-Holmes, Natalia, editor.
Title: Environmental policy in India / Edited by Natalia Ciecierska-Holmes, Kirsten Jörgensen, Lana Laura Ollier, and D. Raghunandan.
Description: Abingdon, Oxon; New York: Routledge, 2020. | Series: Routledge studies in environmental policy | Includes bibliographical references and index.
Identifiers: LCCN 2019040816 (print) | LCCN 2019040817 (ebook) | ISBN 9780367357658 (hardback) | ISBN 9780429341533 (ebook)
Subjects: LCSH: Environmental policy—India. | Environmental management—India. | Environmental protection—India. | India—Environmental conditions.
Classification: LCC HC440.E5 E59 2020 (print) | LCC HC440.E5 (ebook) | DDC 333.70954—dc23
LC record available at https://lccn.loc.gov/2019040816
LC ebook record available at https://lccn.loc.gov/2019040817

ISBN: 978-0-367-35765-8 (hbk)
ISBN: 978-0-429-34153-3 (ebk)

Typeset in Goudy
by codeMantra

Contents

List of authors and affiliations   vii
Acknowledgements   x

PART 1
Institutions and Actors   1

1 Introduction: environmental policy in India   3
NATALIA CIECIERSKA-HOLMES, KIRSTEN JÖRGENSEN,
LANA LAURA OLLIER AND D. RAGHUNANDAN

2 Environmental competencies in India's federal system   17
WILFRIED SWENDEN AND REKHA SAXENA

3 The role India's states play in environmental policymaking   39
KIRSTEN JÖRGENSEN

4 Civil society and state interaction in environment policy in India   60
SUNAYANA GANGULY

PART 2
Environmental policy subsystems in India   87

5 Forest governance in India: achieving balance within
a complex policy subsystem   89
SMRITI DAS

6 India: dilemmas of water governance   111
JOYEETA GUPTA AND RICHA TYAGI

Contents

7 Sustainable energy: prospects and challenges 133
KAUSHIK RANJAN BANDYOPADHYAY, MADHURA JOSHI AND
RAINER QUITZOW

8 Factors shaping the climate policy process in India 158
DENISE FERNANDES, KIRSTEN JÖRGENSEN AND N.C. NARAYANAN

9 Smart sustainable cities 174
SHALEEN SINGHAL AND SOURABH JAIN

PART 3
India within the context of global environmental governance 201

10 India's climate policy: Paris Agreement, NDC and after 203
D. RAGHUNANDAN

11 India's relations with the European Union on
environmental policy 225
DIARMUID TORNEY

12 Environmental politics in India: institutions, actors
and environmental governance 241
NATALIA CIECIERSKA-HOLMES AND KIRSTEN JÖRGENSEN

Index 259

Authors and affiliations

Kaushik Ranjan Bandyopadhyay is an Associate Professor with IIM Lucknow (IIML). Prior to joining IIML, he was principal policy adviser with International Institute of Sustainable Development (IISD) and has been leading the UNEP India Mission towards measuring SDG 12.c.1 on fossil fuel subsidy executed jointly with Ministry of Statistics and Programme Implementation, Government of India.

Natalia Ciecierska-Holmes is developing her PhD project focusing on gender and climate change adaptation in India. She graduated from the Euromaster programme with a degree in European Studies and Politics from the University of Bath, the Humboldt University Berlin and the Freie University Berlin. She has a background in linguistics, languages and politics, and has developed a strong interest in environmental politics and governance in India.

Smriti Das is an Associate Professor at the Department of Policy Studies, TERI School of Advanced Studies, New Delhi, India. Her research interests include public policy processes, institutions and resource politics, forest governance, decentralisation, gender and other cross-cutting issues at the interface of environment and development.

Denise Fernandes is a PhD candidate at the Environmental Studies Programme, University of Colorado, Boulder, USA. Denise holds a Master's in Sustainable Development Practice from TERI University, New Delhi and a Bachelor's in Political Science from St. Xavier's College, Mumbai, India. Her research focuses on climate and environmental justice and inequality, mitigation and adaptation, energy governance and policy initiatives in transitional countries specifically in India and South Asia.

Sunayana Ganguly is currently an Assistant Professor at the Azim Premji University in Bangalore. She received her PhD in Political Science from the Environmental Policy Research Centre Freie Universität Berlin. She has previously worked with the Industrial Ecology Group, University of Lausanne (Switzerland) and the German Development Institute (Bonn). Her work explores environmental governance, civil society, deliberative democracy and sustainable consumption with a focus on South Asia.

Authors and affiliations

Joyeeta Gupta is a Professor of Environment and Development in the Global South at the Amsterdam Institute for Social Science Research of the University of Amsterdam and UNESCO-IHE Institute for Water Education in Delft. She is currently co-chair of the Global Environmental Outlook being coordinated by United Nations Environment.

Sourabh Jain is currently pursuing his doctorate from the Department of Energy and Environment at TERI University, New Delhi, India. His PhD research work focuses on analysing resource efficiency in urban built environment in Indian cities, with a focus on construction and demolition waste management and recycling. His research interests include life cycle analysis, optimisation of circular supply chain, and mathematical modelling of complex systems.

Kirsten Jörgensen is a Senior Lecturer at the Department of Political and Social Sciences, Freie Universität Berlin. She received her PhD in 1996 at Freie Universität Berlin. Her primary fields of interest include comparative environmental politics, European and Indian environmental and climate policy as well as the role of subnational governance. She was coordinator of the Indian-European Multi-level Climate Governance Research Network.

Madhura Joshi leads the work on energy access, green jobs and climate policy work at the Natural Resources Defence Council's India-Program. She has a graduate degree in International Political Economy from the London School of Economics, UK, and an undergraduate degree in Political Science from St. Xavier's College. Her research interests include pathways of sustainable energy transitions in developing countries; energy poverty; energy and climate change governance; and co-benefits-based participatory approaches to climate, energy and development policy-making.

N. C. Narayanan is a Professor at the Centre for Technology Alternatives for Rural Areas (CTARA), IIT Bombay; an associate faculty of the Interdepartmental Programme on Climate Change; and a member of the core faculty group in the newly formed Centre for Policy Studies in IIT Bombay. His research areas are technology and development, public policy process (water reforms and climate change), scaling up technology alternatives and political ecology of resource use.

Lana Laura Ollier is a PhD student at the ETH Zürich and works for the Institute for Advanced Sustainability Studies (IASS) in Potsdam. She graduated in Environmental Policy and Regulation from the London School of Economics and Political Science, and has a broad background in environmental politics, economics and law.

Rainer Quitzow is a Senior Research Associate at the Institute for Advanced Sustainability Studies and a Senior Lecturer in Innovation Economics at the Technische Universität Berlin. He holds a Doctorate in Political Science from the Freie Universität Berlin. His research focuses on sustainable innovation, industrial policy, and governance of the energy transition in Germany and beyond. In particular, he has focused on the internationalisation of emerging renewable energy industries and the changing role of emerging economies in this context.

D. Raghunandan is the Director of the Centre for Technology & Development at the Society for Economic & Social Studies and the President of All India People's Science Network (AIPSN). He also volunteers with the Delhi Science Forum where he contributes to research and campaigns in the areas of Environment, Climate Change & Water Resources, Aerospace and Disarmament & Strategic Affairs. He currently leads the AIPSN campaign on climate change, conducts research and modelling exercises, and has published extensively in India and abroad with a focus on India's climate policy and international negotiations.

Rekha Saxena is a Full Professor at the Department of Political Science, University of Delhi. She did her graduation and postgraduation from Hindu College, and MPhil and PhD from the Department of Political Science, University of Delhi. She started her teaching career from St. Stephen's College. She specialises in the study of Indian and comparative politics with special reference to federal political institutions, constitution, centre–state relations, federalism, elections and party system.

Shaleen Singhal is a Professor at TERI School of Advanced Studies and had been a Visiting Fulbright Professor at Yale University in 2018. He is an architect-planner with a PhD on City Competitiveness that received the Global 2009 Emerald/EFMD award for outstanding doctoral research. His research work and publications lay emphasis on the sustainable redevelopment in cities, ecology-based urban planning, and effective policy and governance for cities in emerging economies like India.

Wilfried Swenden is an Associate Professor/Senior Lecturer in Politics and Co-Director of the Centre for South Asian Studies at the University of Edinburgh. He has worked extensively on multi-level governance and federalism in Europe and South Asia. He recently (2017) completed a Leverhulme International network grant on Continuity and Change in Indian Federalism involving three UK-based and three India-based universities.

Richa Tyagi works as an independent consultant on environmental law and policy in New Delhi. She has worked with organisations like WWF India in the past. She holds an LLB degree from Campus Law Centre, Faculty of Law, University of Delhi and B.A. (Hons.) English from Lady Shri Ram College, University of Delhi. Her interest lies in looking at the intersection of law and conservation of natural resources in the Indian landscape.

Diarmuid Torney is an Assistant Professor in the School of Law and Government at Dublin City University, Ireland. He holds an MPhil and a DPhil (PhD) in International Relations from the University of Oxford. His research focuses on the global politics of climate change and energy, particularly in the European Union, China and India.

Acknowledgements

This book is a product of European–Indian academic exchange and collaboration, and it stems from the sense that there is need for publications about India's environmental policy, both in classrooms and in research contexts. Our thanks go to the authors of the book for their valuable input. We are also grateful to the undergraduate and graduate students at the Freie Universität Berlin, TERI School of Advanced Studies, New Delhi, and Indian Institute of Technology Bombay, Mumbai, who helped to start this book project in the autumn of 2016 and were involved in the first round of reviewing the book chapters in 2017. The book has greatly benefited from insights, inputs and critiques of scholars from the larger comparative environmental politics community and experts on the ground. Funding for the student exchange and workshops was provided by the German Academic Exchange Service (DAAD). Support for the Indian-European Multi-level Climate Governance Research Network (IECGN) came from the Indian Council of Social Science Research (ICSSR, India), the Deutsche Forschungsgemeinschaft (DFG, Germany) and the Netherlands Organisation for Scientific Research (NWO, The Netherlands).

Part 1
Institutions and Actors

1 Introduction

Environmental policy in India

Natalia Ciecierska-Holmes, Kirsten Jörgensen, Lana Laura Ollier and D. Raghunandan

In light of India's rapidly growing economy, environmental policy has become a pressing issue for the country. India's economic liberalisation started in 1991 and has at times triggered double-digit growth rates. Rapid economic growth, industrialisation, growing energy needs, urbanisation and changing consumption patterns are putting increasing pressure on India's natural resources, livelihoods in forest and rural areas, and the quality of air and water. They are also posing health risks.

There are a variety of academic contributions that provide insights into Indian environmental regulation and policy (Chopra 2017a; Jasanoff 1993; Rajamani 2007; Ramesh 2015; Reich and Bowonder 1992). Yet, further insights are needed from a public policy perspective, which helps us to gain a deeper understanding of policy stasis and change, stable and shifting policy paradigms and how that matters, the role played by governments, public administration, legislators, civil society actors, the corporate sector and research in environmental policy. This book offers a fresh perspective by considering environmental policymaking in India in terms of its historic, domestic and international contexts.

The chapters shed light both on the factors that shape India's environmental policy and performance today, and on the dynamics and mechanisms that have been driving policy change over the past four to five decades. In particular, the authors examine the interplay between governmental and non-governmental actors and institutions that are shaping and have shaped environmental governance in India. Their analyses highlight the social, economic and ecological challenges arising from the apparent contradictions between economic growth and environmental sustainability.

Many of the problems India faces as an emerging economy are similar to those faced in industrial countries. However, India's rapid economic growth, and to some extent an environmental race-to-the-bottom, together with population growth, poverty, inadequate infrastructures and social services put pressure on India's natural environment. India ranked 130 among 189 countries in the Human Development Index 2018 (United Nations Development Programme 2018). Nevertheless, economic development also provides the country with opportunities towards a more environmentally sustainable future particularly lying in technological innovation and environmental leapfrogging. Moreover, as we show in the remainder of this book, opportunities for socially inclusive and environmentally sustainable development trajectories also lie in India's vibrant civil society and international cooperation.

The following section sets a frame for this book by showing how environmental policy first emerged as a policy field in India and explores the main characteristics that shape India's environmental policy landscape. Then, the theoretical undercurrents that shape the book's chapters are introduced before presenting an outline of the book's structure.

1.1 The emergence of environmental policy in India

Looking back to the time before the emergence of India's environmental policy, environmental regulation was sparse and fragmented during the first postcolonial phase between 1947 and 1968. Environmental policy first appeared on India's political agenda after the first United Nations Conference on the Human Environment in 1972. This conference gave the initial impulse for the incumbent Prime Minister Indira Gandhi to first develop the field of environmental policy in India. Shortly after the conference, a few environmental regulations and government institutions were established, with India becoming one of the first countries in the world to institutionalise its environmental policy by creating a designated ministry for the environment in 1980. However, it remained largely a symbolic effort and it was not until the devastating industrial disaster in Bhopal in 1984 that the involvement of governmental, civil society and private sector actors in the field increased. This is akin to a number of industrialised countries, in which environmental problems were first addressed in an issue-specific manner as a direct result of environmental catastrophes. The chemical accident in Bhopal in 1984 or the large-scale forest depletion in Germany in the 1980s provides noticeable examples. While industrialised countries continue to move from an end-of-pipe approach towards a pre-emptive policy approach, which regulates pollution at the source, this process has been much slower in India. Following the country's economic liberalisation in the 1990s, environmental issues slowly started to move on to the political agenda.

However, environmental policy and performance in India at the start of the 1990s faced the issues of "bureaucratic inflexibility, unreasonable standards, lax monitoring and enforcement, lengthy court cases" (Jasanoff 1993, 37). In 2018, India had plummeted in the Environmental Performance Index which ranked India among the bottom five countries. Among 180 countries, India had dropped 36 points from rank 141 in 2016 to 177 in 2018 (Wendling *et al.* 2018).

1.2 Features of Indian environmental politics

Indian environmental politics is characterised by a range of features, which will resurface throughout this book. Such features include *institutions*, such as India's centralised federal system, colonial legacies and path dependencies, the impacts of economic liberalisation, neo-liberal growth strategies, and the carbon lock-in of

India's energy economy. Other features are related to *actors* and *ideas*, such as the outstanding importance of the civil society; the different development frames of environmental and climate policy, which include social equity and justice; and the persistent growth first paradigm. Further features are presented by the relevance of forests as *livelihoods* and India's cautious approaches to environmental *leapfrogging*. India's rising importance as an *international player* in climate policy and bilateral relations is significant in various environmental governance contexts.

1.2.1 Institutions

As in many federal systems, such as Germany and the USA, the central government took the lead during the initial phases (starting in the 1970s) of the development of environmental policy. Initially, environmental protection was only hesitantly placed on India's governmental agenda in India's Fourth Five-Year Plan (FYP) (1969–1974), which addressed the challenges and the need for action (Chopra 2017b). Environmental degradation and pollution, soil erosion, water scarcity, and water and air pollution put increased pressure on the government "to accommodate new environmental demands while simultaneously guaranteeing economic growth" (Agrawal and Yokozuka 2002, 240).

But India's unique actor landscape also provides vast opportunities for bottom-up environmental action, testing, experimentation and scale-up in the multi-tiered political system, which includes India's subnational states, the Union territories, cities and rural panchayats (Jörgensen et al. 2015). However, this potential for environmental multilevel governance has not been significantly utilised. India's environmental policymaking and the interplay between national, state and local administrative levels quite often lacked efficacy (Agrawal and Yokozuka 2002). So far, there is also no indication that India's state governments are going to fill the gap by taking environmental protection more seriously by pioneering environmentally sustainable development. That said, it was India's court system, civil society and government entrepreneurs that oftentimes contributed to bringing environmental problems onto the agenda.

Across diverse environmental policy areas, such as forests, water, industry and international climate policy, there are noticeable *legacies of colonial rule* in India's environmental institutions and politics. This concerns India's role at an international level as well as the citizen-state relationship in India. When environmental policy in India emerged in a top-down manner, it was perceived by non-governmental actors as a "neo-colonial" mode of governance that denied citizens simple participatory rights (Jasanoff 1993, 38).

It is not just industrialised economies that have become *locked-into* fossil fuel-based energy systems. Rapidly industrialising countries, such as India, are also beset by technical and institutional *path dependencies*, such as the carbon lock-in, which inhibit environmental and climate protection. A coal-based energy mix combined with a low financial capacity, plus the presence of strong capital and emission-intensive industries, as found in India and China, for example, impedes the transition of the energy sector to a low-carbon economy (Never and Betz 2014).

Coal continues to play an important role in India, and current projections also show an increased usage of coal energy.

Another feature that reoccurs throughout this book is the impact of the *global neoliberal* turn and the effects of the neoliberal economic policy paradigm in India on employment, poverty eradication, social equality and rural development. In the 1990s, neoliberal policies partially diffused in India and were further promoted under the Hindu Nationalist Party influence after 1998. Neoliberal economic rules, such as freedom of markets, deregulation and privatisation, tend to conflict with environmental policy and put pressure on natural resources through exploitation (Harvey 2005). In India, as in other developing countries, the primacies of deregulation and privatisation made it harder to develop sustainable forest and water governance practices and to maintain livelihoods in the forest and mountain areas. Liberalisation in India was often implemented regardless of negative effects on the environment, labour and infrastructures (Bhaduri and Nayyar 1996).

1.2.2 Actors and ideas

Civil society has always played an important role in governing India's development. However, in the 21st century, more groups, interests and organisations are actively influencing India's policy processes (Sil 2014). Environmental activism has become more important and is concerned with a variety of issues. In rural areas, significant activity occurs around environmental disasters; governance for sustainable development, e.g., afforestation programs; and mobilisation against industrial projects threatening the environment and livelihoods. In urban areas, supportive networks disseminating information and carrying out research became more important (Agrawal and Yokozuka 2002, 251). The influence of civil society actors is significant in the framing of policies, in emerging policy paradigms and in policy implementation.

As in other countries, rapid industrialisation and establishment of heavy industry became the centrepiece of India's development policy in the 1960s, thereby subordinating environmental conservation (Chopra 2017a). Indian environmental policy has traditionally been shaped, and continues to be shaped, by the *growth first paradigm*. Following the trajectory of the Environmental Kuznets Curve, the "growth first" paradigm assumes that economic growth first increases pollution and then, as per capita income rises, decreases pollution thanks to the implementation of environmental policy (Stern 2004). This seemed to portray the dominant thinking about environmental policy in India. Economic growth and environmentally sustainable development have traditionally been pitted against each other as opposing ends of the debate on environmental policy. The imperative of India's "growth first" paradigm remained quite unchanged for many decades and subordinated environmental issues including climate change once the phenomenon gained salience (Dubash 2013). This has created an effective barrier for India to follow ambitious environmental policies on a national as well as international level. Moreover, the growth first mantra has prevented India from constructing its own paradigm to promote environmental policies, in general, and climate policies, in particular – an issue that is also faced by other emerging economies. During the 1970s, actors from the industrial sector, large- and medium-sized farms, and India's middle class were not supportive of environmental protection measures and not willing to bear the costs thereof (Agrawal and Yokozuka 2002). In the 21st century, new advocacy coalitions emerged for protecting the climate and the concept of co-benefits of climate mitigation has become an instrument for identifying social and economic win-win options of greenhouse gas mitigation. However, green economy proponents are still in a weak position in India's government, political parties, in the corporate sector and civil society. India's rural actors and communities, rooted in traditional customs and practice, are critical of aggressive economic growth strategies and were considered as proponents for sustainable development (Jasanoff 1993). However, they were unable to significantly change India's industrialisation agenda.

1.2.3 Livelihoods and social inclusiveness

Many people in India are still directly dependent on natural resources for their subsistence. Large sections of the population still inhabit forests or mountainous regions and are directly affected by environmental degradation but also regulation. Thus, in an international comparative perspective, social, economic and ecological functions of the forests, such as livelihood and natural resources, are of special importance in India's forest policy. Social justice and the land rights of forest people are major and recurring neglected issues (Kashwan 2017). Both before and after India's independence, forest policy has been a very important policy subsystem, and the national government has taken on a central role. However, actor constellations have changed recurrently since the 1970s. Varying actor groups, including NGOs, forest dwellers, international donors and actors from the corporate sector, gained access to the policy subsystem. Domestic forest governance is tasked with questions of social justice concerns and customary rights, as well as reconciling environmental aims with social justice and taming economic interests that threaten to undermine the social and ecological dimensions of sustainable forest governance. More broadly, socially inclusive environmental governance has been pursued as a strategy in tangent with decentralisation and participation to empower the local levels and give voice to those formerly excluded from policymaking.

1.2.4 Environmental leapfrogging

Since its independence, India has been consistently committed to technological development (Jasanoff 1993). Under Nehru, a state-governed innovation system for growth was created, which aimed to develop large-scale industrial infrastructures and respective technologies, putting India on a high-carbon development path (Joseph et al. 2014). Since the end of the 1980s, the emergence of India's renewable energy policy framework has opened up opportunities for low-carbon development and increased the scope of environmental leapfrogging.

The discussion about environmental leapfrogging points to the opportunities for developing countries to bypass the phases of fossil fuel-based infrastructure development which shaped economic trajectories in developed countries after the industrial revolution, and to leapfrog to cleaner and greener technologies from the outset (Perkins 2003). Opportunities for environmental leapfrogging in India lie, for example, in renewable energy, smart technologies applied in the context of urbanisation, infrastructure development, transportation and the farming sector. Ideas, such as sustainable development or green growth, generally build on the idea of leapfrogging and point to the potentials lying in technology development and transfer. Since policy learning and technological leapfrogging are important in the context of the Paris climate agreement, these concepts remain pertinent for ongoing research and debate. In addition to discussing technological leapfrogging (see Chapters 3, 7 and 9), the opportunities for institutional leapfrogging through policy learning are also addressed.

1.2.5 India in the context of global environmental governance

Finally, these features would be incomplete without reference to India's rising importance as an *international player* in the global environmental governance system and particularly in the context of climate policy. India's position in the global environmental governance arena has historically been shaped by the North-South debate and the equity principle (Jasanoff 1993). However, India is a global power exerting leadership not only in the context of developing countries but also in the global climate governance system. This feature is explored more specifically in the final chapters of this book.

1.3 Theoretical concepts

In addition to the features that are shaping India's environmental politics, we have selected four theoretical concepts as linking threads, which piece these chapters together and connect description and analysis to theories of the policy process. These are **policy subsystems, policy paradigms, policy change** and **path dependence**. The following sections provide a brief overview of the aforementioned concepts.

1.3.1 Policy subsystems

Policy subsystems emerge around specific policy topics and include actors, which directly or indirectly influence policy processes (Jenkins-Smith *et al.* 2017). The policy subsystem perspective views policymaking as dynamic. Policymakers, as well as a range of other actors with different interests, shape these processes (Howlett *et al.* 2009). Policy subsystems often remain relatively stable over extensive periods of time, with only incremental policy changes. This continuity is brought about by stable institutional factors, actor constellations and governing ideas (Howlett *et al.* 2009).

In India, just like in other countries, environmental policy deals with a large and ever-increasing range of different issues such as quality of air, water, and soil; waste management; protection of nature and forests; and climate change. Due to this heterogeneity, environmental policymaking is becoming more and more specialised, and divided into different policy subsystems. One pertinent example of a policy subsystem is India's forest policy, which existed long before the advent of environmental policy itself. The chapters of this book focus on different policy subsystems related to environmental protection, such as conservation of water and energy, protection of climate and forest, and city development. Viewing issues through the lens of subsystems enable us first to differentiate between environmentally relevant matters and regulatory areas and second to identify the respective set of actors involved in the policy processes and to shed light on their policy beliefs, ideas and interests.

1.3.2 Policy paradigms

Periods of policy stability are marked by relatively stable actor configurations (Sabatier 1988) that have developed a certain consensus "surrounding a policy and the ideas it is based upon" (Hogan and Howlett 2015, 5). "When ideas are widely shared by an entire policy community, they can be called a paradigm" (Baumgartner 2013, 251). Ideas in one policy paradigm differ from those found in another (Hogan and Howlett 2015); however, they are not necessarily incommensurate (Carstensen 2015). Policy paradigms are also mutable and can encompass new ideas. The concept of *policy paradigms*, however, is not without its drawbacks; it has not been used uniformly in policy research, but rather defined and operationalised in many different ways (Wilder 2015). The translation of policy paradigms and ideas into policy cannot be automatically assumed, but it requires empirical investigation (Daigneault 2015).

In this book, the policy paradigm concept helps to shed light on the trajectories of ideas in India's environmental policy subsystems, which are explored in the chapters, considering, among others, the debates about new forms of forest governance, water issues, the co-benefits of climate policy, green growth, and bilateral relations with other countries. Policy ideas are not only challenged in times of crisis but also over a longer period by alternative ideas (Hogan and Howlett 2015). The role of domestic actor constellations, international influences and knowledge in the context of paradigmatic shifts are discussed from the 1970s until today.

1.3.3 Policy change

Based on the assumption that ideas matter and are influential in shaping processes of policy change, policy changes are often connected to changes in the underlying policy paradigms (Hogan and Howlett 2015). While policy continuity can be explained by the strengths of consensus, policy change is rather explained by learning and argumentative discourse. Truly path-breaking changes usually occur as a result of external shocks; however, policy change can also occur as a result of incremental changes over a longer period of time (Rayner 2015, 77). Incremental changes can, for example, occur on the basis of policy-oriented learning, which leads to minor policy changes over an extended period of time (Jenkins-Smith *et al.* 2017).

Environmental policy emerged in different phases in India, which were predominantly marked by stasis, incremental change and occasionally by radical policy changes. Incremental and more radical policy departures from the status quo can be explained by various conditions. One condition under which major policy change is likely to occur is a change in political power relations (Jenkins-Smith *et al.* 2017). A change in the government can open a policy window and offer an opportunity to policy entrepreneurs to place a new proposal on the political agenda. Another is salient events, such as the chemical accident in Bhopal in 1984; this health and environmental disaster placed environmental protection on India's political agenda. Such events can enforce policy processes, modify the political agenda and increase the likelihood that new policies are adopted. Moreover, major policy change can stem from perturbations, such as change in the socioeconomic conditions outside the policy subsystem, regime change, spill-over that occurs from other policy subsystems, and extreme events. Internal policy subsystem events, such as crises, scandals and failure, are also expected to influence debates within the subsystem. However, a salient event or other perturbation might only be a necessary but not sufficient condition; policy change might not occur unless there are actors and mobilising forces to capitalise on the opportunity (Jenkins-Smith *et al.* 2017). As the chapters of this book demonstrate, international factors play a major role in fostering policy change.

1.3.4 Path dependence

Of course, historical conditions do affect future political decision-making (Howlett *et al.* 2009). In some cases, however, it goes beyond that and the policy progress stagnates, whereby current policy decisions reaffirm decisions made in the past, constraining any sort of change (Howlett *et al.* 2009). In some cases, which are explored further in this book, such tendencies have also become apparent in Indian environmental policy. Such a process is most commonly referred to as a path dependency. The lock-into fossil fuel-based energy and transportation systems are examples of a path dependence. Unruh (2000) introduced the concept of "carbon lock-in" to depict ways in which mutually re-enforcing path dependencies of technologies, institutions, and societal norms can constrain climate mitigation policies. Distinguishing between stability to path dependency and the factors that have potentially led to a self-reaffirming policy is an important element in most of the chapters that consider subsystems in this book.

1.4 The structure of the book

This book is divided into three sections. The first section provides a broader overview of the context of environmental politics and policymaking in India. The second section splits into specific policy subsystems, including forest management, water governance, sustainable energy, climate policy and sustainable cities. Finally, in the third section, India's environmental and climate policy is situated within the international context.

1.4.1 Section 1: institutions & actors

Wilfried Svenden and **Rekha Saxena** discuss the political institutions, which set the rules for governmental and non-governmental actors for environmental policy. This chapter sketches the federal backdrop for the division of decision-making power and interplay between the Union Government, India's states and the local level. Despite centralised environmental policy, the dependence on states for policy implementation highlights the significance of intergovernmental collaboration and joint decision-making. The authors, however, point to the remaining limitations for states to co-shape federal environmental policy. For example, consensus and antagonism in the two chambers of India's national parliament, India's bicameral legislature, the Lok Sabha and the Raj Sabha chamber impede and obstruct India's environmental policymaking. A particular focus is also placed on the influence of India's judiciary on the dynamics of environmental governance.

Kirsten Jörgensen looks at India's subnational states which are becoming more important policymakers due to India's changing political economy, economic liberalisation and related decentralisation. The role they play in the country's environmental, climate and green energy governance is slowly changing from that of mere executioner of policy to policymaker in their own right. The states' environmental performance in the traditional areas of environmental pollution control is weak, the political-administrative capacity building is limited, and there is also indication of an environmental race to the bottom. On the other hand, in a few cases, state governments have developed innovative approaches to stimulate green development and create favourable investment conditions. Solar and wind energy deployments in various states provide evidence of this. In doing so, they not only support technological leapfrogging but also facilitate the co-benefit of environmental leapfrogging as a side-effect. India's states only occasionally pioneer green policy innovations and engender others to follow them.

Progressing down to the grassroots level, **Sunayana Ganguly** sheds light on the role of civil society groups in Indian environmental policymaking. While tensions outlined in the previous two chapters between the centralised approaches of the state and actions of the subnational level also manifest in state-society interactions, these interactions are more complex than simply opposing factions. The chapter considers how the organisational structures and actions of civil society movements have changed in India from post-independence to the present day. Moreover, the author's typology of Civil Society Organisations (CSOs) offers a framework for their strategies regarding the state. CSOs have been able to influence the evolution of state policies through partnerships and advocacy, while the state has also played a role in balancing and negotiating both global and domestic demands.

1.4.2 Section 2: policy subsystems

In the second part of the book, contributions follow the underlying theoretical conceptions of path dependence, policy paradigms and policy change within the contexts of different subsystems. These chapters present some of the most pertinent areas required to understand environmental policymaking in India today.

Smriti Das highlights the paradigmatic policy shifts which have occurred in Indian forest policy over the past three decades. Das depicts a shift from centralisation – a legacy from the colonial era – towards more inclusive and democratic forest governance, which manifested in the National Forest Policy of 1988 and the Forest Rights Act of 2006. The chapter presents the complex dynamics at play in Indian forest governance, such as the role of forests as livelihoods, economic interest and the politics of land-use change, social mobilisation, knowledge, international factors and the role of India's forest bureaucracy. Subsequently, the author traces developments in Indian forest governance from the colonial period through the post-development phase after 1980 to the Forest Rights Act and its implementation. The complexity of the forest policy subsystem today is marked by entrenched actor networks who are resistant to change, as well as new networks of actors attempting to drive policy change forward. Emphasising the importance of forests as a resource, the chapter provides readers with the most relevant regulations governing forest use in India and outlines the interactions between agencies and actor networks governing forestry in India.

The chapter by **Joyeeta Gupta** and **Richa Tyagi** presents Indian water governance from a historical perspective and highlights present-day challenges in the current dimensions of Indian water law and policy within its wider organisational structure. The challenges in Indian water governance run deep and relate to conceptions of the nature of water itself, what types of water are to be governed, approaches to governing water, administrative issues and legal ownership and scales of policy programmes. Three key challenges are the multi-sectoral impact of water, water control in terms of public-private actors and fragmented governance. Subsequently, they bridge these findings to prospective visions and the future direction of water governance in the country. This requires Indian policymakers to consider the short-term emphasis on industrial growth and end-of-pipe water strategies. It becomes apparent that the water subsystem is very much interconnected across all sectors, which requires an integrated approach to align policies across energy, agriculture, industry, transport and environment.

The concept of leapfrogging has thus far received the greatest attention within a technological context, as the chapter written on sustainable energy by **Kaushik Bandyopadhyay, Madhura Joshi** and **Rainer Quitzow** shows. Their chapter provides readers with an overview of sustainable energy initiatives in India and outlines how these initiatives interact with, and are influenced by, the broader scope of energy and environmental policy in India. In light of upcoming energy, demographic, economic and infrastructural changes in India, as well as sustainable energy challenges regarding universal energy access, governance and security highlight the herculean task of decarbonisation. Large-scale infrastructure investments are still needed to leapfrog into a low-carbon energy system, while the authors also emphasise the careful negotiation between economic, environmental and social objectives and challenges to enable sustainable energy transitions.

Denise Fernandes, **Kirsten Jörgensen** and **N.C. Narayanan** show that India's climate change policy subsystem evolved against the background of rapid economic growth, poverty eradication and approaches to a low-carbon economy, the latter influenced by the international climate governance system. Since the early 1990s, the growth first paradigm and climate equity have played an important role in framing India's climate policy. Taking shape during three different phases, India's domestic climate policy framework was first triggered by an emerging domestic advocacy coalition and impulses from the international climate processes. The modification of India's initial climate policy paradigm has left more room for new ideas and development strategies, such as the co-benefits of climate policy, renewable energy technologies and environmental leapfrogging.

Shaleen Singhal and **Sourabh Jain** explore how the idea of rendering cities sustainable is envisioned in Indian urban planning processes. The chapter introduces national policy frameworks for sustainable city and smart city development, and provides insights into the role of bottom-up and local initiatives. Indian cities face challenges regarding rapid urbanisation, lacking essential infrastructure, social exclusion, environmental pollution and the impact of climate change. National urban policy frameworks, such as India's Smart Cities Mission from 2014, are also not significantly concerned with strengthening local urban policy capacities. Smart city approaches not only run the risk of promoting "corporate cities" (Hollands 2015), but they also provide significant potential for bottom-up innovation, democratic participation and environmental leapfrogging towards highly efficient, low-carbon and smart technologies. India's current Smart Cities Mission does not yet unleash the full potential for local capacity building and environmental leapfrogging, so still there is scope for future improvements to be made.

1.4.3 Section 3: international context

In addition to looking at the environmental policy system in India from a domestic perspective, the book also considers how it is shaped by international developments. Therefore, the third part of the book addresses environmental and climate policymaking in India within an international context.

Developing upon the different phases of India's climate policy discussed in Chapter 8 in this volume, **D. Raghunandan** provides a detailed examination of both international and domestic climate policies in India. The chapter looks at the development of India's position in international relations and highlights the geopolitical context relevant for India's negotiating stance in international climate fora since the 1990s, as well as its changing climate position from Copenhagen onwards. Questions regarding climate justice regarding the Paris Agreements are raised, particularly regarding the undermining of the "polluter pays" principle by disregarding historical emissions. Looking at the run up to the Paris

Summit in 2015, the chapter provides an analysis of the policy outputs of India's Nationally Determined Contributions (NDC) across various sectors, including energy, forestry, transport and biofuels. Recent developments show the softening of environmental regulation pursued by the present government led by the Bharatiya Janata Party (BJP) actually hampers climate policy.

Diarmuid Torney discusses the long-standing diplomatic relationship between India and the European Union (EU). Over the period since the mid-2000s, environmental issues, including climate change, have occupied a growing place on the agenda of this bilateral relationship, including in joint declarations on climate change and related themes issued at the India-EU summits of 2005, 2008, 2016 and 2017. This chapter traces the development of relations between India and the EU in these policy spheres. It argues that cooperation between India and the EU has been constrained by the somewhat problematic development of the broader India-EU relationship, which was characterised by significant tensions and conflicting priorities on a range of issues. It argues that conflicting climate and environmental policy paradigms between India and the EU constrained fruitful cooperation. However, recent years have seen a gradual convergence of policy paradigms. It is too early to judge the impact of this convergence, but indications from the 2016 and 2017 India-EU summits suggest a more fruitful era of cooperation may be underway.

The final chapter written by **Ciecierska Holmes** and **Jörgensen** discusses the findings of the book chapters against the background of comparative politics literature. Drawing on two strands of literature – Indian politics and comparative environmental politics – it reflects on linkages between India's domestic institutions, actor constellations and international factors with environmental policy as they are significant in the book chapters. Following the structure of this book, it first reflects how centralisation and decentralisation, lacking empowerment of the local level, the transition of the party system, democratic institutions and the judiciary and political-administrative capacity matter in environmental policy. It also considers the role of actor constellations, particularly the role of India's civil society, in policy change. Third, it zooms in on three aspects addressed in the chapters about the policy subsystems forests, water, city development, energy and climate: the importance of livelihoods and social inclusiveness, the potentials of environmental leapfrogging and noticeable shifts in dominant policy paradigms. The third section connects Indian environmental policy with international environmental politics. More recent developments in India's environmental politics after the governmental change in 2014 are considered.

References

Agrawal, A., and Yokozuka, N., 2002. Environmental Capacity-Building: India's Democratic Politics and Environmental Management. *In*: H. Weidner, M. Jänicke, and H. Jörgens, eds. *Capacity Building in National Environmental Policy. A Comparative Study of 17 Countries*. Berlin, New York: Springer.

Baumgartner, F.R., 2013. Ideas and Policy Change. *Governance*, 26 (2), 239–258. 10.1111/gove.12007.

Bhaduri, A., and Nayyar, D., 1996. *The Intelligent Person's Guide to Liberalization.* New Delhi, Toronto: Penguin.
Carstensen, M.B., 2015. Bringing Ideational Power into the Paradigm Approach: Critical Perspectives on Policy Paradigms in Theory and Practice. In: J. Hogan and M. Howlett, eds. *Policy Paradigms in Theory and Practice. Discourses, Ideas and Anomalies in Public Policy Dynamics.* Basingstoke: Palgrave Macmillan, 295–318.
Chopra, K., 2017a. Climate Change Policy in India. In: K. Chopra, ed. *Development and Environmental Policy in India. The Last Few Decades.* Singapore: Springer Singapore, 27–35.
Chopra, K., ed., 2017b. *Development and Environmental Policy in India. The Last Few Decades.* Singapore: Springer Singapore.
Daigneault, P.-M., 2015. Can you Recognize a Paradigm When You See One? Defining and Measuring Paradigmatic Shift. In: J. Hogan and M. Howlett, eds. *Policy Paradigms in Theory and Practice. Discourses, Ideas and Anomalies in Public Policy Dynamics.* Basingstoke: Palgrave Macmillan, 43–60.
Dubash, N.K., 2013. The Politics of Climate Change in India: Narratives of Equity and Co-benefits. *Wiley Interdisciplinary Reviews: Climate Change*, 4 (3), 191–201.
Harvey, D., 2005. *Brief History of Neoliberalism.* Oxford: Oxford University Press.
Hogan, J., and Howlett, M., eds., 2015. *Policy Paradigms in Theory and Practice. Discourses, Ideas and Anomalies in Public Policy Dynamics.* Basingstoke: Palgrave Macmillan.
Hollands, R.G., 2015. Critical Interventions into the Corporate Smart City. *Cambridge Journal of Regions, Economy and Society*, 8 (1), 61–77.
Howlett, M., Perl, A., and Ramesh, M., 2009. *Studying Public Policy. Policy Cycles & Policy Subsystems.* 3rd ed. Don Mills: Oxford University Press.
Jasanoff, S., 1993. India at the Crossroads in Global Environmental Policy. *Global Environmental Change Part A: Human & Policy Dimensions*, 3 (1), 32–52. 10.1016/0959-3780(93)90013-B.
Jenkins-Smith, H.C., s, 2017. The Advocacy Coalition Framework. An Overview of the Research Program. In: C.M. Weible and P.A. Sabatier, eds. *Theories of the Policy Process.* New York: Westview Press, 135–173.
Jörgensen, K., Jogesh, A., and Mishra, A., 2015. Multi-Level Climate Governance and the Role of the Subnational Level. *Journal of Integrative Environmental Sciences*, 12 (4), 235–245.
Joseph, K.J., Singh, L., and Abraham, V., 2014. Dealing with the Innovation – Inequality – the Conundrum: The Indian Experience. In: M.C.C. Soares, M. Scerri, and R. Maharajh, eds. *Inequality and Development Challenges.* New Delhi: Routledge, Taylor & Francis Group, 149–189.
Kashwan, P., 2017. *Democracy in the Woods. Environmental Conservation and Social Justice in India, Tanzania, and Mexico.* New York, NY: Oxford University Press.
Never, B., and Betz, J., 2014. Comparing the Climate Policy Performance of Emerging Economies. *World Development*, 59, 1–15.
Perkins, R., 2003. Environmental Leapfrogging in Developing Countries. A Critical Assessment and Reconstruction. *Natural Resources Forum*, 27 (3), 177–188.
Rajamani, L., 2007. Public Interest Environmental Litigation in India: Exploring Issues of Access, Participation, Equity, Effectiveness and Sustainability. *Journal of Environmental Law*, 19 (3), 293–321.
Ramesh, J., 2015. *Green Signals. Ecology, Growth, and Democracy in India.* New Delhi: Oxford University Press.
Rayner, J., 2015. Is There a Forth Institutionalism? Ideas, Institutions and the Explanation of Policy Change. In: J. Hogan and M. Howlett, eds. *Policy Paradigms in Theory*

and Practice. Discourses, Ideas and Anomalies in Public Policy Dynamics. Basingstoke: Palgrave Macmillan, 61–80.

Reich, M.R., and Bowonder, B., 1992. Environmental Policy in India. Strategies for Better Implementation. *Policy Studies Journal*, 20 (4), 643–661.

Sabatier, P.A., 1998. The advocacy coalition framework: revisions and relevance for Europe. *Journal of European Public Policy*, 5 (1), 98–130. 10.1080/13501768880000051.

Sil, R., 2014. India. In: J. Kopstein, M. Lichbach, and S.E. Hanson, eds. *Comparative Politics*. Cambridge, UK: Cambridge University Press, 339–390.

Stern, D.I., 2004. The Rise and Fall of the Environmental Kuznets Curve. *World Development*, 32 (8), 1419–1439.

United Nations Development Programme, 2018. *Human Development Reports. 2018 Statistical Update*. Available from: http://hdr.undp.org/en/2018-update.

Unruh, G.C., 2000. Understanding Carbon Lock-in. *Energy Policy*, 28 (12), 817–830.

Wendling, Z.A., et al., 2018. *The 2018 Environmental Performance Index*. New Haven, CT: Yale Center for Environmental Law and Policy.

Wilder, M., 2015. What is a Policy Paradigm? Overcoming Epistomological Hurdles in Cross-Disciplinary Conceptual Adaptation. In: J. Hogan and M. Howlett, eds. *Policy Paradigms in Theory and Practice. Discourses, Ideas and Anomalies in Public Policy Dynamics*. Basingstoke: Palgrave Macmillan, 19–42.

2 Environmental competencies in India's federal system

Wilfried Swenden and Rekha Saxena

2.1 Introduction

This chapter examines the responsibilities lying with the formal environmental institutions in India's federal system. India is a federal (technically "union") state, made up of 28 states and 9 union territories. The chapter first demonstrates how environmental competencies were largely overlooked in India's constitution of 1950. A global shift towards environmental awareness during the 1960s and 1970s, and environmental disasters (in particular the Bhopal tragedy in 1984) generated a stronger intervention, especially of the federal government in environmental policy. We demonstrate the mechanisms which enabled the centre to increase its footprint in environmental competencies.

Despite legislative (and fiscal) centralisation, the Indian centre has limited administrative capacity. It relies on the states for the implementation of much of its environmental policy initiatives. In the second section of the chapter, we show how this makes the centre and the states mutually dependent on each other for the delivery of environmental goals. This mutual dependence gives rise to a strong need for intergovernmental collaboration or joint decision-making. We demonstrate that executives, rather than legislatures, take the lead in centre-state collaboration. Furthermore, we show that by and large, institutions of intergovernmental collaboration are somewhat underdeveloped or steered by the central government. This was true for the erstwhile Planning Commission and remains the case for its replacement since 2015; the NITI Aayog. In some cases, the imposition of central preferences can lead to political contestation (especially when the central and state governments are not politically aligned). We refer to land acquisition as an example in which (opposition-) controlled state governments have sought to assert their authority via their control of the Rajya Sabha (federal second chamber) to oppose the relaxing of environmental impact assessments.

If political mediation cannot resolve intergovernmental disputes on environmental issues, court proceedings may appear to be a way out. As we demonstrate in the final part of the chapter, India has seen some centre-state (or inter-state) disputes on environmental issues. Yet from a comparative perspective, attempts to resolve inter-state river water disputes by delegating these to ad hoc tribunals with only a subsidiary role attributed to the Supreme Court stand out. We demonstrate that the track record of these tribunals is mixed at best.

Overall, our chapter demonstrates the extent to which environmental policy in India operates under the shadow of central hierarchy. Yet, the cost of excessive centralisation may instil non-cooperation among the states which (alongside local or urban governments) hold responsibility for much of the policy implementation in environmental policy. Furthermore, centralisation has also reduced the extent to which state and local governments can engage in policy innovation and policy transfer, in spite of the central government's rhetoric propagating "competitive-cooperative federalism".

2.2 Formal distribution of competencies: the rising power of the centre in environmental policy

In federal states, the constitution may distribute responsibilities in environmental policy across different levels of government: the centre and the regions (sometimes referred to as states as in the US and India, or provinces, cantons or *Länder*) may each shape environmental policy in aspects within their area of competence. Yet, constitutions in federal states vary considerably in the extent to which they specify and allocate environmental competencies. Comparative scholars have highlighted four distinctive ways in which this has been done (Selin and Van Deveer, 2012; Srivastava and Datt, 2012: 3). First, in some of the older federations which were forged out of the "coming together" of previously independent states or colonies, such as Australia or the US, the constitution enumerates only the powers of the centre. Non-specified or "residual powers" remain with the states. Since environmental concerns gained salience in the decades after the constitutions of these federal states were put together, environmental competencies primarily resided with the states. However, in time, federal governments have been able to legislate on environmental matters indirectly through their jurisdiction over trade and commerce, financing and external affairs (Srivastasa and Datt). Often, that was made possible through a broader reading of federal competencies in the constitution by the Supreme or Constitutional Court.

Second, in some federal states, environmental matters are tied to ownership of natural resources. Third, in federal constitutions that are relatively easy to amend (for instance only requiring two-third majorities in a bicameral federal parliament and not concurrent majorities by the federal and regional legislatures or special majorities in a referendum) environmental competencies may have been brought into the fold by recurrent constitutional amendment. Fourth, new federal constitutions (such as the Brazilian or South African constitutions) are more likely to give due consideration to environmental issues by inserting measures to protect forests, fauna and flora, control pollution or manage environmental disasters, as they have come into being when environmental issues had become salient already.

In India, the second and third routes were particularly relevant in bringing environmental issues into the constitutional fold. Although the Indian constitution is relatively new (January 1950), it did not make explicit reference to environmental issues (Chakrabarti, 2012: 61–62). Unlike most federal constitutions, Schedule VII of the Indian constitution contains three lists of legislative competencies:

a long list which determines the exclusive central (union) powers, a list specifying powers in which concurrent central-state legislation is possible (but with federal or central dominance or "paramountcy" in case of central-state conflict) and an exclusive list of state powers. Natural resources such as land, water, forests and mineral resources (mines) are attributed to the states under entries 17, 18, 19 and 23 in the constitution. The centre (union government) is made responsible for the regulation of mines and mineral development and of interstate rivers and valleys (ibid.). The Indian federation is not of the "coming together type". Although following independence more than 500 princely states had to be integrated into the Indian union, the new Indian state adopted the rather centralised format of the late colonial Government of India Act (1935) which served as its interim constitution until a new constitution entered into force in 1950 (Swenden, 2017). Following the practice of that Act, residual powers (i.e., those powers not specified in the constitution) are attributed to the centre. As such, the centre also gained legislative competence in air and environment more generally (ibid.).

In time, environmental issues gained more prominence in Indian politics and society. Based on Chakrabarti (2012: 62–64), we can attribute this "paradigm shift" to two dominant causes: (1) a global shift towards environmental awareness from the 1960s and 1970s onward, expressed in important fora such as the UN Conference on Human Environment in Stockholm (1972) and reflected in domestic legislation by major powers, such as the US as in its National Environmental Policy Act, Clean Air Act or Endangered Species Act a.o; (2) environmental disasters which worked as domestic critical junctures, galvanising domestic advocacy of environmental issues and forcing India on a path towards environmental action, such as the enactment of the Environment Protection Act (1986) in the wake of the Bhopal disaster two years earlier. Global and domestic factors pushed powerful Indian politicians like Indira Gandhi and her son Rajiv Gandhi, who succeeded her as Prime Minister in 1984, to take up environmental concerns (see also Ganguli this volume).

The increasing salience of environmental issues led to explicit constitutional amendments. The Indian constitution is not easy to amend, but for much of the post-independence period the Congress Party controlled both chambers of parliament and a majority of the state legislatures. Important amendments affecting the distribution of environmental responsibilities took place in 1976 and 1993–1994. In 1976, the Congress Party dominated both chambers of the union parliament and between 1976 and 1977 even declared a National Emergency, effectively neutralising any state opposition to constitutional change. Environmental issues were brought in for the first time in 1976 when the 42nd amendment inserted Article 48A which endeavours "the State … to protect and improve the environment and to safeguard the forests and wildlife of the country". Yet, this intent opened up scope for significant centralisation since it was accompanied by moving "forests" and "protection of wild animals and birds" from the State List to the Concurrent List; enabling the centre to legislate on these issues and trump conflicting state legislation where necessary. The same amendment also made it a "duty of every citizen of India to protect and improve the natural environment including forests,

Table 2.1 Distribution of legislative competencies in environmental matters as per the seventh schedule of the Indian constitution

Seventh schedule lists Indian constitution	Head (entries)
Union list (exclusive)	Industries (53), oil fields (53), mines and minerals (54), inter-state rivers (56) (fishing and fisheries beyond territorial waters)
State List (exclusive)	Public health (6), agriculture (14), land (18), 21 (fisheries), mines and minerals which are not under union control (23), state industries (24)
Concurrent List (federalism dominance in case of union-state conflict)	Forests (17A), wild animals and birds (17B), economic and social planning (20), population control and family planning (20A)

Source: Sharma and Singh (2018: 630).

lakes, rivers and wildlife and to have compassion for living creatures". Congress also controlled the union government between 1991 and 1996, albeit as a minority government for at least the first half of its tenure. Table 2.1 summarises the distribution of *legislative* competencies between the centre and the states in environmental issues (taken from Sharma and Singh, 2018: 630).

The creation of a third tier of government gained momentum with the assassination of Rajiv Gandhi who had been a long-time proponent of local government. Furthermore, local governments were kept under administrative tutelage of the state (not central) governments, giving the former control of the speed at which they were rolled out within their territories. The 73rd and 74th amendments to the constitution (1992), which introduced (directly elected) panchayats (rural) and urban local government, also expanded constitutional references to environmental issues. Local and urban governments were entrusted with issues, such as water management, soil conservation, drinking water, fuel and fodder, watershed development, sanitation and solid waste management and the protection of the environment amongst others.

The inclusion of these constitutional amendments opened up the possibility of central legislation in environmental affairs. For instance, prior to 1970, central legislation was confined to The Forest Act (1927) and the Factories Act (1948) which India inherited from their British colonisers. Since 1970, additional federal laws have been approved to regulate water and air pollution, wildlife protection, atomic energy, environmental protection and coal mining amongst others.

In addition to these constitutional amendments, the scope for central environmental action has been widened further by the centre's ability to engage in international treaty obligations. This is the case, even in matters which are placed under the state or concurrent legislative list. For instance, energy is a concurrent power. Yet, due to the centre's ability to conclude treaties and international agreements, it has gained the upper hand on issues such as climate change (Jörgensen et al., 2015).

Finally, the Indian states have relatively limited tax capacity, as most taxation is attributed to the centre or shared (in the case of the Goods and Services Tax) between both levels. Strong inter-state variations in fiscal and infrastructural capacity justify fiscal centralisation (Rajaraman, 2017), but this may come at a cost of inter-state innovation in environmental policy. Due to vertical fiscal imbalances (the centre raises more money than it spends and the opposite is true for the states) and horizontal fiscal imbalances (some states are richer than others), the centre has assumed an important role in supporting the states financially. In the process, the centre seeks to equalise fiscal resources between them. Fiscal resources can be disbursed through the Finance Commission or the central government. Finance Commission grants are "non-discretionary" in the main, yet in allocating grants, the Commission takes environmental concerns into consideration. Finance Commissions do so indirectly, for instance by incorporating environmental services in intergovernmental transfers and linking these to land use (forest cover), population density, land size or habitat and cost disabilities tied to excess rainfall, remoteness or hilly terrain (Kumar and Managi, 2009: 3056). They also do so directly by providing some explicit grants-in-aid that are needs-assessed and tied to specific purposes, for instance, waterlogging, coastal zone management, sewerage, sea erosion, arsenic decontamination, water supply in desert areas amongst others (ibid.: 3056). The 13th Finance Commission (2010–2015) earmarked 5 trillion rupees as a green bonus, i.e., special grants for areas with more forest cover. An amount of 5 billion rupees was set aside as a water sector management grant for four years. The purpose of this grant was to incentivise the states to establish an independent regulatory mechanism for the water sector and improved maintenance of irrigation networks. The Commission also recommended a substantial increase in the grants to local bodies to help them meet the challenges of environmental degradation, population pressure, exhaustion of resources and revenue constraints.

In sum, despite the limited responsibilities attributed to the centre in environmental policy at the time of independence, the centre has been able to expand its reach progressively in this area. The mechanisms which made this possible are constitutional amendments expanding the list of exclusively central or concurrent powers; judicial review, international treaty obligations (for instance in climate change) and fiscal federalism.

2.3 Environmental policy and the need for intergovernmental coordination

Despite the increasing centralisation of environmental policy as set out above, the need for centre-state and inter-state coordination is paramount for a number of reasons.

Firstly, legislative centralisation in one policy field has rarely been complete, generating considerable spill-over or externality effects. For instance, although most land resources (land, water and minerals) are placed under the State List, with forests under the Concurrent List, it is the centre which regulates control of these resources. Hence, the Forest Conservation Act requires the states to gain a permit from the centre should they wish to divert forest areas for non-forest purposes (Chakrabarti, 2012: 69). Similarly, the centre controls the "allocation, licensing, operations, royalties and dead rents for mining and de-mining" (ibid.: 70) influencing (and restricting) the revenue which flows back to the mineral-rich states. Mineral-rich states have complained about the lack of compensation to offset the environmental, cultural (infringement of tribal rights) and social costs (forced displacement) of mineral resource extraction (ibid.: 70).

Similarly, although international treaty obligations made the centre the key actor in climate change policy, the union only has "exclusive powers over trade representation, the UN, agreements and conventions with foreign countries, atomic power, mineral and oil resources and control of industries, [whilst] the states control public health and sanitation, agriculture, land improvement and water" (Jörgensen et al., 2015: 269). Therefore, in India, like in the US, climate change action requires centre-state collaboration and coordination (on the US, see Rabe, 2006; Selin and Van Deveer, 2012 for comparative US/EU reflections).

Thirdly, although the centre may dominate the legislation and finance of environmental policy, the states carry the main responsibility for implementing federal environmental legislation. This is in line with the Indian federal system as a whole, in which the centre has gained the upper hand in legislation yet relies on state administrations for much of its implementation. Consequently, the states often outspend the centre, including in policy areas that relate to environmental issues. Rangarajan and Srivastasa (2011: 91) show that the states occupied 89 percent of expenditures in medical and public health, water supply and sanitation; 88 percent in power, irrigation and flood control; 68 percent in agriculture and allied services and about 42 percent in industry and minerals. Therefore, the role of the centre is often confined to monitoring and part-funding the states to ensure compliance with central environmental policy. Thus, the centre often depends on state agencies for the actual implementation thereof. For instance, the states rely on state Environment Protection Authorities for the implementation of central National Environmental Policy.

Finally, even the financing of environmental policy requires centre-state coordination. This is so because apart from Finance Commission grants, as set out above, the central government sets aside a share of its revenue to (co)-fund environmental programmes through the allocation of discretionary central grants. These grants are disbursed through the Ministry of Finance, but their use is determined in conjunction with various sectoral (union) ministries and the NITI Aayog, a federal think-thank which replaced the Planning Commission in January 2015. These so-called "Centrally Sponsored Schemes" or "national development schemes" may fall under the responsibility of the Ministry of the Environment, Forestry and Climate Change, but other ministries may assume important environmental responsibilities as well. An example is the Swachh Bharat Mission (Clean India), initiated by Prime Minister Modi in October 2014. The scheme aims to achieve universal sanitation coverage, a cleaner India overall and the eradication of open defecation in the countryside (as per the Census of 2011, rural household toilet coverage in India was only 32.7 percent). The overall mission is coordinated by the Ministry of Drinking Water and Sanitation which also oversees the implementation of the scheme in the countryside. Yet, the Ministry of Urban Development is in charge of the scheme's implementation in urban areas.

In 2014–2015, the central government supported 66 Centrally Sponsored or National Development Schemes. In an effort to streamline and downsize these schemes (see below), a subgroup of Chief Ministers on the rationalisation of Centrally Sponsored Schemes recommended in 2015 that the central government should prioritise fewer schemes clustered in 11 areas. Two of these areas are directly related to environmental concerns: (1) Drinking Water and Swachh Bharat (Clean India) (2) Wildlife Conservation and Greening. Other areas contain components that touch upon environmental concerns: e.g., rural connectivity; electricity; agriculture, including animal husbandry, fisheries, integrated watershed management and irrigation, nutrition and urban transformation. The Swachh Bharat Mission would integrate two existing Centrally Sponsored Schemes (National Rural Drinking Water Programme and Nirmal Bharat Abhiyan; NITI Aayog, 2015a) whereas five existing schemes would be grouped under the Wildlife Conservation and Greening Rubric: the National River Conservation Programme; the National Afforestation Programme (National Mission for a Green India); the Conservation of Natural Resources and Ecosystems; the Integrated Development of Wild Life Habitats and Project Tiger (NITI Aayog, 2015b). However, the centre continues to rely on the states and local governments for the implementation of these schemes. Furthermore, these schemes are also jointly financed as cost-sharing programmes. For instance, to support the implementation of a scheme such as Swachh Bharat, the centre provides 75 percent of the funding and the states the remaining 25 percent, whereas for the "hilly" (Northeastern states plus Himachal Pradesh, Jammu and Kashmir and Uttarakhand) states that ratio is 90:10, reflecting the more limited infrastructural capacity and comparatively high operating costs within these states due to hilly terrain and low population density.

In sum, externalities, the reliance on state implementation and cost-sharing strengthen centre-state interdependence in environmental policy.

2.4 Environmental policy and the practice of intergovernmental coordination

Although the previous section sets out the case for strong intergovernmental coordination and joint decision-making, the reality often falls short of this. Centre-state coordination can take on two forms: it can bring together executives or civil servants from both levels or members of central and state legislatures. India has a parliamentary system and, as such, political power is concentrated within the parliamentary executive or government (Watts, 1997). Therefore, centre-state relations primarily take the form of inter-executive relations.

The scope for legislators to influence centre-state federalism is limited, although the Rajya Sabha, the federal second chamber, can suspend federal legislation affecting environmental policy.

In what follows, we first set out the (limited) capacity which states have in seeking to influence federal environmental policy which they have to implement. Where such capacity is falling short, centralisation occurs (but also with a higher risk of non-implementation). Alternatively, states may wish to contest central attempts to force them into implementing policies that they do not support. Such intergovernmental contestation is more likely to be played out in the open when the party-political composition of the central and state governments concerned is not aligned. We use the case of the land acquisition act as an example in which political disagreements between the centre and the states affected both the process of intergovernmental coordination at the executive level (in the NITI Aayog) as well as in the legislative arena through the opposition-controlled Rajya Sabha.

2.5 Centre-state relations and executive coordination on environmental issues

In parliamentary systems more so than in presidential systems, power tends to be concentrated among executives. This is so because the legislative and executive branches are fused and the key members of the party or parties (in the case of a coalition) holding office prefer to take up a ministerial posts in the executive or cabinet (which in some parliamentary systems they may or may not combine with a seat in the legislature). Ministers tend to have more bureaucratic or administrative support, which is why they instigate most of the legislation. In a presidential system, on the other hand, the legislative and executive branches are separated, with the executive presidency and legislators holding independent sources of democratic legitimacy. The nature of government (parliamentary versus presidential) also shapes the dynamics of intergovernmental cooperation in a federal system (Watts, 1989). In line with the "executive" nature of parliamentary federalism, state interests may be represented more persuasively in the executive realm, especially where central decisions affect state autonomy through legislation or intergovernmental grants. Federal systems often provide highly institutionalised mechanisms of intergovernmental relations (Bolleyer, 2009). Mechanisms of centre-state coordination also exist in India. They can vary from relatively low-ranked sectorial meetings between civil servants from the states and the centre to occasional high summit inter-ministerial conferences with the participation of the Prime Minister and state Chief Ministers (Saxena, 2013 for an overview).

Although much attention may be devoted to "summit-meetings", the work in terms of policy preparation and the actual implementation of policy is often done by civil servants. At the administrative level, the "oiling and gluing" (Parry, 2012) of centre-state relations can be helped by the existence of the "All India Services" such as the Indian Administrative Services (IAS) and the Indian Forest Services (IFS). IAS and IFS officers occupy the top administrative positions in the central and state administrations. In the case of the IFS, they do so in the relevant union or state forest ministerial department. Although IAS and IFS are central administrative services, civil servants from within both services are "encadred" in the states. As such, they are accountable to the state government which has responsibility for the allocation, promotion and transfers of posts (though the centre regulates their pensions and also recruits and, where necessary, sacks civil servants; Radin, 2007). At the same time, these elite civil servants are tasked with the implementation of central policy in the states. As such, state governments could perceive them as "agents of the centre".

The position of IFS Officers following the enactment of the Forest Conservation Act (1980) and Wild Life Protection Act (1972) illustrates this point. Both acts restrict what hitherto had been a more unqualified power of the states to regulate forests. IFS Officers must enforce the pre-requisites for the diversion of forest land for non-forest purposes. As per the Forest Conservation Act (1980) these pre-requisites are determined by the central government which must give explicit authorisation to the states for the de-reservation of forests or the use of forest land for non-forest purposes. In this matter, the centre is advised by the Forest Advisory Committee in which a direct representation from the states is notably absent (Chaturvedi, 2016: 5–7). Tensions have emerged between IFS officers and state governments where they believe that central policy is obstructing their development potential. Therefore, IAS and IFS officers must thread a fine line between observing political accountability to the state government and overseeing the correct implementation of central policies and guidelines. The fact that IAS and IFS officers belong to the same "corps" and may have been "batch-mates" who serve at a different level could help to alleviate these "split" loyalties.

The representation of state governments is also relevant on issues that affect intergovernmental finance. Building on the example of forestry above, states which have above national average forest coverage have been asking for fiscal compensation by the centre as they feel they are penalised for having to keep India's overall forest coverage at 33 percent. As highlighted above, fiscal compensation can be offered in two forms: either as (mostly) non-discretionary grants determining the centre-state and inter-state distribution of shared tax revenues as recommended by the Finance Commission, or in the form of discretionary grants disbursed by the Ministry of Finance on programmes developed in conjunction with the relevant union sectorial ministries. The Finance Commission, whose experts are appointed by the President for fixed five-year terms, takes the view of state governments into account (in fact, the Commission visits each of the state capitals in the preparation of its report). However, the Commission is without direct state representation. Until 2015, the allocation of discretionary grants was also overseen in part by the Planning Commission. The Planning Commission laid down how much and for which purpose centrally allocated resources could be disbursed as intergovernmental grants to assist in national development programmes and goals. Under the then Bharatiya Janata Party (BJP) central government (2014), headed by Narendra Modi, the Planning Commission was replaced with the NITI Aayog, but largely without the grant-making powers of its predecessor.

The replacement of the Planning Commission with the NITI was meant to enhance the input of the states and contribute towards Prime Minister Modi's goal of strengthening co-operative federalism or "Team India". The states lamented the lack of input in central planning within the erstwhile Planning Commission. Their voice was only heard (and put on record) in the National Development Council, an apex body presided over by the union Prime Minister but with the participation of all Chief Ministers. The National Development Council only enabled the states to air their grievances, usually at a time when complete drafts of the next five-year plans had been in circulation already (Swenden and Saxena, 2017). Similarly, state representations could be articulated during the formulation of Centrally Sponsored Schemes (national development schemes), but only as one among several stakeholders. The relevant programmes would be drafted in the main by representatives of the central ministries involved in the policy and the Planning Commission. Most of the officials in the Planning Commission also belonged to the economic services, unlike the All-India Services, a part of the central administration and therefore less in tune with the needs and aspirations of the states.

The replacement of the Planning Commission with the NITI Aayog has gone hand in hand with the abolition of five years cycles of National Planning and the approval of annual state Plans. The NITI operates more as a policy think-thank at the service of the central government and Prime Minister in particular. Its internal modus operandi creates more opportunities for the temporary employment of outside consultants or junior researchers. Based on the evidence we have, it is highly questionable that the NITI has fundamentally changed the position of the states in their ability to influence central policy (including environmental policy) for which it relies on the cooperation of the states (Swenden, 2019; Swenden and Saxena, 2017). In fact, this body is a poor substitute for the highly institutionalised mechanisms of intergovernmental coordination which have developed in more co-operative federal systems such as Germany or Switzerland (Bolleyer, 2009). This is so despite the creation of ad hoc Regional Councils through which prime regional political actors (Chief Ministers) can cast a stronger influence on policy at an earlier stage in the policy cycle. In 2016, such Councils prepared reports on the "Clean India" Mission and, most importantly, a profound restructuration in the number and funding of Centrally Sponsored Schemes. By and large, this reordering aimed at enhancing the discretion of the states in the implementation of such schemes, whilst reducing the extent of their co-funding by the centre.

The limited ability of state executive actors to influence intergovernmental relations, in general, and environmental policy, more specifically, can be read from the following examples. Firstly, the union government determines which issues should be discussed at the Governing Council (the meeting of all state Chief Ministers, heads of union territories and key representatives of the central government, including the Prime Minister). The union government also determines the policy issues which the Regional Councils should focus on and *which* Chief Ministers are included in its composition (Sengupta, 2015). For instance, of the three Councils that were set up to discuss the Clean India Mission, the restructuring of Centrally

Sponsored Schemes and Skills development in 2015, none were chaired by Chief Ministers representing opposition parties (Sharma and Swenden, 2018). Furthermore, the choice of themes reflected priorities of the federal government. The justification for setting up a Regional Council group to focus on the restructuration of Centrally Sponsored Schemes lies with a Finance Commission decision in 2015 to increase the state component of shared tax revenues by 10 percent (from 32 to 42 percent). This reduced the overall federal resources which can be set aside for "central" consumption, including discretionary intergovernmental grants (which count as a central expense), thus prompting a reduction in the overall number and co-financing of these schemes.

Secondly, unlike the National Development Council before, the Regional Councils lack statutory recognition and their reports are merely advisory. Furthermore, in contrast with the Planning Commission, the NITI plays a limited role in the allocation of discretionary grants to the states, shifting the onus thereof to the Ministry of Finance and the relevant ministerial line departments. The input of state actors is likely to be more and not less restrained there compared with the NITI.

Thirdly, the NITI appears to have engaged more systematically in mapping the practices of the states and has invested in strengthening its capacity to monitor the implementation of federal policies at the state and especially sub-state (district, local government) levels. Seeking to inject some inter-state competition into the political process, it has ranked the states "in terms of doing business, improvement in health, education and water outcomes or more recently sustainable development goals" (NITI, 2017: 113). The NITI also aims to "provide technical and expert assistance to states to improve their performance, [which] includes compilation and dissemination of best-case practices worldwide keeping in view the local Indian conditions" (ibid.: 113). For instance, in 2015, the NITI issued a 300-page "state-benchmarking" or "Good Practices Resource book", listing "best" practices in a range of fields. In the case of environmental policy, this book discussed sewage treatment in Chennai, water security in Sikkim and Kerala, environmental management in the Andaman and Nicobar Islands, forest management in Karnataka, livelihood promotion in Meghalaya, lake restoration in Rajasthan and Karnataka, air quality forecasting in Delhi and sustainable plastic waste management in Himachal Pradesh (NITI, 2015c: 51–106). Towards the end, the book seeks to distil lessons learnt from this inter-state comparison, making the case for states to engage in "Behaviour Change Communication" by suggesting alternative environmental practices beyond merely sensitising citizens to generate more environmental-friendly outcomes (NITI, 2015c: 276). Similarly, based on an evaluation of the Communication Management Water Supply Programme in Gujarat and the Open Defecation Free Villages initiative in Jharkhand, the NITI makes a case for participatory modes of governance in sanitation management (ibid.: 278). However, the NITI only has limited financial resources to reward states for good performance (since it lacks grant-making powers). Furthermore, bench-marking follows "centrally set" parameters or objectives, thus leaving limited space for state initiatives that do not comply with these objectives.

Fourthly, there is no evidence to suggest that the federal government gave significant input to the states in the development of the three-year action plan, the seven-year strategy paper and a 15-year vision document which have come to replace the erstwhile five-year economic plans (Economic Times, 13 April 2017; Swenden, 2019). These documents are also merely advisory (unlike the earlier five-year plans, they do not bind expenditure), and thus the central and state governments are not compelled to put them into action. This, in turn, makes it easier to endorse the Action Plan for central and state governments as Chief Ministers have done in a recent Regional Council meeting of the NITI Aayog. The Plan consists of 24 chapters, of which two focus explicitly on "sustainability" (Chapter 23: environment and forests and Chapter 24: sustainable management of water resources). The annexure to the plan lists the consultation of six and three experts in informing the NITI on the drafting of the environment and forest and sustainable management of water resources, respectively, but again, there is no evidence to suggest that the view of the states was systematically taken into account.

Finally, the NITI also does not appear to have played an important intergovernmental coordinating role on the issue of climate change. States were not involved in shaping India's Intended Determined Contribution in the negotiations leading up to the Paris Agreement (December 2015), even though meeting the emission targets and actions which India pledged to undertake post-2020 require state action. At the same time, since the implementation of the National Action Plan for Climate Change in 2008 (which contained eight National Missions, several of which focused on the promotion of renewable energy) largely depends on adequate state action, states were invited to develop their own state action plans, in alignment with the strategies and goals of the NAPCC and eight Missions. Arguably, State Action Plans were set up to prevent state litigation further down the line. Furthermore, if the NAPCC, National Missions and SAPCC had observed the distribution of competencies, the NAPCC and National Missions should have focused on mitigation of emissions while the states should have emphasised adaptation in areas in which they hold competence such as land, water, coastlines and agriculture. Although by 2014 all states had developed their state action plans, the industrially forward states, in particular Gujarat, Tamil Nadu, Maharashtra and Andhra Pradesh, had made the strongest contribution to renewable energy supply, in particular in wind and solar energy (Jörgensen et al., 2015: 269–272).

2.6 Centre-state relations and coordination on environmental issues by legislative actors

Given the presence of a parliamentary system with highly disciplined political parties, state parliaments play a limited role in intergovernmental coordination. Where they exist, inter-executive agreements or memorandums of understanding on the implementation of national development programmes are not published and Indian state legislatures have played a particularly weak role in scrutinising them. State legislative assemblies also hold very short sessions – in some cases only 11 days per year! (Jensenius and Suryanarayan, 2015; PRS Legislative Research, 2014) and lack select committees to scrutinise their executives, let alone the intergovernmental arrangements in which they engage.

The Rajya Sabha, the national House of States or second chamber, is also not well suited to represent the legislative interests of the states (Saxena, 2019). Unlike the US Senate or German Bundesrat where small states or Lander are over-represented in relation to their share of the overall population, the share of state seats in the Indian Rajya Sabha is more or less in proportion to their share of the Indian population (see Swenden, 2010, for a comparative analysis). Thus, smaller states cannot use the Rajya Sabha as a vehicle to represent their interests in relation to the lower house, in which representation is also mostly according to population. Furthermore, although state legislatures elect the members of the Rajya Sabha, in 2003, the BJP-led National Democratic Alliance succeeded in pushing through a constitutional amendment that dropped the "domiciliary" link with a state as a precondition for senate membership (Saxena, 2014: 394–395). Challenged in the Supreme Court for violating federalism, the Court opined that "it is no part of federal principle that the representatives of the states must belong to that State" (Kuldip Nayar, 2006). This ruling further diluted the ability of senators especially from polity-wide or national parties such as Congress or the BJP to represent the interests of states with which they are associated. Relatedly, because polity-wide parties have a highly centralised organisational structure, members of the Rajya Sabha owe their nomination to the central party leader or executive, not the state party leadership (Shastri, 2006).

However, states are more likely to protest when they are not politically aligned with the central government. They can voice their protest, for instance, by boycotting intergovernmental meetings. Alternatively, since the Rajya Sabha is indirectly elected by state legislatures on the basis of Proportional Representation (Single Transferrable Vote) – unlike the lower house which is elected under first-past-the-post – central governments since 1989 have mostly lacked a legislative majority there. Therefore, opposition parties can withhold consent to legislative proposals in the second chamber which they do not support. They may be more inclined to do so if they feel that government legislation has run into widespread public dissent. Although in ordinary legislation the veto-right of the Rajya Sabha is suspensory, few union governments have gone as far as to trigger a joint session of both parliamentary chambers to resolve bicameral disputes; in part, due to technical requirements which must be met before they can do so. In such a joint sitting, the larger cohort of members of the lower house (and therefore the party in government) would likely carry an overall majority.

In Box 2.1, we use the example of a proposed amendment to the Land Acquisition Bill in 2015 to illustrate how federal opposition parties and non-BJP-ruled states combined to obstruct the central passage of this amendment through the Rajya Sabha. Similarly, we demonstrate how BJP-ruled state governments sought to cooperate with the central government in seeking to work around this legislative deadlock and used the NITI Aayog as a vehicle for this.

BOX 2.1 CASE STUDY – CENTRE-STATE CONFLICT ON LAND ACQUISITION

Although Land is a state subject, the acquisition and requisition of land is a concurrent subject. Opposition to public land acquisition has increased on the grounds that land had been given for development or industrial purposes without proper compensation and attention for environmental concerns. In light thereof, in 2013, the then Congress-led government approved the Right to Fair Compensation and Transparency in Land Acquisition Rehabilitation and Resettlement (LARR) Act (Mohanty, 2016: 4). This act, which was binding on the union and state governments alike, involved the third tier (local government) in the decision-making process. Furthermore, the people who inhabited the land would need to consent to land acquisition: 70 percent if the land were to be developed under a Public-Private Partnership; 80 percent under proposed private ownership. The bill also proposed a state ceiling on the area of agricultural land which could be acquired for development and it introduced a system of fair compensation in which the affected families would be heard. Finally, the acquisition of land which was irrigated and multi-crop was only allowed under "exceptional circumstances", i.e., for the construction of major highways, railways or major district roads, irrigation canals and power lines (Verma, 2015: 18).

After coming into power in 2014, the BJP central government (and many of India's industrial companies) was of the view that the 2013 Act was unworkable and held up important investment projects. In fact, it is argued that under the current law, land acquisition takes on average 59 months (Economic Times, 6 April 2017). To circumvent the veto of the Rajya Sabha (in which Congress and allies defended the 2013 legislation as vital for the protection of small rural landholders and the environment), the BJP sought to amend the process of land acquisition by ordinance instead of legislation. The ordinance would have done away with "a social impact assessment" including environmental concerns, which involved mandatory public hearings and consent of the affected population as stipulated above. It would also have widened the scope within which the state could acquire land without opposition if the land were to be used for atomic energy, railways, electricity, national highways and metro. In the face of continuing opposition in the Rajya Sabha and the public, more generally, the government agreed to withdraw a bill to amend the LARR 2013 and placed its amendments for consideration in a Joint Parliamentary Committee in 2015. Until 2019, government and opposition parties still have not reached a consensus. However, as early as July 2015, the Chief Ministers of three state governments in which the BJP participated expressed a desire to include a provision in the executive ordinance for Land Acquisition which would enable them to pass their own laws. They did so in the Governing Council of the NITI Aayog. The central government took up their concerns and added a provision to the ordinance which gives states the freedom to waive the social impact assessment and forgo consent before acquiring rural land (Verma, 2015: 18). In protest, several Chief Ministers controlled by parties in federal opposition boycotted a meeting of the Governing Council in July 2015 given the discussion of LARR at a time when the issue had still not received parliamentary assent. By September 2018, the number of states who have amended LARR so as to exempt certain projects from consent and a required social impact assessment had grown to eight, five of which are controlled by the BJP (Seetharaman, 2018). Evidently, attempts to act upon this ordinance in contravention of current federal legislation will likely trigger lawsuits by state parties against their government and encounter further protest on the ground. As such, from the government's point of view, the "state route" to land acquisition is only a second-best alternative to an agreed-upon federal law.

2.7 Judicial review and the special case of inter-state river water disputes

Where intergovernmental coordination fails states (or for that matter federal governments) can take recourse to another mechanism: judicial litigation. As is common in federal states, the Supreme Court has played a role in adjudicating environmental disputes between the centre and the state or amongst the states. A detailed review of Supreme Court jurisprudence in this matter falls beyond the scope of this chapter. By and large, judicial litigation is a measure of last resort, as it operates relatively slowly and offers no guarantee to the states that the law will be interpreted in line with their preferences.

Over the years the Supreme Court has built up an important array of cases linked to the environment. On occasion, the Supreme Court has prioritised developmental concerns over environmental rights; but the opposite is also true (see Rajamani, 2007, for a more detailed assessment). Especially after the Emergency (1977), the Court adopted a more activist role in protecting environmental rights, in particular by incorporating these in its readings of fundamental rights provisions such as the right to protection of life and the right to personal liberty (Chakrabarti, 2012: 65) and equality. Especially through the instrument of "Public Interest litigation", the right to potable water, clean environment and sanitation were integrated into the right to life; and in urban centres, the quality of life was assumed to be incompatible with the presence of highly polluting stone crushing units, brick kilns and rice mills (Sivaramakrishnan, 2011: 910). While public interest litigation during the 1970s was still primarily taken up by issues such as bonded labour, child labour, the mentally ill, or women in custodial institutions, since the 1990s it has been primarily taken up by environmental issues (ibid.: 915)

Environmental litigation can come with binding commitments on both the centre and the states. For instance, building on the federal Forest Conservation Act (1980), the Supreme Court in its Godovarman (1996) case and the Centre for Environmental Law (1995) case prohibited the states and authorised federal agencies from opening up forests to private exploitation without review by the courts first. Later on the Supreme Court (rather than executive authorities) ordered the creation of a Central Empowered Committee made up of three federal government officers and two NGO representatives to oversee the implementation of court orders and interim rulings emanating from both judgements (Sivaramakrishnan, 2011: 911). In 2019, demonstrating a clash between environmental rights and personal liberties, the Supreme Court ordered the eviction of at least 1 million tribal citizens across 16 states for breaches of the Forest Right Act (2006), an Act which purported to empower tribals in forest management (Chandra, 2019).

Beyond the more activist role of the Supreme Court in environmental jurisprudence, India stands out for the way in which it has attempted to take inter-state river water disputes largely out of the Supreme Court, delegating initial responsibility to special tribunals instead. More details are provided in Box 2.2.

BOX 2.2 INTER-STATE RIVER WATER DISPUTES

Water is one of India's most precious (and increasingly scarce) resources. The use of water, irrigation and canals is placed under the State List, whereas the regulation of inter-state rivers is a competence of the union parliament. Given that water, unlike other natural resources, is a "mobile resource" and thus in the case of inter-state rivers, the use of water in one state affects the use of water in another state, the central legislature has come to play an important role in regulating the relevant state competencies where these affect inter-state rivers (Salve, 2016: 501–505). Inter-state river water disputes have been quite common. Yet, whereas the Indian Supreme Court is tasked normally with the resolution of centre-state and inter-state disputes (as per Article 131 of the Constitution), in the case of inter-state river water disputes the Constitution has reserved the authority for working out an appropriate dispute resolution mechanism to Parliament. Article 262 specifies that "Parliament may by law provide for the adjudication of any dispute or complaint with respect to the use, distribution and control of the waters of, or in any inter-State river or river valley" and also that "notwithstanding anything in this constitution, Parliament may by law provide that neither the Supreme Court nor any other court shall exercise jurisdiction in respect of any such dispute or complaint".

In 1956, the Parliament passed the Inter-State River Water Disputes Act which provides for the referral of such disputes to a tribunal on the application of a State Government and the satisfaction of the union government that the dispute in question cannot be settled by administrative or political negotiation. In it, water disputes are defined as disputes that pertain to the "use, distribution and control" of "inter-State rivers or valleys". As such, they also contain disputes on the interpretation of inter-State river water sharing agreements or "treaties" and disputes on the levy of water rates (ibid.: 507). The act authorises state governments to request the union government to set up a Water Disputes Tribunal within a year from receiving such a request. The decision of the tribunal is binding on the parties to the dispute and must be published in the Official Gazette. At this point, the Supreme Court can intervene to ensure the enforcement and implementation of the adjudicated dispute. The Supreme Court, despite its lack of statutory power to adjudicate inter-state river water disputes, also has the power to grant interim relief in water disputes (Salve, 2016: 511), should the establishment of an Inter-State river water tribunal not be forthcoming.

Thus far, five inter-state river water tribunals have been established for Narmada, Krishna, Godawari, Cauvery (Kaveri) and Sutlej-Jamuna. In practice, tribunals have sometimes delegated the matter to a commission chaired by a Supreme Court judge. Water disputes have so far been more or less amicably settled, apart from the disputes involving Punjab, Haryana and Rajasthan, and Tamil Nadu and Karnataka. In the last few years, the Cauvery dispute has often found the States of Tamil Nadu and Karnataka at loggerheads, especially in drought years. In some cases, disagreements on how to share the river water between both states underpinned local violence. Failing all political negotiations, the matter has often been provisionally settled by the Supreme Court's intervention. The Cauvery tribunal award was submitted in 2007 but both Karnataka and Tamil Nadu continued expressing discontent, the former more so than the latter. In February 2018, the Supreme Court ordered the Indian central government to set up a Cauvery scheme to decide and implement the sharing of Cauvery waters following the order of the Cauvery Water Tribunal as modified by the Supreme Court. The scheme established a Cauvery Water Management Authority (which will oversee the "storage, apportionment, regulation and control" of Cauvery waters) and Cauvery Water Regulation Committee (which will "monitor the daily water levels, inflows and storage position at major reservoirs storing the Cauvery water") (Deepalakshmi, 2018).

One of the recurrent problems with inter-state river water disputes is the long delay between a request to set up a Tribunal and the actual implementation thereof. In part, this reflects a desire of the union government to settle matters through political negotiations first, but until 2002, the law did not stipulate a time limit of one year beyond which the setting up a tribunal would become mandatory. Another issue concerns the delay between the decision of a tribunal and the actual publication thereof, only after which it becomes mandatory for the riparian states involved in the dispute.

On the whole, the experience with inter-state river water tribunals is mixed. The authority of a tribunal to impose a river-sharing decision is constrained by political imperatives. The Narmada river-sharing agreement is hailed as a "remarkable piece of work, as valuable for its jurisprudence as

(Continued)

it is for its innovative structures created for administering the distribution of waters" (Salve, 2016: 516) between Maharashtra, Gujarat and Madhya Pradesh. In contrast, an authoritative resolution for sharing the Cauvery river between Karnataka, Tamil Nadu, Kerala and Puducherry could not be found until the Supreme Court order in 2018 (and some of its provisions remain disputed).

Ultimately, no inter-state water river dispute can be upheld without state political support. The legislative framework for settling inter-state water disputes could not prevent the unilateral termination in 2004 by the then-Congress Chief Minister of Punjab, Amarinder Singh, of all inter-state river water agreements which Punjab had signed with the riparian states of Haryana and Rajasthan in the 1980s. In response, the President of India referred the matter to the Supreme Court for its advisory opinion. In a major setback to Punjab, it took the Supreme Court until 2016 before ruling that Punjab was bound to share Ravi-Beas river waters with Haryana and other states and comply with its two judgements for completion of the Sutlej-Yamuna Link (SYL) canal. A five-member Constitution Bench headed by Justice Anil R. Dave made the clarification while invalidating the Punjab Termination of Agreements Act 2004, by which the state had terminated its pacts with Haryana, Himachal Pradesh, Rajasthan, Jammu and Kashmir and Delhi for sharing the waters of the two rivers. The SC concluded "… in our opinion, Punjab exceeded its legislative power in proceeding to nullify the decree of this court and therefore, the Punjab Act cannot be said to be a validly enacted legislation," (SCI, 2016: 38). Referring to its 2006 Mullaperiyar dam judgement, the Supreme Court held that a State Legislative Assembly cannot through legislation do an act in conflict with the judgement of the highest court which has attained finality (ibid.: 40).

The difficulty of addressing inter-state river water disputes is likely to arise in the future. Shortly after it came to power in 1998, the BJP-led National Democratic Alliance coalition government proposed the inter-linking of all major rivers of India; a proposal that was taken up by successive Congress-led United Progressive Alliance coalition governments since and by the current BJP majority government. The protagonists of the project argue that it will avoid the paradoxical occurrence of flood and drought simultaneously in various parts of the country by a rational apportionment of water resources throughout the country. Environmentalists, however, argue that it will disturb the ecological balance and bring natural calamities in its trail as well as intensify inter-state disputes and societal conflicts (Mehta and Mehta, 2013). As the above examples demonstrate, these matters are unlikely to be resolved in a political manner alone, especially since the final mode of dispute settlement lies with the Supreme Court of India under its original Jurisdiction (Article 131) and advisory jurisdiction (Article 143).

2.8 Conclusion: environmental federalism under the shadow of central hierarchy

This chapter provided a brief overview of the distribution of environmental competencies in India's highly complex federal system. It demonstrated the extent to which constitutional amendment, international engagements, fiscal federalism and judicial review enabled a gradual centralisation of environmental policy in India.

For many years, legislative centralisation in environmental policy – as in other fields – was made possible by the presence of a dominant party system, in which the Congress Party controlled both federal parliamentary chambers and a majority of state assemblies for most of the time until 1989. Yet, even in the more recent period of central coalition government (1989–2014) few changes were made which strengthened the constitutional footing of the states in Indian federalism, in general, and in environmental policy, more specifically.

Despite the centralisation of environmental policy, the states (and local governments, which due to space constraints were largely left out of our analysis) are important actors in the implementation of environmental policy. Furthermore, they co-fund some of the national environmental programmes. Consequently, the centre has a strong incentive to negotiate with the states through intergovernmental coordination if it wishes to meet its environmental targets. In the second part of the chapter, we demonstrated that intergovernmental mechanisms are not absent, but they tend to replicate the centralised bias which is found in India's federal system, more generally. As is expected from a parliamentary federal system, they also attempt inter-executive coordination rather than inter-legislative coordination. Overall, state-shared rule mechanisms in environmental governance are weak. Their absence can trigger protests, either through mobilising opposition forces in the Rajya Sabha or by embarking on the much longer (and insecure) route of judicial litigation. In the case of inter-state water river disputes, ad hoc courts provide a different mode of dispute resolution, albeit, as we have shown, with mixed success.

In spite of legislative centralisation and limited intergovernmental coordination, Indian federalism provides avenues for environmental policy-learning and transfer. To a very limited extent, this has been encouraged by the central government itself, through its attempts to mobilise the NITI Aayog for the sharing of best practices albeit based on centrally determined objectives. The recent increase in state spending autonomy following the implementation of the XIV Finance Commission report (2015–2020) has also widened the possibility of autonomous but divergent state actions in the environmental domain. Indian states not only vary considerably in their level of financial autonomy but also in their infrastructural capacity. Thus, whatever states have gained in state financial autonomy as a result of the implementation of the XIV Finance Commission report could lead to an increase in inter-state gaps in environmental performance. As the chapter on state practices in environmental policy demonstrates, more financial autonomy can also facilitate the furtherance of environmental goals – for instance through policy innovation in renewable energy. Inter-state differences in topography (forest cover, water flow, potential for solar and wind power) and demography, in modes of state-civil society interactions and in the nature of party competition, may hold further keys to understand diverging state outcomes in environmental policy. The added value of environmental federalism can only be realised if the central environmental policy encourages state innovation and can draw from best state practices in the hope to further sustainable development across the states and India as a whole. Furthermore, given the reliance of the centre on the states and local authorities for the implementation of federal environmental policy, the central government would do well to build-in more robust mechanisms for shared rule and centre-state coordination in environmental policy.

References

Bolleyer, N. (2009), *Intergovernmental Cooperation. Rational Choices in Federal Systems and Beyond* (Oxford: Oxford University Press).

Chakrabarti, P.G.D. (2012), 'Federalism and environmental policy in India', In: P.G.D. Chakrabarti and N. Srivastava, eds., *Green Federalism. Experiences and Practices* (Delhi/Ottawa: TERI/Forum of Federations), 61–71.

Chandra, R. (2019), 'How the FRA is being cut down to size, and tribals with it', *The Wire*, 23 February, https://thewire.in/rights/how-the-fra-is-being-cut-down-to-size-and-tribals-with-it

Chaturvedi, R. (2016), 'India's forest federalism', *Contemporary South Asia*, 24 (1), 1–18.

Deepalakshmi, K. (2018), 'What does the gazette notification on Cauvery scheme say', *The Hindu*, 2 July, www.thehindu.com/news/national/what-does-the-gazette-notification-on-cauvery-scheme-say/article24309460.ece

Economic Times, 'For faster growth in India, change the land acquisition law: official', *The Economic Times*, 6 April 2017.

Jensenius, F.R. and P. Suryanarayan (2015), 'Fragmentation and decline in India's state assemblies. A review, 1967–2007', *Asian Survey*, 55 (5), 862–881.

Jörgensen, K., A. Mishra, and G.K. Sarangi (2015), 'Multi-level climate governance in India: the role of the states in climate action planning and renewable energies', *Journal of Integrative Environmental Sciences*, 12 (4), 267–283.

Kuldip Nayar and Others versus Union of India and Others, Supreme Court Cases (2006), 7 SCC, paras 73, 88, 89.

Kumar, S. and S. Managi (2009), 'Compensation for environmental services and intergovernmental fiscal transfers: the case of India', *Ecological Economics*, 68, 3052–3059.

Mehta, D. and N.K. Mehta (2013), 'Interlinking of rivers in India: issues and challenges', *GeoEcoMarina*, 19, 137–143.

Mohanty, B. (2016), 'Land acquisition, movement actor and federalism. A case study of POSCO' Paper presented at Leverhulme International Workshop on Continuity and Change in Indian Federalism, University of Delhi, December 2016.

NITI Aayog. (2015a), 'Report of the Sub-Group of Chief Ministers on Swachh Bharat Abhiyaan', Delhi: NITI Aayog, October 2015.

NITI Aayog. (2015b), 'Report of the Sub-Group of Chief Ministers on rationalization of Centrally Sponsored Schemes', Delhi: NITI Aayog, October 2015.

Parry, R. (2012), 'The civil service and intergovernmental relations in post-devolution UK', *British Journal of Politics and International Relations*, 14 (2), 285–302.

PRS Legislative Research. (2014), 'Legislative performance of state assemblies', *PRS Blog*, www.prsindia.org/theprsblog/legislative-performance-state-assemblies, consulted December 2018.

Rabe, B.G. (2006), 'Power to the states: the promise and pitfalls of decentralization', In: N.J. Vig and M.E. Kraft, eds., *Environmental Policy. New Directions for the Twenty-First Century* (Washington, DC: CQ Press), 34–56.

Radin, B. (2007), 'The Indian Administrative Service in the 21st century: living in an intergovernmental environment', *International Journal of Public Administration*, 30, 12 (4), 1525–1548.

Rajamani, L. (2007), 'Public interest environmental litigation in India: exploring issues of access, participation, equity, effectiveness and sustainability', *Journal of Environmental Law*, 19 (3), 293–321.

Rajaraman, I. (2017), 'Continuity and change in Indian fiscal federalism', In: C.K. Sharma and W. Swenden, eds., *Special Issue, Continuity and Change in Indian Federalism, India Review*, 16, (1).

Rangarajan, C. and Srivastasa (2011), *Federalism and Fiscal Transfers in India* (Delhi: Oxford University Press).

Salve, H. (2016), 'Inter-state river water disputes', In: S. Choudhry, M. Khosla, and P.B. Mehta, eds., *The Oxford Handbook of the Indian Constitution* (Oxford: Oxford University Press), 502–520.

Selin, H. and Van Deveer, S.D. (2012), 'Federalism, multilevel governance, and climate change politics across the Atlantic', In: P.F. Steinberg and S.D. Van Deveer, eds., *Comparative Environmental Politics* (Cambridge, MA: MIT Press), 341–368.

Sharma, C.K. and Swenden, W. (2018), 'Modi-fying Indian federalism? Centre-State relations under Modi's Tenure as Prime Minister', *Indian Politics & Policy*, 1 (1), 51–82.

Sharma, S. and Singh, A.K. (2018), 'Environmental regulatory authorities in India: an analysis', *Indian Journal of Public Administration*, 64 (4), 627–644.

Shastri, S. (2006), 'Representing the states at the federal level: the role of the Rajya Sabha', In: L. Jörg, P. Paolo and R. Tarchi, eds., *A World of Second Chambers. Handbook of Constitutional Studies on Bicameralism* (Milan: Giuffrè Editore), 587–612.

Srivastava, N. and Datt, D. (2012), 'An introduction to environmental federalism. Experiences and issues in select countries', In: P.G.D. Chakrabarti and N. Srivastava, eds., *Green Federalism. Experiences and Practices* (Delhi/Ottawa: TERI/Forum of Federations), 1–17.

Saxena, R. (2013), 'Intergovernmental relations in India', In: M. Sabharwal and E.M. Berman, eds., *Public Administration in South Asia: India, Bangladesh, and Pakistan* (CRC Press: New York and London).

Saxena, R. (2014), 'The Rajya Sabha. A federal or a secondary chamber?', In: B.D. Dua, M.P. Singh, and R. Saxena, eds., *The Indian Parliament. The Changing Landscape* (Delhi: Manohar), 381–402.

Saxena, R. (2019), 'Reforming the Rajya Sabha', In: Y. Aiyar and L. Tillin, eds., *Special Issue on Indian Federalism for Seminar*, Issue 717, 1 May, 53–59.

SCI (Supreme Court of India). (2016), Advisory Jurisdiction, Special Reference of No1 of 2004 Re: 'The Punjab Termination of Agreement Act', www.indiaenvironmentportal.org.in/files/Ravi-Beas%20River%20waters%20Supreme%20Court%20Order.pdf, accessed 30 August 2019, p. 38.

Seetharaman, G. (2018), 'Five years on, has land acquisition act fulfilled its aim?', *The Economic Times*, 1 September 2018.

Sengupta, M. (2015), 'Modi planning: What the NITI Aayog suggests about the aspirations and practices of the Modi government', *South Asia: Journal of South Asian Studies*, 38 (4), 791–806.

Sivaramakrishnan, K. (2011), 'Environment, law and democracy in India', *The Journal of Asian Studies*, 70 (4), 905–928.

Swenden, W. (2010), 'Subnational participation in national decisions: the role of second chambers', In: H. Enderlein, S. Wälti, and M. Zürn, eds., *Handbook on Multi-Level Governance* (Cheltenham: Edward Elgar), 103–123.

Swenden, W. and Saxena, R. (2017), 'Rethinking central planning. A federal critique of the Planning Commission', In: C.K. Sharma and W. Swenden, eds., *Special issue, continuity and change in Indian federalism, India Review*, 16 (1), 42–65.

Swenden, W. (2019), '"Team India" and the NITI Aayog', In: Y. Aiyar and L. Tillin, eds., *Special Issue on Indian Federalism for Seminar*, Issue 717, 1 May, 28–34.

Verma, S. (2015), 'Subverting the Land Acquisition Act, 2013', *Economic and Political Weekly*, 50 (37), 18–20.

Watts, R.L. (1989), 'Executive federalism: the comparative perspective', In: D.P. Shugarman and R. Whitaker, eds., *Federalism and Political Community. Essays in Honour of Donald Smiley* (Peterborough, ON: Broadview Press), 439–459.

Watts, R.L. (1997), *Comparing Federal Systems in the 1990s* (Kingston-Montreal: McGill-Queen's University Press).

3 The role India's states play in environmental policymaking

Kirsten Jörgensen

3.1 Introduction

India is a large, densely populated federal state which is divided into 29 states and 8 union territories. Policymaking takes place within a relatively centralised federal structure giving great authority to India's Union Government (Lijphart 1996) which can even exercise overriding powers in areas that are constitutionally reserved for the states. The Union Government leverages its significant powers to pass legislation in relevant areas, formulate objectives, shape the national Five-Year Plan which guides the economic development of the country and control India's administrative system. Despite continuous advocacy for greater decentralisation of India's political system (Sáez 2002), in many policy fields the policy paradigm of the superiority of centralised top-down governing by the Union Government has been dominant since India's independence.

However, since India's liberalisation in 1991, the role played by India's states in its development policy has become more relevant, compensating for lacking national initiatives (Sinha 2005). As also described by Swenden and Saxena (see Chapter 2, this volume), over time "significant decentralized traits" have developed, strengthening the political and financial powers of India's federal states (Kohli and Singh 2013, p. 2). In times of political gridlock at the national level and economic stagnation in a number of states, political subnational entrepreneurs have emerged (Rudolph and Rudolph Hoeber 2013). These chief ministers, who were re-elected at least once, were able to boost the regional economic development of their states. One of these regional leaders, Gujarat's former chief minister Narendra Modi, prevailed against the national elites and after a sweeping victory in India's elections in 2014 became the leader of the national government and gained the position of Prime Minister. Relatively higher electoral participation in the states than on the national level highlights the states' strengthened political role becoming the "principle locus of political choice" (Kumar 2013, p. 152). States are increasingly responsible for economic development, welfare and the regulation of industrial relations (Kennedy 2017). Today state action is highly important for industrial and infrastructural development, the energy sector, agriculture and education.

This begs the question of whether the growing economic and political role of India's states also spills over to environmental and climate policy. Mushrooming international comparative literature points to the decisive role subnational states and provinces play, in general, in environmental performance and to an even greater extent in climate action in federal countries (Jörgensen et al. 2015a). As Barry Rabe's studies of US states demonstrated in the 1990s, the growth of their administrative and political capacities and increased state spending on environmental protection challenged the US policy paradigm of the powerful central government in relation to the "lethargic" states (Rabe 2006, p. 34).

India's rapidly growing economy poses huge challenges to the quality of life in urban areas, rural livelihoods and natural resources in India's states. A World Bank study in 2014 found that environmental degradation such as air pollution, water pollution, deforestation and natural disasters cost India $80bn per year or nearly 6 percent of its economic activity. Of that total, 52 percent is attributable to air pollution (World Bank 2014).

The states' environmental action in selected policy subsystems including clean air, waste, renewable energy and energy efficiency will be looked at from four angles: first, from a top-down perspective, we will explore whether and how national policy has helped to increase the environmental, climate and green energy policy capacities of India's states. The states will be regarded as policy implementers. Second, since the 1960s the race-to-the-bottom has been discussed as one likely scenario in which states lower environmental standards to attract investment in environmental federalism research. Drawing on this literature, it will be addressed whether and how India's states obstruct environmental policymaking in India. Third, one strand of comparative environmental politics literature has highlighted the stimulating role subnational states and provinces can play in environmental and climate governance and in the transition to green energy. Within the context of this chapter, a bottom-up perspective will be taken on this issue. We will look at the influence India's states have on India's overall environmental policy capacity building and their role in India's multi-level structures. Selected innovative approaches will be discussed which have been taken by several states to green the economy and to trigger technological leapfrogging. Nowadays environmental and climate governance does not emerge within isolated structures, but rather within global systems. Policy learning and diffusion play an important role in the subnational, national and global spread of approaches that are developed in subnational and national laboratories for experimentation worldwide. Hence, from this fourth angle, horizontal policy learning between India's states and vertical policy learning and diffusion between the states and the national government will be considered. As this chapter aims to introduce selected debates on environmental policymaking in India's states, it will not undertake in-depth studies of the individual topics addressed. The focus of this chapter is on the various ways in which India's states implement, obstruct, shape and also carry forward environmental and climate protection as well as green energy policies. It points to the changing role of India's states in environmental policymaking.

3.2 Environmental policy: the role of the states

Environmental policy from the top down refers to policy directions arising from national governments and legislators. Political arenas for policy formulation and decision making are centered at the national level and national agencies might oversee or guide the implementation of the national policy frameworks at the subnational level. Across the world national governments have, since the United Nations Conference on the Human Environment in Stockholm in 1972, played a major role in the introduction of the new policy domain of environmental protection and they continue to be central actors (Jänicke and Weidner 1997). The perception and policy paradigm of the key role played by central government institutions emerged with relation to the specific nature of environmental problems (Wälti 2010), including the need for environmental research and capacity building, the cross-border character of pollution, the implications of international environmental negotiations and the development of uniform standards to avoid competitive disadvantages for regulated firms.

In India, the central government took the lead during the initial phases of the development of environmental policy. Federal competencies related to environmental protection feature a piecing together of federal state and national competencies. Important areas of policymaking are assigned to the national level. Yet, a number of legislative areas related to the environment, such as public health and sanitation, agriculture, land improvement, water management and mining are, for example, regulated by the state legislatures. Electricity, forests, and economic and social planning fall into a third category of concurrent legislation, where the competencies are shared between the states and the federal level. It is noteworthy that all these areas have linkages to the safeguarding of the natural environment.

Since the beginning of the 1970s, India's legislators have set the major frameworks and institutions for the new policy field of environmental protection in place, giving the states the prominent roles of executors and implementers. Centre pieces of the legislation are the Water (Prevention and Control of Pollution) Act of 1974 and the Air (Prevention and Control of Pollution) Act of 1981, which requires industries to gain consent from state boards.

During the first phase of environmental policymaking, India's national government's leadership function became a stable policy paradigm which influenced the institutionalisation of environmental capacities and the dynamics of environmental policy processes. In the 1960s, a number of states prompted the national government to take action in the water sector, a domain normally reserved for the states' legislators (Gupta 2014). Since the late 1980s, centralisation of environmental protection was also triggered by situational factors, such as the devastating industrial gas catastrophe in Bhopal in 1984, which India's public administration was unprepared for and was blindsided by. The Environmental Protection Act of 1986, which was enacted after the incident in Bhopal, provided the national government with extensive powers to control industrial pollution (Gupta 2014) and set nationwide environmental standards empowering the Union Government rather than the states.

Even where state issues are concerned, the setting of minimum standards is largely pursued in a top-down manner because of the states' lack of capacity to develop their own guidelines for the regulation of pollution from industry and other sectors. States refer to the central guidelines adjusting them to state preferences (OECD 2006).

Although the right to act and to supervise the implementation of environmental law and related areas, such as construction and land use, is in large part down to the states, states still seem to lack the capacity for efficient action.

The major national and subnational agencies responsible for the implementation of India's water protection and clean air legislation are the Central and State Pollution Control Boards (SPCBs), which were established under India's first water law in 1974. The SPCBs mirror the national Central Pollution Control Board, which can assume the powers of the SPCBs in cases of inaction (Jasanoff 1993). Three other services with linkages to environmental performance are also noteworthy, namely India's Administrative Service, the Indian Police Service and the Indian Forest Service. Although personnel are recruited at the national government level, these bodies are under state supervision and answerable both to the states and to the national government (Gupta 2014). SPCBs implement the Water and Air Pollution Control Acts. Before they can be built, industrial plants and projects must often receive consent from the SPCBs. A study from 2009 showed that the SPCBs' refusal rate for such applications varied across state boards; in many cases, it was suspiciously low and the "information collected from boards indicate poor and time-consuming consent management procedure in most boards" (Bhushan 2009, p. 25).

In the 2010s, the SPCBs were reported to have been poorly equipped. They did not have the financial capacity, high-skilled workforce and decision-making scope required to ensure environmental compliance and their monitoring tools were also insufficient (World Bank 2006). Numerous reports filed by governmental agencies think tanks and international organisations have shown that environmental performance continued to be severely hampered by weak administrative capabilities. SPCBs faced capacity challenges; they were not only underfunded but also understaffed in relation to their workload. The weak performance of the SPCBs was also caused by their lack of skilled staff, with lawyers in particular being in short supply. In 2006, the number of people employed by state agencies ranged from between 10 and 800 (OECD 2006, p. 11). The SPCBs' financial resources which consisted of their own income from cess revenues, consent fees and external assistance from the national and the state governments were insufficient (Bhushan 2009, p. 14). Some SPCBs were better equipped than others though, the Maharashtra Pollution Control Board, for example was the best funded and staffed board, while Gujarat's board was not as well-staffed as Maharashtra's but had to monitor the highest number of polluting industries (Bhushan 2009, p. 23).

Environmental performance in India's states still lags far behind national goals. India's National Ambient Air Quality Standards (NAAQS) outlined under India's Air Act and vehicle standards introduced in 1991 and 1996 are being violated. Air pollution control in India relies on one pollution monitoring station for every 2 million people (Pant et al. 2019, p. 51). A Greenpeace study from 2015 points out failures in the design and implementation of the thermal power plant emission standards (Greenpeace India 2016). The study highlights a lack of goal-oriented approaches, regional planning efforts, consideration of interstate pollution and coordination across three government levels, namely the Union Government, state governments and cities.

Since liberalisation, India's Union Government has maintained a dominant position over the states in the making of environmental policy. The features and thematic focuses of India's national environment policy are usually determined and budgeted nationally, such as within the context of India's erstwhile Five-Year Plan. The existing literature about this under-researched topic does not indicate that the centralised environmental policymaking from the top down has stimulated environmental capacity building in the states over time. In particular, the previous fiscal federal structures, which are now slowly changing, have not been helpful in building states' environmental capacity. Hence, it is not surprising that centralised environmental governing is contested. From the view of the states, the burden of implementing centrally initiated policies and legislative measures from parliament has increased without sufficient funding being provided (Finance Commission 2015, p. 60). In its 2015 report, India's Fourteenth Finance Commission suggested strengthening mechanisms of cooperative federalism and in the same vein pointed to the need to integrate economic and environmental concerns (Finance Commission 2015, p. 167). An institutional change meant to strengthen federalist structures and cooperation with the states occurred in 2014 when the newly elected Bharatiya Janata Party (BJP) government replaced the Planning Commission with the National Institution for Transforming India (NITI Aayog) (see Chapter 2, Swenden and Saxena, this volume).

To sum up, the implementation of national regulatory frameworks in India does not effectively address the severe problems of air and water pollution and increasing and diverse waste streams. Effective environmental performance in India is particularly hampered by weak administrative capacities. Aside from insufficient administrative resources, other conditions contribute to the weak environmental performance in India's states as will be addressed in the next subsection.

3.3 Environmental race-to-the-bottom

In India, subnational states and union territories face major challenges related to worsening environmental degradation. Demography, rapid industrial growth and urbanisation are the main culprits for the deteriorating air quality and increasing water pollution, land degradation and waste problems in India's states. The question arises as to whether economic and population growth are the only factors triggering environmental pollution and natural resources degradation or whether lacking political will also hamper the effectiveness of environmental protection. The question of whether subnational states and provinces would rather obstruct environmental protection and for economic reasons race-to-the-bottom has informed the literature about environmental federalism since the 1960s. In the economic debates about federalism, the subnational states and provinces were thought to be the ones that apply "the brakes" and weaken political standards (Engel 1997). Driven by economic inter-state competition and wanting to attract industry, they would not rigorously implement ambitious environmental standards thereby leaving leeway for polluting firms. In the academic debates, the race-to-the-bottom rationale could not be confirmed in empirical studies but could also not entirely be ruled out (Engel 1997; Petschow et al. 2017).

Likewise, for India, there is no easy answer and the literature is inconclusive. In regard to foreign direct investment, the results of a comparative study do not validate the pollution haven hypothesis in the context of India's states (Kathuria 2018). However, oversight of environmental performance of domestic firms is missing. According to widely shared expert opinion, reliable data, which would allow a systematic comparison of environmental performance in India's states is lacking. It is, therefore, not possible to assess improvements and to answer the question of how economic and social development correlate with environmental performance. Also, the course of the Kuznets curve for individual economic sectors or pollutants is not known. Whether a decoupling of economic and social development from emissions, energy intensity and resource consumption in individual sectors is taking place cannot currently be assessed.

A few approaches to measuring environmental performance and ranking India's states have been undertaken (Chandrasekharan et al. 2013; Dash 2011). A comparative study ranked six states, Andhra Pradesh, Sikkim, Himachal Pradesh, Madhya Pradesh and Maharashtra, as the environmentally best-performing states in the year 2012 (Chandrasekharan et al. 2013). Three states out of this group, Maharashtra, Andhra Pradesh and Sikkim, were also ranked in the group of the economically most competitive states in 2011 (Rao and Bird 2014). Overall, environmental performance in the Indian states is very weak.

Air pollution in the states and particularly in urban areas continues to be a major health issue. Regarding air quality, India only ranks 178 out of 180 countries in the Environmental Performance Index 2018 (Wendling et al. 2018). Annual average PM10 concentrations vary across India's states. In 2015, the concentrations of PM 10 exceeded India's standards. This was especially the case in northern and central states in India which saw concentrations up to six times higher than the standard and with Delhi identified as the most polluted state (Pant et al. 2019, p. 49). Electricity production, increased ownership of private cars and the low quality of both vehicles and fuel used are the major drivers of outdoor air pollution. Air pollution is regarded as a national problem (TERI 2016), and initiatives are mainly taken at the Union level. Fast developing states such as Gujarat and Maharashtra have, according to expert opinion, given priority to industrialisation and subordinated environmental protection. Environmental regulations are seen as hindrances in the path to economic growth and development. Various subtypes of particulates (PM) that pose extreme health risks are reaching alarming levels in India's megacities (Pant et al. 2019; TERI 2016). Cities in the rapidly industrialising states of Gujarat, Maharashtra and West Bengal, where polluting industries, such as thermal power stations; iron and steel, cement, pulp and paper, petrochemical and sugar plants; oil refineries; distilleries; and tanneries, are concentrated have the highest levels of the air pollutants sulphur dioxide and oxides of nitrogen. Other states with critical levels include Rajasthan, Andhra Pradesh, Karnataka and Tamil Nadu. India's National Ambient Air Quality Monitoring Programme (NAMP), created by the national government in 2011, aims to develop a nationwide information system about the air quality in India. The designated executing authority is the Central Pollution Control Board (TERI 2016). Some of the cities in India which are most affected have adopted more stringent standards.

In December 2018, the New York Times reported that as millions of Indians watched a televised cricket match between the national teams of India and Sri Lanka, the game suddenly stopped, because one of the Sri Lankan players leaned over and started vomiting. Pollution from solid fuels, the burning of coal and crop residue, and emissions from motor vehicles and poor environmental performance had caused the annual air pollution crisis – a blanket of smog covered the city. Airlines had to cancel flights for several days, schools were shut down and many people had to be hospitalised. India's environmental court, the National Green Tribunal, later criticised Delhi's government for holding a cricket match despite severe air pollution. "Every newspaper has been carrying headlines that the air pollution was going to be higher this week. Still you took no action", the court said. "Are the people of Delhi supposed to bear this?" (Gettleman et al. Dec. 8, 2017).

Environmental activists, representatives of India's environmental court, think tanks and the media point to the problem that policymakers are unimpressed by severe health problems caused by environmental pollution. Both at the national level and in India's states, decision-makers subordinate environmental protection in favour of rapid growth, resulting in pollution and the destruction of wilderness zones among other problems. National and state policymakers do not endeavour to make improvements to environmental performance and are sometimes involved in the dilution of environmental norms. Over the last few years, licensing processes for construction sites were made more lenient and a drastic increase from 45.5 to 73 percent of industrial projects were approved in areas of wildlife (Gettleman et al. Dec. 8, 2017). Obligations for environmental assessments and approvals were also minimised.

According to comparative research, successful environmental policy is brought about by a complex interaction of factors (Jänicke 1997). This includes capacities of governmental and nongovernmental proponents of environmental protection, environmental knowledge and awareness, integrative capacities of the state, the capacity for strategic action, economic-technological framework conditions and political will. Policymakers work within a framework of ideas, intersubjectively held in a given context about the nature of the problems that require attention and objectives that should be pursued (Daigneault 2015, p. 43).

Influenced by global environmental norms, and encouraged by domestic problems, such as the chemical accident in Bhopal, India has set in place elaborate environmental regulatory frameworks. Yet, environmental pollution and the implementation of environmental policy are not an issue that is being tackled by the national and state governments in their day-to-day procedures. Instead, they are driven by developmental concerns and the growth-first paradigm. Between 2016 and 2018, India plummeted in the Environmental Performance Index, from rank 141 to rank 177 out of a total of 180 countries, and the number of deaths caused by PM2.5 are rising (Wendling et al. 2018). There is no indication that the two big parties in India, the Congress party and BJP, or the regional parties are taking more interest in environmental issues, or addressing pressing problems related to the main sources of pollution, such as power generation and transportation for which no simple solutions are at hand. The challenges of handling problems that require costly structural change, and which cannot be easily solved through win-win solutions which have shaped environmental policy success in industrialised countries are huge. An under-researched factor, which might also have influence on lax environmental performance, is corruption. The breaching of environmental norms in the corporate sector is not uncommon and sometimes exacerbated by environmental corruption. Means of corruption are, among others, the recruitment of public employees from monitoring authorities and law enforcement agencies by Indian firms and the execution of orders given by leading state politicians (Jaffrelot 2019). Instances of noncompliance were reported in case studies about Gujarat, where one example led to environmental damages in the form of large-scale destruction of mangroves and the obstruction of creek systems (Jaffrelot 2019). Despite evidence presented by Gujarat's Pollution Control Board, the inspections teams and Gujarat's High Court, which confirmed the lack of compliance in the thermal plants, the Mundra port and other industrial facilities, perpetrators avoided prosecution and punishment (Jaffrelot 2019). In some instances, staff from Gujarat's public agencies and members of India's Administrative Service concerned with noncompliance, and lawyers involved in court cases joined the companies.

According to expert opinion, state governments frequently judge new environmental legislation crafted at the national level through a development lens, mostly ignoring environmental goals. Environmental regulations for mining, forests, wilderness areas and coastal zones are often seen as a barrier to growth. On the other hand, there is interesting evidence that driven by economic and social co-benefits some states have become invested in environmental innovation. The next subsection will take a bottom-up perspective to consider cases, where India's states have undertaken innovative approaches to environmental, renewable energy and climate policy.

3.4 Environmental policy from the bottom up – India's states as policy innovators

Due to their limited administrative-political capacities and the scale of the pollution problem, India's states face difficulties simply acting, never mind pioneering environmental innovations. This was not the case for the US states where their potential for subnational innovation which was unleashed in their climate action in the 2000s was already beginning to show its face at the beginning of the 1990s.

US states' environmental capacities were strengthened during the 1990s, and a few states were able to pioneer innovation in environmental regulatory processes during this period (Rabe 2006).

However, since economic liberalisation, India's states have become increasingly responsible for economic development, welfare and the regulation of industrial relations. In view of their constitutional responsibilities, India's states can develop strategies for various economic sectors, which are of utmost importance for inclusive and environmentally sustainable development. Agriculture, for example, falls under the states' remit. This important economic sector provides employment to 48.9 percent of the workforce and contributes 17.4 percent of the Gross Domestic Product, yet improvements in resource efficiency, conservation and water use through more sustainable forms of agriculture are required. 17.81 percent of the electricity consumed in India goes to agriculture, in 17 states between 40 and 89.2 percent of the land is degraded, and India's states suffer from water pollution and scarcity (TERI 2016, p. 197). India's mountain state Sikkim, for instance, launched an independent innovative initiative in 2003 to pioneer the state's transition to organic farming (Government of Sikkim 20 Feb. 2019). Sikkim's "Organic Mission" is an economic and environmental competition strategy, involving organic standards and regulations, market development for organic food products, the development of an organic farming sector and Bio-Villages and the development of technologies. In 2016, Sikkim became the first fully organic state. Sikkim is regarded a model that can be emulated by other states; however, Sikkim's farmers still face economic challenges due to the lack of local demand for organic products (The Guardian 31 Jan. 2017).

Bottom-up approaches exist, when policy processes evolve at the subnational state level and when the definition of the problems and the design of instruments are shaped by states' actors. Policy change at the state level can be incremental but potentially also involve more radical forms of policy change as the example of organic farming in Sikkim suggests. The debate around laboratories for experimentation (Osborne 1988), according to which subnational states in federal systems sometimes assume a pioneer-like function in policy initiation and implementation, points to innovative policy change taking place. Sometimes the subnational states may compensate for a lack of national policies, as in the case of the US, where in the absence of national climate leadership, the states initiated and instituted separate subnational climate policies during times of national gridlock (Rabe 2004). A number of states began to inventory their greenhouse gas emissions (GHG), create climate action plans, formulate their own GHG-reduction goals and standards, and set up their own regulatory frameworks and funding mechanisms for energy efficiency and renewable energy. The role of the US states as drivers of environmental performance and innovation was explored in environmental studies on subnational state capacities (Rabe 2000; Ringquist 1993).

India's federalist multi-level governance structure certainly provides an opportunity structure for state initiatives. The ideas of cooperative federalism and states' experimentation, as developed by US scholars during the 1930s and 1940s, have been discussed in India as well (Sáez 2002). Various environmentally relevant legislative areas are subject to state regulation, including agriculture, water, waste and land use, or they are a responsibility shared between the states and the Union Government, such as electricity. The early debates about the Indian constitution, however, did not consider, according to Parikh and Weingast (1997), the issue of a certain degree of economic self-rule, which would provide lower levels with the resources needed for independent action (Parikh and Weingast 1997, p. 1609). Yet the amount of financial resources for the states has slowly increased over recent years and the tax revenues going to the states are not tied to federal programs to the same degree as they used to be in the past. The fact that in 2015 India's national budget redistributed a larger share of tax revenues to India's federal states than in the previous year is a further indication of the gradual devolution of powers to India's state governments. In India as in other federal systems, strengthened environmental capacities for the states could counter decreasing environmental ambitions at the national level.

The following section will consider selected state initiatives in which India's states and union territories provide for incremental policy change or even pioneer new policy solutions in India's environmental sector.

3.4.1 Clean air

Civil society actors and the courts played a key role in the introduction of large-scale clean air measures in the Union Territory of Delhi after 1998. The new technology of compressed natural gas (CNG) was comprehensively introduced in Delhi's public transportation fleet (Rajamani 2007). The main drivers behind this policy change were health issues related to Delhi's severe air pollution in the mid-1980s (Puppim de Oliveira and Doll 2016). Agenda-setting was significantly promoted through intense public relations work conducted by the Indian think tank, Centre for Environmental Sciences, which denounced health issues related to Delhi's air pollution and placed the problem on the public agenda (Rajamani 2007). In 1998, India's Supreme Court mandated the use of CNG in public transportation vehicles and instructed Delhi's government to take action.

3.4.2 Waste policy

Waste is another pressing subnational state issue because the amount and diversity of municipal and industrial waste are growing while appropriate infrastructures are mostly missing. Waste policy has long been a neglected issue in India, and the open dumping and burning of waste constitute the primary disposal methods. National framework regulation has emerged rather late, predominantly during the past two decades. Waste management planning at the city and state levels, technological expertise, the development of administrative capacities and, in particular, the creation of appropriate infrastructures for the collection, processing and disposal of waste of all kinds is lacking (Gupta et al. 2015). According to a report from India's Planning Commission, 13 out of the then 28 states and 7 union territories had no waste processing facilities at all in 2011 (Kumar et al. 2017).

As a national strategy was largely missing, various bottom-up initiatives were undertaken to fill the gap and address the severe health and pollution problems resulting from the increasing amounts of all types of waste. Health issues were the main catalyst for the development of solid waste and sewage management systems in Gujarat's city Surat. Administrative and technological initiatives that made Surat one of the cleanest cities in India were taken by networks involving city and state governments after a pneumatic plague epidemic occurred in 1994 (Kapshe et al. 2013).

3.4.3 Low-carbon development

With a rapidly growing renewable energy sector, India is a candidate for a transition to renewable energy and will follow China with "perhaps a ten-year lag" (Mathews 2015, p. 10). Renewable energy policies are well established, are path-dependent and have successfully triggered the diffusion of low-carbon technologies in the wind and solar sector (Jänicke 2012). Renewable energy goals for wind and solar are, however, steadily increasing. International comparative case studies show that subnational states pursue renewable energy policy for perceived economic as well as political advantages (Beermann and Tews 2017; Rabe 2008; Schreurs 2008). Green energy policy, for example, is an area where policymakers at the state level can seek to decarbonise, reducing the use of fossil fuel and instead promoting wind and solar energy. Via green energy policies policymakers can work to reduce local air pollution (Krause 2011), thereby concurrently addressing the global climate problem and generating jobs in the renewable energy sector (Rabe 2008).

India's Union Government has pursued renewable energy policy since the 1970s and reinforced the institutionalisation of this policy field after India's liberalisation in 1991. In 2008, renewable energy policy became an integral part of India's national climate policy. During the first stage of renewable energy policy development in the 1980s, the states were involved in demonstration projects (Chaudhary et al. 2014). Since liberalisation a few of India's states gained increased relevance in the design and implementation of national renewable energy policy (Jörgensen et al. 2015b).

A number of states with locational advantages in the wind and the solar sector including Tamil Nadu, Karnataka, Rajasthan, Maharashtra and Gujarat performed very well in the creation of renewable energy policies. In 2009, nearly a year before the official release of India's national solar mission, the Government of Gujarat (GoG) introduced a solar energy framework and boosted solar power development via fixed preferential tariffs. The national solar mission stimulated India's solar energy market and yielded remarkable growth in capacity allocation across India's states. Achievements were made in terms of capacity, deployment rates, regulatory and policy support, industrial dynamics and the creation of knowledge (Jolly and Raven 2016). Along with the national policy framework, individual state policies were relevant forces in boosting solar energy capacity from 17.8 MW in 2010 to 2.75 GW by July 2014 (Johnson 2015). Among other factors, India's multi-level solar governance has significantly boosted solar development in India.

As in German federal politics (Ohlhorst 2015), in India, renewable energy policy is an area where both a reinforcement of national political objectives by subnational states' measures as described above, as well as a mismatch of national and subnational policies can be identified. Tamil Nadu, which is home to 32 percent of India's installed renewable energy capacity, was an early pioneer of both wind and solar energy policies (Nesamalar et al. 2017). Despite being a leader in the wind energy sector and its enormous wind energy potential, Tamil Nadu has shown reluctance to continue its efforts in this area, scaling back the political promotion of renewable energy. Efforts to redress infrastructural and economic obstacles are insufficient, and the state is not contributing to the realisation of the far-reaching objectives set at the national level (Nesamalar et al. 2017).

India's national Energy Conservation Act 2001 pursues the goal of reducing the energy intensity of the economy. The central strategies addressing energy efficiency in India are the National Mission of Enhanced Energy Efficiency which focuses on industry, the Perform, Achieve, Trade (PAT) scheme and the National Mission for Sustainable Habitat promoting energy efficiency in buildings. Data and studies which could show whether energy intensity across India's states varies do not exist. According to Khosla et al., India's states do on occasion serve as pioneers of policy initiation in energy efficiency, for example in the building sector (Khosla et al. 2017). A few states have focused on specific energy efficiency measures and can be regarded as pioneers with regard to matters such as household energy efficiency, education and influencing behaviour. Andhra Pradesh pioneered a mandatory building energy code that was developed in a consultative process involving public actors and stakeholders from the private sector after a severe power outage in 2012 (Khosla 2016). Andhra Pradesh also pioneered the Light Emitting Diode (LED) street light program and is regarded as a forerunner in data-based governance. Agency for the state's initiatives came in the form of Chief Minister Chandrababu Naidu, who announced the vision for Andhra Pradesh to become one of the three best states in India by 2022 and the best state in terms of inclusive development by 2029.

3.4.4 Climate policy

India's first National Action Plan Climate Change (2008) was developed in a top-down process and was not subject to a wide consultation process. However, there are indications that more dynamic multi-level climate governance structures are emerging (Jörgensen et al. 2015b). First, the greater influence of subnational levels is noticeable in the context of domestic and transnational networks involving NGOs, the corporate sector and donor organisations, all of which are influential at all levels of policymaking (Fisher 2012). Second, India's National Climate Action Plan 2008 does not detail the form regional climate action should take and is complemented by subnational action plans, the State Action Plans on Climate Change (SAPCC) (Jogesh and Dubash 2015; Shukla et al. 2015, p. 11).

Before India's Intended Nationally Determined Contributions (INDCs) were submitted to the United Nations Framework Convention on Climate Change (UNFCCC) in 2015, 32 states and union territories had put in place SAPCCs (Government of India (GOI) 2015).

The INDCs include mitigation and adaptation goals, which have to be implemented by the states. The mitigation targets allow for economic growth and a twofold increase in overall GHG emission levels from the 2010 levels by 2030 (TERI 2016, p. 350) yet strive to reduce the emissions intensity of India's GDP by 33–35 percent by 2030 compared to the 2005 level. As part of its mitigation strategy, India pledged to achieve 40 percent cumulative installed capacity of electric power from non-fossil fuel-based energy resources by 2030. In 2011, Arunachal Pradesh, Odisha, Madhya Pradesh, Maharashtra and Uttrakhand were ranked the highest among India's states with regard to climate mitigation. This ranking was made on the basis of SAPCC, renewable energy growth rates and the electricity intensity of the states' Gross Domestic Product as part of an environmental performance index prepared for the Planning Commission (Chandrasekharan et al. 2013). In the context of state-level climate action planning, the Chief Ministers of Sikkim, Himachal Pradesh and Odisha emphasised environmental issues and "were keen to project their state as environmentally forward thinking" (Dubash and Jogesh 2014, p. 8). In Gujarat, Maharashtra, Sikkim and Odisha, climate policy planning received high-level political support and direct involvement of political representatives and executive heads in the SAPCC (Jörgensen et al. 2015b). Gujarat, in particular, is regarded as a pioneer because of its institutionalisation of a Department of Climate Change.

Innovative approaches taken by the states are related to planning processes and the planning output. Individual states such as Madhya Pradesh attached importance to regional consultations and trying to involve local stakeholders (Jogesh and Dubash 2015, p. 257). The policy output is that the envisaged policy interventions were more incremental than transformational (Dubash and Jogesh 2014, p. 15). Overall, the climate action plans are first and foremost significantly shaped by India's national political strategies "missions" addressed in India's National Climate Action Plan 2008, such as the Jawaharlal Nehru National Solar Mission (JNNSM) and the National Water Mission (Jogesh and Dubash 2015, p. 250).

In addition, state actors have also placed specific regional concerns on the agenda of the states' climate action planning. Electricity transmission and distribution losses in the electricity sector (Odisha), water conservation (Sikkim) and the payment for ecosystem services (Himachal Pradesh) are examples of region-specific issues addressed in the plans (Jogesh and Dubash 2015, p. 250). Concerned by the vulnerability of the state to the melting of Himalayan glaciers, Sikkim institutionalised a State Council on Climate Change and a Glacier and Climate Change Commission. Adaptation measures and necessary precautions to be taken in economic sectors such as agriculture and water management and the tailoring of development strategies according to the vulnerabilities of challenged regions are of high importance in the states' climate action plans. The majority of policy interventions as foreseen in states' climate action plans concern adaptation and resilience building.

India's co-benefits approach to climate mitigation, introduced as a principle in the 2008 National Action Plan on Climate Change, resonates in the states' climate action plan. Renewable energy development, in particular, creates opportunities for economic co-benefits at the subnational level, such as achieving investment and employment through technology and business location strategies. It can in various forms also result in positive environmental and health impacts in urban as well as rural areas, e.g., reducing emissions from cooking and lighting in households. A study of ten climate action plans found that renewable energy had been given emphasis in all of the plans (Jörgensen et al. 2015b). The majority of the initiatives suggested in the state plans studied were incremental in nature and they included a few innovative initiatives. India's National Solar Mission was the policy driver behind a focus on solar energy across the board in all the plans. Yet, objectives linked to non-solar energy resources varied across the states and were related to the advantages of co-benefits that are relevant to the subnational state context, for instance renewable energy applications in agriculture, industry, urban development, transportation, energy, tourism and sustainable habitat. A few states, namely Madhya Pradesh, Karnataka and Kerala, have focused on green tariffs as an innovative, price-based way to promote renewable energy.

Some states that had developed Greenhouse Gas Inventories (GGIs) were requested by the national environment ministry to exclude the GGIs from their state action plans with reference to upcoming international climate negotiations (Dubash and Jogesh 2014, p. 8).

According to Dubash and Jogesh (2014), national support from the top is a necessary condition for the development of effective subnational climate action plans, yet it is not a sufficient condition.

3.5 Environmental leapfrogging

Resource-efficient technological innovation, technology development and diffusion are of utmost importance in the transition processes towards greener and more inclusive development (Jänicke 2012; Perkins 2003). As the examples from agriculture, clean air, waste, energy efficiency, renewable energy and climate protection developed by India's states illustrate, potential does exist in India's states. Subnational governments in India could, for example, exploit the high potential for green construction (Khosla et al. 2017).

More research is needed to provide evidence of Indian states' capacity to trigger environmental leapfrogging. At the moment, technology development is orchestrated by the national government. Yet, various agencies promoting leapfrogging are located at the state level, such as the State Electricity Regulatory Commissions and states' energy agencies. Jharkhand State's climate action plan, for instance, includes the idea of setting up a center to extend technical support to renewable energy development (Jörgensen et al. 2015b).

Examples such as Gujarat's solar and Rajasthan's renewable energy strategy could be regarded as technological leapfrogging with the co-benefit of environmental leapfrogging. Sikkim's approach to organic farming offers an example of deliberate environmental leapfrogging.

Overall, the state governments could potentially take the lead in environmental leapfrogging in areas such as renewable energy, energy efficiency in the industrial and the building sector, organic farming and sustainable transportation. Yet, considering the states' political-economic contexts and motives of the political leadership, environmental leapfrogging is not high up the political agenda. Importantly, the states' fiscal authority is insufficient as they lack the financial resources to realise such technology policies.

3.6 Policy learning and diffusion among India's states

Policy learning, emulation and diffusion are relevant mechanisms advancing environmental and climate governance. Policy learning takes place when policymakers draw lessons from experiences elsewhere in the country or abroad and take up these new ideas in their constituencies. Policy emulation depicts contexts where new policies are modelled fairly accurately on examples found elsewhere. The diffusion of policies is in contrast a much broader concept relating to the many pathways that the diffusion of new ideas and policies locally and globally take (Bennett and Howlett 1992). Subnational policy innovations often serve as models, triggering policy learning and spreading horizontally to other subnational states. Sometimes they serve as models for national policy frameworks resulting in a diffusion of innovations via the national level (Rogers 1962). Empirical research has shown that in the US both innovation and the diffusion of state policies have taken place in a number of policy domains, such as economic development, education, industrial innovation (Osborne 1988), climate protection (Rabe 2008) and the environment (Kern et al. 2005). Policy learning and diffusion in India is under-researched and deserves more attention (Sinha 2015.

Renewable energy policy is a sector in which policy learning nationally and internationally is considered a necessary condition (Jänicke 2017). In India, subnational state programs have also on occasion become templates, such as Gujarat's solar park development which diffused vertically and horizontally. In India, various renewable energy policy frameworks designed by the Union Government utilise a multi-level governance approach and aim to trigger policy learning, emulation and diffusion. The JNNSM (2010) and the National Wind Energy Mission (2014) intend to create new governance structures and processes, aimed at including various levels of government, from the national to the local, the multiple authorities responsible for infrastructure and development, as well as private actors. The JNNSM facilitates objective setting and incentivises deliberation processes, i.e., stakeholder consultations involving public actors from the federal ministries concerned and other governmental levels, as well as private stakeholders from industry, academia and civil society, in order to work towards these objectives. The national policy approach aims to trigger policy-learning from subnational pioneers. The official announcement of the JNNSM indicates, for example, that the government was able to draw lessons from existing state-led solar deployment initiatives and aims to integrate the mission into the existing policy (Government of India (GOI) 30 Jun. 2008, p. 4).

Similarly, innovative approaches to the promotion of solar energy taken by state governments, which might serve as examples for the further development of national frameworks, have been developed in Andhra Pradesh and Rajasthan (Rohankar et al. 2016). The example of Gujarat shows that India's states do not only pioneer policy innovations but that they can also have followers and thus provide leadership. Policy diffusion can potentially take place through horizontal lesson-learning triggered by both transfer organisations such as the SPCBs, the State Electricity Regulatory Commissions, NGOs, the Bureau of Energy Efficiency, the Ministry for Renewable Energy and also international transfer organisations, such as the World Bank. Diffusion can also take place via India's national government, either through regulatory frameworks which draw on the example of state experience or indirectly via voluntary adoption through support mechanisms, incentives and the involvement of national think tanks and governmental institutions. India's "International Solar Alliance" launched in November 2015 at the UNCCC Conference in Paris aims to provide a platform for policy learning, technology transfer and diffusion among countries with solar energy potentials.

Other examples for policy diffusion are Andhra Pradesh's LED program which spread according to interviews "like wildfire", Sikkim's approach to organic farming, Kerala's tourism policy and Joint Forest Management approaches developed in West Bengal which spread to Orissa. In some cases, the central government also took up the policy templates and uploaded them to the national level.

The diffusion of innovative low-carbon policies across Indian states is significant in areas where win-win and co-benefits such as the creation of jobs and revenues can be realized, as for example in the development and diffusion of renewable energy technologies.

3.7 Conclusions

This chapter considers the various ways in which India's states implement, shape, carry forward and also obstruct environmental and climate protection, as well as green energy policies. Building on the presupposition that subnational states are becoming more important policymakers due to India's changing political economy, economic liberalisation and related decentralisation, it examines states' actions in various environmentally relevant subsystems. The increased importance of subnational governments would materialise in independent states' policymaking related to the environment, energy and climate change.

Indeed, the role India's states play in the country's environmental, climate and green energy governance is slowly changing from that of mere executioner of policy to policymaker in their own right. Yet, in contrast to the economic sector where a number of subnational states became active in order to compensate for the ineffectiveness of central measures states have not adopted a prominent position in the combatting of environmental pollution. The states' environmental performance in the traditional areas of environmental pollution control such as the control of industries and the monitoring of air, water and soil is weak. Political-administrative capacity building by the states appears to still be limited and in need of further development. Environmental pollution control, in general, is insufficient and seems to be primarily driven and orchestrated by national institutions.

Alongside weak environmental implementation, there is also indication of an environmental race to the bottom. States rather give priority to fast economic development which becomes apparent in their frequent advocating for dismantling of environmental regulation and exemptions from environmental impact assessments, as in the mining sector and in regard to heavy industry projects.

In view of their constitutional responsibilities, states have the scope to developing green growth strategies for various economic sectors, which would be of utmost importance for inclusive and environmentally sustainable development.

In a few cases enforced by subnational leaders, and motivated by financial pressure and economic co-benefits, state governments have developed innovative approaches to stimulate green development and to create favourable investment conditions. Solar and wind energy deployment in various states provide evidence of this. In doing so, they not only support technological leapfrogging but also facilitate the co-benefit of environmental leapfrogging as a side-effect. The state Sikkim's approach to organic farming offers an example of intended environmental leapfrogging.

However, there is larger potential for state innovation. Subnational governments in India could exploit the high potential for green building and renewable energy in the country's rapidly developing states, union territories and cities. Renewable energy policies offer the greatest socio-economic potential, in the form of, amongst others increased energy security, employment, improvements to the local environment, the development of infrastructure in rural areas and further development of high-tech industries.

In accordance with the federalist idea of "laboratories for experimentation", pioneering state policies serve as a model for national programs. India's states only occasionally pioneer green policy innovations and engender others to follow them and thus provide leadership. In India, subnational state programs have on occasion become templates which have diffused vertically and horizontally. Policy learning across the states as well as nationally and internationally can be considered a necessary condition for improvements in environmental capacity building in India's states.

In the end of the 1990s in the US states, the capacity to develop new solutions for pressing environmental problems was in the ascendance (Rabe 2000). In India, the subnational state capacity to deal with pressing environmental problems is still missing.

References

Beermann, J., and Tews, K., 2017. Decentralised laboratories in the German energy transition. Why local renewable energy initiatives must reinvent themselves. *Journal of Cleaner Production*, 169, 125–134.

Bennett, C.J., and Howlett, M., 1992. The lessons of learning. Reconciling theories of policy learning and policy change. *Policy Sciences*, 25 (3), 275–294.

Bhushan, C., 2009. *Turnaround Reform Agenda for India's Environmental Regulators*. Delhi: Centre for Science and Environment.

Chandrasekharan, I., et al., 2013. Construction of environmental performance index and ranking of states. *Current Science*, 104 (4), 435–439.

Chaudhary, A., Krishna, C., and Sagar, A., 2014. Policy making for renewable energy in India: lessons from wind and solar power sectors. *Climate Policy*, 15, 1–30. 10.1080/14693062.2014.941318

Daigneault, P.-M., 2015. Can you recognize a paradigm when you see one? Defining and measuring paradigmatic shift. *In*: J. Hogan and M. Howlett, eds. *Policy Paradigms in Theory and Practice. Discourses, Ideas and Anomalies in Public Policy Dynamics*. Basingstoke: Palgrave Macmillan, 43–60.

Dash, R., 2011. *Environmental Sustainability – Index for Indian States 2011*. Chennai: Centre for Development Finance.

Dubash, N.K., and Jogesh, A., 2014. *From Margins to Mainstream? State Climate Change Planning in India as a 'Door Opener' to a Sustainable Future*. New Delhi: Centre for Policy Research, Climate Initiative.

Engel, K.H., 1997. State environmental standard-setting: is there a "Race" and is it "to the bottom"? *Hastings Law Journal*, 48, 271–398.

Finance Commission, 2015. *Report of the Fourteenth Finance Commission*. New Delhi: Finance Commission.

Fisher, S., 2012. Policy storylines in Indian climate politics: opening new political spaces? *Environment and Planning C: Government and Policy*, 30 (1), 109–127.

Gettleman, J., Schultz, K., and Kumar, H., 2017. *Environmentalists Ask: Is India's Government Making Bad Air Worse? By Jeffrey Gettleman, Kai Schultz and Hari Kumar* [online]. Available from: www.nytimes.com/2017/12/08/world/asia/india-pollution-modi.html [Accessed 13 December 2018].

Government of India (GOI), 2008. *Jawaharlal Nehru National Solar Mission towards Building Solar India*. New Delhi: Government of India.

Government of India (GOI), 2015. *India's Intended Nationally Determined Contribution: Working Towards Climate Justice*. Bonn: Government of India.

Government of Sikkim, 2019. *Mission 2015 / Sikkim Organic Mission* [online]. Available from: www.sikkimorganicmission.gov.in/mission-2015/.

Greenpeace India, 2016. *Out of Sight: Out of Sight: How Coal Burning Advances India's Air Pollution Crisis*. Bangalore: Greenpeace India.

Gupta, N., Yadav, K.K., and Kumar, V., 2015. A review on current status of municipal solid waste management in India. *Journal of environmental sciences (China)*, 37, 206–217.

Gupta, S., 2014. Environmental policy and governance in a federal framework: perspectives from India. *In*: J. Huang and S. Gupta, eds. *Environmental Policies in Asia: Perspectives from Seven Asian Countries*. World Scientific, 15–42. 10.1142/9789814590488_0002.

Jaffrelot, C., 2019. Business-friendly Gujarat under Narendra Modi: the implications of a new political economy. *In*: C. Jaffrelot, A. Kohli, and K. Murali, eds. *Business and Politics in India*. New York: Oxford University Press, 211–233.

Jänicke, M., 1997. The political system's capacity for environmental policy. In: M. Jänicke and H. Weidner, eds. *National Environmental Policies. A Comparative Study of Capacity-Building*. Berlin: Springer Verlag, 1–24.

Petschow, U., Rosenau, J., and Weizsäcker, E.U. von, 2017. Governance and Sustainability: Routledge. https://www.taylorfrancis.com/books/e/9781351281003

Jänicke, M., 2012. Dynamic governance of clean-energy markets: how technical innovation could accelerate climate policies. *Journal of Cleaner Production*, 22 (1), 50–59.

Jänicke, M., 2017. The multi-level system of global climate governance – the model and its current state. *Environmental Policy and Governance*, 27 (2), 108–121.

Jänicke, M., and Weidner, H., eds., 1997. *National Environmental Policies. A Comparative Study of Capacity-Building*. Berlin: Springer Verlag.

Jasanoff, S., 1993. India at the crossroads in global environmental policy. *Global Environmental Change Part A: Human & Policy Dimensions*, 3 (1), 32–52. 10.1016/0959-3780(93)90013-B.

Jogesh, A., and Dubash, N.K., 2015. State-led experimentation or centrally-motivated replication? A study of state action plans on climate change in India. *Journal of Integrative Environmental Sciences*, 12 (4), 247–266.

Johnson, O., 2015. Promoting green industrial development through local content requirements: India's National Solar Mission. *Climate Policy*, 16 (2), 178–195.

Jolly, S., and Raven, R.P.J.M., 2016. Field configuring events shaping sustainability transitions? The case of solar PV in India. *Technological Forecasting and Social Change*, 103, 324–333.

Jörgensen, K., Jogesh, A., and Mishra, A., 2015a. Multi-level climate governance and the role of the subnational level. *Journal of Integrative Environmental Sciences*, 12 (4), 235–245.

Jörgensen, K., Mishra, A., and Sarangi, G.K., 2015b. Multi-level climate governance in India: the role of the states in climate action planning and renewable energies. *Journal of Integrative Environmental Sciences*, 12 (4), 267–283.

Kapshe, M., et al., 2013. Analysing the co-benefits: case of municipal sewage management at Surat, India. *Journal of Cleaner Production*, 58, 51–60.

Kathuria, V., 2018. Does environmental governance matter for foreign direct investment? Testing the pollution Haven hypothesis for Indian states. *Asian Development Review*, 35 (1), 81–107.

Kennedy, L., 2017. State restructuring and emerging patterns of subnational policy-making and governance in China and India. *Environment and Planning C: Politics and Space*, 35 (1), 6–24.

Kern, K., Jörgens, H., and Jänicke, M., 2005. The diffusion of environmental policy innovations: a contribution to the globalisation of environmental policy. *SSRN Electronic Journal*. https://papers.ssrn.com/sol3/papers.cfm?abstract_id=653583

Khosla, R., 2016. Building energy code lessons from Andhra Pradesh closing the policy gap. *Economic & Political Weekly* 2, 66–73.

Khosla, R., Sagar, A., and Mathur, A., 2017. Deploying low-carbon technologies in developing countries. A view from India's buildings sector. *Environmental Policy and Governance*, 27 (2), 149–162.

Kohli, A., and Singh, P., eds., 2013. *Routledge Handbook of Indian Politics*. Milton Park, Abingdon, Oxon, New York: Routledge.

Krause, R.M., 2011. Policy innovation, intergovernmental relations, and the adoption of climate protection initiatives by U.S. cities. *Journal of Urban Affairs*, 33 (1), 45–60.

Kumar, S., 2013. A shift towards regionalization of Indian politics. *In*: S. Pai, ed. *Handbook of Politics in Indian States. Region, Parties, and Economic Reforms*. Delhi: Oxford India, 147–165.

Kumar, S., et al., 2017. Challenges and opportunities associated with waste management in India. *Royal Society Open Science*, 4 (3), 160764.

Lijphart, A., 1996. The puzzle of Indian democracy A consociational interpretation. *American Political Science Review*, 90 (2), 258.

Mathews, J., 2015. *Greening of Capitalism. How Asia is Driving the Next Great Transformation*. Stanford, CA: Stanford University Press.

Nesamalar, J.D., Venkatesh, P., and Charles Raja, S., 2017. The drive of renewable energy in Tamilnadu: status, barriers and future prospect. *Renewable and Sustainable Energy Reviews*, 73, 115–124.

OECD, 2006. *Environmental Compliance and Enforcement in India: Rapid Assessment*. Paris: OECD.

Ohlhorst, D., 2015. Germany's energy transition policy between national targets and decentralized responsibilities. *Journal of Integrative Environmental Sciences*, 12 (4), 303–322.

Osborne, D., 1988. *Laboratories of Democracy [A New Breed of Governor Creats Models for National Growth]*. Boston, MA: Harvard Business School Press.

Pant, P., et al., 2019. Monitoring particulate matter in India: recent trends and future outlook. *Air Quality, Atmosphere & Health*, 12 (1), 45–58.

Parikh, S., and Weingast, B.R., 1997. A comparative theory of federalism: India. *Virginia Law Review*, 83, 1593–1615.

Perkins, R., 2003. Environmental leapfrogging in developing countries. A critical assessment and reconstruction. *Natural Resources Forum*, 27 (3), 177–188.

Puppim de Oliveira, J.A., and Doll, C.N.H., 2016. Governance and networks for health co-benefits of climate change mitigation: lessons from two Indian cities. *Environment International*, 97, 146–154.

Rabe, B.G., 2000. Power to the states: the promise and pitfalls of decentralization. *In*: N.J. Vig and M.E. Kraft, eds. *Environmental Policy. New Directions for the Twenty-First Century*. Washington, DC: CQ Press.

Rabe, B.G., 2004. *Statehouse and Greenhouse. The Emerging Politics of American Climate Change Policy*. Washington, DC: Brookings Institution Press.

Rabe, B.G., 2006. Power to the states: the promise and pitfalls of decentralization. *In*: N.J. Vig and M.E. Kraft, eds. *Environmental Policy. New Directions for the Twenty-First Century*. Washington, DC: CQ Press, 34–56.

Rabe, B.G., 2008. States on steroids. The intergovernmental Odyssey of American climate policy. *Review of Policy Research*, 28 (2), 105–128.

Rajamani, L., 2007. Public interest environmental litigation in India: exploring issues of access, participation, equity, effectiveness and sustainability. *Journal of Environmental Law*, 19 (3), 293–321.

Rao, G., and Bird, R., 2014. Governance and fiscal federalism. *In*: I.J. Ahluwalia, Kanbur, S.M. Ravi, and P.K. Mohanty, eds. *Urbanisation in India. Challenges, Opportunities and the Way Forward*. New Delhi [u.a.]: Sage India, 203–230.

Ringquist, E.J., 1993. *Environmental Protection at the State Level. Politics and Progress in Controlling Pollution*. Armonk: Taylor and Francis.

Rogers, E.M., 1962. *Diffusion of Innovations*. 4th ed. New York: The Free Press.

Rohankar, N., et al., 2016. A study of existing solar power policy framework in India for viability of the solar projects perspective. *Renewable and Sustainable Energy Reviews*, 56, 510–518.

Rudolph, L.I., and Rudolph Hoeber, S., 2013. The iconization of Chandrababu: sharing sovereignty in India's federal market economy. *In*: S. Pai, ed. *Handbook of Politics in Indian States. Region, Parties, and Economic Reforms*. New Delhi: Oxford University Press, 315–338.

Sáez, L., 2002. *Federalism without a Centre. The Impact of Political and Economic Reform on India's Federal System*. 1st ed. New Delhi [u.a.]: Sage.

Schreurs, M.A., 2008. From the bottom up: local and subnational climate change politics. *The Journal of Environment & Development*, 17 (4), 343–355.

Shukla, P.R., Garg, A., and Dholakia, H.H., 2015. *Energy-Emissions Trends and Policy Landscape for India*. New Delhi: Allied Publishers.

Sinha, A., 2005. *The Regional Roots of Developmental Politics in India*. Bloomington, IN: Indiana University Press.

Sinha, A., 2015. Scaling Up: Beyond the Subnational Comparative Method for India. *Studies in Indian Politics*, 3 (1), 128–133. 10.1177/2321023015575225.

TERI, 2016. *TERI Energy & Environment Data Diary and Yearbook 2015/16*. New Delhi: TERI Press.

The Guardian, 2017. *Sikkim's Organic Revolution at Risk as Local Consumers Fail to Buy into Project* [online]. Available from:. https://www.theguardian.com/global-development/2017/jan/31/sikkim-india-organic-revolution-at-risk-as-local-consumers-fail-to-buy-into-project

Wälti, S., 2010. Multi-level environmental governance. *In*: H. Enderlein, M. Zürn, and S. Wälti, eds. *Handbook on Multi-level Governance*. Cheltenham, Northampton, MA: Edward Elgar, 411–422.

Wendling, Z.A., et al., 2018. *The 2018 Environmental Performance Index*. New Haven, CT: Yale Center for Environmental Law and Policy.

World Bank, 2006. *India: Strengthening Institutions for Sustainable Growth. Country Environmental Analysis*. World Bank.

World Bank, 2014. *India: Diagnostic Assessment of Select Environmental Challenges. An Analysis of Physical and Monetary Losses of Environmental Health and Natural Resources*. Washington, DC: World Bank.

4 Civil society and state interaction in environment policy in India

Sunayana Ganguly

4.1 Introduction

The relationship between the state and civil society is an important process that has shaped the politics and management of the environment in India. Environmental policymaking in India has been historically influenced by a diversity of approaches that are global and local. These approaches are embedded in institutional, social and political processes that have generated sometimes-contradictory impulses and models of conservation and development. The environment, being central to concerns of resource use for both state and society, has therefore been the centre of much negotiation.

The environmental space in India has been shaped by two parallel, often overlapping processes. The first, international laws and treaties that embed or institutionalise particular normative approaches; and second, a strong civil society engaging with a strong centralised state. Global norms elicit responses from both state institutions as well as civil society (Ganguly, 2015) that align these norms to the national terrain, creating new institutions and shaping orientation of both the state and civil society. Some scholars (Bajwa and Bains, 1992; Dwivedi and Khator, 1995) have suggested that institutions related to environmental governance in India emerged as a response to global and external initiatives rather than any long-term vision of domestic policymakers. Others (Shiva, 1991; Sinha, 1998) have argued that demands for environmental governance in India have evolved in the context of social movements. They emerged as a response to the resource-intensive development paradigm that created severe ecological imbalances. Similarly, scholars, such as Migdal et al. (1994), argue that the evolution of governance of natural resources in India is because of the emergence of societal forces, in general, and environmental movements, in particular. However, little work exists on the relationship between state and civil society in forging, negotiating and balancing these competing and diverse interests (Chopra, 2011; Ganguly, 2015).

The historical diversity of thought around the governance of natural resources has led to different models of environmental management that have nurtured heterogeneous civil society organisations (CSOs), orientations and philosophies. These have been classified according to the particular problems and places they are concerned with and the sections of society they involve (D'Souza, 2012; Gadgil and Guha, 2007). Others have formed categories based on conceptions and characteristics of environment problems (Andharia and Sengupta, 1998), while still others (Haydock and Srivastava, 2017) have analysed environmental philosophies based on their main environmental concerns and solutions. While these classifications have captured the diversity of ideologies and philosophies related to the environment, there has been no systematic analysis of how these approaches have undergird institutional orientation and organisation of both civil society and the state.

Haydock and Srivastava (2017) have broadly classified environmental philosophies in India as ones that orient themselves to non-human life or biotic approaches, as well as ones that are more social in orientation. This is similar to a differentiation on the basis of anthropocentrism (Eckersley, 1992) in contrast to Deep Ecology approaches, which emphasises loss of habitat, extinction of species and cruelty to non-human animals (Diehm, 2002). Environmental justice, which has been an influential orientation for some CSOs in India, follows the anthropocentric approach, placing people rather than flora and fauna at the centre of environmental debates. It situates environmental issues within the broader intellectual and institutional framework of human rights and democratic accountability (Bowen and Haynes, 2000; Bryant, 1995), which are distinct from conservation or animal rights that derive from deep ecology approaches. The early western environmental movement aimed to secure and preserve access to natural resources, making the state the agent of conservation. This approach also shaped influential organisations and institutions within the Indian state and civil society. In contrast, environmental movements, described as "the environmentalism of the poor" (Guha and Martínez-Alier, 1997) have two distinguishing characteristics: "they are supported by people engaged in a livelihood struggle, and this struggle is linked to sustainable objectives" (Redclift, 1987, p. 170).

The state has tended towards the centralisation of environmental concerns with its logic mirrored in Indira Gandhi's famous words at the 1972 Stockholm Conference that "poverty is the biggest polluter". This perception of the poor in developing countries causing environmental degradation because of a short-term approach to livelihood security rather than long-term benefits of environmental conservation can be considered a simplistic generalisation (Nadkarni, 2000). Instead, one finds other factors such as the market, weak regulation, weakening of traditional institutions, corruption and state management are all part of a complex nexus of factors that are complicit in environmental degradation. The Indian state has tended to frame questions of environment as subservient to those of growth and development and the alleviation of poverty, instead of seeing development, poverty and environment as part of a holistic relationship. It is also clear that the fallouts of development in the form of environmental degradation fall disproportionately on the poor (Guha and Martínez-Alier, 1997). Thus, in the case of mass movements like Narmada, Chipko or Silent Valley, to name a few, it has been state-led development and economic growth that has been pitted against the "environmentalism of the poor", which emphasises the relationship between ecological and social justice goals.

Civil society has been characterised as a sphere of social life that is public but excludes government activities (Meidinger, 2001). It is used to classify persons, institutions and organisations that have the goal of advancing or expressing a common purpose through ideas, actions and demands on governments (Cohen and Arato, 1992). Its membership is diverse, ranging from individuals to religious and academic institutions to issue-focused groups. These entities range in size and permanence from small, emerging grassroots coalitions to larger, established, better-funded and technically sophisticated formal organisations (Jasanoff, 1997).

The state's approach to environment in India rests on a "complex legacy of colonial and pre-colonial interactions that defines the constraints and parameters within which and from which present thinking and action on development, resource use, and social change have to proceed" (Agrawal, 1992, p. 126). The legacy of the early Nehruvian bureaucratic state, with its emphasis on science and technology has ensured a persistent technocratic approach to the management of the environment (Jasanoff, 1993, p. 32). These institutions, however, have not remained static and have evolved within specific global and local pressures; they have been moulded by global norms and commitments, as well as pressures from within the country, by both grassroots and elites that have struggled to articulate different ideas and trajectories of environmental and developmental progress.

This chapter gives an overview of state-society interaction in the environmental domain since India's independence. It also creates a basic typology of dominant kinds of CSOs present in the environmental domain in India. The analytical framework highlights the importance of viewing the state and civil society as evolving institutions that have specific historical identities, objectives and social histories. This chapter focuses on the interaction between state institutions and civil society in balancing and negotiating different frames of environmentalism in India. In this regard, it outlines the history and trajectories of environmental ideas and narratives that are embedded in both institutions and civil society orientations.

4.2 Theoretical underpinnings

The term environment is often used as a synonym for nature (i.e., the biophysical and non-human environment) and includes both cultural and biophysical elements (Rappaport, 1979). The term environmentalism refers to an explicit active concern with the relationship between the human groups and their environments. The scope and diversity of individuals and institutions around environmentalism in India underscore the complexity and scale of environmental issues. Environmental activism in each country is a result of a specific social, political and economic history (see also Guha and Martínez-Alier, 1997; Jacobs, 2002).

CSOs in India include a diverse range of environmental actors from grassroots organisations and coalitions of conservationists or pollution victims to mature, well-funded, technically expert multinational organisations that resemble of state bureaucracies, but without their political accountability. Some of these affiliations have formed around environmental concerns, while others have incorporated these concerns into broader questions of social development. The different kinds of environmental CSOs display a diversity of form, function, style and expertise, with missions ranging from research to litigation, from lobbying to community education, and from monitoring to natural resource protection. In fact, as Jasanoff argues, "the only structural feature they have in common is their formal independence from the state" (Jasanoff, 1997, p. 580) – this makes the process of building taxonomy a complex undertaking.

The literature on civil society is as disparate as it is diverse. While some scholars argue from a normative perspective for a vibrant and outspoken civil society (Chandhoke, 1995; Gellner, 1994), there are others who favour a strong state that is intertwined with civil society (Hall, 1995; Mahajan, 1999). Some scholars relate civil society with the process of democratisation and political change (Blakeley, 2002) while others focus on its relationship with associations. For the purposes of this chapter, civil society can be understood as a site where "society enters into a relationship with the state" (Chandhoke, 1995, p. 9). CSOs represent different groups and organisations that draw from a diverse base and take a variety of positions between alignment and opposition to the state. The power to participate politically for citizens is given only incrementally by the state and often has to be captured through different avenues. CSOs play an important role in carving out transparent, participatory niches in the rigid and opaque structures of environmental decision-making.

The Indian state has blended modern forms of bureaucratic organisation, competitive electoral politics, participatory forms of governance along with indigenous practices, ideas and institutions and reflects this chequered negotiation in its environment politics (Agrawal and Yokozuka, 2002). The interaction has been characterised as one with a strong (centralised) state facing strong social organisations (Ganguly, 2015). In the face of stalemates between state and civil society that this results in, scholars such as Randeria (2003) have categorised the state as "cunning", selectively furthering some norms and policies, at the expense of others, while simultaneously relying on its perceived weakness to remain unaccountable to citizens. Jasanoff (1993) argues that heterogeneity is not the only characteristic feature of Indian environmental politics, but rather there are some unifying features that cut across strata. One could argue that these unifying features are created by specific institutional and social processes that resonate with the underlying competing philosophies that are present in Indian society and rise to prominence due to a confluence of both global and local developments at critical junctures.

Environmental politics in India can be discussed through two different lenses. One is through the logic of the state that has centralised the control of key resources like water and forests, for example, and secondly through the role of CSOs that co-operate, advocate and align itself with the state at different junctures. The state is subject to a dual conversation that runs parallel to one another, one that is subject to international commitments, obligations and models of resource conservation, the other negotiating these processes against the demands and articulations of civil society. Institutions and policies relating to resource conservation and sustainability embody this dialectic, uneasily shifting between centralisation and decentralisation (see Bhattacharya et al., 2010).

Civil society has both supported and contested the traditional command and control or "fences and fines" orientation of the state. In this approach, local people are excluded from the access and management of protected areas in order to minimise impact and curb illegal encroachment (Brandon and Wells, 1992, p. 1). While this approach garnered support from early conservationists in India, it has been increasingly challenged by CSOs that demanded more dialogue, support and cooperation between the state and local communities.

Strategies for contestation emerged on four different axis; first, CSOs claimed political spaces of representation within the state, where demands could be voiced and deliberated. Second, the movements around the environment that came to be clustered under the influential idea of "environmentalism of the poor" demonstrated that communities in many instances have remained sustainable caretakers of natural resources and can play a role as a bulwark against the state's exploitation of natural resources. Third, CSOs actively began to disseminate alternative visions and pathways on how the relationship between environment and development could be conceptualised formulated and implemented. Fourth, CSOs began to connect local discourses to international ones, building new alliances and interconnections that began transforming both discourse and orientation of natural resource governance at local, state and national levels.

The complexity of state-society relations in India, its layered hierarchies and differences between caste/class/gender among others meant, "inequalities of many kinds exist and compete with each other" (Mohanty, 2002, p. 223). CSOs in India have adjusted their relationship to the state in three different ways, in different phases: first, supporting the state in providing welfare and relief (1950–1960s); second, confronting the state/playing an oppositional role (1970–1980s); third, in an "uneasy" alliance (1990–2000), where it both takes funding from the state and international organisations but also opposes other parts of it (Ray and Katzenstein, 2005, p. 19); and fourth, in opposition and conflict with the state as spaces for state-society deliberation contract (2000–2019). These strategies are often deployed simultaneously, with civil society and the state applying different strategies and narratives to the environmental domain.

4.3 Changing interaction of civil society and state in India

4.3.1 Institutionalizing environmentalism (1950–1960)

The Indian Constitution, as adopted in 1949, did not deal with the subject of the environment or the prevention and control of pollution until the 1976 Amendment. The nature of the interaction between the state and civil society in the environmental sphere post-independence took on several parallel directions. The emphasis on nation-building in the early decades post-independence had pushed models of large-scale industrialisation projects with an emphasis on irrigation, monoculture plantations, hydropower and heavy industries. The poorer and disadvantaged sections of society bore the brunt of displacement (Mohanty and Singh, 2001). In order to address the flagging public sphere, the Central Social Welfare Board (CSWB) was established in 1953 with the objective of promoting voluntary efforts in social welfare. This marked the beginning of government funding to voluntary organisations (VOs) (ibid). VOs were the primary actors, which could be Gandhian or religion-based (both Christian and non-Christian). Other organisations included members of youth and women's clubs, self-help groups, which were introduced and financed by the state, and organisations that were formed on the basis of caste, religion and language. They were involved with the promotion of agricultural and animal husbandry programmes, *khadi* and village industries, co-operative dairies, poultry and fishery units. In many cases, there were both formal and informal connections between these organisations and politicians who had been part of the freedom struggle and shared common belief systems and ideas on development (Sen, 1999). For example, Chandi Prasad Bhatt founded *Dasholi Gram Swarajya Sangh* in Gopeshwar in 1964, which later became a mother organisation to the Chipko Movement. He was influenced by his exchanges with Jaya Prakash Narayan, a Gandhian activist and freedom fighter, in 1956 when he was undertaking a walking tour encouraging self-organisation through India. JP Narayan later led the opposition against Indira Gandhi, forming the Janata Party that became the first non-Congress party to form a government at the Centre in 1977.

The drought and famine experienced by India in the mid-1960s resulted in an emphasis on the basic needs of poor individuals (Ebrahim, 2003, p. 35), and several VOs also emerged in response to this. Many of them were funded by international agencies, especially those whose programmes fit in with the central and state government's programmes and schemes, such as the Integrated Rural Development Programme, and were also provided government support for their work (Ebrahim, 2003, p. 36). Civil society manifested in a large number of self-initiated organisations to create alternate channels for delivery of basic services like health and education. Voluntary organised activities promoting development had a co-operative attitude towards the government as a large number of these organisations had historical links with the ruling Congress Party (ibid).

The institutionalisation of environmental concerns, and specifically, conservation was also taking place at the highest levels of government, with the aid of high-profile conservationists like Salim Ali, JC Daniel, SP Godrej, among others. Organisations like The Bombay Natural History Society (BNHS), set up in 1883, the Botanical Survey of India, which begun in 1892 and reopened again in 1952, the Zoological Survey of India established in 1916 and the Indian chapter of the World Wildlife Fund set up in 1969 acted as influential think tanks with strong links to the government, as well as global funding agencies. Through strong institutional connections, nature conservation was shaped by a handful of elite conservationists, whose ideas resonated with the Nehruvian ideal of scientific modernity and growing centralisation. Both social and intellectual elites cordoned off resources for protection that had historically been common property, such as forests and water.

Until the 1970s, environmental legislation was derived from colonial laws. The Forest Act (1927), as with the Factories Act (1948), was based on a British legislation that outlined a hazardous process as one that could cause "impairment to the health" of people working in factories and "result in pollution to the general environment" (Government of India, 1948, Section 2). Environmental justice was not on the agenda and policies like the 1927 Forest Act denied forest dwellers any rights over forest produce. In other spheres, incremental steps were taken to prevent water pollution in inter-state rivers (River Boards Act, 1956) and prevent cruelty to animals (Prevention of Cruelty of Animals Act, 1960). Thus, the landscape of environmental policymaking in the first two decades after independence remained largely restricted to the bureaucratic structure inherited from the British, consolidating and expanding its influence through elite networks and their interaction with the state.

4.3.2 The emergency and the return of civil society (1970–1980)

During the 1970s and 1980s, a divide emerged between the centralised and technocratic form of environmental management and protection as deployed by the state, set against the emerging organisations around what came to be known as the "environmentalism of the poor" (Guha and Martínez-Alier, 1997). These divergent processes marked the push-pull between the state and civil society in this period. Rebellions, like Chipko (1973) and Appiko (1983) against illegal tree felling in the north and south of India, respectively, were emblematic of organised movements articulating the ecological impact of state-led, monolithic development processes. At the courts, the emergence of the use of Public Interest Litigation in 1979 served as a bridge to redress the breaches by the state by empowering disadvantaged and marginalised citizens.

The critical shift between civil society and the state occurred with the imposition of the Emergency by Indira Gandhi from 1975 to 1977, which saw the democratic state turn dictatorial. This period saw severe curtailments in fundamental rights, the power of the judiciary and the press: it redefined the relationship of citizens with the state, restructured civil society and "made it more alert to transgression of its boundary by the state" (Tandon and Mohanty, 2002, p. 70). It also had a revitalising effect on civil society, which, after 1977 witnessed an increase of activities within traditional social movements involving peasants, workers and students, and also amongst the new social movements (Nepal, 2009) that included environmental groups and women's organisations.

While civil society faced curtailment in the tenure of the Emergency, the environment was a crucial area of concern and interest for Indira Gandhi and she ushered in flagship programs like Project Tiger in 1973, banned the export of tiger and leopard skins and safari hunts and stopped the Moyar Dam that would have inundated the Mudumalai wildlife sanctuary in Tamil Nadu (Rangarajan, 2007). The fines and fences approach that the government was coming to rely on found support among early conservationists who believed that forests were best protected by the state. While this socially repressive regime clamped down on civil liberties, land under forest cover flourished, with the land area under sanctuaries and parks increasing by 4 percent, as compared to one-eighth the figure in 1970 (Rangarajan, 2007). "Forests and wildlife" were also placed on the concurrent as opposed to the states' list where it has remained, which means that it can be legislated on by both the centre and states but in case of a dispute, the centre will prevail.

This marked preference towards state-led conservation came at the cost of displacement and enclosure. Communities that had traditionally depended on the forests for grazing or other non-timber forest products found themselves turned out of their land. At the same time, large-scale industrial projects and agricultural expansion appropriated forestland with the consent of the Centre. This led to grassroots movements that pitted displaced communities against the state and big business (see Bandyopadhyay and Shiva, 1988; Shiva, 1991).

The press and media played a crucial role in supporting civil society's environmental demands with wide-scale reporting and writing on environmental concerns. The "peasants had protested; then, journalists sympathetically reported on these protests" (Guha, 2008, p. 1) with the media becoming a crucial mediator between CSOs and the state. The setting up of the Ministry of Environment and Forests (MoEF) in the 1980s as a response to this widespread support of the green agenda seemed to herald a new and legitimate space for both conservation and environmentalism of the poor and its link to development. A wave of academic interest followed, as think tanks and research institutes began examining links between environment and development and started to become important partners of an expanding environment ministry. Understanding the scientific and social roots of conflict over natural resources was aided by the increasing budgets of the National Committee on Environmental Planning and Coordination (NCEPC) that became the Department of Environment (DOE) and consequently, the MoEF in 1985. In 1983–1984, the DOE had a budget of 27 crore rupees that grew to 850 crore rupees in 2000–2001 (Bhatt, 2004).

In the late 1970s after India's Emergency, the first non-congress government came to power (Janata Government, 1977–1980). They focused on strengthening civil society capacity and influence by creating special roles for VOs (Planning Commission, 1978) and training programs of lower-level functionaries. Special exceptions and incentives were also granted to industries and businesses to involve VOs in their activities in rural areas. Encouraged by institutional incentives, the country witnessed the proliferation of VOs. These provided services to the marginalised in the form of health services, micro-credit and rural banking services, primary education and sanitation (Mohanty and Singh, 2001). To some extent, VOs were also conceived of as partners of the Indian state. For example, the Seventh Five-Year Plan (1985, section 3.14) states:

> Voluntary agencies have been traditionally working in the areas of relief and rehabilitation, education, health and social welfare. But they can also play a useful role in supplementing Government's efforts in other areas such as the provision of drinking water, release and rehabilitation of bonded labor, ground water surveys, development of alternative sources of energy and many other activities relating to rural development and poverty alleviation. Several voluntary agencies have acquired, over the years, professionalism and expertise to provide competent technical services and yet the services of voluntary agencies have not been fully exploited by governmental agencies for the implementation of programmes of welfare and poverty alleviation.

The Seventh Five-Year Plan (1985–1990) also highlighted the negative effect development programs were having on the environment. It reflected that "the need to improve the conditions of our people is pressing; under this pressure many concerned with developmental activities lose sight of environmental and ecological imperatives" (Planning Commission, 1985, section 18.2). For the first time, the plan called out for people working together to improve the quality of the environment and highlighted "securing greater public participation in environmental management" (Planning Commission, 1985, section 18.20). Though implementation of this principle was negligible, it is the first institutional recognition of the fact that effective citizen participation was required in environmental management and conservation.

In 1984, the Bhopal Gas Disaster became a turning point for issues related to environmental justice in the country. On the night of December 2–3, 1984, an explosion at gas tanks storing methyl isocyanate at the Union Carbide India Limited pesticide plant in Bhopal, killed 2,000–4,000 people and maimed about half a million others and their progeny. This became a crucial trigger to environmental jurisprudence in India, highlighting "the polluter-pays principle" and the event became an important precursor to recognising principles such as "sustainable development" and "inter-generational equity". A few activist judges in the late 1970s and early 1980s, in a series of high-profile cases, laid the groundwork for the growth of public interest litigation in India. This resulted in the court taking pro-environmental stands at the behest of

> public spirited citizens which has subsequently led to orders to protect the Taj Mahal from corrosive air pollution, rid the River Ganges of trade effluents, address the air pollution in Delhi, protect the forests and wildlife of India and clear the cities of their garbage.
> (Rajamani, 2007, p. 294)

The 1970s and 1980s saw the development of the Public Interest Jurisdiction (PIL) for the benefit of persons, who, by virtue of their "socially or economically disadvantaged position are unable to approach the court for relief" (Rajamani, 2007, p. 294). PILs offer a collaborative approach, where Judges include numerous parties and stake-holders, form fact-finding, monitoring or policy-evolution committees and arrive at constructive solutions to the problems flagged for their attention by public-spirited citizens. This tool allows judges to design innovative solutions, direct policy changes, catalyse law-making, reprimand officials and enforce orders (Ibid).

The gap between developing a law and enforcement also led to the Environment Protection Act, 1986 (EPA). Before its enactment, only the government could prosecute under Indian environmental laws. The EPA effectively allowed citizens to prosecute offenders (for example, a polluter discharging effluents beyond a permissible limit), provided a 60-day notice is given to the government of the intention to prosecute. In addition, Section 43 of the Air Act (amended in 1987) and Section 49 of the Water Act (amended in 1988) saw the first policies to allow citizen participation in the enforcement of pollution laws.

The 1970s–1980s was emblematic of social movements concerned with environmental questions. Rajni Kothari described this period as a "democratic churning" (1989, p. 58), which brought to the forefront questions around deforestation, displacement, waterlogging, siltation and salinisation. In many cases, voluntary groups from outside the affected area aided local protests. These were often individuals or external groups without any political or institutional affiliation (Swain, 1997). These movements are sometimes rather "simplistically represented as the environmentalism of the poor" (Williams and Mawdsley, 2006, p. 662). Alternatively, these struggles are seen as articulating a cultural opposition to statist understandings of the environment, pitting them against values of holism and the respect for nature (ibid). These articulations have been discussed in scholarship in several ways; as an eco-feminist attack on masculinist science, increasingly embodied by global agri-biotechnology corporations (Shiva, 1991); as part of a far longer history of peasant resistance to the state (Guha, 1989); and on the far right, environmental degradation as further injustice meted out on the Hindu nation due to its colonisation by Muslims and Christians (Sharma, 2012). They have argued that the postcolonial state, like its colonial precursor, privileges the "national" over the local, the urban over the rural, and the "modern" over the "traditional" (Williams and Mawdsley, 2006), but this period saw a reassertion of the voices of the traditionally marginalised, aided by institutional developments.

4.3.3 Liberalizing environmentalism (1990–2000)

It has been argued that environment policy in India had always had its roots in international trends and ideas (Bajwa and Bains, 1992; Dwivedi and Khator, 1995). This was particularly significant in post-liberalisation India that began evaluating domestic questions in light of international debates on the depletion of the ozone, greenhouse gases, climate change, biodiversity loss and the role of forests. Article 253 of the Indian Constitution, for instance, empowered parliament to make any law for the whole country to implement the decision taken at international conferences even for the subjects under the jurisdiction of the states (The Constitution of India, Art. 253, Entries 13–14, List I, Schedule VII). Because India was a signatory to the United Nations Stockholm declaration in 1972, the central government claimed sole jurisdiction over environmental matters based on the fact that environmental rules were derived from international obligations.

The state was cautious in balancing the global environmental agenda with "the aspirations of large masses of poor people" and emphasised that international negotiations should "not impose any burden on developing countries, respecting their sovereign right over their resources". (Planning Commission, 1992, Section 4.16.7). The role of civil society, in particular, was envisaged as support systems, whose role would be strengthened "by directly involving them in the process of identification, formulation and implementation of environmental programmes" (Planning Commission, 1997, Vol. 2, Overview).

Enabled by the state, the 1990s saw a transition in the way civil society was conceptualised. This is mirrored in the terminology – shifting from VOs in pre-liberalisation India to the CSOs of post-liberalisation. This reflects in the changing language of their roles – from the care, welfare envisaged by VOs before the 1990s to empowerment, rights-based activism (Mohan, 2002; Mohanty, 2002). New economic policies and the opening up of the economy in 1991, driven by global institutions favoured the approach of "rolling back of the state" creating a new vacuum that was filled by CSOs, who were seen as potential agents that could support the state in democratisation (Mohanty, 2002). This new space for "participation" was built on a particular interpretation that was "limited to the efficient implementation of project designs and priorities set by national and international environmental experts and bureaucrats" (Randeria, 2008, p. 6). This led to the growing professionalisation of the sector and the growing profile of CSOs, which began to inhabit the public space, between government and society at all levels of society. It also emphasised new forms of partnerships where local communities and government manage resources and share the cost in partnership with one another. One such initiative was the Joint Forest Management (JFM) in the 1980s that expanded in scale and scope in the 1990s (see Chapter 5, Das, this volume).

Activism also deepened with Public Interest Litigations becoming an important tool of regulation with the courts taking on an "activist" role (Rajamani, 2007). The nature of PILs changed, becoming more institutionalised and specialised. CSOs and lawyers began filing them on a regular basis. The courts responded with bolder, more unconventional rulings. With the mainstreaming of narratives around environmental protection, one also saw a steady increase in urban activism around issues of waste, pollution and tree felling, among others. Despite their activism, there was also criticism levelled at the courts for being restrictive in terms of membership, as it was pointed out that its composition of middle-class intellectuals meant that certain value choices were preferred over others, for instance, clean air rather than right to livelihood (Rajamani, 2007). Large-scale mobilisations also led to important central legislations like The Biological Diversity Act (2002), which facilitated access to genetic materials while protecting the traditional knowledge associated with them and The Forests Rights Act (2006), which legally recognise the rights of communities to protect and manage forests.

The 1990s saw the MoEF take some important steps to provide a legal and institutional basis for the management and protection of the environment by way of rules, notification of standards, delegation of powers and identification of agencies. In 1992, after the United Nations Conference on Environment and Development (UNCED), or Earth Summit, held at Rio de Janeiro, the Union Government adopted a National Conservation Strategy and Policy Statement on Environment and Development and outlined a policy of "sustainable development" and the government's "commitment to re-orient policies and action in unison with the environmental perspective" (MoEF, 1992).

Post-liberalisation India also saw the growth of a new consumer class influenced by global cultures of consumption. Many scholars saw these policies of structural adjustment and world market integration as adding to ecological disaster (Sheth, 2004; Shiva, 1991). Others have cautioned against simplistic vilification or glorification of certain demographics. The demand has rather been for an alternative development model, one based around the re-scaling of development projects to the local level, the protection of common-property resources and the restoration (or recreation) of participatory, community-based forms of environmental management (Williams and Mawdsley, 2006).

4.3.4 Subverting environmentalism (2000–2019)

In the decades after liberalisation, India's policy narrative began to shift from poverty reduction to inclusive economic growth and sustainable development. The adoption of new global rhetoric was evident in the Eleventh (2007–2012) and Twelfth (and final) Five-Year Plans (2012–2017), the last before the Niti Aayog was set up in 2015 to replace the Planning Commission. Their focus on sustainable development and inclusive growth deviated from the previous plans, making discursive space for a new paradigm of development – one that theoretically attempts to find a common ground between development and environment (Lele, 1991). It emphasised the role of marginalised communities, but the role of the environment in this marginalisation was not reflected upon. Environment was also instituted as a major cross-cutting national target category (one among six). The focus on innovation, technology was linked to greener technologies and cleaner fuels. The plan also proposed setting up a statutory body on sustainable development that could guide government policies and programmes and reviving committees of concerned citizens as environmental watchdogs (9.1.2). Market orientations of the state are also mirrored in the draft forest policy of 2018 that furthers an economic understanding of forests that privileges forest productivity and public-private partnerships, rather than decentralisation and community participation.

Environmental regulation, in particular, has been systematically weakened with little transparency on the process of environmental monitoring and decision-making (Kohli and Menon, 2009). While policy mechanisms like the Environmental Impact Assessment (EIA) were instituted (1994 and 2006) (see Ghosh, 2013; Kohli and Menon, 2015), their implementation became the core contention between the state and civil society. In particular, critics have pointed out that there is no comprehensive "or systematic integration of the principles of sustainable development into India's policies and programmes. Nor is there evidence that the rate of biodiversity loss has been reduced, or that ecosystem resilience has increased" (Kothari, 2013, p. 10).

The market orientation of the state and its emphasis on a particular model of development – one that is resource-intensive – has sharpened conflict over natural resources. As the economy continues to grow, so must it consume with inputs that range from fossil fuels to mineral ores. Conflicts between the state and people who are dependent on those same resources have often turned violent. For example, farmers of Badkagaon in Jharkhand, India, have been struggling against the National Thermal Power Corporation (NTPC) since 2004, which was when it was allotted coal-mining concessions. In 2016, the police fired on a peaceful sit-in protesting unfair land acquisition killing five (Martinez-Alier et al., 2016). In October 2004, the Orissa government signed an agreement with Vedanta Alumina, a subsidiary of Sterlite Industries (India) (SIIL), to mine bauxite deposit from the Niyamgiri hills, thus ignoring the cultural and livelihood rights of the *Dongaria Kondhas* – the indigenous people who occupy the land. After more than a decade-long agitation attracting international support (Sahu, 2007; The Wire, 23rd April 2018), with the support of the Supreme Court, mining was halted; however, in 2016, a prominent activist from the tribe was murdered. In 2017, it was reported that India was the fourth deadliest country for environmental activists, with 200 documented murders in 2016, a 10 percent rise from 2015 (The Wire, 14th July 2017).

The logic of growth embraced by contemporary governments has treated any impediments to economic development as both subversive and "anti-national" (Kumar, 2016). The state has turned deeply suspicious of environmentalists and indigenous people, advocating for their rights, especially in arenas where their advocacy threatens state access to resources like minerals or energy. It has used policies like the Foreign Contributions Regulation Act to cut off funding for not just domestic CSOs but international ones like GreenPeace advocating on Indian soil. This has led to shrinking spaces for peaceful deliberation, and state and CSO interactions have become increasingly polarised. In addition, institutions that provided independent watchdog functions like the National Green Tribunal (NGT) and the National Board for Wildlife (NBWL) have come under attack since 2014, with the state systematically attempting to dismantle autonomy either through reducing the number of independent members (from 15 to 3 in the case of NBWL) or tweaking the rules by which members of the government could form part of the committee (in the case of NGT). From 2018 to 2019, for example, the State Environment Impact Assessment Authority (SEIAA), which is one of the clearing authorities for EIA, had expired and has not been reconstituted. At the same time, the MoEF has proposed a "re-engineering" of the EIA 2016 notification that commentators suspect will further dilute it. Sharpening its focus on rapid economic growth since 2014, the state has allowed fast-tracking of environmental clearance on industrial projects. By 2019, 99.82 percent of all industrial projects were cleared; 682 out of the 687 projects that were examined by the NBWL. In contrast, under UPA-2, only 80 percent of the projects got clearance – 260 were allowed out of 328 projects (Rathee, 2019). This has weakened both independent assessment processes, as well as deliberation with civil society.

4.4 CSOs and their interaction with the state

Distinguishing between diverse types of environmental organisations in India, one can plot them according to both philosophy and type. NGOs have been defined in the Indian context as "organizations that are generally formed by professionals or quasi-professionals from the middle or lower middle class, either to serve or work with the poor, or to channel financial support to community-based or grassroots organizations (CBOs or GROs) of the poor" (Sen, 1999, p. 332). Building on and conflating the different categorisation made by O'Neill (2014), for the purposes of this chapter, I divide CSO's into (1) CBOs, (2) think tanks, (3) social movement organisations and (4) conservation organisations (see also Costoya, 2007). Business institutions and activities on corporate social responsibility (CSR) have been left out of the mapping, even though they have a growing role in the intersection between state and CSO interactions. This is in order to focus on historically salient actors even though there are overlaps between these different types of organisations.

As seen in the previous section, CSOs have inhabited many different avatars at different moments in postcolonial India, but are also rooted in particular narratives and approaches to the environment. Their role has been to ensure transparency, delivery of services, effectiveness and accountability of existing policies, advocating for change and resisting policies that are perceived as oppressive or impinging on fundamental freedoms, along the four axes previously discussed. Their role involves five strategies with respect to the state: education, persuasion, collaboration, litigation and confrontation. Persuasive strategies involve the bringing of an issue to the attention of authorities, through the collection and presentation of information on the one hand, and petitions on the other. Collaboration entails partnering with the authorities through lobbying of local governmental offices, departments and other decision-making bodies, and confrontation takes the form of rallies, marches, agitations, campaigns and other direct action. Many CSOs will employ these strategies simultaneously, following a "dualistic strategy" where CSOs both cooperate with and confront state actors (Cohen and Arato, 1992; Ganguly, 2015).

4.4.1 CSO typology and relationship to the state

4.4.1.1 Community-based organisations

Community residents have often found it necessary to come together to pool available resources, skills, talents and time for their common good. These organisations are frequently referred to as grassroots or CBOs (Opare, 2007). For these organisations, development activity is centred at the level of the neighbourhood or village and not the nation-state as a whole (Korten, 1987). They are central institutions for building solidarity and social capital (Opare, 2007) and play an important role in generating an inclusive decision-making process, providing members with adequate bargaining power, ensuring increased economic security, promoting community empowerment and serving as channels for organised local development (Rindell and Robinson, 1995; Weinberger and Jutting, 2001).

They have become increasingly important in the environmental domain as both local and foreign organisations push for the involvement of local people in protecting biological diversity and habitat integrity (Kakabadse, 1993; World Wildlife Fund for Nature, 1993). Development organisations, criticised for promoting economically oppressive resource development projects, aim to promote local participation in development (World Bank, 1996). Activists hope to empower local groups in their conflicts with state resource management agencies and national and transnational capital (Colchester and Lohmann, 1993). Indigenous people argue for new models that respect local rights, knowledge and culture (Durning, 1992).

CBOs have played an important role in grassroots work since the 1950s, supplementing government programmes or reaching areas the bureaucracy neglected.

Over time, these organisations fractured into specific networks to form CBOs or people's organisations like Self-Help Groups, farmers and youth groups, village forest committees, user groups and urban resident welfare associations (RWA), among others. Membership is purely voluntary or with a nominal fee. The focus is on empowering marginalised (politically or socially) or under-represented groups like women, scheduled tribes (ST) and scheduled castes (SC). They are local in scope and issue areas, although they may connect to larger discourses like biodiversity conservation and climate change. They are locally networked, often with institutional connections. For example, the village forest committees are envisioned as active partners to the Forest Department.

In the environmental sphere, scholars (Blaikie, 2006; Kellert et al., 2000) document mixed results of Community-Based Conservation (CBC) initiatives. There are several factors that appear to contribute to the success of CBOs; self-organisation has been identified as one critical factor (Gunderson and Holling, 2002; Levin, 1998). Shukla and Sinclair (2010) point to other factors such as providing capacity-building support, increasing access to markets and policymakers, nurturing local leadership, combining local knowledge with scientific knowledge (Berkes et al., 2004; Seixas and Davy, 2008). For examples of successful case studies and characteristics involving CBC, look at Hobley and Shah (1996) who discuss the characteristics of successful functioning of village forest communities in India and Nepal, Shukla and Sinclair's (2010) analysis of the Baripada's forest protection initiative in Maharashtra, and Kumar and Vashisth's (2005) analysis of JFM in Haryana.

4.4.2 Think tanks

The environmental domain in India has historically been perceived as a highly technical field because of the state's emphasis on scientific management of natural resources. Think tanks are organisations that straddle the scientific and/or research communities and the government. Think tanks could be both independent and derive revenues from consulting and research work and may also depend heavily on governments, advocacy groups or corporations for their funding. In India, many researchers of the Indian scientific community also work at public institutes (Mahajan, 1999), which have close institutional links with the state.

Think tanks have evolved over time in post-independent India and could be both independent and established as non-profit organisations or philanthropic operating foundations. Some examples include The Energy and Resources Institute (TERI), Centre for Science and Environment (CSE), Ashoka Trust for Research in Ecology (ATREE), The Council on Energy, Environment and Water (CEEW), policy research institutes located in or affiliated with a university [The Centre for Development and Environment Policy (CDEP), Centre for Environment, IIT Guwhati] and governmentally created or state-sponsored institutes [Indian Institute of Science (IISc), Indira Gandhi National Forest Academy (IGNFA)]. They play a mediating role between the government and public, often resulting in the creating of "issue networks" that could encompass the local, regional, national and international (Scott, 1999). Historically, a Research Programmes Committee, consisting of leading social scientists, was established in the Planning Commission during the First Five-Year Plan (1951–1956) to determine priorities for government support of institutional research relevant to economic planning. At the same time, the Ford Foundation came forward to establish new and strengthen existing institutions. The decade of 1956–1965 saw the establishment of many think tanks to compensate for the absence of a policy research environment in Indian universities and subsequently provide the growing state with data. The 1980s saw another spurt in the growth of think tanks. With the forming of the MoEF, they became part of a shift towards greater institutionalisation of environmental concerns. This was also the period when CSOs and privately supported institutions emerged as research-based policy advocacy groups (Mathur, 2009).

Think tanks act as "policy-brokers" and their main sphere of interaction remains with bureaucrats, rather than decision-makers, who act as "gatekeepers" (Mathur, 2009, p. 17). Given that India is historically bureaucracy driven, it is harder for outsiders to influence policy. A characteristic of these institutes that propose alternative policy pathways is that, apart from conducting research, they play an important advocacy role by publicising their studies in the media and holding seminars for relevant policymakers, "bombarding" them with information (Mathur, 2009, p. 18). These institutions exploit the space between "the state and the sphere of civil society organizations rooted in a participatory politics" (Mathur and Mathur, 2007, p. 603).

Think tanks play an important role in connecting government to activists and CSOs working on the ground, in their analysis and evaluation of policies, as well as identification of implementation gaps. Part of their role as knowledge generators is the creation of conceptual models for practical application. For example, The Energy and Research Institute developed GRIHA (Green Rating for Integrated Habitat Assessment), which was adopted as the national rating system for green buildings by the Government of India in 2007. The annual report of CSE titled "Knowledge based Activism" explains its role as an organisation that generates primary research but also acts as negotiator, facilitator, communicator and trainer of government and citizens.

4.4.3 Social movement organisations

The period of intensified CSO activism in the 1970s saw a number of GROs emerge that came to direct and sustain social movements. According to Zald and McCarthy (1980, p. 2) "A social movement organisation (SMO) is a complex or formal, organisation which identifies its goals with the preferences of a social movement or a countermovement and attempts to implement these goals" (see also Zald and Berger, 1978). Environmental movements have had some scrutiny from theorists (Ray and Katzenstein, 2005; Sangvai, 2007; Shah, 2004) but a distinction can be made between social movement organisations and campaign organisations (Ganguly, 2015). Social movements are informal groupings of people or organisations that "develop in the course of time, and begins with protest or agitation on a particular issue which may not have the 'organization' or 'ideology' for change" (Shah, 2004, p. 10). Social movement organisations respond to a mobilising event, issue or political opportunity to sustain collective action aimed at policy change. The mobilisation around the Forest Rights Act by the National Federation of Forest Peoples and Forest Workers was one such example (Ganguly, 2015). Campaign or Advocacy organisations, on the other hand, are more formalised, less spontaneous and professionalised. For example, organisations like Greenpeace run both local and national campaigns, fulfilling "watch-dog" functions around issues that may otherwise escape public scrutiny and may never gain the momentum of a social movement. Instead, these organisations operate using long term, low-intensity targeted advocacy, which may intensify or add strength to a social movement at particular junctures.

Social movement and campaign organisations could be placed on a spectrum; from city-based advocacy groups with connections to both grassroots and policy-makers (*Kalpavriksh*), to alliances like the *National Alliance of People's Movements* (NAPM) and *Narmada Bachao Andolan* (NDA), to national branches of international organisations (*GreenPeace*) or national advocacy organisations (*Jhatkaa*). Their ideologies have intrinsically been against resource-intensive models of development, giving weight to local experience, yet pulling in strands from the national and international when necessary. Thus, its scope encompasses the "politics of the local", as well as the national and transnational (Sangvai, 2007). This was especially true post-liberalisation, which saw a resistance to the onslaught of multinational capital and intensification of resource exploitation. While social movement organisations pit themselves against the state, their financing comes from diverse sources, which often includes the state. Ironically, the success of social movement organisations often depends on the extent to which the state in which they are located share their pro-poor concerns (Ray and Katzenstein, 2005).

Historically, social movement organisations have focused on poverty alleviation while newer social movements and campaigns from the 1990s have been focused on equity-based arguments and are reconstituting environment claims as rights claims. While distinctions have been made between the environmental priorities of the West (climate change, deforestation) as opposed to issues in Southern countries (desertification, urbanisation, resource conflict) (Gardner, 1995), the cleavages are seldom as neat. In general, resistance has emerged along some well-established fault lines in India. These encompass forest and land-based agitations, conflicts over marine resources, fisheries, aquaculture, industrial pollution, development projects such as dams, power and irrigation projects and mining; industrial projects such as railway, airport and factories; creation of military bases, wildlife sanctuaries and national parks, tourist sites, housing, water and sanitation (Andharia and Sengupta, 1998).

4.4.4 Conservation organisations

According to Visvanathan (2000), environmental discourse in India is often constructed as a pro-environment civil society battling at an anti-environment state. He argues that what we see instead are parallel environmental discourses; one of them is the "ecocratic" and "technocratic" state discourse, which has found a close ally in conservation organisations. This has particular relevance in the history of conservation groups in India whose brand of wilderness protection came to be seen as "elite environmentalism" (Gardner, 1995; Rangarajan, 2001), marked in their different outlook from the "environmentalism of the poor". These organisations have had close institutional linkages with wilderness organisations and ecologists from the West, as well as being well connected to the state. Elite conservationists were traditionally science-based organisations or ecologists, who collaborated with the state to design programs for natural resource management. For example, Salim Ali, the celebrated ornithologist, had a close relationship with the first Prime Minister Jawaharlal Nehru and later his work, influenced Indira Gandhi's views on conservation (Lewis, 2004).

According to Lewis (2004, p. 14), the influence of US ecology and academia on conservation politics in India is indisputable. The number of theories, training programmes, publications, funding, scientists and collaborative projects omnipresent in the country's most influential ecological institutes represents this. This legacy has led to forced relocation of people and even complete villages that were in national parks all over the country. Unlike in the US, which developed the national park model, India did not have open spaces with no or few inhabitants (ibid, 8).

Conservation-oriented organisations can be narrowly or broadly focused. Mawdsley (2004), for instance, paints a broad spectrum encompassing wilderness enthusiasts and anti-slum-dweller organisations, through to social movement leaders and activists, sometimes supporting radical agendas of social and environmental change. Conservation organisations like BNHS and Wildlife Protection Society of India (WPSI), among others, usually work closely with the state in monitoring, studying and training personnel for wildlife protection and natural resource management. They work at both local and national levels and also form part of transnational advocacy and issue networks. These organisations consist of trained ecologists, researchers, scientists, as well as grassroots activists and environmentalists, and are strongly eco-centric. Their funding structures are diverse, through both national and international channels. Their main role is information provision, networking and lobbying. Conservation organisations and the state are often considered allies in legitimising the technocratic and centralised approach of the state. On the other hand, they also act as vocal critics of the state if it strays from its environmental commitments. In forming close formal and informal linkages with the state and in communicating with the discourse that the state understands, conservation groups provide valuable watchdog functions in the realm of nature conservation.

Conservation organisations are often perceived to be closely allied with the urban middle class and by extension the courts. This is significant as "the middle classes exert a disproportionate influence in shaping the terms of public debate on environmental issues through their strong representation in the media, politics, scientific establishment, NGOs, bureaucracy, environmental institutions and the legal system" (Mawdsley, 2004, p. 81). This manifests in a deep divide in discourse between the "people first" and "nature first" trajectories of Indian environmentalism (Table 4.1).

Table 4.1 CSO typology and relationship to the state

Type	Membership	Strategies	Ideology	Issues	Partnerships
Community-based organisation	Voluntary/minimal membership fee Local leaders Self-help groups Forest committees Youth groups User groups	Petitioning Persuasion Bargaining Negotiations Lobbying Confrontation	Anthropocentric/ environmental and social justice	Sustainable livelihoods/ afforestation/natural resource management (NRM)	State/local NGOs
Think tanks	Skilled/hired staff Researchers Technocrats Intellectuals	Mediation Information dissemination Advocacy	Anthropocentric/ ecocentric Environmental and social justice Green capitalism	Multiple issues: Water/climate change/ conservation/sustainable technology/NRM	State/transnational networks/national issue networks/ NGOs/bureaucrats
Social movement organisations	Voluntary Interest groups Middle classes	Lobbying Advocacy Resistance Confrontation Litigation	Anthropocentric/ environmental justice	Displacement/unequal distribution of natural resources/exploitation/ livelihood/destruction of resources	Other social movement and issue groups, scientists, think tanks, intellectuals/ transnational movements
Campaign organisations	Voluntary/ professionalised Advocacy groups Middle classes	Advocacy Demonstrations Petitions Lobbying Litigation	Anthropocentric/ social and environmental justice	Energy/waste/mining/ not in my backyard/ environmental regulation	Civil society/ social movement organisation
Conservation organisations	Scientists/ecologists/ environmentalists Highly trained, Professionals	Information Provision Training Lobbying Litigation	Ecocentric	Wildlife conservation/natural resource management/ animal welfare	State/civil society

4.5 Conclusion

The relationship between the state and civil society in the environmental domain in post-independent India has evolved as a dialogue between the state and civil society, which is sometimes collaborative and at other times conflictual. In understanding CSO interaction with the state, one finds critical shifts at different junctures in history. The 1940–1950s saw an emergence of a collaborative relationship between state and VOs with shared understandings of development. This was also a time where CBOs and conservation organisations enjoyed strong relationships with the state and were able to mobilise their vision into policies and partnerships. The adopting and furthering of the "fences and fines" models of environment policies, as well as models of large-scale industrialisation and its subsequent fallouts, led to large-scale social movements in the 1970–1980s, especially when the state turned dictatorial, throwing into relief questions of livelihood and equity. This period saw an increased growth of social movement organisations that grew in both size and stature over the decades, creating international linkages with global movements, and finding visibility through tools like the PIL that also created spaces for dialogue with the state. As the orientation of the state moved towards liberalisation and then neo-liberalisation in the 1990s, it allowed the state to reconstruct its relationships from partnerships with VOs to carve out provisions for professionalised CSOs that would include service delivery and service provision. This allowed a number of different organisations and think tanks to step into collaborative partnerships with the state. By the late 2000s, the state's growing emphasis on resource-intensive growth sharpened the divide between the demands of CSOs and the expectations of the state, alienating traditional partners like conservation organisations and in many cases weakening institutional partnerships with CSOs.

As environmental concerns came to be articulated by both civil society and the state differently, there was a divergence in the logic of their environmentalisms. The state focused on a technocratic, managerial approach and some CSOs like conservationists became powerful allies of the state, at particular junctures. Other CSOs emphasised a justice-oriented and anthropocentric approach that came to be characterised as the environmentalism of the poor. While the state attempted to balance larger planning goals of growth with the pressures on the environment, it continued to create both opportunities and constraints for civil society. In the face of state command and control structures of environmental governance, a number of different kinds of CSOs came into existence. Some aligned with the state's more managerial view, while others sided with people movements and grassroots resistance to the same, in varying degrees. This led to a heterogeneity of CSOs, of different ideologies, whose work extended across different scales – local, regional, national and international.

At critical junctures in the evolution of state policies, for example, the moment after the Emergency, or in post-liberalisation India, CSOs were able to exert influence through partnerships or advocacy to influence institutional arrangements that aligned with their philosophy and orientation. The state, too, has played a strategic role in balancing and negotiating demands that were both global and domestic. The tension between the historically technocratic approaches of the state with the heterogeneous demands of civil society marks almost every sphere of dialogue around environmental issues. However, one cannot regard the state and society as two continuously separate and opposing factions. Instead one finds several interrelationships and alliances that add to the complexity and evolution of the relationship between the state and CSOs in the environmental domain.

Acknowledgements

The author would like to thank Kirsten Joergensen, D. Raghunandan, Lana Ollier, Natalia Ciecierska-Holmes, Sushmita Pati, Victor Ramraj for their helpful comments on an earlier draft of this chapter. A special thanks also to Sudeshna Baksi-Lahiri for her comments in its earliest drafts.

References

Agrawal, B. (1992) The Gender and Environment Debate: Lessons from India. *Feminist Studies*, 18(1), 119–158. Doi: 10.2307/3178217

Agrawal, A. and Yokozuka, N. (2002) Environmental Capacity-Building: India's Democratic Politics and Environmental Management. In: H. Weidner and M. Jänicke (eds.), *Capacity Building in National Environmental Policy*. Berlin, Heidelberg: Springer. Doi: 10.1007/978-3-662-04794-1_11

Andharia, J. and Sengupta, C. (1998) The Environmental Movement: Global Issues and the Indian Reality. *The India Journal of Social Work*, 59(1), 429–431. Retrieved from www.tiss.edu/view/6/research/the-indian-journal-of-social-work/

Bajwa, G. S. and Bains, M. S. (1992) International and National Efforts for Environmental Protection – An Assessment. In: P. Diwan and P. Diwan (eds.), *201 Environment Administration, Law and Judicial Attitude*. New Delhi: Deep & Deep Publications.

Bandyopadhyay, J. and Shiva, V. (1988) Political Economy of Ecology Movements. *Economic and Political Weekly*, 23(24), 1223–1232. Retrieved from www.jstor.org/stable/4378609

Berkes, F., Seixas, C. S., Fernandes, D., Medeiros, D., Maurice, S., and Shukla, S. (2004) *Lessons from Community Self organization and Cross-scale Linkages in Four Equator Initiative Projects*. Winnipeg: Centre for Community-Based Resource Management, University of Manitoba. Doi: 10.13140/RG.2.1.5026.2480

Bhatt, S. (2004) *Environment Protection and Sustainable Development*. New Delhi: APH.

Bhattacharya, P., Pradhan, L., and Yadav, G. (2010) Joint Forest Management in India: Experiences of Two Decades. *Resources, Conservation and Recycling*, 54(8), 469–480. Doi: 10.1016/j.resconrec.2009.10.003

Blaikie, P. (2006) Is Small Really Beautiful? Community-based Natural Resource Management in Malawi and Botswana. *World Development*, 34, 1942–1957. Doi: 10.1016/j.worlddev.2005.11.023

Blakeley, G. (2002) Civil Society. In: G. Blakeley and V. Bryson (eds.), *Contemporary Political Concepts: A Critical Introduction*. London: Pluto. Retrieved from www.plutobooks.com/9780745317977/contemporary-political-concepts/

Bowen, W. M. and Haynes, K. E. (2000) The Debate over Environmental Justice. *Social Science Quarterly*, 81(3). Retrieved from www.jstor.org/stable/42864015

Brandon, K. E. and Wells, M. (1992) Planning for People and Parks: Design Dilemmas. *World Development*, 20(4), 557–570. Doi: 10.1016/0305-750X(92)90044-V

Bryant, B. (1995) *Environmental Justice: Issues, Policies, and Solutions*. Washington, DC: Island Press. Retrieved from https://islandpress.org/books/environmental-justice

Chandhoke, N. (1995) *State and Civil Society: Explorations in Political Theory*. New Delhi: Sage.

Chopra, D. (2011) Policy Making in India: A Dynamic Process of Statecraft. *Pacific Affairs*, 84(1), 89–107. Doi: 10.5509/201184189

Cohen, J. and Arato, A. (1992) *Civil Society and Political Theory*. Cambridge, MA: MIT Press. Doi: 10.7312/blau17412-080

Colchester, M. and Lohmann, L. (eds.) (1993) *The Struggle for Land and the Fate of the Forests*. Penang: World Rainforest Movement.

Costoya, M. M. (2007) *Towards a Typology of Civil Society Actors: The Case of the Movement to Change International Trade Rules and Barriers. Civil Society and Social Movements Programme*. Project Paper No. 30. October 2007. Geneva: UNRISD. Retrieved from www.unrisd.org/

Diehm, C. (2002) Arne Næss, Val Plumwood, and Deep Ecological Subjectivity. A Contribution to the Deep Ecology–Ecofeminism Debate. *Ethics & the Environment*, 7(1), 25–38. Doi: 10.2979/ETE.2002.7.1.24

D'Souza, R. (2012) *Environment, Technology and Development: Critical and Subversive Essays*. Hyderabad: Orient Blackswan Publications. Retrieved from https://orientblackswan.com/

Durning, A. (1992) Guardians of the Land: Indigenous Peoples and the Health of the Earth. *Worldwatch* Paper 112. Washington, DC: Worldwatch Institute. Retrieved from www.worldwatch.org/node/878

Dwivedi, O. P. and Khator, R. (1995) India's Environmental Policy, Programs, and Politics. In: O. P. Dwivedi and D. Vajpeyi (eds.), *Policies in the Third World: A Comparative Analysis*. Westport, CT: Greenwood Press. Retrieved from https://scholarworks.uni.edu/facbook/231

Ebrahim, A. (2003) *NGOs and Organizational Change: Discourse, Reporting and Learning*. Cambridge, UK: Cambridge University Press. Doi: 10.1017/CBO9780511488566

Eckersley, R. (1992) *Environmentalism and Political Theory: Towards an Ecocentric Approach*. London: University College of London Press.

Gadgil, M. and Guha, R. (2007) Ecological Conflicts and Environmental Movement in India. In: M. Rangarajan (ed.), *Environmental Issues in India: A Reader*. New Delhi: Dorling Kindersley, pp. 385–428. Doi: 10.1111/j.1467-7660.1994.tb00511.x

Ganguly, S. (2015) *Deliberating Environmental Policy in India: Participation and the Role of Advocacy*. London: Routledge. Doi: 10.4324/9781315744476

Gardner, S. (1995) Major Themes in the Study of Grassroots Environmentalism in Developing Countries. *Journal of Third World Studies*, 12(2), 200–244. Retrieved from www.scimagojr.com/

Gellner, E. (1994) *Conditions of Liberty: Civil Society and Its Rivals*. London: Hamish Hamilton. Doi: 10.1017/S0829320100004774

Ghosh, S. (2013) Demystifying the Environment Clearance Process in India. *NUJS Law Review*, July–September (6), 433–480. Retrieved from http://nujslawreview.org/

Government of India. (1948) *The Factories Act*, 1948 (Act No. 63 of 1948), as amended by the *Factories (Amendment) Act*, 1987 (Act No. 20 of 1987).

Guha, R. (2008) The Rise and Fall of Indian Environmentalism. *T. N. Khoshoo Memorial Lecture*, delivered in New Delhi on 24th March 2008.

Guha, R. (1989) *The Unquiet Woods: Ecological Change and Peasant Resistance in the Himalaya*. Delhi: Oxford University Press. Retrieved from www.ucpress.edu/

Guha, R. and Martínez-Alier, J. (1997) *Varieties of Environmentalism: Essays North and South*. London: Earthscan. Doi: 10.4324/9781315070766

Gunderson, L. H. and Holling, C. S. (eds.). (2002) *Panarchy: Understanding Transformations in Human and Natural Systems*. Washington, DC and London: Island Press. Retrieved from https://islandpress.org/

Hall, J. A. (1995) *Civil Society: Theory, History and Comparison*. Cambridge, UK: Polity Press. Retrieved from www.wiley.com/

Haydock, K. and Srivastava, H. (2017) Environmental Philosophies Underlying the Teaching of Environmental Education: A Case Study in India. *Environmental Education Research*, 25(7), 1038–1065. Doi: 10.1080/13504622.2017.1402170

Hobley, M. and Shah, K. (1996) What Makes Local Organisations Robust? Evidence from India and Nepal. *Natural Resources Perspectives*, 11. London: ODI. Retrieved from www.odi.org/

Jacobs, J. (2002) Community Participation, the Environment, and Democracy: Brazil in Comparative Perspective. *Latin American Politics and Society*, 44(4), 59–88. Doi: 10.1111/j.1548-2456.2002.tb00223

Jasanoff, S. (1997) NGOs and the Environment: From Knowledge to Action. *Third World Quarterly*, 18, 579–594. Doi: 10.1080/01436599714885

Jasanoff, S. (1993) India at the Crossroads in Global Environmental Policy. *Global Environmental Change Part A: Human & Policy Dimensions*, 3(1), 32–52. Doi: 10.1016/0959-3780(93)90013-b

Kakabadse, Y. (1993) Involving Communities: The Role of NGOs. In: M. Holdgate and H. Synge (eds.), *The Future of IUCN: The World Conservation Union*, pp. 79–83. Gland: IUCN. Retrieved from www.iucn.org/

Kellert, R. S., Jai, N., and Mehta, S. (2000) Community Natural Resource Management: Promise, Rhetoric, and Reality. *Society & Natural Resources*, 13(8), 705–715. Doi: 10.1080/089419200750035575

Kohli, K. and Menon, M. (2015) Environmental Regulation in India: Moving 'Forward' in the Old Direction. *Economics and Political Weekly*, 50, 20–23. Retrieved from www.epw.in/

Kohli, K. and Menon, M. (2009) *Calling the Bluff: Revealing the State of Monitoring and Compliance of Environmental Clearance Conditions*. New Delhi: Kalpavriksh, Environmental Action Group. Doi: 10.13140/RG.2.1.2866.4164

Korten, D. C. (1987) Third Generation NGO Strategies: A Key to People-Centered Development. *World Development*, 15(Suppl.), 145–159. Doi: 10.1016/0305-750x(87)90153-7

Kothari, A. (2013) Development and Ecological Sustainability in India. *Economic & Political Weekly*, 48(30), 145. Retrieved from www.epw.in/

Kothari, R. (1989) The Indian Enterprise Today. *Daedalus*, 118(4) (Fall), 58. Retrieved from www.jstor.org/stable/20025264

Kumar, S. (2016, February 18) Modi's New Mantra: 'If You're Not With Me, You're Anti-National'. Retrieved April 10, 2018, from https://thediplomat.com/2016/02/modis-new-mantra-if-youre-not-with-me-youre-anti-national/

Kumar, C. and Vashisht, U. S. (2005) Redefining Community–State Partnership in Natural Resource Management: A Case from India. *Development in Practice*, 15(1), 28–38. Doi: 10.1080/0961452052000321550

Lele, S. M. (1991) Sustainable Development: A Critical Review. *World Development*, 19(6), 607–621. Doi: 10.1016/0305-750x(91)90197-p

Levin, S. A. (1998) Ecosystems and the Biosphere as Complex Adaptive Systems. *Ecosystems*, 1(5), 431–436. Doi: 10.1007/s100219900037

Lewis, M. (2004) *Inventing Global Ecology: Tracking the Biodiversity Ideal in India, 1947–1997*. Athens, OH: Ohio University Press. Doi: 10.1093/envhis/12.3.679

Mahajan, G. (1999, May 1) Civil Society and Its Avatars: What happened to Freedom and Democracy? *Economic and Political Weekly*, 34(20). Retrieved from www.epw.in/

Martinez-Alier, J., Demaria, F., Temper, L., and Walter, M. (2016) Trends of Social Metabolism and Environmental Conflicts: A Comparison between India and Latin America. *Journal of Political Ecology*, 23, 238–491. Doi: 10.2458/v23i1.20252

Mathur, K. (2009) *Policy Research Organisations in South Asia*. Working Paper Series 13, Centre for the Study of Law and Governance, Jawaharlal Nehru University, New Delhi.

Mathur, N. and Mathur, K. (2007) Policy Analysis in India: Research Bases and Discursive Practices. In F. Fischer et al. (eds.), *Handbook of Public Policy Analysis Theory, Politics and Methods*, pp. 603–616. London and New York: CRC Press, Boca Rota. Doi: 10.1201/9781420017007.ch39

Mawdsley, E. (2004) India's Middle Classes and the Environment. *Development and Change*, 35, 79–103. Doi: 10.1111/j.1467-7660.2004.00343.x

Meidinger, E. (2001) *Law Making by Global Civil Society: The Forest Certification Prototype*. Buffalo, NY: Baldy Center for Law and Social Policy, State University of New York at Buffalo. Doi: 10.2139/ssrn.304924

Migdal, J. S., Kohli, A., and Shue, V. (eds.). (1994) *State Power and Social Forces: Domination and Transformation in the Third World*, Cambridge, UK, Cambridge University Press. Doi: 10.1017/cbo9781139174268

MoEF. (1992) *National Conservation Strategy and Policy Statement on Environment and Development*. New Delhi: Ministry of Environment and Forests, Government of India (MoEF). Retrieved from www.moef.nic.in/

Mohan, S. (2002) Role and Relevance of Civil Society Organisations. *The Indian Journal of Political Science*, 63(2/3), 193–211. Retrieved from www.jstor.org/stable/42753686

Mohanty, R. (2002) Civil Society and NGOs. *The Indian Journal of Political Science*, 63(2/3), 213–232. Retrieved from www.jstor.org/stable/42753687

Mohanty, M. and Singh, A. K. (2001) *Voluntarism and Government: Policy, Programme and Assistance*. New Delhi: Voluntary Action Network India (VANI). Retrieved from http://planningcommission.nic.in/reports/sereport/ser/stdy_voluntary.pdf

Nadkarni, M. (2000) Poverty, Environment, Development: A Many-Patterned Nexus. *Economic and Political Weekly*, 35(14), 1184–1190. Doi: 10.2307/4409113

Nepal, P. (2009) *Environmental Movements in India: Politics of Dynamism and Transformations*. Delhi: Authorspress. Retrieved from www.authorspressbooks.com/

O'Neill, K. (2014) The Comparative Study of Environmental Movements. In: P. F. Steinberg and S. D. VanDeveer (eds.), *Comparative Environmental Politics: Theory, Practice, and Prospects*. Cambridge, MA: MIT Press. *Global Environmental Politics*, 13(3), 144–146. Doi: 10.1162/glep_r_00189

Opare, S. (2007, April 1) Strengthening Community-Based Organizations for the Challenges of Rural Development. *Community Development Journal*, 42(2), 251–264. Doi: 10.1093/cdj/bsl002

Planning Commission. (1997) *The Ninth Five-Year Plan*. New Delhi: Government of India. Retrieved from http://planningcommission.nic.in/

Planning Commission. (1992) *The Eight Five-Year Plan*. New Delhi: Government of India. Retrieved from http://planningcommission.nic.in/

Planning Commission. (1985) *The Seventh Five-Year Plan*. New Delhi: Government of India. Retrieved from http://planningcommission.nic.in/

Planning Commission. (1978) *The Rolling Plan*. New Delhi: Government of India. Retrieved from http://planningcommission.nic.in/

Rajamani, L. (2007) Public Interest Environmental Litigation in India: Exploring Issues of Access, Participation, Equity, Effectiveness and Sustainability. *Journal of Environmental Law*, 20(2), 334–336. Doi: 10.1093/jel/eqm020

Randeria, S. (2008) Global Designs and Local Lifeworlds: Colonial Legacies of Conservation, Disenfranchisement and Environmental Governance in Postcolonial India. *Interventions: International Journal of Postcolonial Studies*, 9(1),12–30. Doi: 10.1080/13698010601173791

Randeria, S. (2003) Cunning States and Unaccountable International Institutions: Legal Plurality, Social Movements and Rights of Local Communities to Common Property Resources. *Archives Europeennes de Sociologie*, 44, 27–60. Doi: 10.1017/s0003975603001188

Rangarajan, M. (2007) Ideology, the Environment, and Policy: Indira Gandhi. *India International Centre Quarterly*, 33, 50–64. Retrieved from www.jstor.org/stable/23005936

Rangarajan, M. (2001) *India's Wildlife History*. Delhi: Permanent Black. Retrieved from www.orientblackswan.com/

Rappaport, R. A. (1979) Sanctity and Lies in Evolution. In: R. A. Rappaport (ed.), Ecology, Meaning and Religion. Berkeley: North Atlantic Books.

Rathee, D. (2019, April 24) *Environment is the Modi Government's Most Under-Reported Disaster*. Retrieved May 5, 2019, from www.ecologise.in/2019/04/14/dhruv-rathee-environment-is-the-modi-governments-most-under-reported-disaster/

Ray, R. and Katzenstein, M. (eds.). (2005) *Social Movements in India: Poverty, Power and Politics*. Oxford: Rowman & Littlefield, p. 280.

Redclift, M. R. (1987) *Sustainable Development: Exploring the Contradictions*. Routledge: London. Doi: 10.4324/9780203408889

Rindell, R. and Robinson, M. (1995) *Non-Governmental Organisations and Rural Poverty Alleviation*. New York: OUP. Retrieved from https://global.oup.com/

Sahu, G. (2007) People's Participation in Environmental Protection: A Case Study of Patancheru. Working Paper 180, Institute for Social and Economic Change. Retrieved from https://ideas.repec.org/p/sch/wpaper/180.html

Sangvai, S. (2007) The New People's Movements in India. *Economic and Political Weekly*, 42(50), 111–117. Retrieved from www.epw.in/

Scott, J. (1999) Transnationalizing Democracy Promotion: The Role of Western Political Foundations and Think-Tanks. *Democratization*, 6(3), 146–170. Doi: 10.1080/13510349908403625

Seixas, C. S. and Davy, B. (2008) Self-organization in Integrated Conservation and Development Initiatives. *International Journal of the Commons*, 2(1), 99–125. Doi: 10.18352/ijc.24

Sen, S. (1999) Some Aspects of State-NGO Relationships in India in the Post-Independence Era. *Development and Change*, 30, 327–355. Doi: 10.1111/1467-7660.00120

Shah, G. (2004) *Social Movements in India: A Review of Literature*. New Delhi: Sage. Retrieved from https://in.sagepub.com/

Sharma, M. (2012) *Green and Saffron: Hindu Nationalism and Indian Environmental Politics*. Ranikhet: Permanent Black. Retrieved from www.orientblackswan.com/

Sheth, D. L. (2004) Globalisation and New Politics of Micro-Movements. *Economic & Political Weekly*, Januray (3) 45. Retrieved from www.epw.in/

Shiva, V. (1991) *Ecology and Politics of Survival: Conflicts over Natural Resources in India*. New Delhi: Sage Publications. Retrieved from https://in.sagepub.com/

Shukla, S. and Sinclair, A. (2010) Strategies for Self-organization: Learning from a Village-level Community-based Conservation Initiative in India. *Human Ecology*, 38(2), 205–215. Doi: 10.1007/s10745-010-9301-y

Sinha, P. C. (1998) *Green Movements*. New Delhi: Anmol Publications Pvt. Ltd. Retrieved from www.anmolpublications.in/

Swain, A. (1997) Democratic Consolidation? Environmental Movements in India. *Asian Survey*, 37, 818–832. Doi: 10.1525/as.1997.37.9.01p02775

Tandon, R. and Mohanty, R. (2002) *Civil Society and Governance*. New Delhi: Samskriti.

The Wire. (2018, April 23) *Odisha's Niyamgiri Hills – and Its People – Are Still Under Threat*. Retrieved November 10, 2018, from https://thewire.in/rights/odishas-niyamgiri-hills-and-its-people-are-still-under-threat

The Wire. (2017, July 14) *India Fourth Deadliest Country For Environmental Activists, Says Report*. Retrieved November 10, 2018, from https://thewire.in/environment/environmental-activists-deaths-global-witness

Visvanathan, S. (2000) Environmental Values, Policy, and Conflict in India. In *Seminar Understanding Values: A Comparative Study on Environmental Values in China, India and the United States*. Retrieved from www.carnegiecouncil.org/pdf/visvanathan.pdf

Weinberger, K. and Jutting, J. (2001) Women's Participation in Local Organizations: Conditions and Constraints. *World Development*, 29(8), 1391–1404. Doi: 10.1016/s0305-750x(01)00049-3

Williams, G. and Mawdsley, E. (2006) Postcolonial Environmental Justice: Government and Governance in India. *Geoforum*, 37(5), 660–670. Doi: 10.1016/j.geoforum.2005.08.003

World Bank. (1996) *The World Bank Participation Source Book*. Washington, DC: World Bank. Doi: 10.1596/0-8213-3558-8

World Wildlife Fund for Nature. (1993) *Conservation with People*. Gland: WWF International. Retrieved from www.worldwildlife.org/

Zald, M. N. and Berger, M. A. (1978) Social Movements in Organizations: Coup d'Etat, Insurgency and Mass Movements. *American Journal of Sociology*, 83, 823–861. Doi: 10.1086/226634

Zald, M. N. and McCarthy, J. D. (1980) Social Movement Industries: Competition and Conflict Among Movement Organizations. In: L. Kriesberg (ed.), *Research in Social Movements: Conflicts and Change*, Volume 3, pp. 1–20. Greenwich, CT: JAI Press Inc. Doi: 10.4324/9781315129648-7

Part 2
Environmental policy subsystems in India

5 Forest governance in India

Achieving balance within a complex policy subsystem

Smriti Das

5.1 Introduction

One of the most intriguing aspects about forest governance in India is the fact that forests provide livelihoods for large numbers of indigenous people and other communities. Yet, forests are prone to becoming sites of contestation, in which demands for land and the drive for economic growth have often disregarded their roles in livelihoods and biodiversity. Local forest communities have been regarded as destroyers of the forests, when in fact they can contribute to sustaining forest land and preserving species and ecosystem diversity.

During the colonial and a large part of the post-colonial period, forest governance in India was marked by path dependence. The policy discourse at that time was dominated by the idea of a centralised state that prioritised economic development and exercised "eminent domain", investing the power in the state, i.e., the government, to acquire property for public use over the country's forested land. This was exemplified in the post-independence National Forest Policy of 1952, which prioritised national and industrial development over the needs of the forest-dependent local population (Chopra, 2017). The forest subsystem, marked by long-established and entrenched actor networks, resisted any change for a long time in the core beliefs of the policy, resulting in a prolonged *status quo* in the country's forestry sector. However, long periods of policy stability were interrupted by periods of social mobilisation. Claims and political demands were made by relatively dispersed ecosystem people and non-governmental actors constituted by activists, think tanks, civil society organisations (CSOs), scientists, etc. that were distant from the entrenched policy subsystem.

This social mobilisation had discernible influence on discourse and subsequent policy changes. Unlike previous incremental changes, the Forest Policy of India (1988) marked a shift in the paradigm from centralised to decentralised management. The Forest Department played an ambiguous role over this time, shifting from top-down policymaking to become more involved in collaborative forest governance. However, this policy change did not annul the dominant influence of the core actors in the policy network until a later paradigm shift. The framing of discourse on justice and rights materialised in 2004 during the drawing up of the Forest Rights Act. The recognition of "historic injustice" towards "Scheduled

Tribes" and "Other Forest Dwellers" was a milestone indicating this change. The gradual "paradigmatic" policy shift during the last three decades in the Indian forestry sector is perceived as a move towards "democratic and inclusive forest governance" (Kumar et al., 2015). This dynamic shift resulted in new objectives and priorities plus a political and administrative reordering. However, as the chapter will show, the implementation of this policy innovation did not live up to the ambitious democratic goals it set out.

This chapter describes the changing actors and interest coalitions in the colonial, post-colonial and contemporary phases of forest governance in India. The chapter starts by mapping out the complexities of India's forests, for without this context the reader may fail to understand the dynamics of forest governance within multicultural developing societies. It gradually walks the reader through the stages of governance from colonial to modern times, capturing the competing ideas and interests and the settlement of disputes. It also briefly discusses aspects of climate change in the context of forest governance in India.

5.2 Understanding India's forests and its complexities

The most relevant entry point into the question of forest governance is to first understand what the term "forest" means. Two scientific definitions are relevant here: forest cover and forest area. "Forest cover" denotes all land of more than one hectare with a tree canopy of more than 10 percent irrespective of legal status, ownership or land use. By this definition, forest cover also includes land outside recorded forest areas irrespective of the origin of the forest stand (i.e., natural or man-made). "Recorded forest area" denotes all geographic area recorded as "forest" in any government record. This includes reserve forest and protected forest (as constituted under the Indian Forest Act, 1927) along with areas that are recorded as "forest" in any revenue record or are constituted so under any state act or local law. Thus, recorded forest areas could be barren land, degraded land, wetland or even riverbeds. The broad scope of the term "forest" both stems from and allows for different interpretations of what forest is. For example, ecologists' interpretations of a forest being an ecosystem dominated by trees and other woody vegetation is close to the idea of pristine forests, while civil rights activists who have demanded environmental justice and the restoration of the primitive rights of forest-dwelling communities may interpret "forest" as a place of co-existence of homo sapiens and other floral and faunal species. The complexity of the definition of forests is mirrored by the complexity of forest governance in India.

In sharp contrast to large private ownership patterns and areas of wilderness in many developed nations, India's forests are often inhabited by and almost always surrounded by people. Where these people's survival and identity are deeply intertwined with the forest and where forest outcomes impact the well-being of these people, these humans can be referred to as "ecosystem people". Many such groups belong to tribal communities. According to estimates, out of the approximately 85 million tribal people in India, 94 percent reside in and around forests

(Khare, 2012: 260). Both tribal and non-tribal communities are dependent on the forest for a variety of reasons. Many studies, following Jodha's analysis of the role of the commons in semi-arid regions of India (Jodha, 1986, 1990), have analysed rural dependency on forest and community land. According to Lele (2012), the contribution of forestland to the imputed income of rural households was in the range of 10–40 percent depending on the agro-ecological zone, with variations in the income accrued by different classes within the village. Thus, the dependence on forest and other common land is high, though this trend has declined in the past few decades due to outward migration.

Apart from direct-use benefits to the community in the form of firewood, small timber and non-timber forest produce; forests also support the hydrological regime, sequester carbon, conserve biodiversity and regulate micro-climatic variations. The benefits are enjoyed by both local and non-local/off-site beneficiaries (as categorised by Lele, 2012). Local beneficiaries directly engage in forest management, while off-site beneficiaries are unable to due to their geographic remoteness. Since the benefits cannot be simultaneously maximised for all beneficiaries, the management decisions entail trade-offs and are consequential. For example, a management decision prioritising biodiversity conservation may require control over timber extraction; or, a decision to maximise fodder production may lead to a reduction in tree diversity or the availability of firewood (ibid.: 105). Decisions involving land-use change are more complex (for example, using forestland for non-forest uses such as infrastructure development and mining) and have been contested by affected communities and activists, who often find recourse in judicial intervention.

Decisions on trade-offs are inherently political. Arguments justifying first rights have shifted from one side of the spectrum (which prioritises state control) to the other (which legitimises local control). On occasions, there have been moderate positions suggesting the idea of partnership with the market (timber plantations on private forestland) or civil society actors (in the case of joint forest management). However, resolving these conflicts is often difficult because of the complex history of forest governance in the country – a topic that will be examined subsequently in the chapter. It must also be stressed here that India's forests are not spaces of uninhabited wilderness but complex socio-ecological systems that require well-placed governance systems to ensure fair, equitable and sustainable outcomes.

The complexity of decision-making becomes apparent in the changing discourse within three distinct phases of forest governance in India. The changes in actor configurations, policy networks and emergent coalitions help us to understand the changes in the subsystem. The discourse on scientific forestry dominated the colonial period with its underlying objective of revenue maximisation and industrial production (Guha, 1989; Guha and Gadgil, 1989); the postcolonial or post-independence phase could be seen as the development phase that extended the revenue maximisation model for at least the first two decades with a gradual shift from the 1970s onwards towards wildlife and biodiversity conservation (Lele, 2012); the third phase running parallel to the economic liberalisation era exposed the paradox in forest governance. The policy discourse, in this last phase, endorsed participatory governance and sustainable management along with large-scale forest clearance, particularly for extractive industries, resulting in changes in land use and a growing impetus on the private ownership of property. This development was paralleled by the powerful rights-based discourse in Indian forestry which did not result in adequate institutionalisation and implementation of forest rights for forest-dependent communities.

5.3 The colonial legacy and post-colonial development phase in forest governance

Forest policy during the period of British colonial rule was fixated on achieving increased efficiency and the centralisation of power (Buchy, 1998; cf Grove et al., 1998). It is argued that the policies were based on three pillars during this period: appropriation or control of land through the settlement process enshrined in the Indian Forest Act; the development of a quasi-monopoly in hard timber extraction and the control of trade and markets; and the preparation and implementation of working plans (Buchy, 1998: 645). Through the settlement process, the state acquired proprietary rights over land as well as the forest produce. It reserved the right to determine the existence of private rights while asserting the state's prerogative to manage it in the general interest. Assertion of state supremacy was maintained through various laws and operational practices. The Forest Act of 1878 classified the forests of India as "reserve", "protected" and "village" land. "Public interest" became an instrument in the hands of the "annexationist" state to bring more land under its control. There was a drastic reduction in the accessibility of areas due to policies that were not adapted to local socio-ecological conditions. The colonial discourse and the assumptions behind management principles seemed inconsistent with the condition of land in India. For instance, it was not true that access to the resource (forests) was "free". A web of customary relations and institutional arrangements within and between villages controlled the access to the resource (Guha, 1990). The imperial forest historians propagated the view that colonialists saved the forests of South Asia from destruction by indigenous forest users. Guha challenged the view of the imperial historians by arguing that the colonial management practice stemmed from the revenue and strategic needs of the empire (Rangrajan, 1996: 5). There was a bias against the local producers and multi-species forest in the technical strategies of land and forest management (ibid.: 5).

Forest management changed very little during India's transition post-independence as the control over India's forests merely shifted to the Indian state, transferring the same underlying logic the British had devised. The imperial demands of the colonial period were replaced by the demands associated with the Indian state's push for modernisation and economic growth in the post-colonial period and forests continued to be seen from this perspective mainly as an economic resource. The Forest Policy of 1952 catered to the demands of post-war reconstruction schemes, which involved industrial expansion, river valley projects and the development of lines of communication (GoI, 1976). Before and during the green revolution, the national government focused on increasing the domestic production of all agricultural commodities. The Grow More Food campaign that was taken on a planned basis after independence to achieve food sufficiency also authorised diversion of forestland for agricultural purposes. Almost two decades later, during the 1970s, despite conservation goals receiving priority (through policies and laws like the Wildlife Protection Act, 1972, Project Tiger, 1973, and Forest Conservation Act, 1980), the state's primary interest nevertheless remained in increasing its revenues (Saxena, 1995). Thus, for example, under the pretext of forest management, the conversion of "low value" mixed forest to "high value" plantations of commercial species like teak and eucalyptus continued (Saxena, 1995: 8). Moreover, there was a rapid increase in forest-based industries (Guha, 1983: 1888). Forest development corporations were set up to channel institutional finance into the forestry sector (Guha, 1983: 1889). Infrastructure development in these areas received an impetus through the construction of all-weather roads to facilitate transport. The National Commission on Agriculture report (1976) reflected this approach stating: "Production of industrial wood has to be the raison d'etre for the existence of forests" (GoI, 1976).

The state's increasing control over forestland resulted in severe restrictions for the surrounding population. Locals/indigenous communities were discouraged from using the forest. In the entire process, the village commons were neglected (Saxena, 1995) and so were local claims. The Forest Policy of 1952 stated, "... *accident of a village being situated close to a forest does not prejudice the right of the country as a whole to receive the benefits of a national asset*" (GoI, 1952: 3). In the transformation of the forest economy through infrastructure development, institutional financing and enhanced production, the net benefit accrued by individuals (tribal peoples/forest dwellers and those dependent on the forest) was mainly in the form of wages from forest labour. Tribals and other forest dwellers faced severe exploitation at the hands of mercantile interests. Private contractors dominated the trade of forest produce and labour exploitation was rampant (Guha, 1983: 1886).

The Scheduled Areas and Scheduled Tribes Commission (appointed by the President of India in 1960) criticised the gradual extension of government authority over the forests to the detriment of tribal life and economy (Kulkarni, 1987: 2144). Forest officials were reluctant to allow forest communities to exercise rights over land or forest produce, even where there were no trees. Both colonial and post-colonial policies marked ecological transformation which triggered changes in tribal and other forest dwellers' economic situation. Locals started small-scale trade in minor forest produce at their nearest markets and later migrated in search of wage labour. The tribals/forest dwellers resisted the change in their relationship with the forest. Adivasi and peasant struggles in response to forest reservation, a ban on the shifting of cultivation, restrictions on grazing and access to forest produce, the commercial use of forest by contractors and exclusion from protected areas have all been well documented (Arnold, 1982;

Dang, 1991; Gadgil and Guha, 1992; Hardiman, 1996; Kothari et al., 1996; Shiva, 1991; Sundar, 2007, 2012).

The period from the 1970s onwards marked the emergence of "environmental" concerns. The Chipko movement demonstrated that communities would fight to protect the forest (Agrawal et al., 1982). It was a counter-narrative to the ecological destruction through local use arguments in the preceding phase. Significant state response to this movement was a ban on commercial green felling. This phase was also marked by the transfer of the forest from the State List to the Concurrent List by the 42nd amendment to the Constitution of India and then the resulting Forest Conservation Act (FCA) 1980. The transfer of the forest to the Concurrent List implied that both the central government and the states had the power to make laws on the subject. The FCA mandated the central government's approval for any change in the use of forestland (for non-forestry purposes). At the same time, the Wildlife Protection Act (1972) mandated a ban on the hunting of threatened species while creating a network of protected areas. The state's response to the Chipko movement in the form of a blanket ban differed from earlier responses to local protests (Lele and Menon, 2014) which resulted in local concessions being made, as in the case of *Van Panchayats* in Kumaon (Agrawal, 1999), *Mundari khuntkatti* rights in Jharkhand (Upadhayay, 2005) or *Soppinabetta* privileges in North Canara (Saberwal and Lele, 2004). Meanwhile, the struggle between the state and the forest communities (including tribal peoples and other forest dwellers) continued, as demonstrated in forest offense cases and the resistance to the creation of exclusive areas by the state.

Policy change in this phase was mainly incremental, characterised by hierarchical state-centred governance and lacking local empowerment. The Social Forestry Scheme was the precursor of the Joint Forest Management Program. It was introduced in India in the late 1970s with the aim of easing pressure on the forest and making use of all the unused and fallow land. The scheme entailed a plantation programme to cater to the demands of timber, fuelwood and fodder and aimed at reducing pressure on the forests and the people. The top-down approach was, however, ineffective in addressing deforestation and social inclusiveness for small farmers and the poor (Agrawal and Yokozuka, 2002). In contrast, the Joint Forest Management approach initiated by the central government in the late 1980s was more considerate of the need for decentralised forms of forest governance and community-based conservation. It involved collaboration between the forest department and forest people (Kashwan, 2013). While exclusive reserves were maintained and the diversion for developmental purposes continued, local needs were supposed to be met through social forestry and farm forestry. In doing so, the state was responding to the changed rhetoric of "participatory management". Two significant points here were that unlike the previous top-down policy approaches of the earlier periods, the policymaking realm had started to accommodate other ideas and interests. New "discourse coalitions" (Fischer, 1993; Hajer, 1993) emerged whose statements mediated the paradigmatic shifts in the forest policy that are described in the next section.

5.4 Economic liberalisation and India's forest governance paradox (post-1980)

When the ecological imperatives strengthened during the mid-1970s, forest policy aimed to increase the scale of protected areas. Data show that between 1975 and 1990, approximately 400,000 hectares of forestland was brought under strict state protection, which also meant curtailing local people's land-use rights (Khare, 2012: 262). This model did not significantly contribute to biodiversity conservation and alienated many local dwellers. There was a significant decline in the forest area of the country in both quantitative and qualitative terms during this period. A satellite survey by the National Remote Sensing Agency revealed a decline of almost 16 percent in the forest cover between 1972–1975 and 1980–1982 (FSI, 1987: 13). The per capita availability of forest at 0.1 hectares was far less than the global average of 1.01 hectares (Tewari, 1986: 21). The increasing gap between the demand for and supply of wood for fuel and fodder led to an increased incidence of illicit felling and the smuggling of forest produce. Social forestry was unable to address these problems. On the other hand, large areas of forest were also lost to development projects. The diversion of "wasteland" for agriculture also increased the pressure on the forest. The decline in forest cover was exhibited in the higher rate of soil erosion and increase in flood-prone and drought-prone areas.

Responding to exogenous drivers (donor pressure) and endogenous drivers (deforestation and degradation; loss of livelihood), the National Forest Policy of 1988 (NFP 1988) marked a significant departure in the rhetoric of state control. The NFP 1988 placed emphasis on the goals of preservation alongside addressing the demand for fuelwood, fodder and minor forest produce by the tribal population. Subsequently, the Joint Forest Management resolution of 1990 suggested an inclusive approach to forest management. The Joint Forest Management Programme (JFM) claimed to have achieved success through its 1.1 million JFM committees protecting 22.9 million hectares of forest (Lele, 2014). However, studies have pointed to design and implementation issues related to the JFM programme. The impetus for the programme is attributed to exogenous factors, particularly financial incentivisation in the form of bilateral and multilateral grants (ibid.: 41). Although the programme is said to have increased the green cover of degraded areas, there was a decline in the dense forest cover during the same period (Sundar, 2012: 17), and the programme was critiqued for its limited impact in addressing the livelihood needs of communities. Conceptually, JFM institutions adopted the principle of exclusion, and often the idea of participation was restricted to providing opportunities for wage labour. The involvement of communities in local rulemaking was insignificant because the terms of agreement were often unilaterally decided by the Forest Department. The JFM programme fell short of attaining sustainable outcomes on the social, institutional as well as forestry fronts (Lele, 2014: 17). The rhetoric of co-management vis-à-vis data on the performance of the JFM raised several questions regarding its institutional design, including the issues of trust and equity.

The changes in the forestry sector in the 1990s also need to be placed within the context of the period's political-economic structure. Led by global political-economic changes and the influence of neo-liberalism, the reforms in the Indian economy triggered changes in land use and resulted in newer forms of land acquisition. While privatisation and foreign investment were boosted, there was also state withdrawal from welfare functions thereby leading to increased inequality and accumulation by the few. Coercive dispossession in this phase was different from the earlier instances of "development-induced-displacement" that marked the developmental phase. Neo-liberal dispossession took the form of forceful extraction of resources, acquisition of land for new development (like clearing forests and mangroves to create special economic zones), promoting industrial, urban and other uses of land, curtailing access to the forest and the displacement of people. Forests became a hotbed for conflict and contestation between subsistence producers/forest dwellers, capitalist forces (particularly extractive industries) and the state, with the latter being committed to enabling the conditions for profitable investment in the post-liberalisation regime. The conflict was accompanied by a growing trend in the diversion of forestland for non-forest uses, which reached its peak in the post-2000s (Das, 2012). The compensation provided in such cases was inadequate and exclusionary.

While the forestry sector saw competing interests between stakeholders, such as industry, local users and the Forest Department, the mid-1990s also saw active judicialisation of the claim process through the Godavarman case (Sundar, 2012). Subsequent institutional conflicts between the judiciary and the Ministry of Environment and Forests have continued, and the battle is often seen as judicial encroachment into executive and legislative roles. Following this, new institutions emerged, such as the Central Empowerment Committee (CEC) to advise the courts and the Compensatory Afforestation Management and Planning Authority (CAMPA) to oversee how funds collected for compensatory afforestation should be spent. While the diversion of forest continues in accordance with the growth-first paradigm (priority is accorded to growth-led development), there have been questions on whether economic instruments of compensation could actually be effective in reducing deforestation.

BOX 5.1 GODAVARMAN CASE

In 1995, T.N. Godavarman, who was travelling through Gudalur in Tamil Nadu and concerned by the sight of forest/timber felling from large forest areas, filed a writ petition with the Supreme Court of India to protect Nilgiris from illegal timber operation. The Supreme Court expanded the case to ban all kinds of tree felling in any state without prior permission from the central government. The Supreme Court also went on to define "forest" by its dictionary meaning. The Supreme Court's stance on this case has been interpreted as assumption of the roles of policymaker, administrator and interpreter of law and opened a Pandora's box affecting many stakeholders ranging from industry to forest dwellers (Rosencranz et al., 2007). This case, which has been pending in the Supreme Court since 1996, has heard over a thousand interlocutory applications till date.

Evidently, there have always been multiple claims to India's forests. Some of these were legitimised by the state while others were viewed as socially and culturally inferior and not recognised. The claims of subsistence-based economies were not duly acknowledged. This was reflected in the emergence of categories such as "degraded" forest or "wasteland" that could be claimed by the state for "development" purposes and subsumed into "national" needs. The claims of state actors and the business sector were legitimised in the process.

During this process, a new and complex actor constellation emerged, involving both these groups along with the bureaucracy, politicians, donors, media, rights activists and conservationists. This marked a shift from the state-centred bureaucratic actor constellation, dominated solely by the forest departments, to a more diverse policy subsystem with multiple actors and the representation of contesting ideas, of which none dominated.

5.5 The discourse and practice of "forest rights" in India

In the pre-colonial and early post-colonial Indian forestry discourse, the understanding of "forest rights" was restricted to "rights and privileges" as granted by the monolithic state. From a common property resource (CPR) perspective, this was akin to limited access and use rights that are the starting point for survivalist discourse. Graduation from user rights to higher-order rights of proprietorship and ownership requires that the decisions about resource use, resource transformation and alienation rights be entrusted with the community (see Schlager and Ostrom, 1992, for more discussion on property rights). Such a shift would imply a re-conceptualised power relationship in resource governance institutions. But the Forest Conservation Act (1980) and later the judgement in Godavarman case (1996) marked strong centralisation in decision making pertaining to forests and forestland. Though "decentralisation" was claimed in forest policy and efforts like the Joint Forest Management, such reconfiguration was not intended in either the 1988 Forest Policy or the JFM programme. The concept of participation was operationalised mainly through sharing forest protection responsibility with the communities. The JFM programme flourished with continuous inflows of funds for afforestation with wage employment as a by-product of this activity. But the power relation remained intact as the Forest Department controlled the decisions pertaining to resource management and arbitration. Thus, this idea of decentralisation was lopsided and suffered from trust deficit. Technically, the basis of this acclaimed programme was an executive order that could be easily modified, overturned or withdrawn by the executive (Lele, 2014: 45). Local contestations and mobilisation intensified in response to the denial of rights over forests and forest produce, as well as displacement and the exercise of coercive power by the Forest Department. The Commissioner for Scheduled Castes and Scheduled Tribes (SCs and STs) took this spate of evictions and confrontations seriously. During 1988–1989, the Commission's report highlighted that the right to life, which includes right to live with dignity, had been denied for the members of the SCs and STs. The report also emphasised on need to change the way "forests" were conceived from that of "unalterable boundaries" where any tribal inside the forest is a "trespasser" to "land with the people". Upon the recommendations of the Committee, the Ministry of Environment and Forest issued a set of six circulars to all the states and Union territories in 1990. Popularly known as the 1990 circulars, these primarily laid down conditions for the regularisation of "encroachment". They acknowledged that the "encroachment" on forestland by the people was a result of problems in settlement processes, and tribals were facing unwarranted harassment, prosecution and even eviction. There were a series of follow-ups to the 1990 orders, but compliance was low.

While mobilisations continued over conflicts pertaining to rights over forest, forest produce and forest land, the 1990s was marked by contrasting growth politics. There was rapid acquisition and diversion of forestland for non-forest use (see Das, 2012, for trends and discussion on forestland diversion for non-forest use in India). The dismissal of "rights" of forest-dwelling communities over forest and forestland was validated as a necessary "trade-off" to attain economic growth and prosperity. At the same time, the enactment of the Panchayat Extension to Scheduled Areas (PESA) Act of 1996 gave the village assemblies in rural tribal-dominated hinterlands the right to determine appropriate use of natural resources. Also the Supreme Court in the PESA and in the Samatha judgement strengthened the rights of the Gram Sabha over land alienation in the Scheduled areas (refer to the Supreme Court of India judgement in the case Samatha v. State of Andhra Pradesh, 1997, where the Court upheld the right of Gram Sabha over land alienation in the Scheduled areas that were dominated by tribals) (AIR 1997 SC 3297). Yet, in practice, the order was violated through the coalition of powerful interests including politicians, bureaucracy and industry actors.

In 2002, the Ministry of Environment and Forests issued an urgent order of eviction of post-1980 "encroachers" over forestland. The eviction order was criticised for superseding the 1990 guidelines for the regularisation of "encroachment". The order presumably resulted from the failure to differentiate between rightful claimants and "powerful vested interests", thus challenging the very framework for resolution of dispute between the tribals and the forest bureaucracy and intensifying the pressure on the forests. Following massive criticism, the Ministry clarified that there was no change in policy regarding the regularisation of pre-1980 "eligible encroachment". However, this order became the basis for mobilisation against the unrestrained behaviour of the State and intensified the struggle for claiming rights over the forestland. After a long-drawn conflict, in 2004, the "historic injustice" done to tribal and forest-dwelling communities was acknowledged for the first time with orders to discontinue eviction till the identification was complete.

While the passage of the Act was hastened by social and political mobilisation across the country, it was the parliamentary elections of 2004 that signified a "paradigmatic" shift in the history of forest governance in India. The communist parties that became an indispensable part of the UPA (United Progressive Alliance) Government, used its strong arm to shape the National Common Minimum Programme that committed the government to discontinue evictions from forest areas and safeguard the rights of the tribal communities over natural resources (Kashwan, 2017). Amidst social and political mobilisation across various parts of the country, the UPA Government committed to discontinue evictions. The Common Minimum Programme of the UPA in 2004 clearly stated that the eviction of tribal and forest-dwelling communities from forest areas will be discontinued. The demand for a new law strengthened and the Ministry of Tribal Affairs (MoTA) was given the task of drafting the legislation pertaining to forest rights. The draft Bill witnessed significant contestation between the "conservationists" and the "rights activists"; the former debating against forest fragmentation and the latter arguing for justice to displaced and aggrieved communities from the forest consolidation phase. There were several other concerns with the draft Bill, for instance, exclusion of non-Scheduled Tribes from the benefits of the Act. Following severe dissent on some of these issues, the draft Bill was referred to the Joint Parliamentary Committee (JPC). JPC recommendations expanded the purview of the Bill to include non-STs or the "other forest dwellers", extended the cut-off date for rights recognition from 1980 to 2015 and emphasised on due scientific and democratic process for the declaration of protected areas. The recommendations were debated in the two houses of the Parliament and challenged again by the conservation lobby. A group of ministers (GoM) was then entrusted with the task of arriving at a consensus and the legislation was enacted in 2006. The interregnum between the passage of the Act and drafting of rules saw severe contestation till the Rules were finally notified in January 2008.

5.6 The Forest Rights Act (2006) and its implementation

The Scheduled Tribes and Other Forest Dwellers (Recognition of Rights) Act (FRA) in 2006 was a historic piece of legislation that marked a paradigmatic shift in forest governance in India.

> The stated objectives of the FRA are: to recognise and vest the forest rights and occupation in forestland in forest-dwelling Scheduled Tribes and other traditional forest dwellers who have been residing in such forests for generations but whose rights could not be recorded; to provide for a framework for recording the forest rights so vested and the nature of evidence required for such recognition and vesting in respect of forestland.
>
> The Act was significant in its provisions with respect to:
>
> - Defining a comprehensive list of forest rights, including rights to land under occupation for habitation and self-cultivation; community rights such as *nistari* rights; rights over minor forest produce; grazing rights, rights to water bodies; and rights including community tenures of habitat and habitation of pre-agricultural communities;
> - Laying down a framework for the recognition of rights; for decision-making on developmental projects; for the creation of inviolate areas for wildlife conservation; and for the protection, regeneration/conservation/management of any community forest resource.

100 Smriti Das

The FRA had the potential to effectively mediate forest conflicts, provided it was coupled with institutional reorganisation. The implementation of the Act was guided by the rules that were amended in 2012, which laid down an institutional architecture for the effective and timely settlement of rights. The MoTA was chosen as the nodal ministry for the implementation of the Act. At the sub-national (state) level, there was a four-tier structure as depicted in Figure 5.1.

The implementation of the Act was initially hurried through in a few states and the processes made the act resemble an individual land grant scheme, while in other states it was not implemented for a long period. Since there was lack of clarity regarding some provisions of the Act, the state governments drew up their own implementation guidelines based on the local context. Implementation was limited by various challenges. First, there were procedural hurdles, for example, the need for documentary evidence of three generations having resided on forestland (for other forest dwellers). Second, despite the declaratory goals, continued emphasis was placed on individual land rights and community forest rights were disregarded and the claims of other forest dwellers were frequently rejected. Third, micro-politics and conflicts of interests at local governance institutions – the *Gram Sabha* and *Panchayat* – hindered progress. The former comprises of all adult members of the village (over 18 years). *Gram Panchayat* is also a meeting

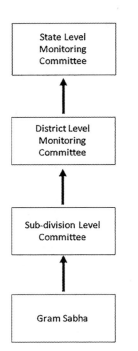

Figure 5.1 Implementation structure of the FRA, 2006.

of adults, with a larger jurisdiction (sometimes even a cluster of villages). *Gram Panchayat* members/representatives are elected through a proper electoral process. Fourth, the declaration of Critical Tiger Habitats and consequent displacement of people without rights settlement was another factor constraining implementation. Some of the reasons have been cited from the author's own FRA-based research studies in different states of the country. While the Act was lauded for its communitarian intent in terms of granting tenure over land held commonly by communities (see Sections 3(1) (a) and 5 of the Act), the capacity for implementation was limited by national level as well as challenges in local institutions.

Despite these issues, the FRA was successful in providing significant legitimisation for the voices and rights of those marginalised in forest governance. For instance, sustained protests helped the *Dongria Kondh* tribe in Niyamgiri hills of Odisha to recover their sacred forests from mining companies; the assertion of community forest rights in the Gadchiroli district of Maharashtra helped to strengthen the livelihoods of local communities through the harvest and sale of bamboo. The communities also demonstrated proficiency in managing the forest while negotiating with the state and market actors to secure their rights. The rules under the Act were modified in response to the implementation experience covering several aspects such as: the definition of community forest rights; decentralisation of NTFP governance; the clarification of claim procedures and eligibility conditions; the conservation and management of community forest resources; and the responsibilities of state and district-level committees. The MoTA also issued guidelines on implementation to the states with the intent of strengthening community forest governance. Yet, the overall progress in the implementation of the act was slow (see Table 5.1).

Implementation data show that only 44.79 percent of the claims have been recognised and respective titles distributed. Almost 45.84 percent of the claims have been rejected, while the rest may be pending. The status report as of September 2018 states that 90.63 percent of claims have been disposed. Upon analysis of the status report, the average area of land under the IFR title was found to be around 2.56 acres (roughly a hectare). Other studies have also shown that the average area of land involved in claims is anywhere between 1.5 and 2 hectares, thus in most cases dispelling the fear of opportunistic land grabbing (Kashwan, 2017) and of forest fragmentation. However, one disconcerting fact relates to the number and nature of the rejections, a topic that has yet to be adequately explored or

Table 5.1 Status of FRA implementation as of 30 September 2018

Number of claims received up to 30 September 2018			Number of titles distributed up to 30 September 2018			Extent of forestland for which titles distributed (in acres)		
Individual	Community	Total	Individual	Community	Total	Individual	Community	Total
4,073,503	146,238	4,219,741	1,818,121	71,714	1,889,835	4,664,948	13,183,785	17,848,733
(96.53%)	(3.47%)	(100%)	(96.20%)	(3.8%)	(100%)	(26.13%)	(73.86%)	(100%)

Source: MoTA, December 2018; https://tribal.nic.in/FRA/data/MPRSep2018.pdf

explained. The state's perspective on this assumes that all rejected cases are illegal or false claims. In my own study on implementation in the state of Rajasthan, Maharashtra and Odisha and upon interaction with communities, it was understood that in many cases the problem is rooted in ineffective (and sometimes undemocratically elected) *Gram Sabha* that is unable to facilitate the claim-making process, administrative oversights and lapses in the verification process and complex procedures. Table 5.1 summons careful interpretation with respect to the community titles as this includes titles under Section 3(1) as well as 3(2); the latter of which does not necessarily include forest "resource" rights. Many of such claims filed under Section 3(2) include land diverted for village infrastructure facilities such as schools, health centres, community burial grounds, etc.

One of the reasons for the slow pace of implementation is a lack of political interest. A more effective explanation, particularly in the context of community forest rights, is that the implementation of the Act is being carried out in an environment where there are competing development pressures, marked by a reluctance towards the redistribution of power amongst local institutions. There are a great number of policy contradictions related to the community ownership of resources. Communal tenures/collective ownership of resources suffered a setback due to development designs that entailed the displacement and impoverishment of tribal communities in forest hinterlands. The tenurial boundaries became obscure as the rights to forestland and produce changed from minimal rights and privileges to almost completely centralised conservation regimes (apart from development projects, which were in the public interest). The assertion of rights over forest hinges on these obscure boundaries which have turned tribal members and other forest dwellers into "encroachers", who were then evicted from their own habitation.

While the Forest Rights Act intends to re-establish tenurial security for the forest-dwelling tribal and other communities, it also means a considerable reorientation of power. There are two major uncertainties that remain associated with the Act: first, whether delays and omissions caused by bureaucratic inefficiencies can deter further mobilisation; and, second, how the fundamental conflict between the neo-liberal ideology of the state and the communitarian intent of the Act be resolved in the interests of social and environmental justice.

5.7 Challenges for forest governance under the National Democratic Alliance (NDA) Government

Differences marked the period between 2004, when the UPA Government first recognised the "historic injustice" regarding the millions of people that were dependent on forest resources for their livelihood, and 2014, when the new right-wing government led by the Bharatiya Janata Party was instated at the Centre. Already during the time of the UPA Government, which was led by the Indian National Congress (INC), tensions within the coalition emerged from the clash between the ideals of social democracy and the pro-reform faction which gradually led to crisis-management strategies. These strategies resembled authoritarian elements of governance (Chacko, 2018: 551), which also affected the implementation of the Forests Rights Act. The second phase of the UPA regime between 2009 and 2014 saw a dilution of benefits of many of the earlier devised schemes. The Ministry of Environment and Forest was even considered as a stumbling block in India's growth story. The interim period was marked by last-ditch efforts by institutions like the National Advisory Council (NAC) to counteract implementation of the Forest Rights Act's support of commercial interests over and above those of indigenous communities. The NAC was instrumental in bringing light of day to rights-based legislation like the Right to Information Act, the Mahatma Gandhi National Rural Employment Guarantee Act and the Forest Rights Act of 2006.

After its landslide victory in 2014, the NDA Government led by the Bharatiya Janata Party built on the failure of the previous government and furthered its authoritarian statist agenda with even more concentration of power at the executive level in the office of the Prime Minister (Chacko, 2018).

The forestry sector in India was not spared the onslaught of the right-wing government. Twice in its regime, first during 2016 and then during 2018, there were attempts by the state to reorient the interests at stake in India's forests. While the recommendations of the 2016 report by the Indian Institute of Forest Management can be dismissed, the Draft Forest Policy 2018 cannot be overlooked for its intent to promote "production forestry" and plantations as the "new thrust area" (Lele, 2018). Shrouded in justification to improve the quality and productivity of India's natural forest, it rationalises public-private partnership (PPP) models in the forestry sector.

> The lands available with the forest corporations which are degraded & underutilized will be managed to produce quality timber with scientific interventions. Public private participation models will be developed for undertaking Afforestation and reforestation activities in degraded forest areas and forest areas available with Forest Development Corporations and outside forests.
>
> There is a need to stimulate growth in the forest-based industry sector. This sector being labour intensive can help in increasing green jobs. Forest corporations and industrial units need to step up growing of industrial plantations for meeting the demand of raw material.
>
> (Draft National Forest Policy, 2018)

The new institutional structure envisaged in the Draft National Forest Policy tends to weaken community forest rights. Community forest rights shall be subsumed under the Community Forest Management Mission. By solely focusing on the synergy between *Gram Sabha* and JFMC (Joint Forest Management Committee), this mission does not fully address the empowerment of local institutions. This draft invited criticism from various quarters and was shelved, possibly in anticipation of intimidating its populist base prior to the elections 2019.

5.8 Responding to global pressures: climate change and governance of forests in India

In parallel with the shifting "rights-based" discourse at the local level, global concerns and influences on subsystem behaviour made the policy arena more akin to multi-level governance. When the Third Assessment Report of the IPCC (IPCC, 2001: 398) predicted serious impact of future climate change on forest ecosystems, it implied not just questions of change in species composition, productivity and biodiversity but livelihood of millions of people that were dependent on forest resources for their livelihood.

Amidst the imperatives of biodiversity conservation, livelihood sustenance and development demands, the statistics of the Forest Survey of India over a decade show an increase in the country's forest cover and a resulting increase in forest carbon stock. These data, however, do not distinguish between forest and other tree/vegetation categories, and include areas such as plantation/orchard vegetation including mango, coffee, coconut, cashew nut and apple (Ravindranath et al., 2014). Thus, the apparent optimism in the potential of India's forest sector to significantly offset carbon emissions in the country (Vijge and Gupta, 2013) has been questioned by Seidler and Bawa (2016) who challenge such assumptions based on the trends in biomass extraction, forest type, rate of afforestation and biomass stocking capacity. They also explore questions related to finance, technical parameters in deciding the reference levels and the monitoring systems, tenurial aspects and resulting benefit-sharing mechanisms. Thus, despite India's significant role in the Conference of Parties (CoP) from Bali (2007) to CoP in Cancun (2010) and the evolution of the concept of Reducing Emission from Deforestation and Forest Degradation (REDD+ where "+" implies additional activities that are explained subsequently), the realisation of all the parameters required for the success of REDD+ projects is uncertain. The Cancun Agreement included five activities under REDD+, namely: (a) reducing emissions from deforestation, (b) reducing emissions from forest degradation, (c) conservation of forest carbon stocks, (d) sustainable management of forests and (e) enhancement of forest carbon stocks (UNFCCC, 2016). During the entire process, the institutional design for REDD+ was supposed to safeguard the interests of the local communities, ensuring their participation and safeguarding biological diversity and the flow of ecosystem services.

The most significant national policy response to deforestation and degradation has been the Green India Mission, which was institutionalised in 2010 as one of the eight missions within the National Action Plan on Climate Change. It had a holistic view of greening, focusing on multiple ecosystem services while stating carbon-sequestration as a co-benefit. But the institutional preparedness to deal with aspects pertaining to trade-offs and convergences between the conservation and livelihood goals, and, monitoring of non-carbon benefits are not adequately addressed (Vijge and Gupta, 2013). This is also evident in the achievement of only two of the REDD+ pilot projects in India so far, both of which are in the north-eastern state of Meghalaya. The Khasi Hills project, initiated by indigenous

Khasi communities, is aimed at watershed restoration through forest restoration activities and reducing pressure on forests, through stimulating shifts from grazing to animal husbandry, use of fuel-efficient stoves and regulations on forest use. The other REDD+ pilot project is in the Garo hills region of Meghalaya, where increased pressure on land had drastically reduced rotation cycles in small-scale slash and burn farming. In 2005, the Wildlife Trust India initiated a community-based natural resource management project in the area, to protect and regenerate the forests between two protected areas using village reserves, enabling wildlife to migrate along a green corridor. The main activities of this project include the establishment of forest plantations, assisted natural regeneration and patrolling to prevent illegal logging and grazing. Given their genesis, both projects clearly prioritise non-carbon benefits, with carbon as an "add-on" benefit rather than a driving motivation; and both involve and seek to empower local communities. The projects have had a significant environmental impact with a reduction in dry season forest fires and improved natural regeneration. The socio-economic impact of these projects is, however, yet to be assessed (Poffenberger, 2014).

Given this policy backdrop, there is the potential for the expansion of REDD+ activities in the country. But there remains a challenge in the form of the continuing struggle between the government and the forest-dependent communities in other parts of the country. In the two north-eastern projects, the strong community tenure rights under the Sixth Schedule of the Constitution have provided the indigenous communities with rights over land and forest through autonomous district councils (Poffenberger, 2014). But the issue of tenure and benefit-sharing mechanisms remains largely unresolved in other parts of the country. India has also committed to creating an additional carbon sink of 2.5–3 billion tons of carbon dioxide equivalent (CO_2 eq) by 2030 through additional forest and tree cover as part of the National Determined Contributions (INDCs). Fulfilment of INDCs requires reforming India's afforestation policies and techniques and issuing proper guidelines for land reclamation, habitat restoration, etc. It would also require the effective implementation of progressive land and forest rights' legislation enabling decentralised governance systems to manage the commons (Seidler and Bawa, 2016).

5.9 The complex policy subsystem and implications for forest governance

The evolution of forest policy and institutions through the colonial to the modern age has seen several phases of continuity or path dependence, as well as policy change at certain points, such as in 2004. Forest policies have continued to see forest dwellers as "destroyers" of the forest and the Forest Department as the "protector". Certain tenets such as encouraging production and commercial forestry even at the cost of village commons (Saxena, 2012) have continued for a long period. Post-independence development planning in India failed to integrate forestry with socio-economic development (with special reference to the forest-dwelling and dependent communities). Forests were about the trees, irrespective of the levels of disturbance or, changing pressure on the remaining forest and its implication for the forest-dependent population. As the REDD+ section shows, international factors also influenced India's forest policy. There was a shift in India's policy paradigm in 1988 with the new Forest Policy. The new discourse was cloaked in the idea of "participation", but there was a lack of political-administrative "buy-in" for the concept. The post-1990 phase in forest governance was strongly influenced by liberalisation and the forest question became closely intertwined with the question of land. Land acquisition by the state, especially where it was transferred to private firms and resulted in displacement overrode other social and environmental concerns (Baviskar, 2012). Conflicts were intensified by land use, climate change and increasing migration that worsened the agricultural and livestock economy as well as regional inequalities. The loss of ecological value in the case of forest land and the fact that social values could not be accommodated resulted in the mobilisation of opposition, as in the case of Niyamgiri mining project in the state of Odisha. Irrespective of policy paradigm changes, the antagonism between industrial stakeholders, conservationists and the rights activists continued, on the premise that forest dwellers were responsible for deforestation and degradation and the new rights regime would adversely influence the sustainability of the forests.

The subsystem complexity was marked by three different aspects: first, the contextual complexity of India's forests. This chapter started with a technical understanding of forests and gradually mapped this to dependencies and inter-sectoral and multi-actor interactions, thereby showing that forests in India are not areas of uninhabited wilderness and, therefore, a single indicator of canopy cover or an area under tree cover cannot capture these complexities. While the pressure on forestland has led to deforestation and forest degradation, these pressures arise at multiple levels (local, regional, global) and are a consequence of multi-level decision-making processes. Thus, while the forest-dependent and -dwelling population may have placed stress upon the forests for their subsistence, there have been other significant causes such as diversion for developmental purposes (including agriculture and infrastructure development) loss due to natural calamities, forest fires (natural and man-made), livestock pressures, poaching, industrial demands and rapid urbanisation. There was no clear plan for how to mitigate the increasing pressure on the forests other than spreading it to non-forest areas (through social and farm forestry) and creating forest and tiger reserves (which were often co-inhabited by humans and other biota). The second relevant aspect is that of shifting policy paradigms and policy changes. A slow paradigmatic shift can be seen through the evolution of rights-based discourse that also resulted in policy change. However, the policy change towards forest rights was dashed in the implementation phases. Therefore, the third aspect highlights the constraints of the implementation of the FRA that has thus far hindered potential community claims. As a short-term remedial measure, this merits improvement in governance and trust paralleled by a reorientation of the implementing machinery to locally contextualise the implementation design and mobilise local communities to take collective action. The Forest Rights Act (2006), in this regard, offers tremendous possibilities by combining rights with responsibilities, but there is need to empower the local level to implement the FRA and mobilise local communities to take collective action. Long-term sustainable forests merit attention to the expanding power of the corporate sector and require the empowerment of forest-dwelling and -dependent communities in order to lead the forest governance model towards a more equitable path of development and social change.

References

Agrawal, A., Chopra, R., and Sharma, K. (1982) *The State of India's Environment: A Citizen's Report*, Centre for Science and Environment, Delhi.

Agrawal, A., and Yokozuka, N. (2002) Environmental capacity-building: India's democratic politics and environmental management. In: H. Weidner, M. Jänicke, and H. Jörgens, eds. *Capacity Building in National Environmental Policy. A Comparative Study of 17 Countries*, Springer, Berlin, New York.

Agrawal, R. (1999) Van Panchayats in Uttarakhand, *Economic and Political Weekly*, 34(39) www.jstor.org/stable/4408446

Arnold, D. (1982) Rebellious Hillmen: The Gudem-Rampa Risings, 1839–1924. In: R. Guha, ed. *Subaltern Studies I*, Oxford University Press, Delhi.

Baviskar, A. (2012) Chapter 3: India's Changing Political Economy and its Implications for Forest Users, In: Rights and Resources Initiative, ed. *Deeper Roots of Historical Injustice: Trends and Challenges in the Forests of India*, Rights and Resources Initiative, Washington, DC. https://rightsandresources.org/wp-content/uploads/2014/01/doc_5589.pdf

Buchy, M. (1998) Chapter 21: British colonial forest policy in South India: An unscientific or unadapted policy? In R. Grove, V. Damodaran, and S. Sangwan, eds. *Nature and the Orient – The Environmental History of South and South East Asia*, Oxford University Press, New Delhi.

Chacko, P. (2018) The Right Turn in India: Authoritarianism, Populism and Neoliberalisation, *Journal of Contemporary Asia*, 48:4, 541–565. DOI: https://doi.org/10.1080/00472336.2018.1446546

Chopra, K. (2017) *Development and Environmental Policy in India – The Last Few Decades*, Springer, Singapore. www.springer.com/in/book/9789811037603

Dang, H. (1991) *Human Conflict in Conservation. Protect Areas: The Indian Experience*, Vikas Publications, Delhi.

Das, S. (2012) Chapter 8: Pressure for conversion of forestland to non-forest uses in India. In Rights and Resources Initiative, ed. *Deeper Roots of Historical Injustice: Trends and Challenges in the Forests of India*, Rights and Resources Initiative, Washington, DC. https://rightsandresources.org/wp-content/uploads/2014/01/doc_5589.pdf

Fischer, F. (1993) Policy discourses and the politics of Washington think tanks. In: F. Fischer and J. Forester, eds. *The Argumentative Turn in Policy Analysis and Planning* (pp. 21–42), Duke University Press, Durham, NC. Cited from Howlett, M., and Ramesh, M. (1998)

FSI. (1987) *The State Forest Report 1987*, Forest Survey of India, Dehradun.

Gadgil, M., and Guha, R. (1992) *This Fissured Land: An Ecological History of India*, University of California Press, Berkeley.

GoI, MoEF. (1952) Forest Policy 1952, Published vide Notification No. 13/52-F, New Delhi, dated 12th May 1952.

GoI (1976) *Report of the National Commission on Agricuture*, 1976, Ministry of Agriculture and Irrigation, Government of India.

Govt of India (2004). Handbook of the Forest (Conservation) Act, 1980. New Delhi: Ministry of Environment & Forests.

Grove, R., Damodaran, V., and Sangwan, S. (1998) *Nature and the Orient – The Environmental History of South and South East Asia*, Oxford University Press, New Delhi.

Guha, R. (1990) An Early Environmental debate: The Making of the 1878 Forest Act, *Indian Economic and Social History Review*, XXVII, 65–84. https://doi.org/10.1177/001946469002700103

Guha, R. (1989) *The Unquiet Woods: Ecological Change and Peasant Resistance in the Himalaya*, Oxford University Press, Delhi.

Guha, R., and Gadgil, M. (1989) State Forestry and Social Conflict in British India, *Past and Present*, 123. www.jstor.org/stable/650993

Guha, R. (1983) Forestry in British and Post British India, *Economic and Political Weekly*, XVIII: 44 and 46, 29 October and 5 November. www.jstor.org/stable/4372653

Hajer, M. A. (1993) Discourse coalitions and the institutionalization of practice: The case of acid rain in Britain. In F. Fischer and J. Forester, eds. *The Argumentative Turn in Policy Analysis and Planning* (pp. 43–76), Duke University Press, Durham, NC. Cited from Howlett, M., and Ramesh, M. (1998)

Hardiman, D. (1996) The fight for the forest. In *Subaltern Studies VIII*. OUP, Delhi.

Howlett, M., and Ramesh, M. (1998) Policy Subsystem Configurations and Policy Change: Operationalizing the Postpositivist Analysis of the Politics of the Policy Process, *Policy Studies Journal*, 26(3): 466–481. https://doi.org/10.1111/j.1541-0072.1998.tb01913.xIPCC.

(2001) *Climate Change 2001: Synthesis Report. A Contribution of Working Groups I, II, and III to the Third Assessment Report of the Intergovernmental Panel on Climate Change* [Watson, R.T., and the Core Writing Team (eds.)]. Cambridge University Press, Cambridge, and New York.

Jodha, N. S. (1990) Rural Common Property Resources: Contributions and Crisis, *Economic and Political Weekly*, 25(26). www.jstor.org/stable/4396434

Jodha, N. S. (1986) Common Property Resources and Rural Poor in Dry Regions of India, *Economic and Political Weekly*, 21(27). www.jstor.org/stable/pdf/4375858.pdf?refreqid=excelsior%3Af29938260f07cf0cc79d699264944733

Kashwan, P. (2017) *Democracy in the Woods – Environmental Conservation and Social Justice in India, Tanzania and Mexico*, OUP, New York.

Kashwan, P. (2013) The Politics of Rights-Based Approaches in Conservation, *Land Use Policy*, 31, 613–626.

Khare, A. (2012) Epilogue. In Rights and Resources Initiative, ed. *Deeper Roots of Historical Injustice: Trends and Challenges in the Forests of India*, Rights and Resources Initiative, Washington, DC. https://rightsandresources.org/wp-content/uploads/2014/01/doc_5589.pdf.

Kothari, A., Singh, N., and Suri, S. (1996) *People and Protected Areas: Towards Participatory Conservation in India*, Sage Publication, New Delhi.

Kulkarni, S. (1987) Forest Legislation and Tribals – Comments on Forest Policy Resolution, *Economic and Political Weekly*, December 12. www.jstor.org/stable/4377847

Kumar, K., Singh, N. M., and Kerr, J. M. (2015) Decentralization and Democratic Forest Reforms in India: Moving to a Rights-Based Approach, *Forest Policy and Economics*, 51(C). https://doi.org/10.1016/j.forpol.2014.09.018

Lele, S. (2018) Smoke in the Woods, *The Hindu* (Online), April 9. www.thehindu.com/opinion/op-ed/smoke-in-the-woods/article23475064.ece

Lele, S. (2014) What is wrong with joint forest management? In Lele and Menon (2014).

Lele, S., and Menon, A. (2014) *Democratizing Forest Governance in India*, OUP, New Delhi.

Lele, S. (2012) Chapter 6: Economic incentives for forest management: products in hand or services in the bush? In Rights and Resources Initiative, ed. *Deeper Roots of Historical Injustice: Trends and Challenges in the Forests of India*, Rights and Resources Initiative, Washington, DC. https://rightsandresources.org/wp-content/uploads/2014/01/doc_5589.pdfPoffenberger, M. (2014) *Khasi Responses to Forest Pressures: A Community REDD+ project from Northeast India*, IUFRO World Series, Volume-32 in Katila et al., Forests under pressure: Local responses to global issues, IUFRO. www.iufro.org/.../ws32.pdf

Rangrajan, M. (1996) *Fencing the Forest: Conservation and Ecological Change in India's Central Provinces 1860–1914*, Oxford University Press, New Delhi.

Ravindranath, N. H., Murthy, I. K., Priya, J., Upgupta, S., Mehra, S., and Nalin, S. (2014) Forest Area Estimation and Reporting: Implications for Conservation, Management and REDD+, *Current Science*, 106(9).

Rights and Resources Initiative. (2012) *Deeper Roots of Historical Injustice: Trends and Challenges in the Forests of India*, Rights and Resources Initiative, Washington, DC. https://rightsandresources.org/wp-content/uploads/2014/01/doc_5589.pdf

Rosencranz, A., Boenig, E., and Dutta, B. (2007) The Godavarman Case: The Indian Supreme Court's Breach of Constitutional Boundaries in Managing India's Forests, *ELR News and Analysis*, 37(1). https://elr.info/sites/default/files/articles/37.10032.pdf

Saberwal, V., and Lele, S. (2004) Localizing Local Elites in Negotiating Access to Forests: Havik Brahmins and The Colonial State 1860–1920, *Studies in History*, 20(2): 273–303. https://doi.org/10.1177/025764300402000205

Samatha v. State of Andhra Pradesh & Ors., A.I.R. 1997 S.C. 3297., JT 1997 (6) SC 449, 1997 (4) SCALE 746.

Saxena, N. C. (2012) Chapter 5: Forests policy in India. In Rights and Resources Initiative, ed. *Deeper Roots of Historical Injustice: Trends and Challenges in the Forests of India*, Rights and Resources Initiative, Washington, DC. https://rightsandresources.org/wp-content/uploads/2014/01/doc_5589.pdf

Saxena, N. C. (1995) *Forests, People and Profit – New Equations for Sustainability*, Natraj Publishers, Dehradun.Schlager, E., and Ostrom, E. (1992) Property Rights Regimes and Natural Resources: A conceptual Analysis, *Land Economics*, 68: 249–262. www.jstor.org/stable/pdf/3146375.pdf?refreqid=excelsior%3Ad778a3443c432f8e5d527faf547b83bf-Seidler, R., and Bawa, K. S. (2016) India faces a long and winding path to green climate solutions, *PNAS*, 113(44). https://doi.org/10.1073/pnas.1616121113

Shiva, V. (1991) *Ecology and Politics of Survival: Conflicts over Natural Resources in India*, Sage Publications, New Delhi. https://uk.sagepub.com/en-gb/eur/ecology-and-the-politics-of-survival/book220564#contentsSundar, N. (2012) Chapter 2: Violent social conflicts in India's forests: Society, state and the market. In Rights and Resources Initiative, ed. *Deeper Roots of Historical Injustice: Trends and Challenges in the Forests of India*, Rights and Resources Initiative, Washington, DC. https://rightsandresources.org/wp-content/uploads/2014/01/doc_5589.pdf

Sundar, N. (2007) *Subalterns and Sovereigns: An Anthropological History of Bastar, 1854–2006*, OUP, Delhi.

Tewari, D. N. (1986) Forests and tribals. In D. Bandhu, and R. K. Garg, eds. *Social Forestry and Tribal Development*, Indian Environmental Society, New Delhi.

UNFCCC. (2016) *Key Decisions Relevant for Reducing Emissions from Deforestation and Forest Degradation in Developing Countries (REDD+) – Decision booklet REDD+*, UNFCCC

Secretariat, February 2016. https://unfccc.int/files/land_use_and_climate_change/redd/application/pdf/compilation_redd_decision_booklet_v1.2.pdf

Upadhayay, C. (2005) Community Rights in Land in Jharkhand, *Economic and Political Weekly*, 40(41) www.jstor.org/stable/4417260

Vijge, M. J., and Gupta, A. (2013) Framing REDD+ in India: Carbonizing and centralizing Indian forest governance? *Environmental Science and Policy*, 38: 17–27. https://doi.org/10.1016/j.envsci.2013.10.012

6 India

Dilemmas of water governance

Joyeeta Gupta and Richa Tyagi

6.1 Introduction

India faces three critical water challenges – a lack of water (and flooding), water contamination and the potential impacts of climate change on the water system. With a population of 1.2 billion rising to about 1.7 billion by 2065 and rapid economic production, per capita utilisable surface (blue) water availability is expected to fall to 25 percent of what it was in 1951 by 2050 (Jain, 2011). Water shortages could lead to a loss of 6 percent of GDP by 2030 (Niti Aayog, 2019). Women spend about 150 million workdays annually in water collection (which could be equivalent to a loss of USD 160 million) (Unilever et al., 2015). Groundwater is overexploited with withdrawal rates in excess of recharge rates. This is leading not only to unsustainable use but also to the risk of land subsidence. Eighty-five percent of such groundwater is used by the agricultural sector (Prabhu, 2012). Several states face severe annual water shortages, and India is fast becoming a water-stressed country. At the same time, water quality is deteriorating with severe impacts on human and ecosystem health. Seventy percent of the water is contaminated putting India 120th out of 122 countries ranked in terms of pollution (Niti Aayog, 2019). The lack of affordable sanitation services has implied that more than half a billion people still practice open defecation and about 200,000 people die annually from water-related disease (Niti Aayog, 2019). Reduced quantities of water also influence the quality of water and this has major impacts on ecosystems and their ability to continue to provide ecosystem services to the Indian people. States score differently in their ability to manage water – with Gujarat scoring relatively high while Meghalaya scores relatively poorly (Niti Aayog, 2019). The expected climate change impacts may exacerbate existing floods and droughts. It will also lead to melting glaciers, changing rainfall patterns, sea-level rise and saltwater intrusion which together will have major impacts on the Indian water system. Floods, droughts, cyclones, thunderstorms and changing rainfall patterns are increasingly being experienced and documented with 1.35 million people displaced from disasters in 2018 alone (Seeds 25, 2019). It should also be noted that transboundary rivers provide more than 50 percent of the water in India (Prabhu, 2012), and India is yet to develop a comprehensive philosophy regarding how it will deal with its riparian partners. Recent newspapers in 2018 report on unilateral statements of

Indian Prime Minister Modi on how to manage the Indus, and of Chinese leadership on how to manage the Brahmaputra – revealing that the crises regard not only water in India but in the entire sub-continent. At the same time, governance will not only have to deal with these problems but also with the complexities of water "ownership" at the central, state and individual levels. Hence, this chapter examines: How does the evolution and current state of water governance in India address current water problems and pre-empt future water challenges? Some of the terms used in this chapter are presented in Table 6.1.

In this chapter, we argue that given the fundamental importance of water to life, ecosystems and the economy, water governance cannot just address the problems of yesterday, but must also anticipate the challenges of tomorrow in order to be effective. Any effort to govern water requires understanding the nature of water, the types of water to be governed, the approach for governing water, how to deal with administrative and water boundaries, how to

Table 6.1 Key concepts in this chapter

Terms	Explanation
Planetary boundaries	The notion of planetary limits to the use of resources and sinks (into which we pollute)
Path dependence	The effect of past decisions, policies and infrastructures on current policy
Riparians	Those who are located on the banks of rivers or share groundwater bodies
Bluewater	Surface and groundwater in water channels
Green water	Water in soils and plants
Grey/black water	Polluted water/sewage
Ecosystem services of water	The supporting, regulating, provisioning and cultural services provided by water and water bodies
Public good	A good that is non-rival (one person's use does not limit the ability of another to use it) and non-exclusive (no one can be excluded from its use)
Sustainable development	Development that meets the needs of the present generations without compromising on the ability of future generations in meeting their own needs
Inclusive growth	Aiming at growth and devising policies to share the fruits of such growth with everyone in society
Inclusive development	Development that aims at social inclusiveness, ecological inclusiveness and relational inclusiveness
Integrated water resource management	Water management that takes all aspects of water use, supply, and linkages to other issues into account
Adaptive water governance	Water governance that takes into account the enormous uncertainties and risks involved in the water sector and allows for continuous adaptation
Nexus approach	A governance approach that takes the relationship between water, food, energy and other sectors into account
Climate proofing	Ensuring that policies and infrastructures take climate change into account

address the demand for water, how to address past legacies such as ownership regimes with respect to water, and what scales are relevant for the governance of water (Gupta, Pahl-Wostl and Zondervan, 2013). Let us briefly explain these here.

First, there needs to be some consensus regarding the discourses about how to treat water – is it a commodity that is subject to market rules, a heritage as in the European Water Framework Directive of 2000, or a glocal public good that should be managed and shared by state(s) in the interest of the public and ecosystems. Such discourses are linked to how society chooses between the different definitions of development: GDP growth, inclusive growth, sustainable development, inclusive development (Gupta, Pouw and Ros-Tonen, 2015), the green economy and translates this into water policy and related instruments. It may have to deal with the notion of local to global planetary boundaries that we have to live within certain ecological limits. Second, in governing water, choices may need to be made regarding the scope of water policy and whether it focuses on blue (surface and ground) water, wastewater, green water (water in soils and plants), atmospheric water (water in the air) and virtual water (the use of water in traded commodities). Thus far, globally, it has been primarily surface and groundwater that has been governed with greywater, black water (sewage), green water and virtual water receiving limited coverage. Third, choices may also need to be made regarding the appropriate paradigm for water governance – integrated water resource management, integrated river basin management, adaptive governance, the nexus approach and the extent to which ecological aspects are incorporated into the governance model. Fourth, choices may need to be made on how to define boundaries between surface and groundwater, between one state and another, between one country and another, between underground aquifers, and so on. Fifth, understanding the nature of demand and the use of water is critical and requires comprehending the role of water in development. Managing water demand requires both incremental and structural changes. Sixth, water governance does not take place within a vacuum – there are long-standing traditions of access to, and ownership of, water; and there needs to be understanding of the *de facto* and *de jure* ownership and/or control of water, how it is linked to land ownership, contracts, leases and/or payments and how it hampers or facilitates water governance. Seventh, scalar issues are critical in water governance, and these concern temporal (time-frame) and spatial (jurisdiction) issues as well as the fit between water governance and the scale of water bodies. Given that the hydrological cycle functions at a global level and is influenced by climate change, there is need also for climate mitigation policy (Vörösmarty et al., 2015). Finally, all the above aspects need to be operationalised in an appropriate toolbox of policy instruments to govern water? These eight issues raise very specific issues in relation to India and the water governance challenges it faces (see Section 6.3).

Some of these broader challenges have, to some extent, been addressed in the global adoption of Agenda 2030 and the Sustainable Development Goals (SDGs) in 2015 (UNGA, 2015). In line with the discourse on inclusive and sustainable development (Gupta and Vegelin, 2016), Goal 6 on water emphasises the need for governance to ensure universal access to affordable drinking water and sanitation services; reduce pollution and the dumping of untreated wastewater; enhance water efficiency; cooperate at a transboundary level; and ensure that water-based ecosystems flourish by 2020–2030. The latter is linked to local planetary boundaries. Goal 6 is interlinked with the achievement of the other Goals and must be achieved in an integrated and indivisible manner.

We argue here that India could consider the advantages of adopting an inclusive development perspective (Gupta and Pouw, 2017). We define inclusiveness as promoting social, ecological and relational inclusiveness – which translates into making sure that water use enhances the well-being of all people in India and neighbouring riparians, is within the boundaries of the physical availability of water in terms of both quality and quantity and does not reduce the availability of water so much that it affects its other ecosystem services, and that politics aims at ensuring social and ecological inclusiveness through relational inclusiveness. In doing so, we expressly move away from the idea of using water only for the highest economic ends, which an (inclusive) growth perspective may lead to. We believe this is the only way that India can avoid a situation in which water is used for short-term economic ends leading to large quantities of concentrated polluted water and leads to path dependency which compromises current and future development.

This paper first describes the state of current water governance in India, then assesses the governance in relation to the eight issues discussed above, before drawing some conclusions.

6.2 Current water governance in India

India's water governance (Cullet and Gupta, 2009) can be traced back to the Indus Valley Civilisation where water was seen as indivisible; watersheds as sacred and protected; and where there were rules for accessing water for personal and irrigation use. The rich and royalty were to provide water to others and pollution was punished (Laws of Manu c200–100 BCE); extensive rules were developed (Kautilya's Arthashastra, c. 300 BCE–300 CE). Thereafter, Islamic conquerors brought Islamic legal principles (Naff and Dellapenna, 2002) which were probably not always enforced (Siddiqui, 1992). Subsequently, British Colonialists transformed society and markets became important (Gadgil and Guha, 1992). Watershed forests were exploited, irrigation enlarged, and the state controlled water and rights to water, while landowners had limited rights to surface water and virtually unlimited rights to groundwater (Getzler, 2004). The state enacted laws on irrigation, embankments, navigation and fisheries. Provinces could regulate water, while the centre regulated inter-state water issues. Post-independence, many of these historical systems coexist in a plural governance system (Singh, 1991) and some are being challenged in court. This section first discusses existing and proposed water law and policy.

6.2.1 Existing water law: federalism and water policy in India

6.2.1.1 The evolution of water law and policy in India since the 1970s

The post-independence Constitution (1947) spells out responsibilities on water with separate powers allotted to the Centre and State. Table 6.2 presents the evolution of water law since the 1970s. A water law was last adopted in 1974,

Table 6.2 Post-independence development of Indian water law

Year	Law/policy	Binding	Key issue
1974	The Water (Prevention and Control of Pollution) Act	Yes	Regulates water pollution
1985	EIA Guidelines for River Valley Projects	No	Framework for assessing the impacts of dams
1986	Environment Protection Act	Yes	Establishes Central Ground Water Authority
1987	National Water Policy	No	Includes estimating water and prioritizing uses
1993	73rd and 74th Constitutional Amendments	Yes	Empowers Panchayats and ULBs to regulate and provide water services
1994	EIA of Development Projects	Yes	Assesses EIAs of big hydropower and irrigation projects
1990s–2000s	State Water Policies adopted Water User's Associations	No	
2002	National Water Policy	No	Enhances institutional framework encouraging participatory approaches
2003	Draft National Policy on Resettlement and Rehabilitation for Project Affected Families	No	Compensates land loss to those displaced
2005	Model Bill to Regulate and Control the Development and Management of Groundwater	No	Includes provisions on Groundwater governance
2006	Notification on EIA	Yes	Strengthens requirements for projects
2007	National Rehabilitation and Resettlement Policy	No	Reduces compensation for displacement
2012	National Water Policy	No	Provides principles for water governance
2016	Draft National Water Framework	No	Provides an overarching framework for water management which can be adapted by states
2016	Model Ground Water Bill	No	A model act which seeks to ensure the protection and regulation of groundwater and establishes authorities for the same

which only covered water pollution. The Environment Protection Act (EPA) (1986) empowers the central government to protect the environment and regulate pollution. Many water problems have been addressed in legal precedents by courts. Bills to modernise water law have been drafted but not yet adopted. At the international level, India has not ratified the 1997 UN Watercourses Convention which governs collaboration with neighbouring water riparians, has several bilateral agreements with Pakistan, Nepal and Bangladesh on watercourses, has an MOU since 2002 with China but has not really revisited these agreements in light of either the Watercourses Convention, the SDGs or the potential impacts of climate change.

A complex web of fragmented organisations may be responsible for the inability of policy to address issues of water governance cohesively. There is no umbrella legislation which governs water law. The existing framework has different principles, rules and precedents adopted over many decades. At the federal level, the key actors are the ministries of water, environment, foreign affairs and the courts. The Union Ministry of Water Resources, River Development and Ganga Rejuvenation makes water law and draft model laws for adoption by states. The National Water Resources Council (NWRC) approves water-related policies including the National Water Policy adopted in 2012. The National Water Board (NWB) reviews the implementation of the National Water Policy and reports to the NWRC. The Central Water Commission, under the NWB, initiates, coordinates and consults State Governments on schemes for flood control, irrigation, navigation, drinking water supply and power development. The National Water Mission under the National Action Plan on Climate Change (NAPCC) aims at integrated water resources development and management to address climate change. It tends to focus on large-scale supply-side approaches using climate change to justify this (England 2018). The Central Ground Water Board (CGWB) develops technology and regulates groundwater resources. The Central Ground Water Authority (CGWA) under the EPA regulates groundwater exploitation to avoid environmental damage and may penalise offenders. The Water Dispute Tribunals adjudicate on inter-state disputes.

The Ministry of Environment, Forests and Climate Change (MOEF), has bodies that regulate environment impact assessments (EIA) and give environmental clearances (EC). Its National River Conservation Directorate implements conservation plans and River Action Plans to improve water quality and river ecosystems. The Ministry of Foreign Affairs regulates transboundary agreements.

We now cover the distribution of powers on water (see Section 6.2.1.2), the right to water (see Section 6.2.1.3), irrigation policy (see Section 6.2.1.4), groundwater (see Section 6.2.1.5), EC (see Section 6.2.1.6) and river interlinking and federal powers (see Section 6.2.1.7). For reasons of space, we do not cover transboundary issues.

6.2.1.2 Constitutional provisions: distribution of powers on water

The Constitution of India (1947) distributes legislative powers between the Union, State and the concurrent list, which empowers both centre and state. The Union may legislate on shipping and navigation on national waterways, and address inter-state water disputes which were further elaborated in the Inter-State Water Disputes Act (1956). States may legislate on water supplies, irrigation and canals, drainage and embankments, water storage, hydropower and fisheries. Aspects not explicitly regulated (e.g., groundwater) have often been resolved in courts. This federal structure has an advantage in aiming at subsidiarity in the area of water policy, but has led to challenges, in particular, with respect to jurisdictional conflicts between the centre and state; and because state-level institutions such as the State Water Pollution Control Boards have been notoriously underfunded and have been unable to implement their mandates (Reich and Bowonder, 1992).

6.2.1.3 The right to water and the role of India's courts

Poor access to potable water has led to litigation where the Supreme Court and many High Courts have held that the human right to water is part of the fundamental "Right to Life" under Article 21 of the Constitution (Upadhyay, 2011), institutionalised in the 73rd and 74th amendments to the Constitution in 1993. The former required states to adopt a Panchayat Raj Act devolving functions, functionaries and funds to panchayats (village governments) to enable "self-governance" on drinking water, water management, minor irrigation and watershed development. The 74th amendment required state governments to constitute urban local bodies (ULBs) with authority for self-governance on water for domestic, industrial and commercial purposes. These amendments brought about significant changes in state laws and were supported by Court judgements (Upadhyay, 2011). In Delhi Water Supply and Sewage Disposal Undertaking v. State of Haryana (1996), the Supreme Court observed that irrigation could not be prioritised over drinking water. In S.K. Garg v. State of UP (1999), the High Court upheld the fundamental right to drinking water and cited the Supreme Court's decision in Chameli Singh v. State of UP that such rights were essential for enjoying human rights under international and national law (Upadhyay, 2011). In Subhash Kumar v. State of Bihar (1999) (Cullet, 2009), the Supreme Court recognised that the right to life included pollution-free water. In Guwahati (Assam), the Court held that the municipal corporation must supply sufficient drinking water, even when there are financial constraints (Upadhyay, 2011). In Vishala Kochi Kudivella Samrakshana Samithi v. State of Kerala (2006), the Kerala High Court stated that lack of resources could not be used to justify not fulfilling the right to water (Cullet, 2007). These decisions require local governments to reconcile the fundamental right to water with the mandate for water supply and management even when they lack resources and have been active in pushing environmental

118 *Joyeeta Gupta and Richa Tyagi*

protection, human rights and capacity building at state level. They also reveal the strong role of local government in addressing key water issues.

However, despite the recognition of the human right to water, the link to the human right to sanitation services as required by the UN General Assembly's adoption of the Resolution on the Human Right to Water and Sanitation (UNGA 2010) has not always been made.

6.2.1.4 Irrigation

The long-term legacy of colonial irrigation laws has meant that the government controls water for public purposes without any consideration for the conservation of the resource (Cullet, 2016). Between 1997 and 2000, some states enacted laws creating Water Users Associations (WUAs) in reaction to the "Participatory Irrigation Management" (PIM) movement (Upadhyay, 2011). However, while these state laws give the WUAs the right to obtain information about water availability, periods of supply and the right to obtain water in bulk from the irrigation department, they failed to make the irrigation department legally accountable when water supply demands were not met. The WUAs could have also been a strong institutional body with powers to regulate the use of water and develop plans for the conservation of water and contribute to better management of water resources but their capacities were never built for that.

6.2.1.5 Groundwater law

Groundwater is regulated under a 1970 Federal draft model bill for state governments revised in 1992, 1996, 2005 (Sankaran, 2009) and more recently in 2016. This stimulated state governments to enact groundwater laws, but most do not redefine private and state property rights in groundwater creating path dependency. The government implicitly suggests that the landholder has rights to groundwater, but the state as groundwater custodian may notify areas of over-extraction, issue permits/licenses for new extractions and penalise offenders. This does not address the historical fact that groundwater is "a right attached to land, which may be restricted by easement" under the Indian Easement Act 1882 (Vani, 2009) and riparian landowners had an unrestricted right to use the groundwater beneath it. However, in 2002, the Andhra Pradesh High Court stated that "Deep Underground Water" is state property under the doctrine of Public Trust (Vani, 2009), going further than the 1997 case where the court held that the landholder has user rights on water in tube wells only if it does not interfere with the rights of other landholders or is not in a groundwater scarce area as that interferes with Article 21 of the Constitution (M.C. *Mehta vs Kamal Nath*: (1997) 1 SCC 388). Therefore, where groundwater is held in public trust, states may legislate on its use. However, there remains critical ambiguity in how far the state and even judges can go in addressing groundwater-related conflicts (see Box 6.1).

BOX 6.1 AMBIGUITY IN GROUNDWATER OWNERSHIP: THE COCA-COLA CASE

The colonial legacy allows landowners to own groundwater under the Easements Act while mandating the state to govern it in the public interest. This ambiguity was challenged in Perumatty Gram Panchayat vs Hindustan Coca-Cola Beverages (P) Ltd in 2003. The Panchayat refused to renew the licence of the local Coca-Cola plant on the grounds of groundwater over-extraction, local environmental problems and drinking water scarcity (Koonan, 2007). The Kerala High Court (Single Bench) decided in favour of the Panchayat stating that the government holds groundwater in trust and cannot allow private parties to overexploit resources (Upadhyay, 2011). The Division Bench of the Kerala High Court overruled this stating that in the absence of a statute prohibiting groundwater use, a person had the right to extract water from his property (Koonan, 2007). This case is still pending in the Supreme Court. Meanwhile, the government has notified the Kerala Groundwater Act (2002) and set up the state groundwater authority.

The central government's limited legislative authority on (ground) water under the Constitution did not, however, prevent it from enacting State Groundwater Acts. The Water (Prevention and Control of Pollution) Act 1974 (Cullet, 2009) regulates and prevents water pollution at national level. The Water Act, amended in 1988, provides for the appointment of central and state boards to regulate pollution and impose penalties for non-compliance. In M.C. Mehta vs Union of India (1997), the Court did not debate whether groundwater was a state or union subject but dealt with the case under the EPA within the purview of the Union Government (Vani, 2009). The Court also ordered the Environment Ministry to constitute a CGWA to regulate groundwater (Sankaran, 2009).

Privatisation of water adds more complexity to the already ambiguous legal understanding of water. Since 1990, the government has promoted the privatisation of water suggested by international financial institutions like the World Bank and the Asian Development Bank (Purohit, 2016). The National Water Policy 2002 also encouraged public-private partnerships (PPP) for planning, development and management of water resources projects (Purohit, 2016). Several public-private partnerships were soon established. An example of a challenging problem is that of Sheonath river. Kailash Soni of Radius Water Limited has a build, own, operate, transfer (BOOT) agreement with the state on the semi-perennial Sheonath river (23.6 km). This agreement was made through a 22-year renewable concession. It empowered Soni to have a monopoly position in selling his water to the highest bidder (mostly industrialists) at the cost of the local farmers. By supplying 4 Ml of water daily, he hopes to recover Rs 600 crores over 20 years. The situation got grim when several farmers and local people rose in protest against the company and government (Bhavdeep, 2002). This case illustrates that the government needs to be careful about the conditions under which it can enter into PPPs and the possible consequences of these. A database maintained by Manthan Adhyan Kendra, a centre set up to research, analyse and monitor water and energy issues, showed that several PPPs in water and sanitation projects were facing challenges in implementation (Kendra, 2013).

A private company will work for profit maximisation. Resource conservation is hardly an objective for it (Thakkar, Lakhani, and Shah, 2017). Groundwater may already be privatised under the applicable laws and this has contributed to a growing water crisis in the country. This crisis can only be ended by treating water as a common pool resource or public good (Thakkar, Lakhani, and Shah, 2017). The Pani Panchayats (a social movement promoting collective management and distribution of water by farmers) of Maharashtra are a good example of managing water as a common resource for everyone. The Panchayats have strict rules on the use of water but by delinking water from land ownership they help to ensure water to landless people, creating a progressive governance system for water. Some positive signs of groundwater recovery resulting from community efforts and policy have been recorded (Mukherjee and Bhanja, 2019). However, the grim news from NITI Aayog (2019) – a government think tank – is that, among other issues, 21 cities in India will have no groundwater by 2020.

6.2.1.6 Environmental clearance

The EIA process initiated around 1976–1977 and revised in 2006 (Ghosh, 2013) evaluates the potential beneficial and adverse environmental, social, cultural and aesthetic impacts of developmental and industrial projects and mandates the central and state authorities to require impact assessment. For example, hydroelectric projects generating between 25 and 50 MW hydroelectric power require a state-level EIA, while larger projects require clearance from the Union MoEF. While the procedure is progressive (Divan, 2009), in the context of hydroelectric projects, it does not adequately include the impact on downstream species migration (e.g., Mahseer in the Subansiri dam in North East India; Vagholikar and Ahmed, 2003); birds (e.g., the National Green Tribunal suspended[1] the EC given to the Nyamjang Chhu project in Arunachal Pradesh in 2012 which affected the Black Necked Crane (Srivastava and Ramachandran, 2016)); biodiversity, wildlife habitat and the catchment area ecology, especially as the Catchment Area Treatment to restore the catchment area post-construction is ineffective (Choudhury and Menon, 2003; Singh and Banerji, 2002); and on culture, demography, cultivation patterns and conservation offsets. Leniency on non-compliance also affects depleting water resources.

The EIA is, therefore, inadequate and being undermined over time and social issues are *de facto* ignored. The toolbox only engages superficially with spatial planning tools, critical for water resource management, demand-side management and/or pollution control upstream. It is argued that "Overall, EIA is used presently as a project justification tool rather than as a project planning tool to contribute to achieving sustainable development" (Panigrahi, 2012: abstract).

6.2.1.7 Inter-state issues: conflicts and river linking

Inter-state conflicts on water sharing are usually resolved through tribunals, but many lead to continuing stress. At present, there are 7 disputes involving 11 states (Niti Aayog, 2019). One interesting case arose when in 2002 Ex-President Abdul Kalam called for interlinking rivers to provide water to a larger population (Mirza, Ahmed and Ahmad, 2008). The Supreme Court applied this in a case on the Yamuna arguing that droughts and floods in different geographical areas could be addressed by linking rivers. States were asked to respond to their stand on river interlinking within a month. The lack of response was construed as consent and the Court passed an order upholding river linking (Sankaran, 2009). This controversial issue (Bandyopadhyay and Perveen, 2002; Iyer, 2004) led Kerala to pass a resolution against such interlinking due to its adverse socio-ecological impacts (PTI, 2014). Nevertheless, the first project under the 30 planned interlinking projects, the Ken-Betwa project has received a go-ahead from the government (Koshy, 2016). This programme will lead to the de-notification of 5,258 hectares of forests, including 4,141 hectares of Panna Tiger Reserve in Madhya Pradesh under the Forest Conservation Act 1980. While the project may be challenged on grounds of a flawed EC (Koshy, 2016), this will not question the authority of the centre in taking this decision.

6.2.2 The expected new water regime in India

India is transitioning to a new water regime. Given limited constitutional authority, the National Water Policy (NWP, 2012) proposed an overarching framework of principles to inspire state water legislation. This framework, in line with the recommendations of international financial institutions, promoted privatisation of water delivery services with full accountability to the democratically elected local bodies (Cullet and Madhav, 2009). It recommended climate change adaptation measures, technologies and practices to local people (PRS, 2012), promoted enhancing water availability for use (e.g., direct use of rainfall, avoiding inadvertent evaporation, interbasin transfer); demand and use management; established the Water Regulatory Authorities for fixing/regulating water tariffs and incentivising efficiency; provided statutory powers to WUAs; and mandated community participation in river/waterbody conservation. It promoted comprehensive water regulation and results from actions since the 12th Plan (Iyer, 2013).

In May 2016, the Union Ministry of Water Resources proposed the Model Bill for the Conservation, Protection, Regulation and Management of Groundwater; the Draft National Water Framework (NWF) Bill and a report called "A 21st Century Institutional Architecture for India's Water Reforms" which suggests restructuring the Central Water Commission (CWC) and Central Ground Water Board (CGWB) into a new National Water Commission (NWC). The latter emphasises an interdisciplinary approach incorporating participatory resource planning and management and including other subject areas like river ecology, agronomy, etc. (Ghosh and Bandopadhyay, 2016). The NWF Bill provides a national legal framework for protecting, conserving, regulating and managing water resources. It defines "water for life" as water needed for the "fundamental right of life of each human being, including drinking, cooking, bathing, sanitation, personal hygiene and related personal and domestic uses", including for women's "special needs" and domestic livestock (NWF Bill 2016). It promotes "River Rejuvenation" through continuous and unpolluted flow of water to maintain water connectivity and reduce adverse human impacts. It calls for integrated river basin development and management (IRBDM), treating the river basin as a whole and aims at holistic management. It's "grade pricing system" for domestic water supply calls for full cost pricing for high-income groups, "affordable pricing" for middle-income people, and a "certain quantum of free supply" for the poor. The framework, although innovative, does not provide sufficient legal protection to water resources but offers legal protection to catchment/watershed areas of surface/groundwater resources against further negative development. While the NFW states that "there shall be minimum interference in existing natural river flows; in the natural state of water bodies and wetlands and in floodplains and riverbeds, which shall be recognised as integral parts of the rivers themselves", the Bill could perhaps be improved by stating that a river conservation zone needs to be determined and earmarked to regulate development in flood plains which provide important ecosystem services including lateral connectivity and habitat to aquatic species, groundwater recharge and flood control. Like the National Aquifer Mapping Project, the NWF Bill could consider calling for mapping the remaining wild rivers to proactively conserve them and ensure socio-economic and ecological benefits.

The Water Ministry's Groundwater Bill 2016 was put up in the public domain in September 2016 with the aim to "ensure groundwater security through availability of sufficient quantity and appropriate quality" and transform groundwater from private property under the Easement Act 1882 to a common pool resource held by the state in public trust. This, of course, amounts to expropriation without compensation. The Bill empowers the Gram Panchayats (village councils) and Nagar Palikas (municipality) to develop participatory and integrated groundwater management plans. It sees "Water for Life" as an integral right of every person within easy reach of the household with the state ensuring this right even when water supply has been delegated to a private body arguing that "such a delegation of water service provision to a private agency will, in no event, constitute the privatisation of water". The Bill introduces priority of use, prioritising the right to water for life, followed by allocation for achieving food security, subsistence agriculture, sustainable livelihoods and ecosystem needs. It demarcates "groundwater protection zones" within a "groundwater security plan" to promote recharge and demand management. However, no strategy for such demand management has been envisioned in the Bill. While the Bill aims at robust groundwater management, it remains to be seen whether decentralised management will be effective since there has been no consensus on its adoption in two years. The Bill may need to build the capacity of Ground Water Committees at lower government levels, prepare detailed strategies for industrial location, groundwater use and water footprints (demand and wastewater management) using instruments that link to the existing regulatory framework (e.g. the Water Cess Act 1977) (Vishwanath, 2016). The Bill ignores the peri-urban areas and, thus, excludes a large portion of future infrastructure development with a considerable impact on groundwater resources. It scarcely addresses issues of adaptation or newer challenges such as pollution from antibiotics.

The River Basin Management Bill 2016 is expected to require River Basin authorities in line with the "River Basin Authority" (RBA) proposed in the NWF Bill (PIB, 2016). The NWF recommends IRBDM and calls for RBAs for each inter-state or sub-basin, and promotes active state participation to ensure sustainable and equitable utilisation of water resources. However, the RBA is confined to creating master-plans for the basins, while such institutions need to be democratic and have adequate regulatory powers to initiate actions to prevent freshwater degradation, penalise violation, continuously evaluate the situation and build capacity to ensure staff that can plan and implement policy (Ghosh, 2016; Ghosh and Bandopadhyay, 2016).

While the Union has proposed these model water laws, these will have to be implemented at the state or sub-state level and powers have been further delegated to rural and urban authorities. However, such delegation of authority may not take into account how upstream users externalise water impacts for downstream users and the conflicts between jurisdictions, both national and international. At the time this chapter went to publishing, the draft bills were yet to be notified even after three years of being circulated by the government.

6.3 Challenges facing Indian water governance

We now assess the progress in Indian water governance in relation to the eight challenges highlighted in the introduction to this chapter.

First, India seems to be in a business-as-usual mode slowly following the route taken by industrialised countries in their development process instead of proactively deciding how water could best be framed and governed given the new realities (i.e., how India could leapfrog into the future, avoid path dependency and develop contextually appropriate solutions). The relationship between India's development strategy and India's water policy has scarcely been explored. India's delay in adopting a new policy runs the risk that water will be the key factor that hampers economic development, because of its influence on human health and ecosystems, to say nothing about how it affects industry, services and tourism, as well as transboundary relations between Indian provinces and India's relations with neighbouring countries. There is a lack of clarity about how to define water. It appears that India is moving towards the public trust doctrine (Vani, 2009) and the sustainable development paradigm on water, but everyday practices are shaped by the continuation of land-related groundwater ownership and the growing neo-liberal capitalist approach advertising "make in India" (Mohan, 2017) which will all require huge amounts of water in the production process. The Uttarakhand High Court recently declared River Ganga and Yamuna as living entities (*Mohd Salim vs State of Uttarakhand and Ors*. WP 126 of 2014). The Cabinet of Madhya Pradesh then declared River Narmada as a "living entity" (Ghatwai, 2017). While such declarations are interesting steps, it is unclear what it will mean in reality. Where India focuses on growth *per se* (a) without adequately incorporating the ecological restraints (planetary boundaries and climate-related issues) into its development paradigm, and (b) signs long-term contracts with international companies, it runs the risk of not only over-exploiting its limited water resources despite platitudes to the contrary, but also of being vulnerable in (inter)national litigation, liability and compensation suits which fall under stringent (inter)national contract law and bilateral investment treaties (cf. Klijn, Gupta, and Nijboer 2009).

Second, it appears that India still differentiates between surface and groundwater, and does not pay much attention to greywater, green water, atmospheric water and virtual water or water used in the production of goods and services. It does not yet have a holistic approach to governing water or taking into account the different ecosystem uses of water. The limits to use are only in relation to groundwater, and there is scarcely any discussion of the multiple ecosystem uses of water or the potential impacts of climate change on water including displacement following ecological disasters.

Third, given that 50 percent of India's waters are from transboundary rivers, there continues to be conflict both with respect to land and water with neighbouring riparian states, and existing agreements are increasingly being repudiated (e.g., the Indus). Equitably sharing these waters with neighbouring states and taking responsibility with respect to causing harm to others is not a top priority as evidenced by India's non-ratification of the UN Watercourses Convention. Efforts to climate-proof agreements with neighbouring states appear not to be discussed. At the same time, inter-state disputes within India have scarcely been settled. The regulation of inter-state rivers is specifically provided for in the Constitution to be under the authority of the Union government. The River Boards Act (1956) is the applicable law for the establishment of river boards to advise state governments on basin management as a whole. However, no river board has currently been set for integrated basin management. Those that exist are for specific projects like the Betwa River Board for the creation of a reservoir and its regulation (Cullet, 2016). The literature on inter-state disputes on water sharing shows that tensions are developing in different parts of India, and these tensions will inevitably require a re-visitation of the role of water in development, extensive demand-side management and rules on pollution. The new River Basin's bill may provide for the groundwork for intra-basin water management but at present it seems quite inadequate to ensure any state action. The Union government is focussed on inter-linking of rivers as the immediate plan for solving the water scarcity issues in the country, a tool that has received severe criticism from water policy experts in the country (Cullet, 2016).

Fourth, in terms of approaches, India has apparently decided to adopt the integrated river basin management approach, but it is unclear how it is going to actually undertake that. How this will affect other ministries on mining, environment, economic development and so forth is not clear.

Fifth, ownership issues are highly contested. The Supreme Court is still wrestling with the issue of whether land ownership allows for virtually unlimited groundwater ownership in the coca-cola case (see Box 6.1). The government is moving towards expropriation of such ownership by clarifying that the state holds water in public trust through changing the law. But such expropriation will require compensation and experiences in Spain suggest that such compensation can be hugely expensive. It is not clear if there will be any compensation for such expropriation. While this might leave farmers without their easy access to groundwater and they may not be able to exercise their right of voice, large companies and multinationals may challenge such expropriation as being a violation of their international investment rights. Furthermore, as long as India allows the privatisation of land and attendant riparian ownership of water under its position with respect to the WTO and investment treaties, this will lead to both land and water grabbing, especially in the absence of a legal decision to the contrary.

Sixth, Indian water law and policy does not appear to have grappled with the causes of water use and pollution to proactively deal with them. Instead, it takes a conservative resource management approach which will fail if it does not deal with the development paradigm that drives water demand and pollution. The focus is on direct users – but even here it's not clear if there is a focus on changing agriculture from, e.g., high to low water-intensive crops. Although water has transitioned from being treated as an "economic good" by the earlier governments to becoming a "common good" and most recently being accepted as a "life good" and India is encouraging demand-side management and enhancing supply, water governance is still focussed on the availability and supply of water. There is no strategy for the sustainable use of water which foresees increasing demand for water in the future, especially in the agricultural, industrial and services sector. While the government's water framework bill suggests treating water as a common resource and moves away from privatisation of the resource as such, it still states that in cases of water services provisioning by private agencies the right to water shall apply. This leaves the supply and management of water open to private agencies. Furthermore, India's fossil fuel-based energy policy itself will require huge amounts of water; different sources of electricity require different amounts of water – with nuclear and thermal power requiring the most, and wind energy requiring the least. However, there is scarcely any debate on this issue.

Moreover, India's role in fossil fuel consumption will also contribute to climate change. Climate proofing national development and water strategies taking both mitigation and adaptation to climate change into account has begun but has a long way to go. The water governance strategy does not appear to deal with floods, droughts, extreme weather events and saltwater intrusion. The discussion of water linking does not reveal an understanding of the diverse ecosystem services of water in different parts of the country nor does it grapple with the bigger issues of seismic risks.

Finally, in relation to issues of administrative scale, while decentralising policies to the local level (cities and villages) is critical for ensuring local level contextual inputs, this will not work if there is no national vision for what needs to be achieved, how water will be shared with neighbouring countries and how this is to be financed. Furthermore, some laws have been in the pipeline for years and every day that India postpones the adoption of these laws, it allows foreign investors who come in under the "Make in India" programme rights to groundwater under the Indian Easements Act. Priority of use with respect to water has only seemingly been addressed with respect to groundwater. While the state at different levels of governance is held responsible for providing access to drinking water and sanitation services under the new laws, it is not clear how sewage will be dealt with. Furthermore, it is not clear how such services are to be provided to squatters in urban slums and landless people elsewhere and transferring the responsibility to urban governments is a piecemeal approach to a much larger problem.

6.4 Conclusions

India's commitment to the SDGs and the Paris Agreement on Climate Change has yet to be translated into India's water policy. This chapter draws the following three key conclusions.

First, existing water policy and the water-related bills do not appear to comprehensively set out a vision for the adaptive governance of water in India taking into account that many flows are transboundary in nature, that climate change affects flows; that the ecosystem services of water need to be maintained in order to ensure the broader impacts on society, that development in different sectors including the agricultural sector needs to be tailor-made based on the availability of water and the strategy on priorities of use, and that there may be many uncertainties. In particular, Indian cities are growing rapidly and infrastructure for cities is expected to develop in the coming two decades. This is a small window for getting the water and sewage infrastructure right for such cities. However, the courts are trying in their own way to address key challenges faced by Indian consumers and producers while the parliament procrastinates.

Second, Indian policy is grappling with the challenge of expropriating land-related water rights without paying huge sums of compensation by using ambiguous language regarding "ownership" of groundwater and the transition to treating water as a common pool resource. It is also ambiguous in its treatment of the privatisation of water, on the one hand, forbidding it and on the other hand making space for the private sector to participate in water and sanitation services. Simply arguing *de jure* that water cannot be privatised may not mean that *de facto* water control does not lie in the hands of the private sector or landowner. Both expropriating rights associated with land and breach of contract with private sector actors bring a very high cost with it. These costs will have to be faced; and the earlier they are addressed the lower they will cost society. Furthermore, the multiplicity of actors, arenas and issues leads to fragmented governance, where power politics may determine water policy outputs, outcomes and impacts especially in the continuing vacuum of clear legally binding guidelines and rules.

Third, decentralisation of water policy is essential in a country of India's size and recognises the need to take local contextual issues into account. However, this needs to occur within an overall science-based vision of how development can proceed and be shared between different sectors, states and people within a water budget. At the same time, adequate resources, knowledge and capacity need to accompany the devolution of power to provincial and local authorities so that they can effectively implement the EIA, run the water organisations, finance stakeholder participation in policymaking, implement policy, and monitor and evaluate policy effectiveness.

This chapter concludes that instead of incrementally developing the water system, policy by policy and court case by court case which may lead to unsustainable path dependency, the government could perhaps think of what kind of a situation India would like to be in, in 2030–2050, given the national to global pressures on water as a resource, the relevant local to global planetary boundaries and backcast to the present. This may make it want to revisit the short-term emphasis on industrial growth at the cost of the well-being of the local farmers and the short-term emphasis on inappropriate growth strategies that are water-intensive and pollute water. Existing water strategies run the risk of being out-of-date even before they are actually implemented.

Note

1 Save Mon Region Federation and Anr. v. Union of India and Ors., Appeal No. 39/2012 before the Principal Bench, National Green Tribunal.

References

Aayog, N. (2019). Composite Water. Management Index: A Tool for Water Management.
Retrieved June 18, 2019, from https://niti.gov.in/writereaddata/files/document_publication/2018-05-18-Water-index-Report_vS6B.pdf
Advanced Centre for Water Resources Development and Management (ACWADAM). (2010). Pani Panchayat: A model of groundwater management – A presentation by ACWADAM. Retrieved June 16, 2019, from https://www.indiawaterportal.org/articles/pani-panchayat-model-groundwater-management-presentation-acwadam
Bandyopadhyay, J. & Perveen, S. (2004). Interlinking of rivers in India: Assessing the justifications. Economic and Political Weekly, 39(50), 5307–5316. Retrieved from https://www.jstor.org/stable/4415896?seq=1#metadata_info_tab_contents
Bavinck, M. & Gupta, J. (2014). Legal pluralism in aquatic regimes: A challenge for governance. COSUST, 11, 78–85. doi: doi.org/10.1016/j.cosust.2014.10.003
Bhavdeep, K. (2002). This Man owns the River. Retrieved May 22, 2019, from www.outlookindia.com/magazine/story/this-man-owns-the-river/
Cullet, P. (Ed.). (2007). Sardar Sarovar Dam Project: Selected Documents. Aldershot: Ashgate.
Cullet, P. (Ed.). (2009). Water Law, Poverty, and Development: Water Sector Reforms in India. Oxford: Oxford University Press. doi: 10.1093/acprof:oso/9780199546237.001.0001
Cullet, P. (2016). Water law in India: Overview of existing framework and proposed reforms. IELRC Working Paper. Retrieved. September 22, 2016, from www.ielrc.org/content/w0701.pdf

Cullet, P. & Gupta, J. (2009). India: Evolution of water law and policy. In J. Dellapenna & J. Gupta (Eds.), The Evolution of the Law and Politics of Water. Dordrecht: Springer Verlag (pp. 157–174). doi http://doi.org/10.1007/978-1-4020-9867-3_10

Cullet, P. & Madhav, R. (2009). Water law reform in India: Trends and prospects. In R. R. Iyer (Ed.), Water and the Laws in India (pp. 511–534). New Delhi: SAGE Publications India Pvt Ltd. doi 10.4135/9788132104247.n19

Divan, S. (2009). Contours of EIA in India. In R. R. Iyer (Ed.), Water and the Laws in India (pp. 390–413). New Delhi: SAGE Publications India Pvt Ltd. doi 10.4135/9788132104247.n15

Doniger, W. & Smith, B. K. (Trans. & Eds.) (1991). The Laws of Manu (ca. 200 BCE). New York, NY: Penguin.

England, M. I. (2018). India's water policy response to climate change. Water International, 43(4), 512–530. doi: 10.1080/02508060.2018.1450569

Gadgil, M. & Guha, R. (1992). The Use and Abuse of Nature. New Delhi: Oxford University Press.

Getzler, J. (2004). A History of Water Rights at Common Law. Oxford: Oxford University Press. doi: 10.1093/acprof:oso/9780199207602.001.0001

Ghatwai, M. (2017). Madhya Pradesh Assembly declares Narmada living entity. Indian Express. Retrieved June 12, 2010, from http://indianexpress.com/article/india/madhya-pradesh-assembly-declares-narmada-living-entity-4639713/

Ghosh, S. (2013). Demystifying the environmental clearance process in India. NUJS Law Review, 6(3): 433–480. Retrieved from www.cprindia.org/sites/default/files/articles/03shibanighosh.pdf

Ghosh, N. (2016). Draft water bills: Address gaps through comprehensive research agenda. Retrieved, September 12, 2016, from www.orfonline.org/expert-speaks/draft-water-bills-address-gaps-through-comprehensive-research-agenda/

Ghosh, N. & Bandopadhyay, J. (2016). Sustaining the liquid mosaic. Longer steps needed. Economic and Political Weekly, 51(52), 20–24. Retrieved from https://www.researchgate.net/publication/311861730_Sustaining_the_Liquid_Mosaic_Longer_Steps_Needed

Gupta, J. (2016). Geopolitics of the new earth: Towards sharing our ecospace. In S, Nicholson, & S, Jinnah (Eds.), New Earth Politics (pp. 271–292). Cambridge, MA., MIT Press.

Gupta, J., Pahl-Wostl, C., & Zondervan, R. (2013). 'Glocal' Water Governance: A multi-level challenge in the Anthropocene. Current Opinion in Environmental Sustainability, 5(6): 573–580. doi: 10.1016/j.cosust.2013.09.003.

Gupta, J. & Pouw, N. (2017). Towards a transdisciplinary conceptualization of inclusive development. COSUST, 24: 96–103. doi: 10.1016/j.cosust.2017.03.004

Gupta, J., Pouw, N., & Ros-Tonen, M. (2015). Towards an elaborated theory of inclusive development. European Journal of Development Research, 27(4), 541–559. doi doi.org/10.1057/ejdr.2015.30

Gupta, J. & Vegelin, C. (2016). Sustainable development goals and inclusive development. International Environmental Agreements, 16(3), 433–448. doi: 10.1007/s10784-016-9323-z

Iyer, R. R. (2004). River-linking project: Many questions. In M. Patkar (Ed.), River Linking: A Millennium Folly? (pp. 9–19). Mumbai: National Alliance of People's Movements.

Iyer, R. R. (2013). Why a national water framework law. The Hindu. Retrieved, October 2, 2016, from www.thehindu.com/opinion/lead/why-a-national-water-framework-law/article4280263.ece

Jain, S. K. (2011). Population rise and growing water scarcity in India – revised estimates and required initiatives. Current Science, 101(3), 271–276. Retrieved from http://re.indiaenvironmentportal.org.in/files/file/water.pdf

Kautilya (ca. 300 BCE). The Arthashastra (L.N. Rangarajan trans. 1992). Delhi: Penguin.

Kendra, M. A. (2013). Database PSP in Water, Sanitation, Solid Waste Management and Sewerage Projects. Retrieved, June 13, 2019, from www.manthan-india.org/wp-content/uploads/2015/04/DatabasePSP-March-2013.pdf

Klijn, A. M., Gupta, J., & Nijboer, A. (2009). Privatising environmental resources: The need for supervision. Review of European Community and International Environmental Law, 18(2), 172–184. doi: 10.1111/j.1467-9388.2009.00639.x

Koonan, S. (2007). Legal Implications of Plachimada – A Case Study. Retrieved, June 13, 2019, from www.ielrc.org/content/w0705.pdf

Koshy, J. (2016). Ken-Betwa, a threat to wildlife? The Hindu. Retrieved, May 13, 2019, from www.thehindu.com/news/national/Ken-Betwa-project-a-threat-to-wildlife/article14414566.ece

Menon, M., Vagholikar, N., Kohli, K., & Fernandes, A. (2003). Large dams in North East India: Rivers, forests, people and power. Ecologist Asia, 11(1), 71–73.

Mirza, M., Ahmed, A. U., & Ahmad, Q. K. (2008). Interlinking of rivers in India: Issues and Concerns. Boca Raton, CRC Press.

Mohan, S. (2017). State of the state: Politics of power shifts and shifting power of the state in India. COSUST, 24, 42–46. doi: 10.1016/j.cosust.2017.02.012

Mukherjee, A. & Bhanja, S. N. (2019). An untold story of groundwater replenishment in India: Impact of long-term policy interventions. In A, Singh, D, Saha & A, Tyagi (Eds.), Water Governance: Challenges and Prospects (pp. 205–218). Singapore, Springer. doi: 10.1007/978–981-13-2700–1_11

Naff, T. & Dellapenna, J. W. (2002). Can there be a confluence? A comparative consideration of western and Islamic fresh water law. Water Policy, 4(6), 465–489. doi:10.1016/S1366-7017(02)00041-7

Prabhu, S. (2012). India's Water Challenges, Atlantic Council. Retrieved, May 17, 2017, from www.files.ethz.ch/isn/154067/PrabhuBrief.pdf

Press Information Bureau, Government of India Ministry of Water Resources. (2016). National Water Framework Law. Retrieved, May 13, 2017, from http://pib.nic.in/newsite/PrintRelease.aspx?relid=148369

PRS. (2012). Report Summary: Draft National Water Policy 2012. Retrieved, July 11, 2019, from www.prsindia.org/parliamenttrack/report-summaries/summary-on-draft-national-water-policy-2012-2431/

PTI (Press Trust of India). (2014). Kerala not to allow Interlinking of Rivers, The Business Standard, Press Trust of India. Retrieved. July 10, 2019, from www.business-standard.com/article/pti-stories/kerala-government-oppose-interlinking-of-rivers-117050900564_1.html

Purohit, M. (2016). Privatisating India's water is a bad idea. The Wire. Retrieved. May 13, 2019, from https://thewire.in/politics/water-privatisation

Reich, M. R., & Bowonder, B. (1992). Environmental policy in India. Strategies for better implementation. Policy Studies Journal, 20(4), 643–661.

Sankaran, K. (2009). Water in India: Constitutional perspectives. In R. R. Iyer (Ed.), Water and the Law in India (pp. 435–474). New Delhi, Sage Publications India Pvt Ltd,. doi: 10.4135/9788132104247.n17

SEEDS. (2019). The Face of Disaster 2019: Beyond Response to Build a Sustainable Future. Retrieved, July 18, 1019, from https://reliefweb.int/sites/reliefweb.int/files/resources/THE%20FACE%20OF%20DISASTERS%202019.pdf

Siddiqui, I. A. (1992). History of water laws in India. In C. Singh (Ed.), Water Law in India (pp. 289–319). New Delhi: Indian Law Institute.

Singh, C. (1991). Water Rights and Principles of Water Resources Management. Bombay: N.M. Tripathi.

Singh, S., & Banerji, P. (2002). Large Dams in India: Environmental, Social and Economic Impacts. New Delhi: Indian Institute of Public Administration (IIPA).

Srivastava, R., & Ramachandran, N. (2016). Sustainable development: Towards a new paradigm for India. European Journal of Sustainable Development, 5(4), 51–60. doi: 10.14207/ejsd.2016.v5n4p51.

Thakkar, H., Lakhani, A., & Shah, M. (2017). Should we privatise water? The Hindu. Retrieved, January 14, 2018, from www.thehindu.com/opinion/op-ed/should-we-privatise-water/article18161255.ece

UN General Assembly). (2010). General Assembly Resolution 64/292, The Human Right to Water and Sanitation. A/64/292 (28 July 2010) Retrieved from www.undocs.org/A/RES/64/292

UN General Assembly. (2015). General Assembly Resolution A/70/L.1, Transforming Our World: The 2030 Agenda for Sustainable Development. A/RES/70/1. Retrieved from https://undocs.org/A/RES/70/1

UNHRC (United Nations Human Rights Council). (2010). General Assembly Resolution 15/9, Human rights and access to safe drinking water and sanitation. A/HRC/RES/15/9. Retrieved from www.right-docs.org/doc/a-hrc-res-15-9/

Unilever, Sunlight, Oxfam, NextDrop, an&d WaterAid. (2015). Every Woman Counts, Every Second Counts: Water for Women. Retrieved, July 10, 2019, from www.unilever.com/Images/slp_water-for-women-march-2015_tcm244-423659_en.pdf

UN Ramsar Convention on Wetlands of International Importance especially as Waterfowl Habitat, Ramsar 2 February 1971, as amended by the Paris Protocol of 3 December 1982 and the Regina amendments of 28 May 1987.

UN Watercourses Convention. (1997). United Nations Convention on the Law of the Non-Navigational Uses of International Watercourses. Reprinted in 36 ILM 700 (21 May 1997, entered into force 17 August 2014).

Upadhyay, V. (2011). Water rights and the new water law in India: Emerging issues and concerns in a rights based perspective. In India Infrastructure Report 2011, Water: Policy and Performance for Sustainable Development (pp. 56–66). Oxford: Oxford University Press,.

Vagholikar, N. & Ahmed, M. F. (2003). Tracking a Hydel Project. The story of lower Subansiri. The Ecologist Asia, 11(1), 25–32.

Vani, M. S. (2009). Groundwater law in India. A new approach. In R. R. Iyer (ed.), Water and the laws in India (pp. 435–474). New Delhi, Sage Publications India Pvt Ltd. doi: 10.4135/9788132104247.n17

Vishwanath, S. (2016). A model Groundwater Bill. The Hindu, July 9. Retrieved, July 10, 2019, from www.thehindu.com/news/national/kerala/A-model-groundwater-bill/article14478750.ece.

Vörösmarty, C. J., Hoekstra, A. Y., Bunn, S. E., Conway, D., an&d Gupta, J. (2015). What scale for water governance: Fresh water goes global? Science 349(6247), 478–479. doi: 10.1126/science.349.6247.478-a

Court Cases

M.C. Mehta v. Kamal Nath (1997) 1 SCC 388.
Subhash Kumar v. State of Bihar, AIR 1991 SC 420.
Narmada Bachao Andolan v. Union of India, Writ Petition (Civil) No. 319 of 1994, Supreme Court of India, Judgment of 18 October 2000, AIR 2000 SC 3751
Narmada Water Disputes Tribunal, Final Order and Decision of the Tribunal 1979
Writ Petition (Civil) No: 512/2002
Hindustan Coca-Cola Beverages (P) Ltd v. Perumatty Gram Panchayat, 2005(2) KLT 554
The Cauvery Water Disputes Tribunal, final order available at http://wrmin.nic.in/writereaddata/Inter-StateWaterDisputes/FINALDECISIONOFCAUVERYWATERTRIBUNAL4612814121.pdf
M.C. Mehta Vs UoI (1997) 11 SCC 312
Gautam Uzir & Anr. V. Gauhati Municipal Corp. 1999 (3) GLT 110.
Para 6 of the affidavit–in–opposition filed by Gauhati Municipal Corporation and quoted in 1999 (3) GLT 110
Delhi Water Supply and Sewage Disposal Undertaking v. State of Haryana (1996) 2 SCC 572: AIR 1996 SC 2992
Article 243W of the Constitution of India, relating to powers, authority, and responsibilities of municipalities
National Consumer's Protection Samiti and Anr v. State of Gujarat & Ors. 1994 (2) GLR 1043
Networking of rivers In re: (2004) 11 SCC 358, (2004) 11 SCC 359, (2004) 11 SCC 360, (2004) 11 SCC 363
M.C. Mehta v. Union of India 1997 (11) SCC 312)
Rambabu M.P. v. District Forest Officer, AIR 2002 A.P. 256
Vishala Kochi Kudivella Samrakshana Samithi v. State of Kerala, 2006(1) KLT 919
S.K. Garg v. State of UP, 1999 ALL. L. J. 332
Chameli Singh v. State of UP, (1996) 2 SCC 549: AIR 1996 SC 1051
Subhash Kumar v. State of Bihar, AIR 1991 SC 420
Narmada Bachao Andolan v. Union of India, AIR 2000 SC 3751
Hindustan Coca-Cola Beverages (P) Ltd v. Perumatty Gram Panchayat, 2005(2) KLT 554
Mohd Salim v. State of Uttarakhand and Ors. *2017 SCC OnLine Utt 367* (WP 126 of 2014)

Other Government Materials

Andhra Pradesh Farmers Management of Irrigation Systems Act (1997).
Andhra Pradesh Water Resources Development Corporation Act (1997).
Bengal Embankment Act (1855).
Bihar Irrigation Act (1997).
Constitution of India (1947).
Draft National Development, Displacement and Rehabilitation Policy (2005).
Draft National Policy on Resettlement and Rehabilitation for Project Affected Families (2004).
Draft National Water Framework (NWF) Bill (2016).
Easement Act (1882).
Embankment Regulation (1829).
Environment Protection Act (1986).
Government of India Act (1935).
Guidelines for Environmental Impact Assessment of River Valley Projects (1985).

Indian Easements Act (1882).
Indian Fisheries Act (1897).
Indus Waters Treaties (1960).
Inter-State Water Disputes Act (1956).
Karnataka State Water Policy (2002).
Land Acquisition Act (1894).
Madhya Pradesh Irrigation Act (1931)
Madhya Pradesh Regulation of Waters Act (1949).
Maharashtra Management of Irrigation Systems by Farmers Act (2005).
Maharashtra State Water Policy (2003).
Maharashtra Water Resources Regulatory Authority Act (2005).
Model Bill to Regulate and Control the Development and Management of Ground Water (2005).
Model Groundwater Bill, 2016, available at http://wrmin.nic.in/writereaddata/Model_Bill_Groundwater_May_2016.pdf
National Rehabilitation and Resettlement Policy (2007).
National Water Policy (1987).
National Water Policy (2002).
National Water Policy (NWP).
Draft National Water Framework (NWF) Bill (2016).
Northern India Canal and Drainage Act (1873).
Northern India Ferries Act (1878).
Notification on Environmental Impact Assessment of Development Projects (1994).
Notification on Environmental Impact Assessment of Development Projects (2006).
Rajasthan Farmers' Participation in Management of Irrigation Systems Act (2000).
Rajasthan Irrigation and Drainage Act (1954).
Rajasthan State Water Policy (1999).
River Basins Bill (2016).
River Boards Act (1956).
The Andhra Pradesh Water, Land and Trees Act (2002).
The Karnataka Ground Water (Regulation for protection of sources of drinking water) Act (1999).
The Kerala Ground Water (Control and Regulation) Act (2002).
The West Bengal Ground Water Resources (Management, Control and Regulation) Act (2005).
Uttar Pradesh Water Policy (1999).
Water (Prevention and Control of Pollution) Act (1974).
Water (Prevention and Control of Pollution) Act (1974), available at www.ielrc.org/content/e7402.pdf (Last accessed on 21 September 2016).
Water Cess Act.

7 Sustainable energy
Prospects and challenges

Kaushik Ranjan Bandyopadhyay, Madhura Joshi and Rainer Quitzow

7.1 Introduction

Energy has often been referred to as the "Missing MDG" (Williams 2009)! Despite the essential role of energy in development, energy was conspicuous by its absence from the set of eight time-bound and quantified targets as specified in the erstwhile Millennium Development Goals (MDGs, agreed to at the United Nations (UN) Millennium Summit in September 2000). The world had to wait another 15 years before energy finally secured an "official entry" into the United Nation's 2030 Agenda for Sustainable Development, adopted by the UN in September 2015. The seventh Goal of the 2030 Agenda (SDG7) aims to ensure universal access to affordable, reliable, sustainable and modern energy. The following three key targets under SDG7 are:

- to ensure universal access to affordable, reliable and modern energy services (Target 7.1);
- to increase substantially the share of renewable energy in the global energy mix (Target 7.2); and
- to double the global rate of improvement in energy efficiency (Target 7.3).

Only a few months later, the landmark Paris Agreement on climate change, reached in UNFCCC COP21, set the aim of keeping the global temperature increase from pre-industrial levels well below 2°C and pursuing efforts to limit it to 1.5°C. With 3,013.8 MtCO2e, India is the fourth largest emitter of greenhouse gas in the world, while being the ninth largest economy. Almost half of the emissions come from electricity production, based almost completely on fossil fuels, especially coal (Ahluwalia et al. 2016, p. 16; Dubash and Joseph 2015, p. 9). Joining the global initiative against climate change, India committed to three Intended National Determined Contributions (INDCs): (1) by 2030, a 33–35 percent reduction in the emission intensity of GDP from 2005 levels, (2) an increase in non-fossil-fuel-based electricity capacity to 40 percent by 2030 and (3) an increase in the forest cover to absorb 2.5–3 billion tonnes of CO_2 by 2030 (Ahluwalia et al. 2016, p. 1).

Achieving SDG7 in India while meeting its climate goals is not only critical for reaching global targets, it also represents a considerable challenge. It will take place within the context of at least three parallel transition processes on the sub-continent – demographics, urban and infrastructural. An estimated 10 million people are expected to enter the job market annually in the next two decades (FICCI and EY 2013), and India's middle class is expected to grow by around 83 million by 2025 (UNDESA 2014). The country's urban population is projected to almost double between 2014 and 2050. An unprecedented expansion in infrastructure will be required to meet the current unmet and future needs of India's rapidly growing urban centres. India also has the dubious distinction of housing the largest proportion of global poor (30 percent), around 24 percent of the global population without access to electricity, and around 30 percent of the global population relying on solid biomass for cooking (GoI 2015). Despite being the fourth largest emitter of greenhouse gas in the world, India's per capita emissions are below the global average.

Against this backdrop, this chapter examines India's sustainable energy challenges by building upon three key pillars of energy policy in India: access, governance and security. The paper also assesses the potential to decouple energy consumption from CO_2 emission. In Section 7.2, the chapter begins with a progress review of SDG7 in India; Section 7.3 provides an overview of potential co-benefits of renewable energy and energy efficiency in India, which may act as additional drivers of related policies. It contrasts this with the inertia in the fossil-based energy sector, most notably coal. Section 7.4 carries out a critical examination of governance and regulatory structures of the energy sector in India and assesses its role in perpetuating lock-in effects and path dependencies within its sector. Section 7.5 provides concluding remarks.

7.2 Policies to promote the SDG for energy in India

India faces a daunting challenge of catering to the needs of a population with varying levels of income and inclusion levels, both socially and financially. On the one hand, there exist multifaceted programmes that have been designed particularly to improve the quality of life of the poorest, such as support for providing a reliable life-line supply of electricity and for shifting households from conventional, polluting methods of cooking to using improved cookstoves and liquefied petroleum gas (LPG). On the other hand, there is heavy influx in use of energy-dependent household appliances, increased demand for cooling and other services across the economy. Given the diversity in needs and the low energy consumption base in the country, India's energy consumption and concomitant CO_2 emissions are projected to grow rapidly in tandem with economic growth. In view of this, the Government of India (GoI) has adopted a policy approach that aims to meet the energy demand of its citizens without allowing the carbon emissions to grow concomitantly. This approach relies on three key elements that are contained in SDG7: increasing energy access, promoting renewable energy and enhancing energy efficiency.

7.2.1 Ensuring universal access to modern energy services

7.2.1.1 Access to power

To date, efforts to increase access to electricity for lighting still rely primarily on conventional grid extension. Progress in doing so has been substantial in recent years. In August 2015, the Modi government announced a new scheme aimed at achieving 100 percent village-level electrification within 1,000 days (Jain et al. 2018). In April 2018, this goal had been achieved, implying that at least 10 percent of households in previously unelectrified localities had gained access to electricity. In India, a village is considered as electrified if the basic infrastructure is in place; power is being supplied to schools, health centres and other public places; and at least 10 percent of households are receiving electricity (Deendayal Scheme 2016). In order to deal with the challenges of the last mile connectivity, the government launched a new scheme called Pradhan Mantri Sahaj Bijli Har Ghar Yojana – "Saubhagya" on 25 September 2017. The scheme aimed to provide connections to all households in India by December 2018 (Jain et al. 2018). According to online data provided by the government, 99.9 percent of households had been electrified by mid-2019.

These figures do not, however, provide any insights into the quality and affordability of electricity, which remains a significant problem, in particular for poor households. A joint initiative by the central government and the states entitled "24×7 Power for All" seeks to provide continuous electricity supply to all household categories. Realizing this goal represents a much more complex challenge than the expansion of grid-infrastructure alone. In the past, cross-subsidisation schemes have prioritised the provision of low-cost power to the poor over investments in the quality of supply. This, in turn, reduces the capacity of low-income communities to translate access to power into productive uses, curtailing their ability to pay higher prices for power. Moreover, the burden of cross-subsidisation disproportionately falls on Electricity Distribution Companies (discoms) on poorer Indian States with higher numbers of poor households. Small- and medium-sized businesses in these regions have to shoulder higher tariffs and lower quality service that results from financially ailing discoms (Swain and Dubash 2019).

The Central government has initiated measures to address these issues. These include proposed amendments to the National Tariff Policy that would make subsidies a joint responsibility of Central and State governments and that would shift to a progressive load and consumption-based tariff (Swain and Dubash 2019). The latter would be of particular benefit to smaller businesses by shifting the financial burden of cross-subsidisation to larger consumers. More substantial progress on the issues remains a challenge, however. The provision of low-cost electricity to rural areas remains an important building block of so-called "redistributive welfarism". This term describes a political economy, where state-level politicians build their electoral success on the provision of low-cost but poor-quality power. The central government has sought to address this challenge since the 1990s when it launched a reform agenda, which included the creation of regulatory agencies. While important progress has been made in stimulating private investment in generation capacity, a breakthrough in solving the challenges of the ailing discoms remains elusive (Dubash et al. 2019).

7.2.1.2 Clean cooking

The data from the latest Indian Census for 2011 reveal that dependence on solid fuels continues in an unabated manner. More than 80 percent of the rural population still relies on traditional fuels, like firewood, crop residue, cow dung and lignite with important health and safety implications. As per the latest Census Report, 87 percent of the rural households and 26 percent of the urban households depend on biomass for cooking (Niti Ayog 2017b). A programme to promote improved cookstoves based on traditional biomass (known in national vernacular Hindi as Unnat Chula Abhiyan) represents one important approach to tackle these challenges. However, the adoption of these stoves has so far been rather low in India. Reasons include a mismatch between the design of the technology and user expectations, low willingness to pay due to low awareness and low perceived benefits (Mobarak et al. 2012), inadequate supply of appropriate technologies and fuels and the absence of an enabling market and financing environment (Arun 2015).

In addition, the use of biogas as an alternate fuel for cooking is being promoted via the National Biogas and Manure Management Programme (NBMMP). NBMMP seeks to provide renewable energy services to households across the country by facilitating the deployment of family-sized anaerobic (biogas) digesters. Key challenges that have impeded its effective implementation have been the limited understanding of the technology amongst the users, feedstock availability and high upfront costs (Rahaa et al. 2014).

Finally, liquid propane gas (LPG) has been successfully introduced in many urban areas, but the penetration rate is abysmally low in rural areas. The installation of LPG has been made convenient due to subsidisation under several government schemes, like Rajiv Gandhi Gramin LPG Vitaran Yojana, Pradhan Mantri Ujjwala Yojana and the PAHAL (DBTL) Scheme. The Ujjwala scheme, in particular, provides LPG connections to below poverty line households as an alternative to conventional cookstoves burning wood in an inefficient manner. Ujjwala has the twin objectives of energy access and public health improvement as traditional biomass use leads to respiratory and cardiovascular problems. Yet, the monthly refill of the cylinder continues to be a problem, due to the high cost of refill as well as the arduous task of carrying the cylinder to the nearest refill station in many remote areas (Bansal et al. 2013). Around 85 percent cite high upfront costs and high refill costs as barriers to regular LPG use (CRISIL 2016). The lack of synergy among the various programmes to promote clean cooking represents an additional factor hampering their success (Jain et al. 2015).

7.2.2 Promoting renewable energy

In its Nationally Determined Contribution (NDC), the country has pledged to achieve about 40 percent cumulative installed capacity from non-fossil-fuel-based energy resources by 2030, and to increase by five times its renewable energy capacity from 35 (as of March 2015) to 175 GW by 2022 (see Box 7.1 for details) (MoEFCC 2015; MoNRE 2017). Although the achievement of the 2022 targets seems to be a tall order, considerable strides have been made in augmenting the share of renewable energy in the energy mix of the country (Aggarwal 2017). As of July 2019, much remains to be done: a total of 81 GW of renewable energy capacity has been installed, with 29 GW of solar power, 36 GW of wind power, 9 GW of bio-power and 4.5 GW of small hydropower (MoNRE 2019). In June 2019, an over-subscribed auction conducted by the Solar Energy Corporation of India Ltd. (SECI) yielded tariffs of INR 2.54–2.55 (USD 0.036–0.037) per kWh (Renewables Now 2019a). In an auction held in December 2018, wind tariffs came in at INR 2.82–2.85 (USD 0.035–0.039) per kWh. With these reductions in tariffs, renewables are now at par with coal power tariffs, which average at INR 3–5 (USD 0.047–0.077 cents) per kWh for domestic coal and at INR 5–6 (USD 0.077–0.093) per kWh for imported coal (Renewables Now 2019b).

India's renewable energy sector is dominated by large hydro with a growing share of wind and solar energy. India has a longstanding track record in the development of wind energy. It ranks fourth in the world in total installed capacity, behind China, the USA and Germany (REN21 2019). Its global leadership in the sector was built on a combination of central and state-level incentives, which led to the expansion of wind energy in selected Indian states from the early 1990s. A study by Schmid (2012) reinforces that national- and state-level policies have played a significant role in promoting renewable energy policy for a sample of nine Indian States. Results from the study suggest that the Electricity Act 2003 along with the passing of the Tariff Policy 2006, state-level policies, quantity-based instruments and a greater participation of the private sector has been largely instrumental in promoting the development of installed capacity from renewable energy power. Another study by Jörgensen et al. (2015) indicates that variation could be observed in the sectors and areas that are identified for the application of renewable energy, suggesting that the states are taking advantage of co-benefits that are relevant to the regional context.

Apart from some early advances in off-grid solar energy applications, India was a relative laggard in the development of solar energy. The sector started gaining momentum with the launch of the National Solar Mission (NSM) under the National Action Plan on Climate Change (NAPCC) in 2010, which targeted the development of 20 GW of solar energy capacity by 2022. The government has, however, revised the target in 2017 to 100 GW of installed solar power capacity. This has been complemented by an initiative to promote solar parks as well as policy initiatives in selected states. Solar parks aim to provide dedicated land with the required infrastructure for grid-connected solar energy generation and are developed jointly by SECI and responsible State governments. Currently, 34 solar park projects with a total of 23 GW of capacity have been approved in 21 Indian states. They are supposed to deliver 40 GW of solar power or 40 percent of targeted capacity. As of March 2019, a total of 9 GW had been auctioned, of which 5 GW had been commissioned (Seetharaman and Chandrasekaran 2019).

While utility-scale, grid-connected solar energy constitutes the mainstay of India's solar capacity, rooftop and off-grid systems are beginning to increase their share. This is mainly the result of demand from industrial and commercial users who seek to supplement relatively expensive power from the grid with investments in private rooftop systems. In addition, a number of states have started experimenting with rooftop and off-grid schemes. Maharashtra, a relatively wealthy state with significant agricultural production, is supporting a solar feeder scheme to provide farmers with supplemental day-time power. Madhya Pradesh is experimenting with an auction scheme that invites bids for aggregated rooftop solar projects. A first auction has yielded tariffs as low as INR 1.58 (USD 0.022) per kWh, albeit including yearly increases of 3 percent over 25 years (Shidore and Strauss 2019).

7.2.3 Enhancing energy efficiency in India

Despite advances in recent years, boosting energy efficiency still offers significant low-hanging fruit in India. A recent study estimates that 86 percent of India's potential to mitigate greenhouse gas emissions lies in energy efficiency measures (Ahluwalia *et al.* 2016). The bulk of this can be captured in the industrial and transport sectors and to a lesser degree in buildings. All three sectors are expected to experience strong growth over the next decades, with urbanisation being an important driver. Hence, promoting the efficient use of energy will have a major impact. In addition, enhanced energy efficiency and switching to solar water pumps for irrigation in agriculture can support reductions in subsidised energy consumption in the sector.

7.2.3.1 Energy efficiency in industry

In the industrial sector, India has introduced, among other initiatives, an innovative market-based energy efficiency trading mechanism called Perform, Achieve and Trade (PAT). It represents a flagship programme of the Bureau of Energy Efficiency (BEE) under the aegis of the National Mission for Enhanced Energy Efficiency (NMEEE), one of the eight missions under the NAPCC (Bandyopadhyay 2016). The PAT scheme resembles a cap and trade mechanism and involves trading in energy-saving certificates between energy-intensive industrial production units identified as designated consumers (DCs). The first cycle of PAT (2012–2013 to 2014–2015) covered 478 plants (called "designated consumers" or DCs) in eight energy-intensive industrial sectors accounting for one-third of total energy consumption in the country (Bandyopadhyay 2016). The first PAT Cycle succeeded in over-achieving its target by around 30 percent, resulting in energy savings of 8.67 MTOE. The thermal power sector has been the only laggard and fell short of its target by 5 percent. However, Phase 1 was dominated by low-cost retrofit projects (65 percent). The focus was primarily on driving utility and component efficiency rather than process and/or systems efficiency (AEEE et al. 2016). For PAT Cycle-II (2016–2017 to 2018–2019), three new sectors, namely Railways, Refineries and discoms, have been added. The target of this cycle is to achieve an overall energy consumption reduction of 8.869 MTOE from 621 DCs in 12 sectors. These consumers account for around 50 percent of India's industrial energy use (Sethi 2017). The success of Phase II is largely contingent upon process innovation, availability of low-cost finance and trading of energy-saving certificates (ESCerts).

7.2.3.2 Energy efficiency in buildings

By 2050, India's urban areas are likely to see an addition of around 400 million people leading to a doubling of energy demand (United Nations 2016). In addition, around two-thirds of the building infrastructure required to meet this rising demand is still to be built (Kumar et al. 2010). This large-scale urbanisation presents a tremendous opportunity for investing in energy-efficient infrastructure. For instance, if all states in India were to adopt energy-saving building codes such as Leadership in Energy and Environmental Design (LEED) or Green Rating for Integrated Habitat Assessment (GRIHA) and leading developers go beyond minimum code requirements for commercial buildings, an estimated 3,453 TWh of electricity can be cumulatively saved by 2030 (ASCI and NRDC 2014). With more than 20 million square miles, India ranks third in the world for LEED certified buildings. As of mid-2018, around 12 states had adopted energy conservation building codes (ECBC).

A small set of appliances fans, televisions, refrigerators, air-coolers, air conditioners and water heaters contribute about 50–60 percent of the total residential electricity consumption in India (Chunekar et al. 2017). To promote more efficient energy use by households, the BEE has established an obligatory Standards and Labelling (S&L) programme to eliminate lower-efficiency appliances through mandatory standards that are periodically tightened. The programme currently has mandatory efficiency ratings for eight appliances and voluntary ratings for an additional 13. For large-scale adoption of energy-efficient appliances, complementing this programme with behavioural interventions and bulk procurement will be crucial (Chunekar and Kelkar 2017).

To target efficient lighting appliances, India has also introduced the Domestic Efficient Lighting Programme (DELP). Its main objective is the promotion of efficient lighting appliances. Under this scheme, every grid-connected consumer with a metered connection can acquire LED bulbs at about 40 percent of the market price from their respective Electricity Distribution Company. This scheme is also performing well with over 300 million LEDs distributed and an estimated energy savings of over 40 million kWh of energy per year (GoI 2019).

7.2.3.3 Energy efficiency in agriculture

The agriculture sector in India consumes about 170 Billion Units (BU) of electricity, accounting for around 18 percent of the total electricity consumption in India. This electricity is mainly used to run pump sets for irrigation purposes. As Indian agriculture is dependent on the vagaries of the monsoon, the farmers prefer pump sets as a more reliable source of irrigation. Typically, the pump sets used for agricultural purposes are inefficient in terms of overall energy performance. Since the users receive virtually free electricity, there is neither an incentive to opt for more efficient but more expensive pump sets nor to adopt other energy-saving agricultural practices. Hence, energy efficiency measures are not only important for reducing greenhouse gas emissions, but they represent an important vehicle for reducing the financial burden resulting from the cross-subsidisation of rural electricity tariffs.

It is estimated that a reduction of electricity consumption by 25–30 percent could be achieved by replacing existing inefficient pump sets with BEE star-labelled efficient pump sets. An Agriculture Demand Side Management (AgDSM) programme, if properly designed and implemented, has the potential of influencing the behaviour of the consumers, thereby modifying their consumption (FICCI and ICFI 2016). Jörgensen et al. (2015) have shown that six out of ten state-level climate action plans focused on applying renewable energy in the agricultural sector with a particular emphasis on energising pump sets, technical modernisation of the agricultural sector, and usage in cold storages. In particular, there is a lot of emphases to replace the existing pump sets, either run by diesel/kerosene fuels or by grid-based electricity, with solar energy run pump sets. The Kisan Urja Suraksha evam Utthaan Mahabhiyan (KUSUM) scheme announced in 2018 aims to promote the instalment of over 1.75 million standalone and 1 million grid-connect solar-powered agriculture pumps in collaboration with state governments. The objective of this scheme is to help reduce, if not completely replace, reliance on both diesel and electricity for agriculture while providing a cost-effective solution for irrigation to farmers in the long run. In addition, KUSUM aims to promote around 10 GW of ground-mounted grid-connected decentralised renewable energy plants by 2022. If the targets of the scheme are met, the government estimates about 27 million tonnes (MT) of CO_2 emissions savings and about 1.2 billion litres of diesel savings per annum (CCEA 2019). Bringing discoms on board, bringing down the cost of solar pumps, increasing local service centres and local information centres, focussing on skill development to help farmers transition, promoting micro-irrigation practices, and promoting water-harvesting measures transition are a few measures which can help this scheme's successful implementation. The states of Chhattisgarh, Haryana, Karnataka, Kerala, Rajasthan and Tamil Nadu have adopted approaches for applying renewable energy in farm applications.

7.2.3.4 Energy efficiency in the transport sector

India's transport sector is growing rapidly to serve the needs of its growing urban middle class. It accounts for 14 percent of India's energy consumption (IEA 2015). While relatively moderate compared to the global average of approximately 25 percent

(EIA 2016), energy consumption in the sector is now growing the fastest among the end-use sectors. The country's low-average vehicle penetration (32 vehicles per 1,000 people in 2015) makes it one of the world's most attractive auto markets (Raj 2016).

The government has taken initiatives to put in place fuel efficiency and emission standards for a new fleet of vehicles. Emissions standards based on the Euro norms were first introduced in the year 2000 (labelled Bharat Stage in India). On 1 April 2017, the Supreme Court of India brought the Bharat Stage VI vehicular emission standard (equivalent to Euro 6) into effect and banned the production of vehicles that do not comply with the newly launched standards. This represented an acceleration of the previously planned roll-out. As per the revised timeline imposed by the government, automakers and fuel suppliers are expected to leapfrog straight to BS-VI norms by 1 April 2020 – in line with the promises India made in its INDC (Sasi 2017). Additionally, the GoI finalised the country's first passenger vehicle fuel-efficiency standards on 30 January 2014 (MoP 2014) and notified "Energy Consumption Standards for Motor Vehicles" on 23 April 2015 under the Energy Conservation Act 2001. Related energy savings by the end of 2025 are estimated to be 22.97 MTOE (Wadhwa 2017).

For commercial heavy-duty vehicles, the GoI finalised fuel-efficiency standards in August 2017 but fell short of implementing the standard due to pressure from the automobile industry lobby (Kaur and Mukherjee 2018). The standards are the government's response to India's rapidly growing commercial vehicle sector, to be followed by standards for heavy-duty vehicles (IEA 2015).

Railways are considered a relatively benign mode of transport as compared to road transport when considered in terms of energy intensity and emissions. A study carried out by the Asian Institute of Transport Development (AITD) observed that the energy consumption on different inter-city rail sections in the case of freight traffic varied between 10.28 and 25.01 percent of the energy consumed by road transport in parallel stretches of state and national highways (AITD 2002). In the case of passenger transport, the energy consumption on rail varied between 78.77 and 94.91 percent of the energy consumed by road transport (Bandyopadhyay 2010). Hence, promoting railways for both intercity passenger and freight transport will reduce energy consumption significantly. In addition, objectives to promote efficient mass transit systems like metro rail in India's growing urban centres have been articulated in the National Urban Transport Policy and the National Smart Cities Mission.

7.3 In pursuit of the multiple benefits of low-carbon development

While India has made important strides towards a low-carbon development pathway, the challenges ahead remain daunting. Nevertheless, the Indian government has shown increasing ambition for low-carbon development scenarios. In addition to reducing greenhouse-gas-emissions, this can provide essential co-benefits, tackling urgent socio-economic and environmental problems in India (Chaturvedi and Samdarshi 2011, Rai and Victor 2009, Sen et al. 2016, Ürge-Vorsatz et al. 2014).

This narrative of climate co-benefits has played a key role in India's climate policy stance. Climate mitigation is to be pursued when it coincides with national development priorities. This rationale is central to the National Action Plan on Climate Change, which endorses the notion that the pursuit of development objectives can at times yield climate policy gains (Dubash and Khosla 2015). The following section briefly outlines some of the expected co-benefits – and hence drivers – of low-carbon development in India. It concludes with a brief discussion of fossil-based – and in particular coal-based – power generation and to what extent low-carbon energy sources are likely to replace rather than merely supplement these high-carbon sources of energy in India.

7.3.1 Benefits of renewable energy in India

India has seen a manifold increase in its renewable energy ambitions. This is linked to the government's industrial policy goals. Increasing investments in renewable energy, particularly through domestic manufacturing, represents one of the focus areas of the government's Make in India initiative, launched by the Modi government in 2014. This has made the mobilisation of investment from both foreign and domestic sources a key priority. A key aim of the initiatives is to boost employment in the renewable energy sector. According to studies, the solar and wind energy sector have the potential to create over 330,000 jobs by 2022 (CEEW and NRDC 2017, Rajya Sabha 2018). An additional synergy of Modi's ambitious promotion of renewable energy is its role in positioning the country as a global leader and building international partnerships with other leading countries. India's role in jointly launching the International Solar Alliance with the French government is a case in point (Shidore and Busby 2019).

Renewable energy production can also have a positive effect on energy security and price stability (Narula et al. 2017). India's fossil fuels are likely to last about 50 more years, if the consumption patterns continue to grow at the existing rate. Renewable energy can lengthen this process and generate power in a decentralised and distributed manner, meeting competitively the power requirements of a large number of small and medium enterprises (Chaturvedi and Samdarshi 2011, Kumar and Madlener 2016, p. 281). Moreover, the import share for consumed energy in India 2012 was almost 40 percent (Bambawale and Sovacool 2011, Parikh and Parikh 2011). A low-carbon-scenario permits a reduction to a 22 percent import rate by 2027 (Ahluwalia et al. 2016). This is a desirable outcome, especially considering the high volatility of international energy prices. And the decentralised character of renewables can mitigate the high vulnerability of the Indian energy infrastructure (Garg et al. 2015, Narula et al. 2017).

Finally, a shift from fossil fuels to the use of renewable energy sources can protect the environment and health of the population by reducing local air pollution and lowering water consumption in water-stressed areas. The WHO reported that 13 of the 25 most polluted cities in the world are in India. A more recent study published in Lancet estimates that more than half a million Indians have died prematurely in 2015 due to particulate matter 2.5 ($PM_{2.5}$) air pollution

(NDTV 2017). Against this background, replacing coal-based power generation with renewable energy has the potential to generate substantial co-benefits for public health. Moreover, over half of India's groundwater resources are overexploited. In the absence of mitigating measures, water use in the energy sector is projected to substantially increase over the next decades. Due to its substantially lower water requirements compared to fossil-bases power generation, renewable energy can play a key role in reducing water stress in India (Ferroukhi et al. 2018).

7.3.2 Benefits of energy efficiency in India

Like the co-benefits from renewable energies, energy efficiency can improve energy security and lower energy prices. Efficiency can increase industrial productivity and lead to overall economic growth, bringing positive social effects. Energy efficiency also reduces local pollution and helps preserving natural resources (IEA 2015). The following areas have been identified to hold substantial impact potential in India: mining, electricity generation, transmission and distribution, pumping water, industrial production and processes, transport equipment, mass transport, building design, construction, heating ventilation, lighting and household appliances (Parikh and Parikh 2011). In a scenario with aggressive development of renewables, nuclear, hydroelectricity, gas and increased energy use efficiency and transport efficiency, Parikh and Parikh (2011) estimate a reduction in the annual growth rate of commercial energy from 6.1 to 5.2 percent and together with a reduction in CO_2 emissions of 30 percent by 2030 and an annual GDP growth rate of 8 percent.

7.3.3 From multiple benefits of low-carbon energy to a low-carbon development pathway?

These multiple benefits of renewable energy and energy efficiency have spurred important advances towards meeting SDG7 and promoting climate-friendly energy technologies in India. However, in parallel, the expansion of high-carbon energy generation technologies aimed at meeting India's unmet and underserved energy demand persists. The government expects capacity additions of 22.7 GW coal-based power between 2017 and 2022 and a further 25.5 GW from 2022 to 2027 (MoP 2018). To ensure the availability of foreign and domestic coal supplies, the government is promoting both the exploitation of additional domestic reserves and investment in overseas coal mines, notably in Australia (Rosewarne 2016). By 2020, the government aims to double coal production capacity to 1.5 billion tonnes (BT).

In recognition of the high levels of CO_2 emissions from coal-based power, the Indian government has begun to support more efficient supercritical coal-based power generation technology. From the 13th Five Year Plan for 2017–2022, the government plans to allow only supercritical power plants. Moreover, the specific requirement for additional coal-based power plants is determined based on the rate of expansion in non-fossil-based capacity. In further support for a shift from coal to renewable energy, the Indian government introduced a Clean Energy Cess in 2011, a tax on coal, lignite and peat produced in the country. Since the introduction the cess was progressively increased from INR 50 to INR 400 per metric tonne (Sinha 2016).

While a step in the right direction, this is not likely to have a major impact on the further expansion of coal-based power in India. While investments in low-carbon development have already led to a relative decoupling of CO_2 emissions from economic growth, it remains highly uncertain when India might reach a peak in annual CO_2 emissions and hence the absolute decoupling of emissions from GDP growth. Unlike China, which has committed to reach the peak in its annual CO_2 emissions in 2030, India has not committed to such a target till date. For now, the Modi government has instead opted for a strategy that focuses its efforts on the expansion of low-carbon energy without concomitant efforts to phase out its highly polluting coal-based power generation.

7.4 Towards an energy governance for a low-carbon pathway in India

Avoiding a high-carbon development pathway will be largely contingent upon changes in the governance of India's energy system. In view of this, the section discusses three major areas in need of substantial changes to place India on a more sustainable development trajectory in the energy sector. First, development planning will have to do away with its current supply-side bias. Instead, it requires an integrated approach, where supply and demand considerations are addressed on an equal footing. Second, it requires the development of an institutional landscape, which is able to tackle multi-objective, multi-sectoral planning. Third, India will have to address the financial sustainability of its electricity sector, currently hampered by its structurally underfunded state-level discoms. The three points are elaborated in more detail below.

7.4.1 Integration of supply and demand

Traditionally, the acute challenges of energy access and the need for securing growth and development for the country have led to an uncritical focus on increasing supplies without consideration of the energy-consuming sectors in India's energy planning. Section 7.2 highlights that demand-side measures can lead to immense energy savings. These will have strong implications on the country's future energy trajectory. However, the historical focus on energy scarcity with a supply-side bias has led to an emphasis on increasing supplies across all sources – coal, oil, gas, nuclear, renewables, etc., which continues today. Current policies targeting the development of energy resources, including coal, oil, gas as well as renewables, highlight a similar approach (see Box 7.1 for some of the targets).

Examining the targets in the coal and renewables sector highlights the need for rethinking India's energy narrative. The government has a target of doubling coal production capacity to 1.5 BT by 2020 and also plans to achieve 175 GW of installed renewable energy capacity by 2020, a five-fold increase in its renewables ambition since 2011. However, the extent of coal and renewables required will change under different scenarios. While most energy models predict a high reliance on coal for India, the range varies between 896 MT and 1.22 BT (Shegal and Tongia 2016). On the other hand, the draft National Electricity Plan released by the Central Electricity Authority (CEA) in 2018 states that no additional coal-based power generation capacity will be required up to 2027, given the existing planned capacity addition targets and projects in renewable energy, nuclear, large hydro and coal-based power already under construction (MoP 2018).

The mismatch between demand and supply considerations has the potential to exacerbate unsustainable infrastructure lock-ins and can lead to stranded and infructuous investments (Joshi and Khosla 2016). In fact, infrastructural loans (from power generation to steel to telecom) have been one of the key reasons for India's current banking sector crisis (Mehta 2016, Reserve Bank of India 2016). A sectoral credit stress test undertaken by the Reserve Bank of India (2016, p. 29) highlighted that "the shocks to the infrastructure segment will impact the profitability of banks considerably, with the most significant effect of the single factor shock being on the power and transport sectors".

Due to its modular nature, renewable energy may not only offer a low-carbon alternative to large-scale coal-based power generation. It may also provide a more flexible solution for providing targeted electricity supply where it is most needed. The recent market and policy developments in favour of solar energy applications tailored to specific commercial uses are promising in this regard.

BOX 7.1 KEY ENERGY SUPPLY TARGETS

- Increase production of coal to 1.5 BT /year by 2020[i] from 638.18 MT in 2015/16
- 10 percent reduction in oil and gas imports by 2022 or increase production to 20 percent of total oil/gas consumption. Oil consumption in 2015/16 was 184.67 MT
- LNG receiving capacity to double by 2022
- 10 percent ethanol blending in petrol by 2020
- Achieve 175 GW of installed RE by 2022 – Solar: 100 GW, Wind: 60 GW by 2022, Biomass-based Energy: 10 GW, Small Hydro: 5 GW[ii]
- 63 GW of Nuclear energy by 2030 from current levels of 5.8 GW
- Add 6.9 GW generation capacity from large hydro projects by 2020; and aggressively pursue large hydro[iii]
- Enhance production of Coal Bed Methane gas

    Sources: [i]Niti Ayog (2017a), [ii]MoC (2015), [iii]GoI (2015).

7.4.2 Institutional capacity for integrated policy-making

The regulatory structure of the energy sector in India, as with many countries, is quite fragmented, comprising multiple institutions across levels of governance (national, sub-national, local) with overlapping areas of jurisdiction (see Annexure 7.1). Traditionally, the control on energy policies has been spread over five fuel-based sub-sectoral ministries – coal, petroleum and natural gas, new and renewable energy, power and nuclear. Historically, climate change has not formed a part of energy governance. However, the establishment of the NAPCC in 2008, structured around the theme of "co-benefits", allowed climate considerations to be a part of energy and developmental policies. As a result, the Ministry of Environment, Forests, and Climate Change and its related institutions and boards have also become important players in India's energy governance architecture. Integrating climate change consideration across ministries and agencies will be crucial, as India continues to expand its infrastructure and building stock to meet the demands of its growing urban, middle-class population while increasing efforts to satisfy the basic needs of its large poor population.

The focus on sub-sectoral energy ministries prompts a silo-based approach, with each ministry seeking to meet higher targets of production, and distributions, however, with little integration with energy-consuming sectors. This fragmentation of the regulatory structure remains one of the key challenges for individual policy problems. For example, policies aimed at enabling a transition to cleaner cooking devices have been enacted at the national level by ministries such as Ministry of Petroleum and Natural Gas, Ministry of New and Renewable Energy; Ministry of Environment and Forests, Ministry of Rural Development; and at the state level by different ministries, each with its own set of targets. The multiplicity of actors with poor inter-ministerial and inter-governmental coordination, multiple targets with a focus on distribution instead of usage and inadequate institutional reviews of past policies have contributed to limited improvements in the sector (Balachandran 2011; Joshi and Bhardwaj Forthcoming). The scale and scope of energy, climate and development problems require policy considerations, which span sectors and ministries. An integrated consideration of India's multiple objectives in decision-making requires institutional structures and capacities which allow for multi-objective planning and effective regulatory institutions, which can oversee sectoral developments and control entrenched interests.

The NAPCC, with its focus on climate benefits of development actions, or co-benefits, and the subsequent state climate action plans provided an institutional platform to mainstream climate concerns in energy and development planning (MoEFCC 2008). Since then, several planning documents, and state- and city-level initiatives have explored co-benefits and green growth. More recently, India's climate pledge ahead of Paris Agreement in 2015 also made the link between energy, climate and development explicit. These various plans and policies have led to a proliferation of institutional structures, both at the central and state level, to explicitly examine climate implications of policies. Dubash and Joseph (2016) in their study on climate institutions discuss that institutional structures have incrementally changed, but manpower and capacity within these organisations remain constrained (see Table 7.1). While it is difficult to select a benchmark for

Table 7.1 Personnel working on climate change in key ministries in 2014

Ministry	Section	Administrative levels in ministries			
		Special/ Additional/ Joint Secretary/ Scientist (G)	Director/ Deputy/ Secretary/ Scientist (D, E, F)	Under secretary/ Scientist (C)	Section officer/Desk officer
Environment and Forests	Climate Change Unit (CCU)	1	3	1	1
Environment and Forests	National Green India Mission (NMGI)	2	1	1	NA
External Affairs	UNES (United Nations Economic and Social) Division	1	1	0	0
Finance	Climate Change Finance Unit (CCFU)	1	1	1	0
Power	National Mission on Enhanced Energy Efficiency (NMEEE)	3	8	0	0
New and Renewable Energy	Jawaharlal Nehru National Solar Mission (JNNSM)	2	2	NA	NA
Science and Technology	National Mission on Strategic Knowledge for Climate Change (NMSKCC)	1	2	NA	NA
Science and Technology	National Mission for Sustaining the Himalayan Ecosystem (NMSHE)	1	2	NA	NA
Water Resources	National Water Mission (NWM)	3	2	1	NA
Urban Development	National Mission on Sustainable Habitat (NMSH)	NA	NA	NA	NA
Agriculture	National Mission for Sustainable Agriculture (NMSA)	NA	NA	NA	NA

Source: Authors, based on Dubash and Joseph (2016).

the staff strength required to perform a range of complex sub-national, national, and international coordination and implementation tasks, the capacity indicated in Table 7.1 seems inadequate.

The complex nature of governance of the energy sector in India has also led to questions on the effectiveness and independence of regulators in the sector. Over the last decade or so, independent regulatory authorities have emerged starting with the electricity sector (both at the central and state levels), and in oil and gas (Dubash 2011). The role and functions of the regulators, such as ensuring that the development of the sector is in line with the objectives of the country, overseeing compliance with environmental standards and procedures and ensuring fair competition, will assume significance in moving towards more sustainable pathways and meet India's climate, energy and development objectives.

However, regulators in the country are under-resourced and under-staffed. In addition, existing energy regulators in the country face challenges in functioning independently and insulating themselves from political interference. For instance, the independence and effectiveness of the Petroleum and Natural Gas Regulatory Board (PNGRB) has been questioned for a number of reasons. First, there is limited independence in selecting officials as its members are appointed by the government. Second, while the views of the board and the government have clashed on several occasions, the board has frequently been forced to back down (Bose 2016). Third, overlapping areas of jurisdiction and clarity on the role of the regulator appear to be missing (Sen and Mukherjee 2015). Fourth, it has no control over deciding the location of refineries, nor does it have a mandate on granting operating licenses. Unlike regulators in the financial or telecom sector, the PNGRB does not have the right to exercise any control on pricing or even regulate it, nor a significant say in infrastructure developments, constraining its functions as an effective regulator of the sector. While there are discussions to clarify the role of PNGRB and vest it with penal powers, these changes and how they manifest themselves in practice remain to be seen (Mishra 2017).

Even regulators that are relatively more independent have limitations that could impact the health of the sector. The Central Electricity Regulatory Commission (CERC) and the State Regulatory Electricity Commission (SERC), created under the Electricity Regulatory Commissions Act (1998) and given more teeth under the Electricity Act (2003), are one of the better examples of regulators in the energy sector. Nevertheless, there are limitations to the autonomy of these institutions, particularly in matters of subsidy and taxation. The Electricity Act, 2003 states that the "right to grant any subsidy to any consumer or class of consumers in the tariff determined by the SERC remains with the state government". This has led to the politicisation of tariffs, for example, granting free-power or concessional rates to certain sectors. These decisions are often taken for political reasons with little consideration for the financial health of the sector (Pargal and Banerjee 2014). Such politics coupled with inadequate data on the real amount of subsidy being provided to the agriculture sector or even the cost during off-peak hours has resulted in the fact that the SERCs are virtually powerless in improving the financial health of the state distribution companies.

Finally, the coal sector in India entirely lacks a regulator. A Coal Regulatory Authority (CRA) bill was proposed and introduced in the parliament in December 2013 (GoI 2013). However, the provisions of the bill, such as appointment and removal of members of the CRA by the government and tariff regulation powers, are restricted to providing advice to the government on methodologies (PRS Legislative Research 2018). Meanwhile, the state-run company Coal of India (CIL) de facto determines prices with government approval, raising concerns amongst critics with some voices fearing a replication of past regulatory issues (Dutta 2014).

7.4.3 Creating an enabling environment for financial sustainability in the electricity sector

A significant challenge for the expansion of energy access in India can be attributed to the poor financial health of its discoms. This takes on additionally urgency when considering the need to modernise and expand the grid to facilitate the integration of variable renewable energy within a low-carbon development pathway as well as the need to substantially increase the quality of service, in particular, for poor households. This, in turn, is the key for enabling a virtuous cycle where access to reliable and affordable power boosts the ability of poor consumers to pay for power by enabling productive uses of electricity. The discoms' poor financial health is due to insufficient revenue collection, which hampers investment in the distribution grid infrastructure and curtails an increase in customer base.

Balancing affordability and financial viability require tariffs to be set high enough, so that a utility's total revenue base – across all its consumers – allows for full cost-recovery while ensuring that low-income customers are not required to pay more than they can bear (Banerjee et al. 2016, UNDESA 2014). India has been grappling with the problems of financially ailing discoms, due to state-level subsidies and cross-subsidies for domestic consumers as well as unmetered connections for agriculture coupled with inefficient billing and inadequate revenue collection. State governments usually provide subsidies to discoms for selling electricity to consumers at less than the procurement cost or for free in some cases. However, subsidy payments by states are not made regularly, adding to the financial woes of the discoms.

Hence, reviving the health of the power sector depends largely on efficient provisioning of electricity and restoring the health of discoms that are reeling under financial stress. The Indian government has already come out with a new scheme for revival of discoms known as Ujjwal Discom Assurance Yojana (UDAY). This is particularly important in the context of India's assertion in the INDC, where the country has emphasised improving the efficiency of the power sector. Besides UDAY, the GoI also introduced the Integrated Power Development Scheme (IPDS) to support the reduction in aggregate technical and commercial (AT&C) losses, the establishment of IT-enabled energy accounting and auditing systems and the improvement in billed energy based on metered consumption. Irregularities in billing consumers can be particularly devastating for poor consumers and is directly linked with collection efficiency. In particular, delays in administering bills result in high, accumulated bills, which have led to increased default rates among poor customers (Swain and Dubash 2019).

7.5 Concluding remarks

The ambitious scale and scope of the policies and programmes discussed in Section 7.2 have the potential to lead India towards a low-carbon pathway. Recent auctions for renewable energy indicate that the costs of renewables are now on par with coal-based electricity. Environmental and social co-benefits of low-carbon development pathways are additional drivers which have the potential to accelerate low-carbon transitions.

In light of the three major transitions that are underway in India – demographic, urban and infrastructural – the coming years have the potential to reorient India's energy sector by redirecting investments toward low-carbon infrastructure. This way India could leapfrog into an energy system dominated by more environmentally sustainable, low-carbon energy technologies. If current government targets for fossil-based energy generation are realised, however, India risks replicating the lock-in in unstainable energy infrastructure, which prevails in much of the industrialised world. To avoid new lock-ins in high-carbon pathways, the resolution of three broad issues is crucial.

First, the energy governance in India has a heavy supply-side bias with insufficient integration between demand and supply considerations. The dichotomy of high renewable and fossil-fuel-based targets without a clear picture of future demand pathways is worrying. Leapfrogging into a low-carbon energy system will depend upon large-scale infrastructure investments that are yet to occur. But the mismatch between demand and supply has the potential to worsen the stranded assets problems, create infructuous lock-in and potentially reduce the confidence in government policies.

Second, institutional capacities for integrated policy-making are currently inadequate for addressing the multiple challenges that India faces. Policymakers will have to combine policies that address the challenges resulting from rapid demographic change, urbanisation and infrastructure expansion with a transition to a low-carbon economy. Current governance mechanisms in the energy sector in India can encourage a silo-based, all-of-the-above approach and have the potential to hamper a critical review of policy decisions. Existing capacity and regulatory constraints make it hard to implement policies, which seek to work across sectors. Negotiating India's multiple objectives and challenges, with supporting institutional structures will play a part in enabling sustainable transitions. If unresolved, these challenges have the potential to create new lock-ins and path dependencies at a time where a low-carbon development pathway is starting to look like a realistic alternative to the outdated fossil-based paradigm. While it is unlikely that this will stop India's transition to a low-carbon economy, it may significantly slow it down.

Third, the financial health of the electricity utilities will play an important role in achieving India's developmental goals and moving towards a low-carbon future. In the absence of bold action to confront these financial challenges, India is unlikely to meet both its climate and energy access targets.

Finally, the policy challenges outlined in this chapter are underpinned by an Indian political economy, in which the Central government has had limited capacity to fundamentally alter the institutional framework in the sector. Despite regulatory reforms, state-level governments still retain an important degree of autonomy in determining the development of their power sectors. Moreover, state-level politics have demonstrated substantial inertia in sustaining the model of redistributive welfarism that characterises the plight of state-level discoms (Swain and Dubash 2019). The strong push from the Modi government in both expanding access to the electricity grid and in deploying renewable energy across the country alone will not fundamentally alter this. However, these developments do have a significant disruptive potential, which could be harnessed to drive further improvements. The combination of increased household-level electrification and low-cost renewable energy offers potential synergies. It creates both increasing pressure on States to modernise their discoms and opportunities to meet rural electricity demand through low-cost, tailor-made renewable energy applications.

References

AEEE, Sustainability Outlook, and Shakti, 2016. *Tracking the Perform-Achieve- Trade Scheme for Energy Efficiency*. New Delhi: Alliance for an Energy-Efficient Economy, Sustainability Outlook Market Access & Insights Team, and Shakti Sustainable Energy Foundation. Available from: www.aeee.in/wp-content/uploads/2016/03/PAT-Pulse_Jan-2016_final-for-print.pdf [Accessed 17 Jul 2019].

Aggarwal, M., 2017. India to Be Third Largest Solar Market in 2017: Report. *Live Mint* [Online], 10 May. Available from: www.livemint.com/Industry/9U7aHwYKlhmQGASjSqiavN/India-to-be-third-largest-solar-market-in-2017-report.html [Accessed 17 Jul 2019].

Ahluwalia, M., Gupta, H., and Stern, N., 2016. *A More Sustainable Energy Strategy for India*. Working Paper 328. New Delhi: Grantham Institute on Climate Change and the Environment; ICRIER; LSE India Observatory.

AITD, 2002. *Environmental and Social Sustainability of Transport: Comparative Study of Rail and Road*. New Delhi: Asian Institute of Transport Development (AITD).

Arun, S. 2015. *Bundling Improved Cooking and Lighting Technology for Energy Access*. New Delhi: The Energy and Resource Institute (TERI). Available from: www.teriin.org/policybrief/files/ImprovedCooking/files/downloads/Bundling_Technology.pdf [Accessed 17 Jul 2019].

ASCI and NRDC, 2014. *Building Efficient Cities: Strengthening the Indian Real Estate Market Through Codes and Incentives (2014)*. New Delhi: Administrative Staff College of India and Natural Resources Defense Council. Available from: www.nrdc.org/international/india/files/real-estate-efficiency-codes-IB.pdf [Accessed 17 Jul 2019].

Balachandran, P., 2011. Dynamics of Rural Energy Access in India: An Assessment. *Energy*, 36 (9), 5556–5567.

Bambawale, M.J. and Sovacool, B.K., 2011. India's Energy Security: A Sample of Business, Government, Civil Society, and University Perspectives. *Energy Policy*, 39, 1254–1264.

Bandyopadhyay, K.R., 2016. *Emission Trading in India: A Study of Two Schemes*. Kitakyushu: Asian Growth Research Institute. Available from: www.agi.or.jp/workingpapers/WP2016-03.pdf [Accessed 17 Jul 2019].

Bandyopadhyay, K.R., 2010. Reconciling Economic Growth with Low Carbon Mobility in India. *India Infrastructure Report 2010*. Chennai: IDFC Limited. Available from: www.idfc.com/pdf/report/Chapter-15.pdf [Accessed 17 Jul 2019].

Banerjee, S.G., et al., 2016. *Regulatory Indicators for Sustainable Energy: A Global Scorecard for Policy Makers*. Washington D.C.: The World Bank. Available from: http://documents.worldbank.org/curated/en/538181487106403375/pdf/112828-REVISED-PUBLIC-RISE-2016-Report.pdf [Accessed 17 Jul 2019].

Bansal, M., Saini, R.P., and Khatod, D.K., 2013. Development of Cooking Sector in Rural Areas in India: A Review. *Renewable and Sustainable Energy Reviews*, 17, 44–53.

Bose, P.R., 2016. Oil Regulator Opposes Govt's Move to Give GAIL the Run of Eastern Gas Grid. *The Hindu Business Line* [Online], 27 November. Available from: www.thehindubusinessline.com/companies/oil-regulator-opposes-govts-move-to-give-gail-the-run-of-eastern-gas-grid/article9391789.ece [Accessed 17 Jul 2019].

CCEA, 2019. *Cabinet Approves Launch Kisan Urja Suraksha evam Utthaan Mahabhiyan*. New Delhi: Cabinet Committee on Economic Affairs. Available from: http://pib.nic.in/PressReleaseIframePage.aspx?PRID=1565274 [Accessed 17 Jul 2019].

CEEW and NRDC, 2017. *Greening India's Workforce: Gearing up for Expansion of Solar and Wind Power in India*. New Delhi: The Council on Energy, Environment and Water and the Natural Resources Defence Council. Available from: www.nrdc.org/sites/default/files/greening-india-workforce.pdf [Accessed 17 Jul 2019].

Chaturvedi, A. and Samdarshi, S.K., 2011. Energy, Economy and Development (EED) Triangle: Concerns for India. *Energy Policy*, 39, 4651–4655.

Chunekar, A., Varshney, S., and Dixit, S., 2017. *Residentional Electricity Consumption in India: What Do We Know?* Pune: Prayas Energy Group. Available from: www.prayaspune.org/peg/publications/item/331.html [Accessed 17 Jul 2019].

Chunekar, A. and Kelkar, M., 2017. *The Efficiency of Appliances. Plugging in: Electrcity Consumption in Indian Homes*. New Delhi: Centre for Policy Research and Prayas Energy Group. Available from: http://cprindia.org/news/6546 [Accessed 17 Jul 2019].

CRISIL, 2016. *Assessment Report: Primary Survey on Household Cooking Fuel Usage and Willingness to Convert to LPG*. New Delhi: Petroleum Planning and Analysis Cell.

Deendayal Scheme. 2016. *Definition of Electrified Village*. New Delhi: Deendayal Upadhyaya Gram Jyoti Yojana. Available from: www.ddugjy.gov.in/portal/definition_electrified_village.jsp [Accessed 17 Jul 2019].

Dubash, N.K., 2011. From Norm Taker to Norm Maker? Indian Energy Governance in Global Context. *Global Policy*, 2, 66–78.

Dubash, N.K. and Joseph, N.B., 2016. Evolution of Institutions for Climate Policy in India. *Economic and Political Weekly*, 51 (3), 44–54.

Dubash, N.K. and Joseph, N.B., 2015. *The Institutionalisation of Climate Policy in India: Designing a Development-Focused, Co-Benefits Based Approach*. New Delhi: Center for Policy Research.

Dubash, N.K. and Khosla, R., 2015. Neither Brake nor Accelerate: Assessing India's Climate Contributions. *Economic and Political Weekly*, 50 (42), 10–14.

Dubash, N.K., Swain, A.K., and Bhatia, P., 2019. *The Disruptive Politics of Renewable Energy*. New Delhi: Centre for Policy Research.

Dutta, I., 2014. Coal Regulatory Authority Little More than Eye-Wash. *The Hindu* [Online], 28 March. Available from: www.thehindu.com/business/Industry/coal-regulatory-authority-little-more-than-eyewash/article5845188.ece [Accessed 17 Jul 2019].

EIA, 2016. *International Energy Outlook 2016*. Washington D.C.: US Energy Information Agency (EIA).

Ferroukhi, R., et al., 2018. *Water Use in India's Power Generation: Impact of Renewables and Improved Cooling Technologies to 2030*. Abu Dhabi, Washington D.C.: IRENA and World Resources Institute.

FICCI and ICFI, 2016. *Agricultural Demand Side Management (Ag-DSM) Program in India*. New Delhi: Federation of Indian Chambers of Commerce and Industry and ICF International. Available from: http://ficci.in/spdocument/20804/White-Paper-AgDSM-Workshop.pdf [Accessed 17 Jul 2019].

FICCI and EY, 2013. *Reaping India's Promised Demographic Dividend — Industry in Driving Seat*. New Delhi: Federation of Indian Chambers of Commerce and Industry and Ernst and Young. Available from: www.ey.com/Publication/vwLUAssets/EY-Government-and-Public-Sector-Reaping-Indias-demographic-dividend/$FILE/EY-Reaping-Indias-promised-demographic-dividend-industry-in-driving-seat.pdf [Accessed 17 Jul 2019].

Garg, A., Neswa, P., and Shukla, P.R., 2015. Energy Infrastructure in India: Profile and Risks under Climate Change. *Energy Policy*, 81, 226–238.

GoI, 2019. *National Ujala Dashboard*. New Delhi: Government of India. Available from: www.ujala.gov.in/ [Accessed 17 Jul 2019].

GoI, 2015. *India's Intended Nationally Determined Contribution: Working Towards Climate Justice*. New Delhi: Government of India at UNFCCC. Available from: www4.unfccc.int/submissions/INDC/Published Documents/India/1/INDIA INDC TO UNFCCC.pdf [Accessed 17 Jul 2019].

GoI, 2013. *The Coal Regulatory Authority Bill, 2013*. New Delhi: Government of India. Available from: http://164.100.47.4/BillsTexts/LSBillTexts/Asintroduced/149_2013_LS_Eng.pdf [Accessed 17 Jul 2019].

IEA, 2015. *India Energy Outlook*. Paris: International Energy Agency (IEA).

Jain, A., Choudhury, P., and Ganesan, K., 2015. *Clean Affordable and Sustainable Cooking Energy for India: Possibilities and Realities Beyond LPG*. New Delhi: Council for Energy Environment and Water (CEEW).

Jain, A., et al., 2018. *Access to Clean Cooking Energy and Electricity: Survey of States 2018*. New Delhi: Council on Energy, Environment and Water (CEEW).

Jörgensen, K., Mishra, A., and Sarangi, G.K., 2015. Multi-Level Climate Governance in India: The Role of the States in Climate Action Planning and Renewable Energies. *Journal of Integrative Environmental Sciences*, 12 (4), 267–283.

Joshi, M. and Bhardwaj, A., [Forthcoming]. *Lessons from Applying Multi-Criteria Analysis: A Case-study on Rural Cooking Energy Transitions* [Working Paper]. New Delhi: Centre for Policy Research.

Joshi, M. and Khosla, R., 2016. India: Meeting Energy Needs for Development While Addressing Climate Change. *In*: S. Roehrkasten, S. Thielges and R. Quitzow, eds. *Sustainable Energy in the G20 – Prospects for a Global Energy Transition*. Potsdam: Institute for Advance Sustainable Studies.

Kaur, B. and Mukherjee, P., 2018. Fuel Efficiency Standards: Did Centre buckle under pressure from industry? *DownToEarth*, 25 Jun. Available from: www.downtoearth.org.in/news/air/fuel-efficiency-standards-did-centre-buckle-under-pressure-from-industry--60583 [Accessed 17 Jul 2019].

Kumar, S. and Madlener, R., 2016. CO_2 Emission Reduction Potential Assessment Using Renewable Energy in India. *Energy*, 97, 273–282.

Kumar, S., et al., 2010. *Developing an Energy Conservation Building Code Implementation Strategy in India*. New Delhi: United States Agency for International Development (USAID), USAID ECO-III Project.

Mehta, S., 2016. Infrastructure, Metal and Textile Sector Have Contributed Most to the Stressed Loans. *The Economic Times* [Online], 28 Jun. Available from: http://economictimes.indiatimes.com/news/economy/finance/infrastructure-metals-and-textile-sector-have-contributed-most-to-the-stressed-loans/articleshow/52957612.cms [Accessed 17 Jul 2019].

Mishra, T., 2017. Ministry to Revamp Oil and Gas Regulatory Board to Minimise Conflict. *The Hindu Business Line* [Online], 16 Feb. Available from: www.thehindubusinessline.com/economy/policy/ministry-to-revamp-oil-and-gas-regulatory-board-to-minimise-conflict/article9547335.ece [Accessed 17 Jul 2019].

Mobarak, A.M., et al., 2012. Low Demand for Nontraditional Cookstove Technologies. *Proceedings of the National Academy of Sciences (PNAS)*, 109 (27), 10815–10820.

MoC, 2015. *CIL Gearing up for One Billion Tonne Coal Production Mark*. New Delhi: Ministry of Coal. Available from: http://pib.nic.in/newsite/PrintRelease.aspx?relid=121779 [Accessed 17 Jul 2019].

MoEFCC, 2015. *India's Intended Nationally Determined Contribution Is Balanced and Comprehensive: Environment Minister. India to Reduce the Emissions Intensity of Its GDP by 33 to 35 Per Cent by 2030 from 2005 Level. India to Create Additional Carbon Sink of 2.5 to 3 Bi*. New Delhi: Ministry of Environment, Forest and Climate Change. Available from: http://pib.nic.in/newsite/PrintRelease.aspx?relid=128403 [Accessed 17 Jul 2019].

MoEFCC, 2008. *National Action Plan on Climate Change*. New Delhi: Ministry of Environment, Forest and Climate Change.

MoNRE, 2019. *Physical Progress*. New Delhi: Ministry of New and Renewable Energy. Available from: https://mnre.gov.in/physical-progress-achievements [Accessed 17 Jul 2019]

MoNRE, 2017. *Year End Review 2017 – MNRE*. New Delhi: Ministry of New and Renewable Energy. Available from: http://pib.nic.in/newsite/PrintRelease.aspx?relid=174832 [Accessed 17 Jul 2019].

MoP, 2018. *National Electricity Plan*. New Delhi: Ministry of Power, Central Electricity Authority.

MoP, 2014. *Notification 10/7/2008-EC*. New Delhi: Ministry of Power. Available from: www.egazette.nic.in/WriteReadData/2014/158019.pdf [Accessed 17 Jul 2019].

Narula, K., et al., 2017. Sustainable Energy Security for India: An Assessment of the Energy Supply Sub-System. *Energy Policy*, 103, 127–144.

NDTV, 2017. Air Pollution Caused Half a Million Deaths in India in 2015: Study. *NDTV* [Online], 31 Oct. Available from: www.ndtv.com/food/air-pollution-caused-half-a-million-deaths-in-india-in-2015-study-1769169 [Accessed 17 Jul 2019].

Niti Ayog, 2017a. *Draft Three Year Action Agenda*. New Delhi: Niti Ayog.

Niti Ayog, 2017b. *User Guide for India's 2047 Energy Calculator: Cooking Sector*. Niti Aayog. Available from: http://indiaenergy.gov.in/iess/docs/Cooking.pdf [Accessed 17 Jul 2019].

Pargal, S. and Banerjee, S.G., 2014. *More Power to India: The Challenge of Electricity Distribution*. Washington D.C.: The World Bank.

Parikh, J. and Parikh, K., 2011. India's Energy Needs and Low-Carbon Options. *Energy*, 36, 3650–3658.

PRS Legislative Research, 2018. *The Coal Regulatory Authority Bill 2013*. New Delhi: PRS Legislative Research. Available from: www.prsindia.org/billtrack/the-coal-regulatory-authority-bill-2013-3046/ [Accessed 17 Jul 2019].

Rahaa, D., Mahanta, P., and Clarke, M.L., 2014. The Implementation of Decentralised Biogas Plants in Assam, NE India: The Impact and Effectiveness of the National Biogas and Manure Management Programme. *Energy Policy*, 68, 80–91.

Rai, V. and Victor, D.G., 2009. Climate Change and the Energy Challenge: A Pragmatic Approach for India. *Economic and Political Weekly*, 44 (31), 78–85.

Raj, A., 2016. India's Passenger Vehicle Density to Nearly Double by 2020. *Live Mint* [Online], 8 Feb. Available from: www.livemint.com/Companies/vbNU9FS9PDU5UPpUSkGYTN/Indias-passenger-vehicle-density-to-nearly-double-by-2020.html [Accessed 17 Jul 2019].

Rajya Sabha, 2018. Employment Opporunity in Solar and Wind Energy Sectors. *Unstarred QUestion No -1576*, 31 Jul. New Delhi: Government of India quoting CEEW and NRDC 2017. Available from: http://164.100.47.5/qsearch/QResult.aspx [Accessed 18 Oct 2018].
REN21, 2019. *Renewable Energy 2019: Global Status Report*. Paris: REN21.
Renewables Now, 2019a. Indian Solar Tender Awards 1.2 GW at INR 2.54/kWh. *Renewables Now* [Online], June 13. Available from: https://renewablesnow.com/news/indian-solar-tender-awards-12-gw-at-inr-254kwh-report-657862/ [Accessed Jul 17, 2019].
Renewables Now, 2019b. Lowest Bid in SECI's Tranche-VI Wind Auction Hits INR 2.82/kWh – Report. *Renewables Now* [Online], 18 Feb. Available from: https://renewablesnow.com/news/lowest-bid-in-secis-tranche-vi-wind-auction-hits-inr-282kwh-report-643266/ [Accessed 17 Jul 2019].
Reserve Bank of India, 2016. *Financial Stability Report December 2016*. Mumbai: Reserve Bank of India.
Rosewarne, S., 2016. The Transnationalisation of the Indian Coal Economy and the Australian Political Economy: The Fusion of Regimes of Accumulation? *Energy Policy*, 99, 214–223.
Sasi, A., 2017. Bharat Stage-VI in 3 Years: Race over Speedbumps. *The Indian Express*, 27 Feb. Available from: http://indianexpress.com/article/explained/death-by-breath-bharat-stage-iv-bs-iv-bs-vi-in-3-yrs-race-over-speedbumps-4545456/ [Accessed 17 Jul 2019].
Schmid, G., 2012. The Development of Renewable Energy Power in India: Which Policies have been Effective? *Energy Policy*, 45, 317–326.
Seetharaman, G. and Chandrasekaran, K., 2019. Government's Solar Park Push is Running into Land Acquisition and Transmission Challenges. *The Economic Times*, 28 Apr. Available from: https://economictimes.indiatimes.com/industry/energy/power/governments-solar-park-push-is-running-into-land-acquisition-and-transmission-challenges/articleshow/69074597.cms?from=mdr [Accessed 17 Jul 2019]
Sen, S. and Mukherjee, P., 2015. Supreme Court Rules PNGRB Cannot Fix Gas Retail Price: The Judgement Came in Response to the Dispute between PNGRB and Indraprastha Gas. *Live Mint* [Online], 2 Jul. Available from: www.livemint.com/Money/FHRzht5OY7DijmlMZgZbvL/Indraprastha-Gas-surges-16-on-favourable-Supreme-Court-ruli.html [Accessed 17 Jul 2019].
Sen, S., et al., 2016. Renewable Energy Scenario in India: Opportunities and Challenges. *Journal of African Earth Sciences*, 122, 25–31.
Sethi, G., 2017. *Workshop on SDG7: Affordable and Clean Energy*. New Delhi: Niti Aayog. Available from: www.niti.gov.in/writereaddata/files/Girish%20Sethi.pdf [Accessed 17 Jul 2019].
Shegal, A. and Tongia, R., 2016. *Coal Requirement in 2020: A Bottom-Up Analysis*. New Delhi: Brookings India.
Shidore, S. and Busby, J.W., 2019. What Explains India's Embrace of Solar? State-led Energy Transition in a Developmental Polity. *Energy Policy*, 129, 1179–1189. Available from: https://doi.org/10.1016/j.enpol.2019.02.032 [Accessed 17 Jul 2019].
Shidore, S. and Strauss, R.S., 2019. *Bright Future? Fourth Annual Review of Solar Scale-Up in India*. New York: Council on Foreign Relations. Available from: www.cfr.org/blog/bright-future-fourth-annual-review-solar-scale-india [Accessed 17 Jul 2019].
Sinha, A., 2016. Union Budget 2016–17: Coal Cess Doubled to Fund Ministries, Green Drives. *The Indian Express* [Online], 2 Mar. Available from: http://indianexpress.com/article/india/india-news-india/union-budget-2016-17-coal-cess-doubled-to-fund-ministries-green-drives [Accessed 17 Jul 2019].
Swain, A.K. and Dubash, N.K., 2019. *Beyond Poles and Wires: How to Keep the Electrons Flowing?* New Delhi: Centre for Policy Research.

TERI, 2013. *TERI Energy Data Directory and Yearbook (TEDDY) 2012/13*. New Delhi: The Energy and Resources Institute.

UNDESA, 2014. *World Urbanisation Prospects: The 2014 Revision, Highlights*. New York: United Nations, Department of Economic and Social Affairs. Available from: https://esa.un.org/unpd/wup/Publications/Files/WUP2014-Highlights.pdf [Accessed 17 Jul 2019].

United Nations, 2016. *World Urbanization Prospects, 2014 Revision*. New York: United National. Available from: http://esa.un.org/unpd/wup/Highlights/WUP2014-Highlights.pdf [Accessed 17 Jul 2019].

Ürge-Vorsatz, D., et al., 2014. Measuring the Co-Benefits of Climate Change Mitigation. *The Annual Review of Environment and Resources*, 39, 549–582.

Wadhwa, D., 2017. *Fuel Economy Norms for Transport Sector*. New Delhi: Ministry of Power. Available from: www.ecmaindia.in/Uploads/image/84imguf_Sh.SaurabhDiddiMs.DeepshikhaWadhwa(BEE).pdf [Accessed 17 Jul 2019].

Williams, M., 2009. Energy Missing Millennium Goal – U.N. Climate Chief. *Reuters* [Online], 21 Jan. Available from: https://in.reuters.com/article/india-energy/energy-missing-millennium-goal-u-n-climate-chief-idINDEL27013420090121 [Accessed 17 Jul 2019].

Annexure

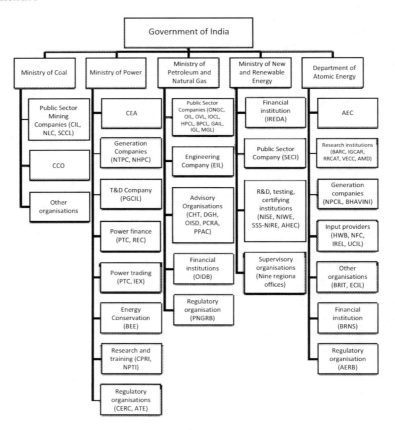

AHEC – Alternate Hydro Energy Centre; AEC – Atomic Energy Commission; AERB – Atomic Energy Regulatory Board; AMD – Atomic Minerals Directorate for Exploration and Research; ATE – Appellate Tribunal for Electricity; BARC – Bhabha Atomic Research Centre; BBMB – Bhakra Beas Management Board; BEE – Bureau of Energy Efficiency; BHAVINI – Bharatiya Nabhikiya Vidyut Nigam Ltd; BHAVINI – Bharatiya Nabhikiya Vidyut Nigam Ltd; BPCL – Bharat Petroleum Corporation Ltd; BRIT – Board of Radiation and Isotope Technology; BRNS – Board of Research in Nuclear Sciences; CCO –Coal Controller's Organization; CEA – Central Electricity Authority; CERC – Central Electricity Regulatory Commission; CESC – Calcutta Electric Supply Corporation Ltd; CHT – Centre for High Technology; CIL – Coal India Ltd; CPRI – Central Power Research Institute; DGH – Directorate General of Hydrocarbons; discom – distribution company; DVC – Damodar Valley Corporation; E&P – Exploration and Production; ECIL – Electronics Corporation of India Ltd; EIL – Engineers India Ltd; EOL – Essar Oil Ltd; GAIL – Gas Authority of India Ltd; GSPC – Gujarat State Petroleum Corporation Ltd; HPCL – Hindustan Petroleum Corporation Ltd; HWB – Heavy Water Board; IEX – Indian Energy Exchange; IGCAR – Indira Gandhi Centre for Atomic Research; IGL – Indraprastha Gas Ltd; IOCL – Indian Oil Corporation Ltd; IREDA – Indian Renewable Energy Development Agency Ltd; IREL – Indian Rare Earths Ltd; MGL – Mahanagar Gas Ltd; NEEPCO – North Eastern Electric Power Corporation Ltd; NFC – Nuclear Fuel Complex; NHDCL – NHDC Ltd; NHPC – National Hydroelectric Power Corporation Ltd; NISE – National Institute of Solar Energy; NIWE – National Institute of Wind Energy; NLC – Neyveli Lignite Corporation; NPCIL – Nuclear Power Corporation of India Ltd; NPTI – National Power Training Institute; NTPC – National Thermal Power Corporation Ltd; OIDB – Oil Industry Development Board; OIL – Oil India Ltd; OISD – Oil Industry Safety Directorate; ONGC – Oil and Natural Gas Corporation Ltd; OVL – ONGC Videsh Ltd; PCRA – Petroleum Conservation Research Association; PGCIL – Power Grid Corporation of India Ltd; PNGRB – Petroleum and Natural Gas Regulatory Board; PPAC – Petroleum Planning and Analysis Cell; PTC – Power Trading Corporation of India Ltd; R&D – Research and Development; REC – Rural Electrification Corporation; RIL – Reliance Industries Ltd; RRCAT – Raja Ramanna Centre for Advanced Technology; SCCL – Singareni Collieries Company Ltd; SEBs – state electricity boards; SECI - Solar Energy Corporation of India; SERC – State Electricity Regulatory Commission; SJVN – Satluj Jal Vidyut Nigam Ltd; SSS-NIRE – Sardar Swaran Singh National Institute of Renewable Energy; T&D – transmission and distribution; THDCIL – THDC India Ltd; transco – transmission company; UCIL – Uranium Corporation of India Ltd; VECC – Variable Energy Cyclotron Centres.

Source: Updated by the Authors based on TERI (2013).

8 Factors shaping the climate policy process in India

Denise Fernandes, Kirsten Jörgensen and N.C. Narayanan

8.1 Introduction

In 2015, a heatwave killed thousands of people in the three Indian states of Andhra Pradesh, Telangana and Odisha and temperatures hit a high of 48°C in some Indian cities. In the summer of 2018, in the state of Kerala, more than a million people were affected by the severe flooding during the monsoon season. Heatwaves and floods highlight the broader problem that climate change poses to India. The 2018 Global Warming of 1.5 Degree Special Report commissioned by the Intergovernmental Panel on Climate Change (IPCC) presents mounting evidence that if the average global temperature rises by more than 1°C compared to the temperature in 2018, India will be at the receiving end of some of the most damaging climate extremes (IPCC 2018). Climate change, though rapidly developing, is often difficult to perceive, which in turn makes it difficult to politicise. It poses enormous challenges to political agenda-setting and decision making. Global in scale and long term in scope, it threatens the economic foundations of the carbon locked-in industrialised countries and the industrialising world, its life forms and its energy and transportations systems (Unruh 2000).

To countries of the newly industrialising world, climate change presents a special challenge. Striving to cover steadily growing energy demands and to provide equal access to electricity for underprivileged parts of the population, it is tempting to neglect the call for climate mitigation and postpone action. The reluctance towards climate mitigation in developing countries is enhanced politically by climate justice concerns. In contrast to the future greenhouse gas emissions (GHGE) which will be predominantly produced in the global south, the historical responsibility for climate change lies with the global north. Industrialised countries have contributed disproportionately to the emission of greenhouse gases (GHG) and thereby to the global problem giving industrialising nations grounds to assert that they have a legitimate right to increased demand in the energy sector; greater access to and a more reliable energy supply; economic development and poverty eradication (Dubash *et al.*, 2018).

The primary objective of this chapter is to describe the development of climate policy in India and to explain the factors that influenced the domestic climate policy process. The focus is on climate mitigation policies, which consist of actions to reduce GHGE and limit global warming. Section 8.1 introduces current comparative climate politics literature and the knowledge available about the factors shaping climate mitigation policy in industrialised and industrialising countries and maps out the factors which shape domestic policy output in a general sense. Section 8.2 first outlines the unique challenges faced by climate policy development in India and then provides an overview of India's climate policy over the last three decades. A chronological overview of climate policy development in India is provided, and the process is divided into three main phases according to significant policy change. Policy shifts over this time period are outlined and factors that affected policy discussed, building on relevant literature on India's climate policy. Section 8.3 will focus on the link between knowledge, institutions and the climate policy process.

8.2 Comparative climate politics – factors shaping domestic policy responses

Domestic climate policy achievements and failures cannot simply be explained by rising prosperity as the environmental Kuznets curve would suggest. Contrary to comparative politics theories, the presence or absence of democratic institutions is also an insufficient explanation (Bernauer and Böhmelt 2013). A variety of conditions and mechanisms need to be considered. Comparative climate politics research has identified a number of conditions that shape the climate policy output in different countries. The literature identifies factors that are linked to "under-reactions" (Peters et al., 2017, p. 612) of governments to the challenges presented by climate change as well as factors that are supportive of proportionate and ambitious climate policies (Bernauer and Böhmelt 2013).

Unruh (2000) introduced the concept of carbon lock-in to depict the dilemma of climate mitigation policies. Unfavourable conditions, which impede the institutionalisation of climate mitigation policies, are caused by the technological and institutional carbon lock-in. Industrialised economies have become locked into fossil fuel-based energy and transportation systems (Unruh 2000, 2002). Rapidly industrialising countries are also beset by technical and institutional path dependencies, which inhibit mitigation policy. A coal-based energy mix combined with low financial capacity, as well as the presence of strong capital and emission-intensive industries – such as in India and China – constrain the transition of energy sectors to a low-carbon economy (Never and Betz 2014). Developing economies with substantial poverty rates have greater difficulty placing climate mitigation high on the political agenda. Across the board, the insufficiency of domestic policy responses to climate change is linked to the complexity and cross-sectoral character of the climate problem and the need to address all the CO_2-emitting sectors in fragmented political administrative structures (Peters et al., 2017), in which diverse ministries often pursue conflicting objectives and interests.

In contrast, significant leverage for domestic climate action can be derived in both industrialised and industrialising countries from aspects of global climate governance and domestic factors (Jänicke 2017). International climate conferences are external events that frequently lead to climate issues being placed higher up domestic political agendas. Comparative studies also show that the institutionalisation of domestic climate policy has been boosted in great part by lesson-learning from international pioneers at the city and country level (Bulkeley 2013). Climate policy is also driven by new knowledge about the economic co-benefits. Industrial policies promoting renewable energy and energy-efficient technologies (Jänicke 2017; Never and Betz 2014) are important drivers of climate mitigation policy and indicate a shift towards a low-carbon development. Ideas, knowledge and science are all key factors for climate policymaking and policy-oriented learning (Never 2012, 2015). Emerging domestic climate advocacy coalitions involving public and private actors, and in particular non-governmental organisations (NGOs) and researchers, are reported to have influenced policy paradigms and policy change in the BRICS countries of China, India and Brazil (Aamodt and Stensdal 2017). Key individuals within organisations can play an important role in (Never 2015; Peters et al., 2017; Peterson et al., 2008) triggering changes in the dominant policy paradigm and promoting policy change.

On balance, climate politics relies on the actor constellation involved and whether or not climate protection proponents – climate advocacy coalitions – have access to policymaking channels. Different sequences of the climate policy process emerge against the background of the interplay between the international climate process and domestic factors and also depend on the way economic interest, development concerns, climate equity and technological options are discussed. Climate knowledge, produced by the IPCC and domestic climate research organisations is an important driver of the domestic and international climate process. Critical knowledge about the harmful impacts of climate change and the vulnerability of certain countries and regions is of utmost importance and can trigger policy change. In the next subsection, we will discuss climate policy development in India.

8.3 Climate policy development in India and factors influencing it

Due to India's sheer size (it has an estimated population of 1.3 billion), it is paradoxically both the world's third-largest GHG contributor and a member of the group of countries with the lowest per capita emissions. More than 300 million people still lack electricity or reliable electricity supply. As a rapidly developing country, it is home to 30 percent of the world's poorest people and, therefore, in the country's development strategies, emphasis is placed on inclusive development (Shukla et al., 2015).

India's climate policy subsystem is torn between the priorities of rapid economic growth, poverty eradication and moves towards a low-carbon economy (Jörgensen 2017). Stable influential factors that remain constant over longer periods of time include the need to eradicate poverty including energy poverty and India's carbon lock-in. India's National Action Plan Climate Change stresses the overriding priority of economic and social development and of maintaining high growth rates (Government of India, Prime Minister's Council on Climate Change 2008). Despite India's Intended Nationally Determined Contributions (INDCs) outlining ambitious goals for the growth in renewable energy supply, the use of coal and oil will also grow in order to cover India's rapidly increasing electricity demand. Carbon-based fuels and in particular coal-fired electricity generation will continue to increase by nearly 4 percent per year until 2022 (International Energy Agency 2017). India's power sector is caught in the carbon lock-in (Never and Betz 2014; Unruh 2000) reflecting the path-dependence of the country's coal-centred energy mix (see Chapter 7, Bandyopadhyay, Joshi and Quitzow, this volume).

India's energy policy cannot be reformed easily because it struggles with political and administrative fragmentation constraining policy change and effective implementation, which is often a challenge in all fields not just that of energy policy in India (Bang et al., 2015).

However, with regard to factors, which can spur the development of climate policy, India has a long-standing and continuous history of renewable energy policy which was initially driven by energy security concerns. Today renewable energy policy belongs to the central pillars of the country's climate action strategy. India aims to increase non-fossil fuel-based energy resources to 40 percent of the installed electric power capacity by 2030 (Government of India (GOI) 2015). After India's liberalisation in 1991 and the passing of India's Electricity Act in 2003, the Tariff Policy of 2006 and state-level policies have fostered the development of installed capacity from renewable energy sources in the country (Chaudhary et al., 2015; Schmid 2012). The potential economic and technical benefits of climate action, and the economic potential of Clean Development Mechanisms (CDMs) (Fisher 2012; Michaelowa and Michaelowa 2012; Shukla and Dhar 2011) became more obvious in the early 1990s, which is reflected in the growth of India's co-benefits and green growth debate (Dubash et al., 2018).

More changeable conditions, which significantly influenced the domestic policy process in India, include international factors, such as the United Nations Framework Convention on Climate Change (UNFCCC) negotiation process (Dubash et al., 2018). Moreover, India also saw a political spill-over from domestic green industrial policies, renewable energy policy, in particular, spurring climate policy. Domestic NGOs, think-tanks and policy entrepreneurs also played roles, forming a like-minded actor coalition, and inserting new knowledge and ideas into the domestic discourse.

Since the 1990s, a durable and widely undisputed policy paradigm shared by government officials and NGOs has played a critical role in India's climate policy: global "climate equity", which implies that climate change was a problem created by industrialised countries which therefore should be held to account first (Dubash 2013; Isaksen and Stokke 2014). The related development first, or "growth first" theory holds that India's first priority as a former colony and developing country should be development and poverty reduction and that these aims should not be hampered by emission reduction goals.

The Indian climate policy landscape has undergone significant change over the course of the last 25 years. From its cautious entry into national and international discourse in the early 1990s, the status of climate policy has over the years gained central prominence. A diverse set of factors have exerted their influence and driven this transformation. While this transitional pathway is not clear-cut, a few broad changes are discernible enough to permit a coherent division of the process into three major phases.

In the following sections, three different phases of domestic climate policy will be outlined; periods of policy stability and policy change will be highlighted; and factors affecting policy shifts over these time periods will be discussed. External factors such as the stages of the UNFCCC process, the interplay between domestic and international factors and political demands directed towards India by industrialised countries and the developing country coalitions will be considered, as will domestic factors such as new technological developments and related domestic interests articulated by the corporate sector; the public perception of climate change as a threat or opportunity; and demands formulated by NGOs. This section will also explore the continuous interaction between political agenda-setting and policy formulation with the international climate process (its course and major decisions), plus how Indian domestic actors from the field of research and academia, the state-level, NGOs and the corporate sector have become more influential in the shaping of climate policy (Aamodt and Stensdal 2017).

8.3.1 1990–2006 India's climate policy paradigm emerges

Climate policy first appeared on India's governmental agenda in the 1990s thanks in large part to the international climate negotiations resulting from the passing of the United Nations climate convention in 1992. Government action focused on the emerging international climate regime and framed the subject as a purely international issue, leading to the establishment of a negotiating team that was influenced by both governmental actors and NGOs (Michaelowa and Michaelowa 2012). Climate equity guided the development of India's negotiating position (Fisher 2012), sealing the domestic debate off from new insights about potential development advantages climate mitigation could bring about, including environmental, social, economic and health benefits (Dubash et al., 2018).

Often perceived as obstructionist because it continued to resist binding goals and obligations for developing countries, India was nonetheless able to demonstrate international leadership (Jörgensen 2017). Spurred on by domestic NGO activists, in 1991 India exerted cognitive leadership by introducing the equity principle to the international climate negotiations, which was met with great approval by fellow industrialising countries (Dutta et al., 2015). India also became an entrepreneurial leader and rule maker and managed to introduce the "common but differentiated responsibility" (CBDR) wording into international treaties in 1992. India and China took the lead in the negotiating group of developing countries (G77) (Gupta et al., 2015) in the run-up to Conference of the Parties (COP) 1 in Berlin in 1995 by insisting on the differentiated architecture of the treaties, thus leaving developing countries free from obligations. In contrast, domestic climate policy did not exist in India prior to 2007.

India's private sector paid increasing attention to the problem of climate change, in particular, with regard to its impact on business and as a potential hindrance for growth (Das 2012; Pulver 2012). Actors from India's industrial sector gradually realised the economic opportunities lying in climate mitigation policy and therefore favoured the introduction of the market-based CDM in the Kyoto Protocol after the COP 8 which was held in Delhi in 2002. Subsequently, India modified its position, dipping "half a toe in the water" (Dubash 2013, p. 192) by agreeing to the introduction of the CDM in the Kyoto Protocol.

Overall, the distinguishing characteristic of the first phase of India's climate policy process spanning the period from 1990 to 2006 is the development and influence of a domestically uncontested climate policy paradigm. The principles of equity and development-first have informed India's international negotiating position since the 1990s; in fact, India became a deal-maker in international negotiations, inserting the Common But Differentiated Responsibility (CBDR) wording into the international climate treaties. In addition, the beginnings of domestic advocacy for climate mitigation were spurred on by business interests, due to the linking of economic opportunities offered by finance and technology transfer and international climate cooperation.

8.3.2 2007–2013 Developing domestic climate policy

From 2007 onwards, national climate strategies have diffused significantly across developing countries boosted by the upcoming 2009 United Nations Climate Change Conference in Copenhagen (Iacobuta et al., 2018). Likewise, India has seen the emergence of a climate policy geared towards domestic mitigation and adaptation emerge. India's government has made fewer commitments in international climate negotiations than it has actually carried out in domestic climate action (Betz 2012). In 2007, India's incumbent Prime Minister Manmohan Singh announced that per capita GHGE in India will never exceed those of the Organization for Economic Co-operation and Development (OECD) nations. In the same year, he also established a National Advisory Panel which was mandated to develop a national climate strategy. The National Action Plan on Climate Change (NAPCC) was launched in 2008. It included national objectives such as the promotion of renewable energies ("Solar Mission") and energy efficiency ("Enhanced Energy Efficiency") (GOI 2008). A rapid development of climate policy measures in India occurred, and the number of newly introduced energy regulations and programmes increased.

Domestic climate policy was increasingly driven by India's pressing energy security concerns and a growing scientific consensus about the impacts of climate change (Dubash 2013; Gupta et al., 2015). Actor constellations changed and the basic ideas and assumptions that had informed India's initial climate policy paradigm from the beginning were less widely shared. A newly emerging domestic climate advocacy coalition and policy entrepreneurs such as the incumbent environmental minister Jairam Ramesh supported policy change and a modified negotiation position (Aamodt and Stensdal 2017).

A change in perspective on the economic and development threats of climate mitigation policy was crystallised in the anchoring of the "co-benefit" principle into India's NAPCC in 2008. Initially introduced by the IPCC into global climate research and policy consultation, the co-benefit method explores the economic, social and environmental advantages lying within climate mitigation measures. India's adoption of this principle signalled a shift in the domestic climate policy paradigm and it also provided for important institutional change stimulating new thoughts and research about the potential benefits of climate mitigation in the form of development and green economic growth (Dubash et al., 2013; Khosla et al., 2017). India's reading of the co-benefit approach followed the lines of the "development first" principle. In contrast to the approaches taken in developed countries, which try to achieve climate mitigation goals by promoting a low-carbon economy, India's NAPCC focuses on the climate mitigation potential contained within economic development (Mayrhofer and Gupta 2016). Titled "Faster, more inclusive and sustainable growth", India's Twelfth Five-Year Plan (2012–2017) outlined the need for a low-carbon strategy for inclusive growth "in order to improve the sustainability of its growth process, while carbon mitigation will be an important co-benefit" (Planning Commission of India 2013, p. 117). A slight modification of India's international position took place at the 2009 Copenhagen Summit when a new alliance of rapidly growing countries appeared and committed to energy intensity targets. The new group was led by China and included the BRICS countries Brazil, South Africa, China and India. Driven by increasing demands by the international community and developing country coalitions India pledged to voluntarily decrease its 2005 levels of emission intensity by 20–25 percent by 2020 (Ministry of Environment and Forests 2010).

In conclusion, in the second phase of India's climate policy process international factors also have played a major role in triggering domestic policy processes. A newly developed domestic climate advocacy coalition and the incumbent environmental minister spurred on the policy change of greater openness towards climate mitigation.

8.3.3 2014–2018 Policy process and policy change

The 2015 United Nations Climate Change Conference in Paris stimulated a reformulation of climate policy resulting in India's INDC, which was submitted shortly before the COP21. Led by the new Bharatiya Janata (BJP) government, which came into power in 2014, the policy process differed from previous policy phases. For example, climate researchers and NGOs had less access to policy-formulation (Aamodt and Stensdal 2017) during this period. Moreover, following the BJP's rise to power in 2014, the question arose as to whether Prime Minister Modi would pursue an aggressive industrialisation strategy or whether he would, as his book Convenient Action suggested, strive to set up a national climate and environment-compatible growth strategy and develop new approaches to low-carbon development (Modi 2011). During his time in power Modi has opted for the former option as can be seen by developments such as the dismantling of environmental legislation, the relaxing of restrictions on the licensing of environmentally harmful mining activities and the banning of environmental organisations (Gettleman et al., Dec. 8, 2017).

Surprisingly, India's INDC indicated in part a policy shift towards quite ambitious environmental goals. First, a rather moderate new goal for the reduction in the emissions intensity of GDP by 33–35 percent by 2030 (compared to 2005). Second – and even more importantly – a highly ambitious goal for renewable energy, in which non-fossil fuels should make up a 40 percent share of the installed electricity mix by 2030. The third goal was additional carbon reductions of 2.5–3 billion tons through an increase of forest cover. The goal to enhance solar power capacity to 100 GW by 2022 particularly stands out. It is linked to a remarkable international initiative taken by India at the 2015 Paris Climate Conference, namely the creation of an International Solar Alliance involving more than 120 countries, including several African nations (Government of India (GOI) 2015). India's National Electricity Plan, December 2016, indicated that India's growing energy demand could potentially be met without building new coal power stations (GOI 2016).

In 2018, India had a fully-fledged climate policy framework. Mitigation as well as adaptation measures is included both in the National Action Plan Climate Change and in the climate action plans which were designed by India's states (Jogesh and Dubash 2015; Jörgensen et al., 2015). Targets and instruments for renewable energy and energy efficiency as well as a number of policy strategies operating under the term "Missions", which are linked to India's climate action plan, have been set in place. In the third phase, the concept of low-carbon and inclusive economic growth is present, though it does not appear consistently as a common goal and guideline of the energy policy. The potential co-benefits of poverty reduction, access to energy, health improvements and educational advantages offered by climate mitigation and, in particular, India's solar mission have not yet been fully realised (Dutta et al., 2015; Jaeger and Michaelowa 2015; Quitzow 2015). The promotion of renewable energy policies is less contested than the scaling down of carbon-intensive power infrastructure as considered in the Draft National Energy Policy (2017) and the Three Year Action Agenda (2017–2018 to 2019–2020) (Climate Action Tracker 03 December 2018). At the very least, India will have to double its energy consumption by 2030 in order to meet its growing energy needs. Despite the ambitious goal of increasing the share of non-fossil resources in installed power capacity to 40 percent by 2030, India cannot easily escape the carbon lock-in and eliminate fossil fuels from its energy mix entirely.

All told, a combination of factors have shaped the different phases of India's climate policy process between 1990 and 2018. International factors such as the UNFCCC process, political demands made of India by industrialised countries and the developing country coalitions were important. Domestic factors such as interests in clean development technology, financial arguments from the corporate sector and the public perception of climate change as a threat have had a significant impact on India's policy process. Domestic actors from the field of academia and research, from the state-level, NGOs and the corporate sector have become more influential in shaping climate policy (Aamodt and Stensdal 2017). Political agenda setting and policy formulation interacted continuously with the course and decisions within the international climate process.

During the second and third phases, India's initial climate policy paradigm was modified. It was no longer as clear cut; a unified position amongst the actors within India's climate policy subsystem is no longer recognisable. The basic ideas of equity and development are still relevant, but climate mitigation is no longer a taboo. Renewable energy policy, in particular, is no longer assumed to hamper economic growth and development. The idea of the co-benefit concept, which combines economic development with climate mitigation, added a new perspective, partially softening formerly incompatible positions. However, the notion that poverty reduction and climate mitigation can be complementary is still not a widely shared idea (Jaeger and Michaelowa 2015) as it is in the case of growth and poverty reduction.

8.4 Knowledge

8.4.1 Knowledge, agency and policy in climate governance in India

Ideas, knowledge and policy-oriented learning are, alongside other factors such as interests and institutions, of importance for policy processes. The field of climate policy-oriented learning and the conditions influencing the political processing of climate knowledge is still under-researched (Bernauer 2013). Yet, comparative research shows that policy change can to a substantial degree be explained through the "presence or absence and the strengths of the climate knowledge system" (Never 2015, p. 146). Changes in climate policy, in particular, depend on information about the extent of expected climate impacts and feasible opportunities for climate mitigation and adaptation.

Climate knowledge is not merely developed in the context of governmental institutions or on behalf of governments. Networks involving non-state experts, research organisations, NGOs and the corporate sector can play an important role in producing knowledge and stimulating policy learning by themselves. As we will outline, domestic NGOs and think-tanks have played an important role in the production and interpretation of knowledge in India. Climate advocacy coalitions can be found not only in India but also in Brazil and China. They are important in mobilising knowledge about climate change in Brazil, China and India and in stimulating climate policy learning (Aamodt and Stensdal 2017; Dubash 2013). In India, the work of NGOs and think-tanks was more influential than academic climate science research.

The IPCC, for example, is an international epistemic community that has triggered policy learning through the dissemination of knowledge and the creation of a scientific consensus. IPCC reports were influential in the context of India, channelling new insights via domestic actor constellations.

In this subsection, we will identify the knowledge and agency that influenced India's climate policy process and point to two cases where knowledge was significant for policy change. There has been a selective use of knowledge in India's climate policy process. However, two cases of climate policy change have been identified in which knowledge significantly influenced India's climate process. Interestingly, in both cases, India's domestic NGOs and think-tanks played a significant role. In the following section, we will first shed light on India's climate science capacities and then explore two examples of how these actors have shaped India's climate process.

8.4.2 Knowledge agencies in India in the climate change process

Climate science and research received a boost in 1998 at the international level with the formation of the IPCC to influence the UNFCCC process. At that point, India had a well-developed scientific research base and infrastructure, with higher education institutes (science and engineering) and national laboratories under the umbrella of the Council of Scientific and Industrial Research (CSIR) (Kandlikar and Sagar 1999). Scientific knowledge was advanced with particular emphasis placed on a technical and economic analysis of the implications of and ways to abate (Kandlikar and Sagar 1999) climate change. Between 2005 and 2009, Indian scientists produced around 391 publications on climate science (Alex and Preedip Balaji 2010). The government also set up the Indian Climate Research Programme (ICRP) for data collection and the assessment of climate science. Research and the production of knowledge-based research have become more important since the National Mission for Strategic Knowledge of Climate Change (NMSKCC) was introduced in the context of India's National Climate Action Plan 2008. Large numbers of scientists have been working on climate issues, yet up until 2010 the scientific landscape was fragmented and the influence of scientists on the policy process was "often informal and adhoc" (Never 2012, p. 379).

The single largest disciplinary group of climate researchers in India consists of climatologists and meteorologists with physicists, chemists, biologists, ecologists and agronomists involved in various aspects of climate science but acting on an independent and disciplinary level (Kandlikar and Sagar 1999). Another large group of researchers in India is involved in modelling, scenario building and the econometrics of climate change, energy and carbon emissions (Dubash *et al.*, 2018). The role of universities and the Indian Institutes of Technology (IITs) in policy and decision-making was limited and scholars were consulted only when certain scientific input was required. Policy researchers from non-governmental research institutions, consultancies and international donor agencies have played a slightly more influential role during policy formulation, planning and strategy building. A mainstream think-tank, The Energy and Resources Institute (TERI), became more involved with the international negotiation process in the mid-2000s after its incumbent director general became head of the IPCC in 2002 (Bidwai 2012). Up until 2007, TERI used to be a central actor within India's fragmented climate-change network (Never 2012). Interaction between domestic researchers and policymakers has intensified since 2007 during the formulation of India's first

NAPCC. Responsibility for climate change was assumed by the Prime Minister's Office (PMO) in 2007 and a high-level advisory group – the PM's Council on Climate Change (PMCCC) – was institutionalised. The PMCCC provided little scope for detailed analytical input, resulting in no marked increase in research capacity to inform policy (Dubash and Joseph 2015). The policy arena was also seen as "inadequately inclusive of civil society" (Aamodt and Stensdal 2017, p. 121).

8.4.3 Bringing the third-world critique to the climate negotiation process

The first example of knowledge-driven policy change occurred at the beginning of the 1990s when India championed the CBDR approach. Indian NGOs successfully incorporated the concept of the "third-world critique" into the domestic and international climate process and eventually the negotiation table. The Centre for Science and Environment's (CSE) report "Global Warming in an Unequal World" was an Indian research initiative showcasing domestic research work as a response to western scientists' attribution of methane emissions to the developing world (Agarwal and Narain 1991). It countered a report by the World Resources Institute by emphasising the historical contribution to the stocks of GHGs by industrialised countries, the need for a per capita approach and for a distinction between "survival emissions" and "luxury emissions" (Dubash 2013, p. 192). NGOs such as the CSE and TERI exerted influence on the Indian government's position in the international negotiations and on "a broader national consensus" (Dubash 2013, p. 192). Thereby the inclusion of the CBDR argument in the international climate negotiations stemmed from knowledge produced by NGOs.

8.4.4 A climate advocacy coalition emerges

The second example of knowledge-driven policy change occurred from 2007 onwards, in the form of a causal process. The process started with the 2007 IPCC report, which pointed to India's vulnerability. Knowledge provided by the IPPC 2007 fourth assessment report was the major factor that led to the formation of a new policy advocacy coalition consisting of think-tanks, and NGOs who believed that the current negotiating position needed to change (Aamodt and Stensdal 2017; Never 2012). For the first time, this actor constellation pointed to the need for big developing countries to also address mitigation, indicating a break from the earlier consensus which rejected mitigation. Eventually in 2009, a policy window of opportunity for broader participation in the climate policy process opened when Jairam Ramesh took office as the Minister of Environment and Forests (MoEF) in 2009. From 2009 to 2011, climate advocacy actors' new ways of thinking resonated with his leadership of the MoEF.

This phase was marked by a transition to co-benefits, sustainable development and a win-win approach (Dubash *et al.*, 2013; Isaksen and Stokke 2014) as Ramesh emphasised the concepts of the "environment", "sustainable development" and "voluntary emission reduction". Some senior negotiators and influential civil society groups pointed to the need for a separation of international and domestic climate policy concerns (Dubash and Joseph 2015). Focus was placed on scientific knowledge and infrastructure to guide and inform policy. The period 2009–2011 was characterised by new forms of interactions between divergent research groups in the policy process and the use of different scientific knowledge was encouraged to draw up the plans for the different climate change missions. According to Aamodt and Stensdal (2017), the co-benefit approach which highlighted the economic advantages of energy efficiency and renewable energy ensured continuity within the development of India's climate policy.

Prior to 2009, climate policy had predominantly been constructed as a diplomatic matter (Dubash et al., 2018), designed and discussed in closed circles, mainly influenced by "an externally-driven agenda" (Raghunandan 2012, p. 127). A small group, commissioned by the Government of India, which was led by the MoEF and the Ministry of External Affairs included negotiators, bureaucrats and leading experts from selected organisations and played a significant role in the negotiation process (Michaelowa and Michaelowa 2012). The domestic mainstream think-tank TERI was quite dominant in the field of climate research and policy-making with their research fellows including a former ambassador and top-level bureaucrat (Bidwai 2012; Dubash and Joseph 2015). Little or no public debate took place on addressing societal perspectives, vulnerability to climate change and environmental degradation (Bidwai 2012), topics that have not had as much electoral mobilisation as the issues of growth and development.

In contrast, in 2007, more stakeholders from India's corporate sector and civil society appeared on the scene. Industry organisations like the Confederation of Indian Industries (CII) emerged in the policy subsystem (Isaksen and Stokke 2014; Thaker and Leiserowitz 2014). The CDM process encouraged the business community to insert research cells within large companies for the production of GHG inventories and reporting.

This phase saw a slightly greater role of science in the policy process and the business sector became a driving force in India's climate policy process (Never 2012). A higher regulatory density indicated that significant policy learning had occurred in the areas of energy efficiency and renewable energy policy (Never 2012).

8.5 Conclusions

Climate change presents enormous challenges to India. The country will suffer from some of the worst climate extremes, posing great risks to food security, health and livelihoods. In addition, the country must also balance the two goals of economic development – moving people out of poverty and providing access to electricity – and climate mitigation. The move towards a low-carbon economy is particularly difficult as India's power sector relies heavily on a coal-based energy mix leading to a carbon lock-in. India's climate policy has undergone significant change over the course of the last 25 years. From the early 1990s up until today, climate equity has played an important role in shaping both India's domestic and international climate policy discourse. In the international context, it was India, who placed the principle of Joint but Differentiated Responsibility on the climate negotiation agenda.

The development of India's climate policy from the 1990s until 2018 featured different phases of policy stability and policy change, caused by domestic as well as international factors, and the interaction between the two. Impulses from the international climate system and, in particular, the IPCC reports, and related to this, India's domestic climate advocacy coalition which emerged after 2007 have stimulated the development of India's climate policy.

The distinguishing characteristic of the first phase of India's climate policy process spanning the period between 1990 and 2006 is the development and influence of a domestically uncontested climate policy paradigm. Guided by the principles of equity, and development-first, it has informed India's international negotiating position. India became a deal-maker by inserting the CBDR concept into the international climate treaties. Aside from this, the beginnings of domestic advocacy for climate mitigation materialised, spurred on by the economic opportunities presented by finance and technology transfer which were linked to international climate cooperation. However, India's government made fewer commitments during international climate negotiations than it did in its domestic climate action.

In the second phase of India's climate policy process, from 2007 onwards international factors have also played a major role. Yet, a newly emerging domestic climate advocacy coalition, along with policy entrepreneurs such as the incumbent environment minister Jairam Ramesh supported policy change. A change in perspective on the economic and development threats of climate mitigation policy were crystallised in the anchoring of the "co-benefit" principle into India's NAPCC in 2008. The focus on both the economic co-benefits of domestic mitigation and the development of a domestic climate advocacy coalition in India promoted policy change.

During the second and third phases, there was a modification to India's initial climate policy. This paradigm is no longer as clear-cut as it previously had been and it is difficult to identify a unified position among the actors within India's climate policy subsystem. The basic ideas of equity and development are, however, still relevant and climate mitigation is no longer a taboo. Renewable energy policy, in particular, is no longer assumed to hamper economic growth and development. However, the notion that poverty reduction and climate mitigation can be complementary is still not as widely shared an idea as that of the complementary nature of growth and poverty reduction.

Comparative research shows that policy change can to a substantial degree be explained through an increase in knowledge; climate policy, in particular, depends on information about the extent of expected climate impacts and feasible opportunities for climate mitigation and adaptation. Two cases of climate policy change where knowledge significantly influenced India's climate process have been identified. Interestingly, in both cases India's domestic NGOs and think-tanks played a significant role. The first example of policy change occurred at the beginning of the 1990s when India championed the CBDR approach. The second one occurred from 2007 onward. Until 2007, climate policy was predominantly designed and discussed in closed circles. Since then the climate policy subsystem has seen science play a slightly greater role in the policy process. A change in

India's domestic climate policy discourse became particularly apparent after the IPPC's 4th assessment report which pointed to India's vulnerability and stimulated the formation of a new climate policy advocacy coalition in India, consisting of think-tanks, NGOs and scientist who believed that the current position needed to be changed.

By 2018, India had achieved a fully-fledged climate policy framework; however from 2014 to 2018, the BJP government pursued an aggressive industrialisation strategy that dismantled environmental legislation, relaxed restrictions on the licensing of environmentally harmful industrial activities and showed a lack of emphasis on low-carbon development and clean-air policies.

References

Aamodt, S., and Stensdal, I., 2017. Seizing policy windows. Policy influence of climate advocacy coalitions in Brazil, China, and India, 2000–2015. *Global Environmental Change Part A: Human & Policy Dimensions*, 46, 114–125.

Agarwal, A., and Narain, S., 1991. *Global warming in an unequal world: A case of environmental colonialism*. New Delhi: Centre for Science and Environment.

Alex, P., and Preedip Balaji, B., 2010. Mapping climate change research in India: A bibliometric approach. In 6th International Conference on Webometrics, Informetrics, Scientometrics, Mysore (India), 19–22 October 2010 [Conference paper]. http://eprints.rclis.org/15301/

Bang, G., Underdal, A., and Andresen, S., eds., 2015. *The domestic politics of global climate change. Key actors in international climate cooperation*. Cheltenham: Edward Elgar Pub. Ltd.

Bernauer, T., 2013. Climate change politics. *Annual Review of Political Science*, 16(1), 421–448.

Bernauer, T., and Böhmelt, T., 2013. National climate policies in international comparison: The Climate Change Cooperation index. *Environmental Science & Policy*, 25, 196–206.

Betz, J., 2012. *India's turn in climate policy: Assessing the interplay of domestic and international policy change* [online]. GIGA. Available from: http://www.econstor.eu/bitstream/10419/57188/1/689598971.pdf [Accessed 8 September 2015].

Bidwai, P., 2012. Climate change, India and the global negotiations. *Social Change*, 42(3), 375–390.

Bulkeley, H., 2013. *Cities and climate change*. London: Routledge.

Chaudhary, A., Krishna, C., and Sagar, A., 2015. Policy making for renewable energy in India: lessons from wind and solar power sectors. Climate Policy, 15 (1), 58–87. 10.1080/14693062.2014.941318.

Climate Action Tracker, 2018. *India – country summary*. Available from: https://climateactiontracker.org/countries/india/ [Accessed 13 December 2018].

Das, T., 2012. Climate change and the private sector. *In*: N.K. Dubash, ed. *Handbook of climate change and India. Development, politics, and governance*. Abingdon, Oxon, New York: Earthscan, 246–253.

Dubash, N.K., 2013. The politics of climate change in India: Narratives of equity and cobenefits. *Wiley Interdisciplinary Reviews: Climate Change*, 4(3), 191–201.

Dubash, N.K., and Joseph, N.B., 2015. *The institutionalisation of climate policy in India: Designing a development-focused, co-benefits based approach*. New Delhi: Centre for Policy Research.

Dubash, N.K., et al., 2013. Indian climate change policy. Exploring a co-benefits based approach. *Economic & Political Weekly EPW* June 1, xlviii(22), 47–61.

Dubash, N.K., et al., 2018. India and climate change: Evolving ideas and increasing policy engagement. *Annual Review of Environment and Resources*, 43(1), 395–424.

Dutta, V., et al., 2015. Evaluating expert opinion on India's climate policy: Opportunities and barriers to low-carbon inclusive growth. *Climate and Development*, 8(4), 1–15.

Fisher, S., 2012. Policy storylines in Indian climate politics: Opening new political spaces? *Environment and Planning C: Government and Policy*, 30(1), 109–127.

Gettleman, J., Schultz, K., and Kumar, H., 2017. *Environmentalists Ask: Is India's Government Making Bad Air Worse?* By Jeffrey Gettleman, Kai Schultz and Hari Kumar [online]. Available from: https://www.nytimes.com/2017/12/08/world/asia/india-pollution-modi.html [Accessed 13 December 2018].

Government of India (GOI), 2015. *India's intended nationally determined contribution: Working towards climate justice.* Government of India.

Government of India (GOI), 2016. *Draft National Electricity Plan* [online]. Available from: http://www.cea.nic.in/reports/committee/nep/nep_dec.pdf [Accessed 7 February 2019].

Government of India, Prime Minister's Council on Climate Change, 2008. *National Action Plan on climate change.*

Gupta, H., Kohli, R.K., and Ahluwalia, A.S., 2015. Mapping 'consistency' in India's climate change position: Dynamics and dilemmas of science diplomacy. *Ambio*, 44(6), 592–599.

Iacobuta, G., et al., 2018. National climate change mitigation legislation, strategy and targets: A global update. *Climate Policy*, 18(9), 1114–1132.

Intergovernmental Panel on Climate Change (IPCC). 2018. *Global Warming of 1.5°C. An IPCC special report on the impacts of global warming of 1.5°C above pre-industrial levels and related global greenhouse gas emission pathways, in the context of strengthening the global response to the threat of climate change, sustainable development, and efforts to eradicate poverty.* Geneva: IPCC, World Meteorological Organization. Available from: https://www.ipcc.ch/sr15/ [Accessed 10 November 2019].

International Energy Agency, 2017. *Coal 2017* [online]. Available from: https://www.iea.org/coal2017/ [Accessed 7 February 2019].

Isaksen, K.-A., and Stokke, K., 2014. Changing climate discourse and politics in India. Climate change as challenge and opportunity for diplomacy and development. *Geoforum*, 57, 110–119.

Jaeger, M.D., and Michaelowa, K., 2015. Global climate policy and local energy politics: Is India hiding behind the poor? *Climate Policy*, 1–12.

Jänicke, M., 2017. The multi-level system of global climate governance – the model and its current state. *Environmental Policy and Governance*, 27(2), 108–121.

Jogesh, A., and Dubash, N.K., 2015. State-led experimentation or centrally-motivated replication? A study of state action plans on climate change in India. *Journal of Integrative Environmental Sciences*, 12(4), 247–266.

Jörgensen, K., 2017. India: The global climate power torn between 'growth-first' and 'green growth'. In: R.K.W. Wurzel, J. Connelly, and D. Liefferink, eds. *The European Union in International climate change politics. Still taking a lead?* London, New York: Routledge, Taylor & Francis Group, 270–283.

Jörgensen, K., Jogesh, A., and Mishra, A., 2015. Multi-level climate governance and the role of the subnational level. *Journal of Integrative Environmental Sciences*, 12(4), 235–245.

Kandlikar, M., and Sagar, A., 1999. Climate change research and analysis in India: An integrated assessment of a South–North divide. *Global Environmental Change Part A: Human & Policy Dimensions*, 9(2), 119–138.

Khosla, R., Sagar, A., and Mathur, A., 2017. Deploying low-carbon technologies in developing countries. A view from India's buildings sector. *Environmental Policy and Governance*, 27(2), 149–162.
Mayrhofer, J.P., and Gupta, J., 2016. The science and politics of co-benefits in climate policy. *Environmental Science & Policy*, 57, 22–30.
Michaelowa, K., and Michaelowa, A., 2012. India as an emerging power in international climate negotiations. *Climate Policy*, 12(5), 575–590.
Ministry of Environment and Forests, 2010. *India: Taking on climate change. Post-Copenhagen domestic actions*. Delhi: Ministry of Environment and Forests.
Modi, N., 2011. *Convenient action: Gujarat's response to challenges of climate change*.
Never, B., 2012. Who drives change? Comparing the evolution of domestic climate governance in India and South Africa. *Journal of Environment & Development*, 21(3), 362–387.
Never, B., 2015. *Knowledge systems and change in climate governance. Comparing India and South Africa*. New York: Routledge.
Never, B., and Betz, J., 2014. Comparing the climate policy performance of emerging economies. *World Development*, 59, 1–15.
Peters, B.G., Jordan, A., and Tosun, J., 2017. Over-reaction and under-reaction in climate policy: An institutional analysis. *Journal of Environmental Policy & Planning*, 19(6), 612–624.
Peterson, T.D., McKinstry, R.B., Jr., and Dernbach, J.C., 2008. Developing a comprehensive approach to climate change policy in the United States that fully integrates levels of Government and economic sectors. *Virginia Environmental Law Journal*, 26, 227–269.
Planning Commission of India, 2013. *Twelfth Five Year Plan (2012–2017) Faster, More Inclusive and Sustainable Growth* [online]. Available from: http://planningcommission.gov.in/plans/planrel/12thplan/pdf/12fyp_vol1.pdf [Accessed 6 March 2018].
Pulver, S., 2012. Corporate responses to climate change in India. In: N.K. Dubash, ed. *Handbook of climate change and India. Development, politics, and governance*. Abingdon, Oxon, New York: Earthscan, 254–265.
Quitzow, R., 2015. Assessing policy strategies for the promotion of environmental technologies: A review of India's National Solar Mission. *Research Policy*, 44(1), 233–243.
Raghunandan, D., 2012. India's climate policy. Squaring the circle. *IDS Bulletin*, 43, 122–129.
Schmid, G., 2012. The development of renewable energy power in India: Which policies have been effective? *Energy Policy*, 45, 317–326.
Shukla, P.R., and Dhar, S., 2011. Climate agreements and India: Aligning options and opportunities on a new track. *International Environmental Agreements: Politics, Law and Economics*, 11(3), 229–243.
Shukla, P.R., Garg, A., and Dholakia, H.H., 2015. *Energy-emissions trends and policy landscape for India*. New Delhi: Allied Publishers.
Thaker, J., and Leiserowitz, A., 2014. Shifting discourses of climate change in India. *Climatic Change*, 123(2), 107–119.
Unruh, G.C., 2000. Understanding carbon lock-in. *Energy Policy*, 28(12), 817–830.
Unruh, G.C., 2002. Escaping carbon lock-in. *Energy Policy*, 30(4), 317–325.

9 Smart sustainable cities

Shaleen Singhal and Sourabh Jain

9.1 Introduction

Cities now are vital settlements for the survival of humanity and provide scope for the expansion of future life on this planet. The vitality and viability of human exertion towards global sustainability shall also be determined by the future of our cities. The pace of urbanisation worldwide has been increasing with rising consumption of resources and pollution. In 1800, just 5 percent of the global population lived in urban areas. In industrialised countries, this increased to just under 15 percent in 1900. In 2008, over half of the world's population lived in cities. It is now predicted that around 68 percent of the world's population will live in urban areas by 2050 – an increase of 2.5 billion people and almost 90 percent of this population growth will occur in Asia and Africa (UN DESA 2018a). Several Asian cities simultaneously demonstrate dichotomous phenomena, including poverty and wealth, formality and informality, and new and modern skylines along with historic and dilapidated core areas (Bharne 2013). The BRICS nations (Brazil, Russia, India, China and South Africa) constitute a major share of the global urban population and are also among the fastest-growing economies in terms of urbanisation (Chen et al. 2014, UN DESA 2018a). However, the nature of rapid urbanisation varies with the level of existing development in a country and its cities. Unlike advanced economies, where higher urbanisation translates into higher economic wealth (Chauvin et al. 2017), the relationship is more complex in emerging economies where rapid urbanisation does not always lead to rapid economic growth (Chen et al. 2014). With limited resources and rising urban populations, emerging economies need innovative policy measures to meet the goals of sustainable urban development.

Among emerging economies, urbanisation in India is on the rise and so too are related challenges and potential opportunities. India is projected to contribute 17–18 percent of global urban growth by 2050 (UN DESA 2018a). The urban population of India is projected to increase at an annual rate of 2 percent and increase from 472 million in 2019 to 876 million in 2050 (UN DESA 2018a). India will have seven megacities and the number of million-plus population cities is expected to increase from 61 in 2018 to 71 by 2030 (UN DESA 2018a). It is also expected that the average population size of million-plus cities will increase from

3 million in 2011 to 4 million by 2030, while the average population size of smaller urban settlements shall increase from 39,000 in 2008 to 55,000 by 2030 (Sankhe et al. 2010, Census of India 2011a).

The physical infrastructure, social, environmental, institutional and governance-related challenges are also increasing with urbanisation in India. Megacities in the country are already becoming material-intensive and suffer from pollution and water-stress related problems (CPCB 2015, Kennedy et al. 2015, Li et al. 2015). Like several emerging as well as mature economies, India has already overshot its national ecological carrying capacity, thereby increasing the possibility of resource scarcity in the future (Global Footprint Network 2015). There is an ever-increasing gap in demand and supply of basic services, such as water supply, solid waste management, sanitation and wastewater treatment, public transportation, and affordable housing (Gore and Gopakumar 2015). These issues are evidenced by performance indicators, such as the Human Development Index (HDI), where India ranked 130th (an HDI value of 0.64) out of 189 countries and territories in 2017 (UNDP 2018). This places India in the "medium human development" category – the HDI value has increased from 0.427 to 0.640 (up by 49.8 percent) between 1990 and 2017. India ranks 177th out of 180 on the Environmental Performance Index (EPI), which assesses a country's performance on parameters such as the quality of urban infrastructure, forest and water resource management practices, air quality, and progress on climate change (Wendling et al. 2018). Other critical institutional and financial challenges include inadequate revenue generation for investment in basic infrastructure and limited institutional capacity (Aijaz 2007, Vaidya 2009, FICCI 2014).

This chapter explores the trajectories of urban policy in India and emphasises the importance of a paradigm shift necessary to promote environmental leapfrogging (see Chapter 1, Ciecierska-Holmes, Jörgensen, Ollier and Raghunandan, this volume) for resource efficiency, particularly through built environment and infrastructure domains, albeit by the transformation in governance. The second section of the chapter presents important urban policy changes that occurred between India's independence and the most recent years. Section 9.3 examines challenges, such as limited public participation, inequitable government support, potential gentrification, lack of capital investments and other hurdles in the way of transformation to smart and sustainable cities in India. Section 9.4 advocates for a paradigm shift for cities to leapfrog with a focus on physical infrastructure and urban governance. Section 9.5 draws conclusions for the chapter.

9.2 The trajectories of urban policy in India

Since the country's independence in 1947, urban development policy in India has evolved in three phases and is influenced by both domestic and international factors. This section traces this transformation in urban development over three time periods: post-independence to economic liberalisation in 1991; post-economic liberalisation; and third, after the change in government in 2014. International factors triggering the decentralisation debate in India were, for example, the launch of Local Agenda 21 following the 1992 Rio Summit, in which Chapter 28 of the Agenda 21 makes reference to local urban governance. After 2014, the new Hindu nationalist BJP government took charge at the federal level and initiated the Smart Cities Mission (SCM) in 2015 with a renewed emphasis on development in cities. India also became a signatory of the Paris Climate Agreement and UN Sustainable Development Goals-2030, both of which are likely to influence urban growth in India.

9.2.1 Post-independence era

Historic events, such as the Partition of India and Independence in 1947, as well as the end of World War II in 1945, provide the backdrop for urban policies during the early post-independence years. Due to the influx of refugees from Pakistan and employment opportunities created during World War II, the interval between 1941 and 1951 witnessed haphazard urban population growth by more than 50 percent and an acute shortage of housing (Planning Commission of India 1951, Census of India 2001). These factors resulted in overcrowding and the creation of many sub-standard houses and slums, which lacked essential amenities, such as drinking water, sanitation, lighting and ventilation.

The main policy changes in India's urban policy debate resonate in India's Five-Year Plans (see Table 9.1). The first three Five-Year Plans from 1951 to 1966 lacked clearly defined objectives and targets for urbanisation. The government prioritised rehabilitating refugees, increasing the housing supply, setting minimum standards for housing construction, eradicating slums, promoting town and country planning, setting up an autonomous housing board and advisory body on building and materials research, and enhancing governance capacity at the local level for housing development (Jacobson and Prakash 1968). Due to financial constraints, national policymakers in this period paid limited attention towards capacity building of local government bodies. In the Fourth Five-Year Plan (1969–1974), the development of urban drinking water, sanitation and drainage infrastructure was also included (Planning Commission of India, 1969, 1974, 1980b). Balanced urbanisation was first addressed in the Sixth Five-Year Plan (1980–1985), with the recognition of urban environmental issues, such as air and water pollution, loss of water bodies and agricultural land. The Sixth and Seventh Five-Year Plans (1980–1990) also focused on environment and cultural heritage aspects (Planning Commission of India 1980a).

9.2.2 Post-economic liberalisation (1991)

After India's economic liberalisation in 1991, urban governance adopted a financially top-down and administratively bottom-up approach. The responsibility of establishing town planning organisations, preparing master plans for each important town or city, and enacting and implementing urban legislation was that of state governments while the role of the central government was only advisory (Planning Commission of India 1956, 1961). The recognised role of the central government was to envision a national development agenda, assess its impact on

Table 9.1 Key urban-focused policy changes across Five-Year Plans in India

Year	Central urban plan/policy	Focus area	Key issues identified	Proposed measures
1951	1st Five-Year Plan	Housing	Inadequate supply, poor quality and high cost of housing	Financing; control of prices of key building materials
1956 1961	2nd Five-Year Plan 3rd Five-Year Plan	Housing and urban planning	Same as above for housing; haphazard urban development	Same as above for housing; master plans and integration of peri-urban region into urban planning
1966	4th Five-Year Plan	Housing, urban services and urban governance	Same as above for housing; poor coverage of water supply and sanitation; lack of effective urban governance	Set up Housing and Urban Development Finance Corporation; local taxation and increased support from the state government
1974	5th Five-Year Plan	Housing, urban services and urban governance	No specific issues identified	Continuation of earlier policies for housing and water; master plans for cities other than metro cities
1980 and 1985	6th and 7th Five-Year Plans	Slum housing and balanced urban development	Lack of amenities in urban slums; scattered development within urban boundaries; limited development of small and medium-sized towns; lack of clean water supply and waste management	Changes in land-use laws to reduce cost of housing; slum development rather than slum relocation; funding for integrated urban development for small and medium-sized towns
1992	8th Five-Year Plan	Housing and urban services	Poor coverage of urban services	Adoption of National Urban Housing Policy; changes in laws to increase the supply of land
1998	9th Five-Year Plan	Sustainable urban development	Urban poverty and shortage of affordable housing; lack of decentralisation; unsustainable practices in building practices	Urban employment schemes and funds for housing; more fiscal and administrative power to urban bodies; use of eco-friendly building materials and energy-efficient buildings
2002	10th Five-Year Plan	Sustainable urban development	Lack of health and education facilities; weak urban governance; urban water pollution	Autonomy to urban bodies and protection from interference; Funding for social welfare schemes for urban areas; emphasis on management of urban solid and liquid waste
2007	11th Five-Year Plan	Sustainable urban development	Shortage of funds faced by urban bodies; air pollution; urban waste issues	National urbanisation policies; urban regeneration initiatives (JNNURM); National Urban Transport Policies; National Urban Sanitation Policy
2012	12th Five-Year Plan	Sustainable urban development	Poor urban water management; energy inefficiency; poor performance monitoring framework	Integration of water supply, groundwater and sewage treatment policies; digitisation of land records; energy-efficient lightings and renewable energy in cities; key performance indicators

urban development, provide financial support and technical advice to states and municipalities, and expand training and education facilities related to urban development (Planning Commission of India 1956, 1961, Routra 1993). Since rural areas constituted over 80 percent of the national population, priority was often given to rural development over urban development. Resources for urban development were limited due to widespread rural poverty and lack of basic services in rural areas. Sustainable development resonated in India's policy even as early as the 1980s with a focus on basic services to fulfil "human needs" and later was also addressed through the Brundtland Report in 1987 (Shaw 2018). Goals included 100 percent coverage of urban households by piped water supply by 1991, 100 percent coverage of Class I towns with sewerage facilities and toilets, aligning with the UN's International Water Supply and Sanitation Decade of 1980s. Formulated targets still have not been met.

Following India's economic liberalisation, several additional urban issues emerged that were incorporated into the national urban policy agenda. Environmental issues arose during the 1990s and 2000s, such as traffic congestion, carbon emissions, climate change and energy demand. Policymakers recognised the importance of balanced urbanisation and launched several policies, such as the National Urban Transport Policy (2006), National Action Plan on Climate Change (NAPCC) (2008) and the Solar Cities Program (2014).

The absence of effective governance at the local level along with the poor implementation of policies and programmes lead to new thinking about urban governance regarding effective implementation and the importance of democratic decentralisation (Planning Commission of India 1992, 1997). India's policy planners acknowledged that municipal bodies were financially, administratively and politically weak and had not been able to play an effective role in development of urban infrastructure (Planning Commission of India 1985). They indicated that implementation processes needed to be changed from "ad-hoc and isolated" to an integrated approach (Planning Commission of India 1992). In 1992, the 74th Constitutional Amendment Act (CAA) was the first major reform to reflect the importance of local governments or urban local bodies (ULBs) with the intention of bringing decentralised governance to urban areas at par with the Panchayat Raj system in rural areas as introduced by the 73rd Constitutional Amendment. Previously, urban governance had mostly been considered in a bureaucratic top-down administrative framework. The 74th Constitutional Amendment recognised ULBs as a third tier of government, granted them constitutional status and incorporated their functions, duties, responsibilities and jurisdiction in national structure (Chakrabarti 2001, Batra 2009). However, the 74th Amendment was ineffective as metropolitan planning committees (MPCs) were not set up or were only formed in a few states with a delay of several years (e.g., in West Bengal and Maharashtra). Neither the state governments nor municipal authorities and planners were interested in this policy reform and regarded it rather as an additional burden and not as an enabling mechanism (Sivaramakrishnan 2013). This meant that the expected positive features, such as spatially integrated planning and infrastructure provision, environmental conservation and resource mobilisation, did not materialise.

Due to the inadequacy of government resources, the importance of stakeholder involvement and the inclusion of the private sector in developing public infrastructure was recognised (Planning Commission of India 1997, Sahasranaman and Kapur 2014). India's judicial system played an active role in emphasising the "right to clean environment" and the government's obligation to protect the health of its citizens (Véron 2006). A significant policy initiative that followed was the launch of the flagship Jawaharlal Nehru National Urban Renewal Mission (JNNURM) in 2005, which aimed to close investment gaps and implement urban reforms to improve infrastructure, basic services for the poor and community participation (GoI JNNURM 2011). Central to the JNNURM was the aim to shift the role of the state from one of a provider to that of a facilitator and regulator of urban policy. However, it only generated partial success (Sivaramakrishnan 2013) and weak participation from cities. Only limited transformation could be achieved, and mainly in large cities (Kundu 2014).

Sustainable city development gained prominence in 2007, particularly in the context of sustainable buildings. Think-tanks, such as The Energy and Resource Institute (TERI), came up with ideas for a national Green Rating for Integrated Habitat Assessment (GRIHA) for buildings and an Urban Services Environmental Rating System (USERS) for the local bodies (Shaw 2018). Over the years, performance monitoring and performance-based resource allocation to ULBs have also become an integral part of urban governance. During this period, varied dimensions of sustainability were integrated into the government's policy initiatives, such as the NAPCC in 2008 and under the NAPCC, the launch of the National Mission on Sustainable Habitat in 2010 that stressed energy efficiency of buildings, urban waste recycling, shifts towards public transport and the integration of climate change objectives into planning processes. Before the new BJP government came into power in 2014, India had already emphasised urban strategic planning, ideas of smart growth and had considered the initiative of a smart city strategy (Shaw 2018).

9.2.3 Government change in 2014

Since 2014, there has been an emphasis on the smart city approach. Sustainable urban development and smart city approaches became two distinct concepts (Dirks and Keeling 2009, Randhawa and Kumar 2017). In the (most recent) 12th Five-Year Plan document, smart cities were referred to as an engine of economic growth that generates employment and meets rising aspirations of people for a better quality of life by providing access for everyone to basic services of clean water, sanitation, sewage, solid waste management, safe and affordable public transport systems, and affordable housing while preserving the sustainability of the urban environment (Planning Commission of India 2012). The SCM was launched in 2015 with the objective of uplifting cities by strengthening their core infrastructure and providing a clean and sustainable quality of life using "smart" solutions (MoUD 2015). The strategies envisioned under the SCM focus on retrofitting (of the existing built environment), redevelopment (replacement of inefficient built environments and infrastructure) and city extension (greenfield development through the introduction of new and smart built environment solutions in a previously uninhabited area). The SCM also includes a Pan-city initiative aiming to use information and communication technology (ICT) and related interventions to implement smart solutions to the existing city-wide infrastructure (MoUD 2015). A total of 100 cities have been selected through four rounds of a smart city competition. Other urban policy initiatives launched by the current government include a restructured version of past programmes with varied approaches and focal points: these include the Atal Mission for Rejuvenation and Urban Transformation (AMRUT), National Heritage City Development and Augmentation Yojana (HRIDAY), Pradhan Mantri Awas Yojana – Housing for All (Urban) and The Swachh Bharat Mission – Urban (SBM-U). However, the SCM appears to have received greater attention than these other initiatives from the government itself, domestic media and discourse as well as international institutions. The SCM reflects a minor shift in India's urban development policy by including a possibility of addressing issues in existing urban spaces rather than just focusing upon greenfield development.

Having traced these three phases of India's urban development policy, it suffices to say that India's goals of urban development have not changed significantly, and the government continues to prioritise the provision of housing for all, access to basic urban services and the eradication of urban poverty across most cities. Since the 1992 constitutional amendment, the decentralisation mantra to empower the local level has not been sufficiently implemented. Despite the emphasis on a bottom-up participatory approach, the significance of community-based organisations and non-government organisations only appears to have gained marginal power. It is evident that the introduction of SCM has focused on outputs, investment, technology integration and sustainability in the selected 100 cities. However, due to several challenges, including institutional capacity and coordination, the urban development sector in India is far from comprehensively meeting the aspired goals.

9.3 Smart and sustainable cities in India

The concept of smart sustainable cities has emerged internationally as a new policy paradigm to promote the utilisation of smart technologies and related aspects for improving efficiency, quality of life and the sustainability of citizen welfare (Höjer and Wangel 2014). However, some authors critique the growing trend towards what Hollands (2015, p. 61) calls "corporate and entrepreneurial governance" in the smart cities approach. Albino et al. (2015) have focused on the meaning of "smart" in the context of cities while examining definitions, dimensions, performance and initiatives relating to smart cities. They highlight that the smart city concept has been aggressively used in several Asian countries to create new cities, such as Masdar City in the United Arab Emirates, Songdo in South Korea and greenfield smart cities in China, whereas the North American smart cities are predominantly located in existing urban centres.

In contrast, a sustainable city is broadly described in terms of environmental, social and economic achievements of a city (Bibri and Krogstie 2017). Particularly in the context of cities of the global South, it is important not only to reflect on the ecological footprints, carrying capacity and resource consumption but also to encompass social dimensions (Parnell et al. 2018) such as social capital (Singhal et al. 2013). While the global debate on sustainability included climate change resilience, resource efficiency and other environmental aspects, the scope of environmental sustainability in cities in India prior to 2014 had been focused on land-use planning, solid and liquid waste management, air quality management, and energy efficiency (Planning Commission of India 2011). Internationally, there have been distinctions (de Jong et al. 2015) as well as synergies (Bibri and Krogstie 2017, Martin et al. 2018) between sustainable city and smart city approaches for urban development, yet in the context of cities in emerging economies, it is imperative to identify and harness convergences between the two approaches, aiming to address overlapping challenges and opportunities. A synergy that will be subsequently discussed in Section 9.4 is the option of environmental leapfrogging offered by the smart cities project. This would require targets and incentives.

The rest of this section outlines several key issues in Indian urban development policy, many of which follow business-as-usual urban policies and practices. The current urban development policies and practices demonstrate the continuity of previous policies with only limited variation in the urban development paradigm under the SCM. A qualitative comparison of the differences as well as similarities between the pre- and post-2014 urban development paradigm in India is presented in Table 9.2.

Table 9.2 Similarities and differences in urban development policies

Urban issue	Similarities between pre- and post-2014 urban development policies	Differences between pre- and post-2014 urban development policies
Governance structure	Mostly top-down; central- and state-level agencies-controlled funds and power One-time funds provided by the central government Limited empowerment of existing local bodies	SPV created with representatives from all levels of government as an execution agency It is still feared that SPVs, additional parastatal agency, may further weaken urban local governance
Public participation	Public did not play much of a role in policymaking	Under SCM, civic engagement sought online and offline, through local meetings, for proposal preparation
Environmental sustainability	Support for renewable energy and public transport	40 GW of rooftop solar target; most are likely to be installed on buildings in urban areas
Social equity	Support for affordable housing Big cities received most of the funding	Emphasis on area-based development with possible risks of gentrification
Basic urban services delivery	Not sufficient investment in urban water supply Limited provisions of user charges and emphasis on behavioural change	Emphasis on citywide initiatives Clean India and toilets for all initiatives to help in waste management

Source: Based on Ahluwalia (2017), Praharaj et al. (2018), Smith et al. (2018).

9.3.1 Conditions for success and constraints of sustainable urban development

In India, there is discordance between urban policy discourse from academics, decision-makers and business circles and the complex realities on the ground (NIUA 2014, Randhawa and Kumar 2017, Sharma and Rajput 2017). This discourse has limited reach and impact on practices dealing with urban complexities in the country.

The implementation of the SCM in India requires more effective governance structures (Praharaj *et al.* 2018). More attention is needed on vertical integration of policy goals, cooperation between the national level, the states and municipal agencies, and most importantly, the involvement of the local level (Varma and Singhal 2016). Strengthening local institutional capacity is a vital theme that requires greater focus. Ambiguity appears in the objectives outlined for India's SCM that aims to develop compact, sustainable and inclusive communities – promising everything and nothing at the same time (Smith *et al.* 2018).

9.3.1.1 Ineffective local urban governance

Local city governments play an important role in constructing necessary infrastructure, providing public services and conveniences in a sustainable manner, planning and regulating sustainable development in urban areas, mobilising resources for development of communities and in integrating social, economic and cultural development (Mohanty 2016, Srinivasan 2016). However, to fulfil that role, local governments need to have necessary legislative and fiscal powers to influence urban development (Mohanty 2016). But India's urban governance structure remains top-down and cities lack administrative and legislative powers (Ahluwalia 2017). In addition, the financial conditions of many urban bodies in India continue to deteriorate (Mohanty 2016). Despite the passage of the 74th CAA, many states have failed in devolving decision-making power and functions to ULBs and in sharing adequate financial and other resources, which has left ULBs at the mercy of state governments (Chakrabarti 2001, Nandi and Gamkhar 2013, Acolin *et al.* 2014, Kundu 2014). Furthermore, the SCM has created a new public-private entity of Special Purpose Vehicle (SPV) for each targeted city to fulfil the objectives of the SCM, making the urban development process more complicated and top-down. The SCM transfers the roles and responsibilities of urban development to the SPV while limiting the role of municipal governments. This has caused scepticism among researchers about the process, scope and effectiveness of the initiative. Many fear that SPVs implementing the SCM risk diluting the spirit of the participatory and bottom-up structure of urban governance and may benefit only a small section of society rather than promoting inclusive and diverse urban development (Hoelscher 2016, Ahluwalia 2017).

Despite contrasting views on the success and failure of the initiative, the SCM certainly has raised the priority of the urban development agenda at the national policy level in the past few years. Yet, similar to previous urban development initiatives such as JNNURM (Nandi and Gamkhar 2013, Kundu 2014), the current urban development praxis also provides limited emphasis on empowering local administration and institutions (Praharaj et al. 2018) to steer cities towards potential sustainability. With limited or no innovation in the governance framework, Indian cities shall not be able to realise the aspired goal of making cities smarter and sustainable.

9.3.1.2 Scarcity of capital investments

Transforming existing cities into sustainable ones requires significant investment. It is estimated that India would need to invest approximately Rs. 50 lakh crore (US$ 780 billion) between the fiscal years 2018 and 2022 to build its infrastructure sustainably (Crisil Infrastructure Yearbook 2017). Many cities face a severe shortage of funds to even provide basic urban services (Acolin et al. 2014). There is a need for cities to develop innovative financial mechanisms to expand and maintain urban development projects. Harvey (2012), however, pointed out that the availability of capital alone would not support urban projects without sound mechanisms for utilising the surplus capital.

Indian cities lack both capital and effective institutions to utilise the funds appropriately. The central and state governments release grants to cities based on certain monitoring and regulatory requirements that are often challenging. The support from the central government is limited to the financial and planning aspects of cities. Yet, due to the inadequacy of manpower, local governments depend on state-level agencies for the actual execution of projects (Praharaj et al. 2018). Due to poor coordination among different agencies, as well as multiplicity of agencies, city authorities struggle to procure adequate funding for development. To improve the potential for capital investments, cities also need to improve existing partnership models, though public-private partnerships have so far made limited contributions to the urban development sector (Mathur et al. 2009, HPEC 2011, Ullah 2016). To gain true financial stability and autonomy (Chattopadhyay 2015) and enhance their competitiveness (Singhal et al. 2013), cities must pursue a sustained reform agenda along with strategic resource mobilisation plans.

SCM in India attempts to address both issues through seeking foreign direct investments and developing partnerships with many countries. Since the launch of SCM, major countries, including the USA, Germany, Japan, and other European countries, have shown interest in providing technical and financial support for the smart cities project (Minz 2016). India's smart cities initiative encourages public-private partnerships and it is estimated that India's SCM requires an investment of USD 150 billion, 80 percent of which is expected to come from national and international private players (Chaudhry et al. 2018, WEDC 2018). However, much of the financial support and investment are likely to be in form of debt, raising several concerns. Indian cities need to learn from international examples and be cautious not to rely on excessive debt-financing infrastructure projects. Many cities around the world, including in Asia, managed to grow quickly by borrowing money from domestic and international borrowers, creating "bubbles" in many cases (Harvey 2012). Such growth benefited only a few, and when bubbles burst, working class and poor suffered the most, for example, in Thailand during 1997–1998. Such examples show that debt-trap urban development often leads to privatisation of profit and socialisation of losses (Harvey 2012).

9.3.2 Limited public participation

9.3.2.1 The use of ICTs under the SCM

Information and communication technologies play an important role in the SCM policy context. Over the past decade, development and the application of ICTs permeated most aspects of the lives of people living in cities (Smart Cities Council India 2016). It is expected that the high penetration of ICTs and digital literacy would be conducive to people's involvement in city development (Rexhepi et al. 2018). However, the use of ICTs has divided opinion. According to Ahluwalia (2017), although ICTs are necessary, urban problems in India cannot be solved with technology alone, but a combination of aspects, such as smart technology, resource efficiency, behavioural changes, efficient and smart governance, people's participation, and accountability. Indeed, despite the focus on ICTs, Smith et al. (2018) indicate that smart city projects are predominantly focusing on public health and safety rather than on utilising cutting-edge communication and technology.

Despite the centrality of ICT, observations show that among cities selected under the SCM, online participation rates of people were lower in cities that had higher digital literacy (Praharaj et al. 2018). Furthermore, higher literacy and employment also did not guarantee higher online engagement of people for the SCM (Praharaj et al. 2018). Other studies have indicated that people, particularly youth, use ICTs mainly for entertainment rather than to engage in governance (Dong and Ji 2018). It is argued that for better engagement of citizens, including increased participation in e-governance, better political willingness is essential, going beyond mere access to digital media (Mukhtarov et al. 2018). India's SCM promotes ICTs and multiple digital platforms, such as MyGov.in, yet with limited attention to empowering local governments and residents.

9.3.3 Environmental sustainability

9.3.3.1 Long-term climate change risks ignored

Cities in India require explicit integration of the impacts of climate change within their local urban development agenda (Singhal et al. 2010). Furthermore, many cities in India are vulnerable to unpredictable rainfall patterns, sea-level rise and rise in average temperature (Sharma and Tomar 2010, Schellnhuber et al. 2012). Although environmental aspects of cities have become part of the urban policy agenda, the main thrust of policies continues to focus on improving basic urban services, such as drinking water, sanitation and waste management. The focus in praxis has, therefore, been more on socio-economic development and poverty eradication rather than dealing with sustainability and climate change mitigation issues (MoEFCC 2015, Dubash 2017). Existing urban policies including the SCM fail to integrate long-term risks to urban areas from climate change. Policymakers and researchers focusing on climate change mitigation have argued that adaptation to urban climate issues needs to be prioritised (Bai et al. 2018, Chu 2018) as cities in India are experiencing negative impacts of climate change (Selvaraj et al. 2016). The adaptation strategies in cities require rethinking society-government relationships, developing risk and hazard management systems, and building climate-resilient urban infrastructure (Revi 2008, Chu 2018). It is vital that cities in India, like other cities, prepare and implement climate compatible plans (Dhakal et al. 2017) which complement the targeted development agenda.

9.3.3.2 Improper land management and green infrastructure

Cities are concentrated zones of human development, making land a prime resource in urban areas. Limited availability and poor management of land in urban areas in India is one of the major obstacles in promoting sustainable cities. Integrating green infrastructure and concepts of resource self-sufficiency with land management as part of urban planning tends to play a key role in the preservation of the local environment. The benefits of green infrastructure, the role and value of local ecosystem services, and the local production of resources in solving many urban issues have also been recognised (Bolund and Hunhammar 1999, Jim and Chen 2009, Baró et al. 2015). In cities in India, however, the focus has been on the built environment as opposed to green infrastructure and management of open areas. Multiple development dimensions compete for limited amounts of land as a resource and, thus, call for trade-offs or raise conflicts. Urban expansion, including construction of housing and much-needed roads in India, has occurred on agricultural land, wetland and other natural areas (Pandey and Seto 2015, Ramachandra et al. 2016). Preserving land for its natural setting reduces its availability for urban development uses and peri-urban agriculture, thus creating land-use conflicts and socioeconomic concerns. The ever-increasing demand for the built environment requires the construction of infrastructure and buildings, often raised on arable land and ecologically sensitive areas (Seto et al. 2012, Pandey and Seto 2015).

9.3.4 Social inclusiveness

9.3.4.1 Inequitable distribution of government support

Urbanisation in India has been fragmented and unbalanced due to factors such as limited investment, top-down governance, and regional, cultural and political differences. Recent urban policies seem to be following the trend in a different format. The SCM also ultimately aims to engage with and benefit only a small fraction of urban population in India (Figure 9.1). Cities selected under the SCM predominantly are large and better-off, while many small to medium-sized cities with poor coverage of basic urban services have been ignored (Smith et al. 2018).

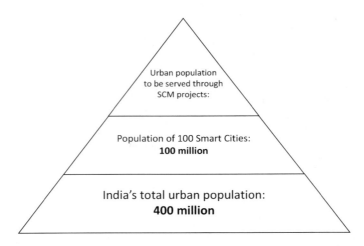

Figure 9.1 Focus on limited urban population under SCM (MoHUA 2017, Source: Based on Chaudhry *et al.* 2018); data are for area-based development (ABD) projects and 90 cities selected till 2017; ABD projects received over 80 percent of total SCM funds (Chaudhry *et al.* 2018).

9.3.4.2 *Potential gentrification*

The SCM proposes area-based development (ABD) (retrofitting existing areas or greenfield development) and Pan-city initiatives for each city selected. The emphasis is on substantial investment in housing risks neglecting the development of slums and poverty-stricken urban areas (Doshi 2015, Hoelscher 2016). For example, the New Delhi Municipal Corporation is one of the cities selected under the SCM, and is one of the wealthiest and financially sustainable municipal corporations in India, serving 300,000 people, just a small fraction of around 20 million living in the whole of Delhi. Moreover, more than 80 percent of allocated funds under the SCM are being spent on ABD projects (Chaudhry *et al.* 2018). In many cities, the majority of the population belongs to low-income groups, but only 13 percent of funds have been allocated for affordable housing projects. It is, therefore, expected that the SCM is likely to benefit only a small fraction of the urban population and may contribute to gentrification.

9.3.5 *Urban services delivery*

9.3.5.1 *Poor urban service delivery mechanism*

The current urban service delivery framework is inadequate and unable to accommodate the entire needs of increasing population in cities in India (HPEC 2011, Praharaj *et al.* 2018). Issues such as flooding, traffic congestion, waste accumulation on roads, deteriorating air and water quality, inaccessible sewerage networks and the proliferation of diseases (e.g. asthma, dengue chikungunya, swine flu, etc.) have adversely affected the quality and efficiency of citizen welfare

(World Economic Forum 2016). Water scarcity in urban areas has become increasingly prominent due to negligible rainwater harvesting, pollution, overconsumption, inadequate water supply and maintenance (HPEC 2011, Bholey 2016). Non-extensive waste management and sanitation facilities have resulted in open defecation practices by over 50 million people (PricewaterhouseCoopers and Save the Children 2015). Most services provided by ULBs lack accountability and meet limited pressure from communities to improve standards of delivery and these problems have aggravated. For instance, in most cities, the per capita water supply for the majority of the urban population is between 70 and 90 litres per capita per day (lpcd), much lower than the norm of 135 lpcd (MoUD 2008, Shaban 2008). On average, only 51 percent of sewage is treated in million-plus cities, while in smaller cities, a range of only 8–32 percent of sewage is treated before being discharged into and, thus, polluting rivers and other water bodies (CPCB 2009, 2015). Moreover, the rapid rise in personal vehicles ownership in cities has contributed to traffic congestion, road accidents, poor urban air quality and urban sprawl over past few decades (IIHS 2011, Singh 2012). Inclusive urbanisation concerns are reflected through the estimated housing shortage of over 18 million affordable units during 2012 (MoHUPA 2012). The number of towns reporting slums increased from 1,743 in 2001 to 2,613 in 2011, and the population living in slums increased from 52 million in 2001 to 65 million in 2011 (Census of India 2011b).

City authorities' main focus used to be on building physical infrastructure, rather than environmentally sustainable services. However, this scenario has started to change in recent years. The Ministry of Housing and Urban Affairs has recently created indicators to measure social, environmental and economic liveability in cities (MoUD 2017). There are, however, limited provisions to encourage the ICT-enabled delivery of urban services. It is important that cities adopt advanced technology integration and information management: for service delivery, to enhance the capacity of municipal bodies, to reform institutional set-up to manage multiple jurisdictions, to promote transparency and to create data-driven knowledge platforms for implementing best practices (Shoeb and Manishankar 2017). ICT can facilitate monitoring water inputs and outputs in real time to track water consumption and water generation. In cities, such as Singapore, data-driven approaches to urban services have substantially improved the efficiency of water distribution (Zubizarreta et al. 2016). Many cities around the world are using ICT to manage urban mobility, smart cards for payment and real-time monitoring of traffic (Zubizarreta et al. 2016). The inclusion of monitoring mechanisms, such as water and energy metres and sensors to monitor consumption, can help local authorities in optimising resources.

9.4 Comparison of three cities under the SCM

The general challenges of transformation under the SCM are further explained through the example of a comparison of three cities selected under the SCM (Table 9.3). Each of the three cities is unique. Indore has been among the fastest-growing cities in the country and has been rated as the cleanest city in the

Table 9.3 Comparison of three cities chosen under the SCM

Parameters	Indore	Lucknow	Amravati
SCM mission			
Area-based development	Rejuvenation and redevelopment of a heritage site at the centre of the city	Rejuvenation and redevelopment of an area covering less than 1 percent of the city area	Greenfield area within greenfield city will be equipped with advanced ICTs, aiming to balance environmental, social and economic aspects
City-wide solution	Use of ICTs for solid waste management, transport and governance	Use of ICTs for transport, street lighting and governance	Use of ICTs for water management; aims to use 100 percent of wastewater
Total budget	₹ 6,000 cr	₹ 2,053 cr	₹ 1,900 cr
Government sources of funding	25 percent of funding from the central and state governments	90 percent of the funding from the central and state governments	70 percent of funding from central and state governments
Other sources of funding	Annual user charges and local tax; premium on private land and the sale of public land after real estate redevelopment; short-term loans	Annual user charges and local tax and higher taxes from properties under areas-based development area; short-term loans	5–6 percent through PPP projects; local revenues through taxes, user charge and advertisements; 20–25 percent from loans from multilateral banks (World Bank, JICA, ADB, etc.)
Unique features	Significant improvement in MSW management BRTS system operational	Emphasis on non-motorised transport E-governance to enhance government's response ICTs for public safety River cleaning for riverfront development	"Prevention is better than cure" approach Focus on happiness Special focus on water management
Risks	Gentrification of city Water supply and management getting limited attention Limited focus on non-motorised transport, even though the city is highly populated and polluted	ICTs may exclude many people due to low penetration of internet and limited digital literacy Gentrification of city Restricted access to river water for people outside area-based development initiatives	Significant amount of capital investment Execution uncertainties Suboptimal allocation of limited government funds as the city would serve less than 1 million people
International cooperation	The UK would provide support in planning, transport and energy infrastructure	N/A	Singapore would provide support in planning and in seed development phases

Source: (i) Smart City Proposals, documents and city profiles available on www.smartcities.gov.in; (ii) https://in smartcitiescouncil.com/cities/lucknow; (iii) https://india.smartcitiescouncil.com/cities/indore); (iv) http://pib.nic. newsite/PrintRelease.aspx?relid=156166; (v) Amravati international cooperation (Keng and Kumar 2018); and (vi) dore international cooperation (Deloitte 2016).

past two consecutive years. Amravati is among the first greenfield cities expected to be fully equipped with ICT from the outset and received extensive support from the state government. Lucknow is a popular tourist destination but experiences severe water and air pollution. Although at various stages of development, all three cities reflect unique challenges and risks of the SCM.

Indore: Indore is known as the commercial capital of the Indian state of Madhya Pradesh and is also the largest city in the state. The city performs better on many economic, social and basic urban service parameters when compared with rest of the country. Indore has been ranked the cleanest city in the country two years in a row as per the two most recent surveys conducted by New Delhi Ministry of Urban Development (MoUD). Among the chosen smart cities, Indore has envisaged ambitious projects to be undertaken under the SCM with a focus on urban mobility, e-governance and solid waste management. However, several challenges remain. First, most of the funds are dedicated towards redevelopment of Rajwada, under ABD, leaving many Pan-city initiatives underfunded. Second, although it has elected ULBs, much of the administrative control of physical infrastructure lies with the state government. Third, the city still relies on state and central governments for funding as local sources of funding remain limited.

Lucknow: Lucknow is one of the heritage and tourist-centric cities in the state of Uttar Pradesh. The city is among the very few cities in India which has dedicated tracks for bicycles. Similar to other SCM cities, Lucknow has adopted a multi-dimensional development plan which focuses on liveability, e-governance, renewable energy and physical infrastructure. However, over 70 percent of funds will be invested in ABD initiatives with Pan-city projects receiving the rest. The Qaiserbagh area, selected for ABD, covering only 1 percent of the total city area, is slated to receive the majority of the funds under the SCM. Most of the Pan-city funds are intended for the installation of ICTs, such as video surveillance cameras, smart street lighting, traffic monitoring systems and e-governance. An overwhelming reliance on ICT excludes many people due to low penetration of the internet among the population. In addition to this, using e-governance requires digital literacy, which will lower participation from urban poor and low-income groups who are in most need of government services.

Amravati: Amravati is a greenfield city designated to be the capital of Andhra Pradesh, and it is yet to be built. It is envisioned that the city will be among the most advanced in India. Furthermore, there is scope for avoiding many problems of existing cities during the design phase, and solutions could be implemented from the beginning. Governance of Amravati could differ from existing cities through preventative rather than reactive measures. Nevertheless, building the city from scratch requires significant capital investment and would have to tackle implementation uncertainties. One can argue that building greenfield cities is a suboptimal allocation of limited government funds; funds which could be used to address numerous other issues faced by many other cities in the state. Furthermore, Amravati is expected to accommodate 500,000 people by 2025, and even if this number may double, it reflects that a significant amount of resources shall be invested for serving a population of less than a million people, which shall be a highly skewed distribution of resources.

9.5 Scalability for megacities

Most of the urban population in India will live in non-megacities, but the country will have seven megacities, cities with a population greater than 10 million, supporting over 130 million people by 2030 (UN DESA 2018b). A few cities, e.g., Surat and Pune, shall have populations over 8–9 million but less than 10 million (UN DESA 2018b). Thus, it is expected that soon nearly 150 million people will live in megacities in India. Megacities present a different set of opportunities and challenges for encouraging sustainable development. The three cities discussed above are medium to large cities. Some of the SCM initiatives mentioned in Table 9.3 can be scaled and implemented in megacities, such as Delhi and Mumbai. Megacities can capitalise on financial resources, multicultural human capital, knowledge, and international cooperation – which are not readily available in small or medium-sized cities. Further, these cities are major commercial and tourism hubs, and most companies have their head-offices located in such megacities. Consequently, these cities can be major recipients of the benefits of corporate social responsibility, aimed at addressing lack of affordable housing, sanitation, waste management and other initiatives for improving social and environmental sustainability (Raimi et al. 2018). While Delhi and Mumbai are megacities, they are also an aggregation of smaller cities and, thus, resonate with the three identified SCM cities on parameters discussed in Table 9.3. Such polycentric urban regions offer several opportunities. With the right context of proper urban infrastructure and governance capacity, small and medium-sized cities can offer much higher economic potential than megacities (Frick and Rodríguez-Pose 2018). Optimal integration can harness the network of closely located smaller cities to benefit the megacity from economy-of-scale (Meijers et al. 2018).

It may appear logical for megacities to scale up solutions successfully implemented in smaller cities, but such an approach may not be effective for several reasons. First, megacities such as Delhi and Mumbai are physically single entity cities but divided into multiple municipal corporations, each independently governing a portion of the city. The formulation of uniform policies for, for instance, land-use, waste management or local transport, is a challenge because of the existence of multiple decision-making bodies. These problems are worsened by the fact that spatial unevenness of population distribution and infrastructure availability is much higher in megacities, leading to non-uniform delivery of urban services to urban and peri-urban areas (Jain et al. 2019). Thus, despite the possibilities of higher resource-use efficiency, uniform governance of complex mega-urban systems presents a huge challenge (Marull et al. 2015). Second, megacities have much higher population density, which offers multiple benefits of economy of scale but often leads to overcrowding with a burden on infrastructure. Overcrowding contributes to property encroachment and safety risks, and existing infrastructure is inadequate to support the population (Rajagopal and Sachitanand 2017). The external costs of overcrowding, for example, of time lost and inconvenience through an inefficient public transport system (including bus rapid transit system (BRTS)) may greatly exceed benefits derived from economy of scale (Varghese and Adhvaryu 2016). So, for example, the costs of overcrowding in BRTS are less likely to occur in Indore than in Delhi or Mumbai. Similar effects may occur for many ICT-based solutions such as smart-parking for urban space management, particularly because of lack of discipline, higher costs and poor supporting infrastructure (Patel 2018). Although other cities face similar obstacles in implementing ICT-based solutions, the challenges are magnified in megacities.

9.6 Environmental leapfrogging

In many cities in the global South, rapid population growth is outpacing development and putting unprecedented pressures on resources. However, there is potential for environmental leapfrogging towards less resource-intensive structures, which can be incorporated into the smart cities concept. A key potential pathway for leapfrogging is through enhancing the resource efficiency in cities, an area that has attracted minimal attention so far in current policy discourse and practice. Concomitant to this aspect, the built environment, in particular, is one of the fastest-growing sectors, one of the highest in cumulative resource intensity, and has a significant existing and potential footprint in urban and peri-urban areas in India. With newer impetus for cities under the SCM, significant opportunity exists for selected cities to make comprehensive efforts to leapfrog for resource efficiency and inspire other cities in India to be smart and sustainable. Limited emphasis has been placed on application of resource efficiency strategies so far through the SCM and other urban programmes.

The strategies envisioned under the SCM focus on retrofitting (of existing built environment), redevelopment (replacement of inefficient built environment and infrastructure) and city extension (greenfield development by introduction of new and smart built environment solutions in a previously uninhabited area). Innovative strategies and actions if implemented comprehensively through the SCM and other urban-focused initiatives, such as HRIDAY, AMRUT, Housing for All (Urban) and The Swachh Bharat Mission – Urban can create significant opportunities for leapfrogging through redevelopment and retrofitting of the existing built environment and infrastructure or through new greenfield development in cities. Aspects such as greater implementation of energy and material efficiency and focused building codes in planned new and redeveloped areas require greater attention. It is estimated that around two-thirds of buildings in India that will exist in 2030 are yet to be built (Kumar et al. 2010, Khosla et al. 2017), and if this phenomenal built environment remains unregulated, then energy demand in the buildings sector could increase by 700 percent by 2050, compared with 2005 levels (GBPN 2014, Khosla et al. 2017).

In its current form, the SCM does not provide an opportunity structure for technological advancement to promote energy and material efficiency measures through the built environment and infrastructure upgrading. Although the SCM addresses retrofitting and redevelopment in existing cities to a limited degree, which is a current priority in India, less emphasis is placed on housing the additional 400 million urban inhabitants (by 2050) in a sustainable manner – a potentially detrimental urban scenario. Demonstrable integration of a resource-efficient strategy through programmes such as SCM and Housing for All (Urban) is imperative.

India's co-benefits principle laid down in the NAPCC could be a trigger for environmental leapfrogging strategies to address the win-win options for cities (Sharma and Tomar 2010, Beermann et al. 2016). Integrating principles of resource efficiency and the circular economy into urban development that simultaneously provide socio-economic and environmental benefits to inhabitants (including the urban poor) of aspiring smart cities can provide effective measures for addressing existing and future challenges (Ghisellini et al. 2016). For example, sustainable management of urban waste, including construction and demolition waste recycling (Jain and Singhal 2016), utilisation of waste-to-energy technologies (Kalyani and Pandey 2014) and wastewater recycling (2030 Water Resources Group 2016), can provide co-benefits, such as saving material and energy, creating employment for local communities and augmenting the city's access to resources. Government policies alone are insufficient and innovative business models and market-driven strategies are required for a transition towards resource efficiency and a circular economy (Goyal et al. 2016).

Efficient governance is an essential component to steer transformations in cities towards sustainable development. Decentralised urban governance is a necessary condition for sustainable urban development. Power and responsibilities need to be devolved to local governments responsible for providing infrastructure and services. Despite the decentralisation mantra over more than two decades, there has been limited noticeable difference in actual public praxis of empowering local governments. In its current format, the SCM appears to be yet another lost opportunity to promote a transformation for longer-term benefits. Currently, there are two key insufficiencies: there is too little foresight beyond achieving immediate tangible results in targeted cities and too little focus on strengthening the local institutional framework with a capacity to plan and commission smart development initiatives. What is needed is local capacity building and empowerment, as well as a change in the approach to implementation by policy decision-makers, elected representatives and city managers.

Role of Other Civic Actors: for cities in India to leapfrog towards resource efficiency and long-term sustainability, the actor-networks of city officials and private and civil society need to converge in terms of understanding, strategies and actions. Independent organisations including non-governmental organisations (NGOs) and local community associations (LCAs) can catalyse urban development towards smart and sustainable cities. Such groups highlight socio-economic and environmental issues in urban areas, which are often neglected by mainstream civil and public agencies. For example, the Delhi government has collaborated with LCAs and NGOs to spread health and safety awareness of waste management and improve the municipal waste management system in the city (Talyan et al. 2008), and some NGOs have represented rights of waste pickers and other marginalised stakeholders in a waste management system (Demaria and Schindler 2016). Non-government actors have also voiced against environmental impacts of megaprojects in cities, for example Yamuna riverfront, in Delhi, and their impacts on the informal economy run by slum dwellers (Follmann 2015).

Not-for-profit groups are also perceived to be transparent, gender-sensitive and people-centric. For example, they have also been entrusted for designing and overseeing a slum redevelopment housing project in the city of Trivandrum, Kerala (Williams et al. 2018). A few such actors, e.g., Housing and Lands Rights Network (HLRN), have also raised concerns that SCM has excluded vulnerable and marginalised people living in cities from the development process. For many reasons, including the need for land for infrastructure development and urban beautification, this has resulted in the eviction of many people from their settlements (Chaudhry et al. 2018).

Further, many organisations have played a key role in researching and providing knowledge for sustainable urban development. The National Institute of Urban Affairs (NIUA), with assistance from the government, had been instrumental in providing research and capacity building support to many urban bodies. Research and development based organisations such as Development Alternatives, the Deutsche Gesellschaft für Internationale Zusammenarbeit (GIZ) and TERI have collaborated with the government of India to address many sustainability-related challenges (Sekhar et al. 2015, Banerjee et al. 2016). The Indian Council for Research on International Economic Relation (ICRIER) suggested that cities must also account for social costs, which include health costs, productivity losses, etc., resulting from poor quality of urban services and growing environmental impacts.

Democratically elected governments at various governance levels will dominate the urban development in India and citizens will continue to hold the government accountable in whatever form they can. However, an individual citizen may not be aware and powerful enough to voice against certain government policies. In such cases, independent organisations and LCAs can complement and empower citizens' concerns in cities, act as a bridge between government and citizens, or work independently to draw the attention of citizens and government towards issues and push them to address the problems (Sen 1999, Harriss 2007).

9.7 Conclusion

India is likely to contribute 17–18 percent of global urban growth by 2050, and its cities are in greater focus now with increasing demographic and economic potential. Newer programmes, missions and approaches have been introduced over time by the current and previous governments which reflect urban policy transformations in India but with limited changes in priorities and outcomes. The lack of decentralisation and empowerment of the local urban governments belong to the major constraints of more sustainable urban development in India.

Apart from addressing the lack of local urban governance capacities, there is a need for a paradigm shift to enable Indian cities to leapfrog for resource efficiency, to become smart and sustainable. India's SCM has the potential to trigger such leapfrogging through the built environment and infrastructure domains.

However, the existing governance structure and implementation processes require transformation for long-term benefits.

Scholarly debate has been critical regarding SCM's implementation and neglect of inclusive urban development. There is apprehension that SCM may also contribute to gentrification, widen disparities between large and small cities, weaken decentralised governance structure and may exclude the digitally illiterate. There is also acknowledgement, however, that SCM has provided renewed impetus to the urban development agenda through the policy discourse. A critical governance issue is the centralisation of power at the national level and the concomitant need to empower government at the city level. The current multi-level governance structure across national, state, city-region and city institutions needs to be realigned to deal effectively with the urban challenges in India.

The approach to transform urban settings to smart sustainable cities must facilitate the ongoing policy praxis to advance beyond a focus on traditional output indicators and to address critical dimensions of human development, sustainable consumption and knowledge-based urban development. It is an exciting time for urban development in India, but the many challenges can only be met by employing comprehensively sustainable methods. Leapfrogging in thinking, strategy, action and evaluation for sustainability is essential to influence the quality of life of the current and future billion urban population.

References

Acolin, A., Chattaraj, S., and Wachter, S.M., 2014. Urban governance and development of informality in China and India. *In*: E. Birch, S. Chattaraj, and S. Wachter, eds. *Slums: How informal real estate markets work*. Philadelphia: University of Pennsylvania Press.

Ahluwalia, I.J., 2017. Urban governance in India. *Journal of Urban Affairs*, 41 (1), 1–20.

Aijaz, R., 2007. *Challenges for urban local governments in India*. London, UK: Asia Research Centre, London School of Economics and Political Science, No. 19.

Albino, V., Berardi, U., and Dangelico, R.M., 2015. Smart cities: Definitions, dimensions, performance, and initiatives. *Journal of Urban Technology*, 22 (1), 3–21.

Bai, X., Dawson, R.J., Ürge-Vorsatz, D., Delgado, G.C., Salisu Barau, A., Dhakal, S., Dodman, D., Leonardsen, L., Masson-Delmotte, V., Roberts, D.C., and Schultz, S., 2018. Six research priorities for cities and climate change. *Nature*, 555, 23–25.

Banerjee, A., Paterok, K., Saluja, M.S., Arora, R., Satpathy, I., Malik, J.K., Arora, N., Kapur, S., Saluja, S., Bhattacharjya, S., Sekhar, A.R., Varsha, D., Nagrath, K., and Rathi, V., 2016. *Material consumption patterns in India: A baseline study of the automotive and construction sectors*. New Delhi: GIZ.

Baró, F., Haase, D., Gómez-Baggethun, E., and Frantzeskaki, N., 2015. Mismatches between ecosystem services supply and demand in urban areas: A quantitative assessment in five European cities. *Ecological Indicators*, 55, 146–158.

Batra, L., 2009. *A review of urbanisation and urban policy in post-independent India*. New Delhi: Centre for the Study of Law and Governance, Jawaharlal nehru University, No. 12.

Beermann, J., Damodaran, A., Jörgensen, K., and Schreurs, M.A., 2016. Climate action in Indian cities: An emerging new research area. *Journal of Integrative Environmental Sciences*, 13 (1), 55–66.

Bharne, V., 2013. *The emerging Asian city: Concomitant urbanities and urbanisms*. New York: Routledge.
Bholey, M., 2016. India's urban challenges and smart cities: A contemporary study. *Scholedge International Journal of Business Policy & Governance ISSN 2394–3351*.
Bibri, S.E. and Krogstie, J., 2017. Smart sustainable cities of the future: An extensive interdisciplinary literature review. *Sustainable Cities and Society*, 31, 183–212.
Bolund, P. and Hunhammar, S., 1999. Ecosystem services in urban areas. *Ecological Economics*, 29 (2), 293–301.
Census of India, 2001. *Census data 2001*. New Delhi: Office of the Registrar General & Census Commissioner.
Census of India, 2011a. *Provisional Population Totals, Census of India 2011: Urban Agglomerations and Cities* [online]. Available from: www.censusindia.gov.in/.
Census of India, 2011b. *Primary census abstract for slum*. New Delhi: Office of the Registrar General & Census Commissioner.
Chakrabarti, P.G.D., 2001. Urban crisis in India: New initiatives for sustainable cities. *Development in Practice*, 11 (2/3), 260–272.
Chattopadhyay, S., 2015. Financing India's urban infrastructure. *Journal of Infrastructure Development*, 7 (1), 55–75.
Chaudhry, S., Saxena, S., and Kumar, D., 2018. *India's smart cities mission: Smart for whom?cities for whom?* New Delhi: Housing and Land Rights Network.
Chauvin, J.P., Glaeser, E., Ma, Y., and Tobio, K., 2017. What is different about urbanization in rich and poor countries? Cities in Brazil, China, India and the United States. *Journal of Urban Economics*, 98, 17–49.
Chen, M., Zhang, H., Liu, W., and Zhang, W., 2014. The global pattern of urbanization and economic growth: Evidence from the last three decades. *PLoS One*, 9 (8), 1–15.
Chu, E.K., 2018. Urban climate adaptation and the reshaping of state–society relations: The politics of community knowledge and mobilisation in Indore, India. *Urban Studies*, 55 (8), 1766–1782.
CPCB, 2009. *Status of water supply, wastewater generation and treatment in class-I and class-II towns of India*. Delhi: Central Pollution Control Board (Ministry of Environment and Forests, Govt. of India).
CPCB, 2015. *River stretches for restoration of water quality*. Delhi: Central Pollution Control Board (Ministry of Environment and Forests, Govt. of India).
Crisil, 2017. *Crisil infrastructure yearbook*. Mumbai: Crisil Limited.
Demaria, F. and Schindler, S., 2016. Contesting urban metabolism: Struggles over Waste-to-Energy in Delhi, India. *Antipode*, 44 (2), 293–313.
Dhakal, S., Shrestha, A., Singhal, S., Moloney, S., Vaughter, P., Darnsawasdi, R., Kim, S.M., Pharino, C., and Haryono, E., 2017. *Tracking climate actions for climate compatible development in cities*. UNU-IAS Policy Brief, No. 4.
Dirks, S. and Keeling, M., 2009. A vision of smarter cities: How cities can lead the way into a prosperous and sustainable future. [online]. Available from: https://www.ibm.com/downloads/cas/2JYLM4ZA.
Dong, C. and Ji, Y., 2018. Connecting young adults to democracy via government social network sites. *Public Relations Review*, 44 (5), 762–775.
Doshi, S., 2015. Rethinking gentrification in India: Displacement, dispossession and the spectre of development. *Global gentrifications: Uneven development and displacement*. Chicago: Policy Press, 101–119.
Dubash, N.K., 2017. Safeguarding development and limiting vulnerability: India's stakes in the Paris Agreement. *Wiley Interdisciplinary Reviews: Climate Change*, 8 (2), e444-n/a.

FICCI, 2014. *FICCI report on urban infrastructure in India*. New Delhi: The Federation of Indian Chambers of Commerce and Industry (FICCI).

Follmann, A., 2015. Urban mega-projects for a 'world-class' riverfront – The interplay of informality, flexibility and exceptionality along the Yamuna in Delhi, India. *Habitat International*, 45 (3), 213–222.

Frick, S.A. and Rodríguez-Pose, A., 2018. Big or small cities? On city size and economic growth. *Growth and Change*, 49 (1), 4–32.

Ghisellini, P., Cialani, C., and Ulgiati, S., 2016. A review on circular economy: The expected transition to a balanced interplay of environmental and economic systems. *Journal of Cleaner Production*, 114, 11–32.

Global Buildings Performance Network (GBPN), 2014. *Residential buildings in India: Energy use projections and savings potential, India*. Ahmedabad: CEPT University.

Global Footprint Network, 2015. Ecological wealth of nations [online]. Available from: http://www.footprintnetwork.org/ecological_footprint_nations/.

GoI JNNURM, 2011. *Jawaharlal Nehru National Urban Renewal Mission: Overview* [online]. Available from: http://jnnurm.nic.in/wp-content/uploads/2011/01/PMSpeechOverviewE.pdf.

Gore, C.D. and Gopakumar, G., 2015. Infrastructure and metropolitan reorganization: An exploration of the relationship in Africa and India. *Journal of Urban Affairs*, 37 (5), 548–567.

Goyal, S., Esposito, M., and Kapoor, A., 2016. Circular Economy Business Models in Developing Economies: Lessons from India on Reduce, Recycle, and Reuse Paradigms. Thunderbird International Business Review, 60 (5), 729–740.

Harriss, J., 2007. Antinomies of empowerment. Observations on civil society, politics and urban governance in India. *Economics & Political Weekly*, 42, 2716–2724.

Harvey, D., 2012. Rebel cities: From the right to the city to the urban revolution. New York: Verso.

Hoelscher, K., 2016. The evolution of the smart cities agenda in India. *International Area Studies Review*.

Höjer, M. and Wangel, J., 2015. Smart sustainable cities: Definition and challenges. In: M.L. Hilty and B. Aebischer, eds. ICT Innovations for Sustainability. Switzerland: Springer International Publishing, 333–349.

Hollands, R.G., 2015. Critical interventions into the corporate smart city. *Cambridge Journal of Regions, Economy and Society*, 8 (1), 61–77.

HPEC, 2011. *Report on Indian urban infrastructure and services*. New Delhi: High Powered Expert Committee (HPEC).

IIHS, 2011. Urban India 2011:Evidence. The India Urban Conference: Evidence and Experience (IUC). Bangalore: The Indian Institute for Human Settlements (IIHS).

Jacobson, L. and Prakash, T., 1968. Urbanization and regional planning in India. *Ekistics*, 25 (148), 158–165.

Jain, M., Korzhenevych, A., and Sridharan, N., 2019. Determinants of growth in non-municipal areas of Delhi: rural–urban dichotomy revisited. Journal of Housing and the Built Environment, 34 (3), 715–734.

Jain, S. and Singhal, S., 2016. An example of construction and demolition waste recycling in New Delhi. Switch Asia Magazine, 36–39.

Jim, C.Y. and Chen, W.Y., 2009. Ecosystem services and valuation of urban forests in China. *Cities*, 26 (4), 187–194.

de Jong, M., Joss, S., Schraven, D., Zhan, C., and Weijnen, M., 2015. Sustainable–smart–resilient–low carbon–eco–knowledge cities; making sense of a multitude of concepts promoting sustainable urbanization. *Journal of Cleaner Production*, 109 (Supplement C), 25–38.

Kalyani, K.A. and Pandey, K.K., 2014. Waste to energy status in India: A short review. *Renewable and Sustainable Energy Reviews* 31, 113–120.
Kennedy, C.A., Stewart, I., Facchini, A., Cersosimo, I., Mele, R., Chen, B., Uda, M., Kansal, A., Chiu, A., Kim, K., Dubeux, C., Lebre La Rovere, E., Cunha, B., Pincetl, S., Keirstead, J., Barles, S., Pusaka, S., Gunawan, J., Adegbile, M., Nazariha, M., Hoque, S., Marcotullio, P.J., González Otharán, F., Genena, T., Ibrahim, N., Farooqui, R., Cervantes, G., and Sahin, A.D., 2015. Energy and material flows of megacities. *Proceedings of the National Academy of Sciences*, 112 (19), 5985–5990.
Khosla, R., Sagar, A., and Mathur, A., 2017. Deploying low-carbon technologies in developing countries: A view from India's buildings sector. Environmental Policy and Governance, 27, 149–162.
Kumar, S., Kapoor, R., Rawal, R., Seth, S., and Walia, A., 2010. Developing an energy conservation building code implementation strategy in India. *Proceedings of the 2010 ACEEE Summer Study on Energy Efficiency in Buildings*, 8, 209–224.
Kundu, D., 2014. Urban Development Programmes in India: A Critique of JnNURM. Social Change, 44 (4), 615–632.
Li, E., Endter-Wada, J., and Li, S., 2015. Characterizing and contextualizing the water challenges of megacities. *Journal of the American Water Resources Association*, 51 (3), 589–613.
Martin, C.J., Evans, J., and Karvonen, A., 2018. Smart and sustainable? Five tensions in the visions and practices of the smart-sustainable city in Europe and North America. Technological Forecasting and Social Change, 133, 269–278.
Marull, J., Font, C., and Boix, R., 2015. Modelling urban networks at mega-regional scale: Are increasingly complex urban systems sustainable? Land Use Policy, 43, 15–27.
Mathur, O.P., Debdulal, T., and Rajadhyaksha, N., 2009. *Urban property tax potential in India*. New Delhi: National Institute of Public Finance and Policy.
Meijers, E., Hoogerbrugge, M., and Cardoso, R., 2018. Beyond polycentricity: Does stronger integration between cities in polycentric urban regions improve performance? Tijdschrift voor Economische en Sociale Geografie, 109, 1–21.
Ministry of Housing and Urban Affairs (MoHUA), 2017. *Rajya Sabha question no. 1311: Beneficiaries under Smart Cities Mission*.
Minz, S., 2016. Know the countries that are helping India become smart [online]. Available from: https://www.proptiger.com/guide/post/the-foreign-hand-in-making-indian-smart.
MoEFCC, 2015. India: First biennial update report to the United Nations Framework Convention on Climate Change. New Delhi: Ministry of Environment, Forest and Climate Change.
Mohanty, P.K., 2016. Financing cities in india: municipal reforms, fiscal accountability and urban infrastructure. New Delhi: SAGE Publications India.
MoHUPA, 2012. *Report of the technical group on urban housing shortage (TG-12)*. New Delhi: Ministry of Housing and Urban Poverty Alleviation (MoHUPA).
MoUD, 2008. National urban sanitation policy. New Delhi: Ministry of Urban Development.
MoUD, 2015. *Smart Cities Mission: Statement & Guidelines* [online]. Available from: http://smartcities.gov.in/upload/uploadfiles/files/SmartCityGuidelines(1).pdf.
MoUD, 2017. *Livability standards in cities*. New Delhi: Ministry of Urban Development.
Mukhtarov, F., Dieperink, C., and Driessen, P., 2018. The influence of information and communication technologies on public participation in urban water governance: A review of place-based research. Environmental Science & Policy, 89, 430–438.
Nandi, S. and Gamkhar, S., 2013. Urban challenges in India: A review of recent policy measures. Habitat International, 39, 55–61.
NIUA, 2014. *NIUA Dialogues* [online]. Available from: http://pearl.niua.org/dialogue-series.

Pandey, B. and Seto, K., 2015. Urbanization and agricultural land loss in India: Comparing satellite estimates with census data. *Journal of Environmental Management*, 148, 53–66.

Parnell, S., Elmqvist, T., McPhearson, T., Nagendra, T., and Sorlin, S., 2018. Introduction. In: T. Elmqvist, X. Bai, N. Frantzeskaki, C. Griffith, D. Maddox, T. McPhearson, S. Parnell, P. Romero-Lankao, D. Simon, and M. Watkins, eds. The Urban Planet: Knowledge Towards Sustainable Cities. New York: Cambridge University Press.

Patel, L., 2018. *Automated Parking Lots Fail to Deal with City's Parking Woes* [online]. Available from: https://ahmedabadmirror.indiatimes.com/ahmedabad/others/automated-parking-lots-fail-to-deal-with-citys-parking-woes/articleshow/65060742.cms.

Planning Commission of India, 1951. Chapter 35: Housing. In: *1st Five Year Plan*. New Delhi: Government of India.

Planning Commission of India, 1956. Chapter 26: Housing. In: *2nd Five Year Plan*. New Delhi: Government of India.

Planning Commission of India, 1961. Chapter 33: Housing and urban and rural planning. In: *3rd Five Year Plan*. New Delhi: Government of India.

Planning Commission of India, 1985. Chapter 12: Housing, urban development, water supply, and sanitation. In: *Seventh five year plan*. New Delhi: Government of India.

Planning Commission of India, 1992. Chapter 13: Urban development. In: *Eighth Five Year Plan*. New Delhi: Government of India.

Planning Commission of India, 1997. Chapter 3.7: Housing, urban development, water supply, and civic amenities. In: *Ninth Five Year Plan*. New Delhi: Government of India.

Planning Commission of India, 2012. Chapter 18: Urban development. In: *12th Five Year Plan*. New Delhi: Government of India.

Praharaj, S., Han, J.H., and Hawken, S., 2017. Urban innovation through policy integration: Critical perspectives from 100 smart cities mission in India. City, Culture and Society, 12, 35–43.

Raimi, L., Adelopo, A.G.O., and Yusuf, H., 2018. Corporate social responsibility and sustainable management of solid wastes and effluents in Lagos megacity Nigeria. Social Responsibility Journal, 15 (6), 742–761.

Rajagopal, D. and Sachitanand, R., 2017. *Mumbai: A City Brought to Its Knees by the Burden of Its Success* [online]. Available from: https://economictimes.indiatimes.com/news/politics-and-nation/mumbai-a-city-brought-to-its-knees-by-the-burden-of-its-success/articleshow/60988261.cms.

Ramachandra, T. V, Bharath, H.A., Vinay, S., Kumar, U., Venugopal Rao, K., and Joshi, N. V, 2016. Modelling and visualization of urban trajectory in 4 cities of India. *32nd Annual in-house Symposium on Space science and Technology, ISRO-IISc-STC*.

Randhawa, A. and Kumar, A., 2017. Exploring sustainability of smart development initiatives in India. International Journal of Sustainable Built Environment, 6 (2), 701–710.

Revi, A., 2008. Climate change risk: An adaptation and mitigation agenda for Indian cities. Environment and Urbanization, 20 (1), 207–229.

Rexhepi, A., Filiposka, S., and Trajkovik, V., 2018. Youth e-participation as a pillar of sustainable societies. Journal of Cleaner Production, 174, 114–123.

Routra, J.K., 1993. Urban and regional planning in practice in India. Habitat International, 17 (3), 55–74.

Sahasranaman, A. and Kapur, V., 2014. The practice of PPP in urban infrastructure. In: I.J. Ahluwalia, R. Kanbur, and P.K. Mohanty, eds. *Urbanisation in India: Challenges, opportunities and the way forward*. India: Sage Publications.

Sankhe, S., Vittal, I., Dobbs, R., Mohan, A., and Gulati, A., 2010. *India's urban awakening: Building inclusive cities sustaining economic growth*. Delhi: McKinsey Global Institute.

Schellnhuber, H.J., Hare, W., Serdeczny, O., Adams, S., Coumou, D., Frieler, K., Martin, M., Otto, I.M., Perrette, M., and Robinson, A., 2012. Turn down the heat: Why a 4 C warmer world must be avoided. Washington D.C.: World Bank.

Sekhar, A.R., Varsha, D., Nagrath, K., Rathi, V., Banerjee, B., Saluja, M.S., Arora, R., and Becke, U., 2015. *Resource efficiency in the Indian construction sector: Market evaluation of the use of secondary raw materials from construction and demolition waste*. New Delhi: Deutsche Gesellschaft für Internationale Zusammenarbeit (GIZ) GmbH.

Selvaraj, K., Pandiyan, J., Yoganandan, V., and Agoramoorthy, G., 2016. India contemplates climate change concerns after floods ravaged the coastal city of Chennai. *Ocean and Coastal Management*, 129, 10–14.

Sen, S., 1999. Some aspects of state-NGO relationships in India in the post-independence Era. *Development and Change*, 30(2), 327–355.

Seto, K.C., Güneralp, B., and Hutyra, L.R., 2012. Global forecasts of urban expansion to 2030 and direct impacts on biodiversity and carbon pools. *Proceedings of the National Academy of Sciences*, 109 (40), 16083–16088.

Shaban, A., 2008. Water poverty in urban India: A study of major cities. *Seminar Paper UGC-Summer Programme*.

Sharma, D. and Tomar, S., 2010. Mainstreaming climate change adaptation in Indian cities. *Environment and Urbanization*, 22 (2), 451–465.

Sharma, P. and Rajput, S., eds., 2017. *Sustainable smart cities in India: Challenges and future perspectives*. Cham, Switzerland: Springer.

Shaw, A., 2018. Towards sustainable cities in India. In: J. Mukherjee, ed. *Sustainable urbanization in India*. Cham, Switzerland: Springer, 23–37.

Shoeb, S. and Manishankar, P., 2017. *A study on the usage of ICT for the Smart City Mission, India*. Bangalore: Indian Institute of Management.

Singh, S.K., 2012. Urban transport in India: Issues, challenges, and the way forward. *European Transport* (52), Paper n° 5, ISSN 1825-3997.

Singhal, S., Berry, J., and McGreal, S., 2010. Linking regeneration and business with competitiveness for low carbon cities lessons for India. In: S. Basu, R. Sarkar, and A. Pandey, eds. *India infrastructure report 2010: Infrastructure development in a low carbon economy*. New Delhi: Oxford University Press.

Sivaramakrishnan, K.C., 2013. Revisiting the 74th Constitutional Amendment for better metropolitan governance. *Economic and Political Weekly*, 48 (13), 86–94.

Smart Cities Council India, 2016. Smart cities India readiness guide: The planning manual for building tomorrow's cities today. Mumbai: Smart Cities Council.

Smith, R.M., Pathak, P.A., and Agrawal, G., 2018. India's "smart" cities mission: A preliminary examination into India's newest urban development policy. Journal of Urban Affairs, 41 (4), 518–534.

Srinivasan, R., 2016. Local government in India: past, present, and future perspectives. In: *Comparative Studies and Regionally-Focused Cases Examining Local Governments*. Hershey, PA: IGI Global, 228–258.

Talyan, V., Dahiya, R.P., and Sreekrishnan, T.R., 2008. State of municipal solid waste management in Delhi, the capital of India. *Waste Management*, 28 (7), 1276–1287.

Ullah, A., 2016. Prospects of smart cities development in India through public private partnership. *International Journal of Research in Advent Technology*, 4 (1), 23–32.

UN DESA, 2018a. *World urbanization prospects: The 2018 revision*. New York: United Nations Department of Economic and Social Affairs, Population Division.

UN DESA, 2018b. *The World's cities in 2018—data booklet*. New York: United Nations Department of Economic and Social Affairs.

UNDP, 2018. *India Ranks 130 on 2018 Human Development Index* [online]. Available from: www.in.undp.org/content/india/en/home/sustainable-development/successstories/india-ranks-130-on-2018-human-development-index.html.

Vaidya, C., 2009. *Urban issues, reforms, and way forward in India*. New Delhi: Department of Economic Affairs, Ministry of Finance, No. 4.

Varghese, V. and Adhvaryu, B., 2016. *Measuring overcrowding in Ahmedabad buses: Costs and policy implications*. 11th Transportation Planning and Implementation Methodologies for Developing Countries, TPMDC 2014, 10-12 December 2014. Mumbai: Transportation Research Procedia.

Varma, A. and Singhal, S., 2016. Significance of Cultural Dimensions in Urban Planning Process for Sustainability of Pilgrimage Towns in India. In: A. Goswami and A. Mishra, eds. *Economic Modeling, Analysis, and Policy for Sustainability*. Hershey, PA: IGI Global, 327–350.

2030 Water Resources Group, 2016. *Circular economy pathways for municipal wastewater management in India: A practitioner's guide*. Washington, DC: 2030 Water Resources Group.

WEDC, 2018. *India's Smart Cities Initiative Offers Investment Opportunities* [online]. Available from: https://wedc.org/export/market-intelligence/posts/india-smart-cities-initiative-offers-investment-opportunities/.

Wendling, Z.A., Emerson, J.W., Esty, D.C., Levy, M.A., and de Sherbinin, A., 2018. *2018 environmental performance index*. New Haven, CT: Yale Center for Environmental Law & Policy.

Williams, G., Omankuttan, U., Devika, J., and Aasen, B., 2018. Enacting participatory, gender-sensitive slum redevelopment? Urban governance, power and participation in Trivandrum, Kerala. *Geoforum*, 96, 150–159.

World Economic Forum, 2016. *Reforms to accelerate the development of India's smart cities shaping the future of urban development & services*. Geneva: World Economic Forum.

Zubizarreta, I., Seravalli, A., and Arrizabalaga, S., 2016. Smart City Concept: What It Is and What It Should Be. *Journal of Urban Planning and Development*, 142 (1), 1–8.

Part 3

India within the context of global environmental governance

10 India's climate policy
Paris Agreement, NDC and after

D. Raghunandan

10.1 Introduction

In Chapter 8, Fernandes, Jörgensen and Narayanan provided an overview of India's domestic climate policy over the last three decades, described policy shifts, and drawing on comparative climate politics literature, discussed factors that affected policy change. The present chapter takes a closer look at India's international and domestic climate policies and examines their interplay with the international climate negotiation process. It discusses the outcomes, again in both international and domestic contexts, and the extent to which they matched up to the goals set by India in the respective scenarios and it highlights that the current international ambitions to limit temperature increase to 2°C are grossly insufficient.

The first section examines how India's position in international negotiations took shape, especially in response to global climate politics involving a contestation between developed and developing countries over climate justice and equitable sharing of the atmospheric carbon space between nations. It highlights India's own evolving foreign relations and geo-political interests, a factor not often encountered in the literature. The section also deliberates over the disregard of the serious projected climate impacts India would face (see Box 10.1) as an important driver of India's negotiating stance. In this context, the section also analyses what it views as a paradigm shift in India's negotiating position in the run-up to the Copenhagen Summit in 2009, key elements of this shift and the different factors that brought it about. The important role played by think tanks in India in bringing science and other knowledge to bear on policy options for India is highlighted.

Against this background, the next section looks at the Paris Agreement (PA) and seeks to understand its implications for India. The question of adequacy of pledges made by different countries, especially developed nations, for meeting the global goal of restricting temperature rise to 2°C is discussed, in particular how the forward-looking perspective of the PA that ignores historical emissions constrains developing countries such as India.

A fairly detailed analysis of India's Nationally Determined Contributions (NDC) tabled, as required, before the Paris Summit in 2015 then follows. The policy outputs as regards different quantitative and other commitments made are

BOX 10.1 CLIMATE IMPACTS IN INDIA

Current and expected climate impacts in India have been delineated in India's official Second National Communication to the UNFCCC (NATCOM2) of 2012 and in the rather detailed Reports of the Indian Network on Climate Change Assessments (INCCA) of 2010 prepared by various governmental scientific agencies. Highlights are briefly summarised here.

Global average temperature rise of 1.5°C–2°C is expected in the near to medium term, notwithstanding mitigation measures under the PA which kick in only in 2020. India has already experienced substantial climate impacts and further impacts are expected in the near future.

India is expected to experience rise in average surface temperature of around 1.5°C–2°C by 2030, with higher temperatures in winter and spring, and rise in the minimum temperature. While total quantum of precipitation may not change much, rainfall distribution is expected to vary both spatially and seasonally, with a decrease in the number of rainy days and a substantial rise in the number and intensity of heavy rainfall days. The heaviest rainfall days have happened during 1961–1980 with an alarming rise of intensity during 1980–2009, as also witnessed in the 2018 and 2019 monsoon seasons. Delays in onset and withdrawal of the southwest monsoon have already been observed, and this trend is expected to consolidate. While most Himalayan glaciers are retreating, more in the east than in the west, direct causality cannot be ascribed to climate change alone, and other factors including local pollution may also contribute.

These variations in temperature, rainfall patterns, hydrological systems and related crop behaviour consequent are expected to have a considerable impact on agriculture in which 68% of land vests with small farmers and 60% cropland area is rainfed. Pre-existing vulnerability of agriculture and people dependent upon it will be exacerbated by climate change.

Incidents and intensity of both floods and droughts are expected to increase. Food production is expected to drop by 20–40% by 2050, especially in wheat but also in rice, maize, sorghum and soyabean. Protein content may also drop.

Fish stocks too will display variations in location, even if total volumes may not drop much. Livestock, especially ruminants, are expected to respond negatively to warming, with milk yields expected to decline 1.5% by 2020 and 13.5% by 2050.

These impacts on agriculture are expected to result in a 10–20% drop in farm incomes and a 5% drop in gross domestic product (GDP). Food security, especially of poorer sections of the population, is expected to be severely threatened.

> India will also experience sea-level rise and impacts on habitats and livelihoods of populations in coastal areas stretching over thousands of kilometres. Urban areas are expected to experience severe strain on infrastructure due to extreme weather events. Increase in disease-carrying vectors and their spread to new areas will likely increase the disease burden especially affecting already vulnerable infants, children, the infirm and the elderly.
>
> India effectively pressed the argument of equity between nations, but did so chiefly so as to avoid being subject to counter-pressures on its own emissions, rather than to push for developed countries to take on a higher share of the emissions reduction burden on the grounds of equity. In the words of one commentator, India thus used equity as "a shield … but not as a sword" (Rajamani 2011). On both counts, India's official negotiating stance resulted in missed opportunities and a weaker outcome for itself.

examined, along with some discussion on missed policy options. The section unpacks the different targets delineated so as to appraise the extent to which they address multiple objectives as would be desirable for transformative outcomes, in particular, domestic equity, an issue scarcely encountered in the debate. The section also once again interrogates the apparent lack of attention in the NDC to addressing climate impacts and building climate resilience.

A last brief section also looks at other environment policies of the present government led by the Bharatiya Janata Party (BJP), which came to power in 2014 to replace the earlier coalition government led by the Congress Party, and which was re-elected in 2019 with an even larger mandate than before. The effort here is to understand the development trajectories of the two political formations and examine the differences, if any, made by the respective political–ideological preferences.

10.2 India and the road to Paris

India's positions in the international negotiations have evolved since the Rio conference in 1992, with several phases in between, as discussed by Fernandes, Jörgensen and Narayanan (see Chapter 8, this volume).

During the early period when the United Nations Framework Convention on Climate Change (UNFCCC) was itself being drawn up in the 1990s, the problem was recognised as a global issue with growing understanding based on science. However, while the notion of burden-sharing between countries was slow to take off, India rightly championed the cause for developing nations. These nations were waging a highly unequal battle with developed countries who were geo-politically dominant, well-equipped with scientific data and who were seeking to build a case for placing considerable responsibility for greenhouse gas (GHG) emissions on developing countries (Agarwal and Narain 2012, Dasgupta 2012). India saw this in terms of the global political economy, and as a concerted effort by industrialised countries to advance their own interests. As a country ranking broadly with least developed countries (LDCs) in terms of per capita energy consumption, emissions and most development indicators, India correctly grounded the issue of burden-sharing on equity, which was posed as being based on per capita emissions of each country and on the historical responsibility of developed nations for the problem of climate change, which had mostly been caused by their GHG emissions since the industrial era (ibid.). This perspective led to the emissions control architecture of the Kyoto Protocol (KP) based on common but differentiated responsibility (CBDR). This outlined emission reduction targets for developed countries only, which were obliged to provide financial and technological assistance to developing countries to enable mitigation and adaptation actions.

In this early period, India also played an important role in clarifying scientific issues, for example, by undertaking independent studies and countering efforts to shift the major blame for anthropogenic GHGs away from the fossil fuel-based economic activities and lifestyles of the global North to methane from paddy cultivation and animal husbandry in developing countries (Parashar et al. 1996).

The above approach by India toward the international climate negotiations also framed its policy-making processes as part of its structures and mechanisms for global diplomacy and international relations, largely run within the Indian government by the Ministry of External Affairs.

During the long period following the broad agreement on the KP in 1997 until it was fully fleshed out and ready for ratification in 2005, India did little to formulate new ideas or perspectives for the subjects under discussion. Instead, it established what has been characterised as a defensive posture in international negotiations, warding off perceived threats to equity in the form of efforts to transfer greater share of the burden to developing countries or to deny the financial and technical assistance promised in the KP. These efforts even led India to occasionally adopt positions along with climate-denier countries (Raghunandan 2002) and it sought to shift the emphasis from mitigation to adaptation in order to bring funds to developing countries. A common thread to both these broad phases was India standing alongside other developing countries in opposition to the US and other developed nations (Dasgupta op. cit., Ghosh 2012).

The turn of the new millennium and the release of the Fourth Assessment Report of the Inter-governmental Panel on Climate Change (IPCC) in 2007 coincided with several major developments, both within India and in its external relations with major powers. This saw a paradigm shift in India's international negotiating position on climate change. Along with other developing countries, India's previous stance had been to refuse to undertake any emission reduction commitments. In doing so, it had maintained a strict firewall between developed and developing countries' obligations due to the onus for climate change lying squarely on the former, and it adopted a firm stance against the US and other developed countries, which were seen to be attempting to shift the burden for emission reduction to developing countries and thus impeding their economic progress. During this shift, however, India started seeking common ground with the US and other developed nations. In doing so, it breached the developed–developing firewall and committed itself to emission reductions.

Several factors, both international and domestic, came together to influence this paradigm shift, which much of the academic literature does not adequately reflect.

From the mid-1990s onward, a clutch of large developing countries embraced globalisation and witnessed high economic growth, which prompted substantial changes in the geo-political realm that had already been shaken up by the collapse of the Soviet Union and its allied Eastern European bloc. The spectacular economic growth of China also saw it raise its political influence to dramatic new heights. New alliances and groupings were emerging in the world. This process saw the US and other major developed country powers seek to draw the so-called emerging powers into their orbit on the major geo-political and global economic issues of the day, including the issue of climate change. Led by the US, the G7 grouping of big powers first brought Russia into a G8 and then roped in major developing countries, such as China, India and Brazil into a G8+5 "major economies forum", which gradually morphed into a larger G20 grouping of major developed and developing countries. In these Summits, the US reasserted itself in the global climate debate by pressuring allies and others into supporting its positions, in keeping with the forceful stance of the then George W. Bush administration.

For its part, India, earlier widely perceived to be close to the Soviet Union, was now avidly pursuing a strategic alliance with the US, which soon found concrete expression in a defence agreement and a nuclear deal. Looking to align its positions with those of the US in various international fora, including in relation to climate change, India went along with several new US-led formulations at successive G8+5 Summits, which presaged and acted virtually as first drafts for the new emissions control architecture that was to emerge at climate negotiations summits from Copenhagen to Paris (Raghunandan 2008, 2009, 2009a, 2012, Sengupta 2012). In a signed opinion piece published during the Copenhagen conference, then US Secretary of State Hillary Clinton made clear that the US was working to a plan continuing through the Bush and Obama administrations, and wanted to bring India and China into a single climate treaty framework for all countries. She underlined that success at Copenhagen required that "all major economies, developed and developing, need to take robust action to reduce their carbon emissions" and that the US had taken the lead to bring about such a framework through initiatives such as the "Major Economies Forum… and agreements at the G-20" meets (Clinton 2009).

Scientific findings from the Fourth Assessment Report of the IPCC (IPCC/AR4) and a torrent of other studies following it all conveyed that the tipping point for irreversible climate change was dangerously close and called for urgent and drastic emissions reduction, which were also quantified. These had far-reaching effects on perceptions worldwide, with special implications for India, and also shaped opinion within India.

Island states perceived a real existential threat, while LDCs foresaw grave challenges compounding the developmental problems they already faced. With their recent spurt in growth, large developing countries, including India, found it difficult to continue staying passively behind the Kyoto firewall and came under increased pressure from both developed and developing countries, especially LDCs and island states, to take on substantial emissions reductions. While reorienting its foreign policy toward a strategic partnership with the US, India had not fully grasped the major change in the perspective of Island States, LDCs and other smaller developing countries, who increasingly saw the large developing countries, now sitting at the high table with major, mostly developed world powers as part of the problem, too. India was perhaps worst affected, since China, Brazil, South Africa and Indonesia had already declared their own mitigation targets in the run-up to Copenhagen. India came face-to-face with this change in perception at the Durban Summit in 2013. Having almost single-handedly stalled the Summit for a whole day by resisting that mitigation obligations becoming legally binding, India found itself completely isolated, also from its former developing country allies whose cause it had championed (Raghunandan 2012a). Grenada's lead delegate and spokesperson for the island states, in response to India's plea that it wanted more leeway for development without committing to binding emission controls, lamented that India seemed to be conveying that "while they develop, we die" (Black 2012, cited Raghunandan 2012a).

However, apart from this temporary shift in emphasis at the Durban Summit, possibly prompted by changes in the leadership of India's Ministry of Environment, India's official position had indeed undergone a paradigm shift from Copenhagen onward. This was driven, as argued above, mostly by a realignment of India's foreign policy toward that of the US, but also by a significant shift in public opinion in India. The IPCC/AR4 had, while calling for deep absolute emission cuts by developed countries, also called upon developing countries to "deviate below their projected baseline emissions" (IPCC 2007: 89–90). Some civil society organisations and academics analysed available data on historical and contemporary emissions by different countries and came to the conclusion that whereas India was indeed not historically responsible for the problem of climate change, its position in the world now called for it to be part of the solution; it should offer to slow down its emissions growth trajectory and leverage this position to press for deeper emissions cuts by developed countries (Raghunandan et al. 2007). Breaking from the earlier paradigmatic Indian position from the very beginning of the UNFCCC negotiations, this position soon gathered considerable momentum. On the eve of the Copenhagen Summit, a petition was launched against the Indian government from numerous prominent civil society organisations, experts, scholars and social movements in India (Campaign for progressive climate policy in India 2009). Here, India did indeed shift its stance at Copenhagen and announced that it would reduce its emissions intensity by 20–25% by 2020 compared to then prevalent levels.

We may conclude this section with two additional observations regarding India's negotiating position as it evolved before Copenhagen and thence to Paris.

India may not face the existential threat faced by small island nations due to climate change and consequent sea level rise, but it lies in one of the worst climate-affected regions of the world according to successive IPCC reports and its own National Communications to the UNFCCC (IPCC 2007a: 470–506). Yet, India never really factored in the current and foreseeable impacts of climate change the country would face into its international negotiating position in the way the LDCs or the small island states had consistently done. India did not press developed countries to urgently undertake deep emission cuts so that the severity of climate impacts on India could be reduced. In the process, India lost potentially powerful leverage (Raghunandan 2013).

10.3 The Paris Agreement context

The PA sets the context in which India's emissions reduction commitments and its other domestic climate related actions conveyed in its NDC are to be understood.

The PA was greeted with euphoria in most official circles; many civil society observers and activist groups greeted it as a triumph of perseverance and political will, even while conceding that it was not the best possible outcome. The PA certainly represents a breakthrough in the limited sense that it ties more than 195 nations to some commonly agreed and binding framework for concerted actions to control GHG emissions underlying climate change. It is the broadest recognition backed by governments of the reality of human-induced climate change, not a minor achievement considering the amount of deliberately spread scepticism in major economies, especially in the US, and of the need for a low-carbon pathway to tackle it. The PA thus signals the beginning of the end of business-as-usual development activities based on fossil fuels and affirms that a transition to renewable energy and environmentally sustainable development is now seriously underway.

Yet, this is a limited success and masks fundamental deficiencies, ignoring which will bode ill for what is certain to be an uphill struggle to contain the climate crisis. The reality is that the self-congratulatory and celebratory remarks made by many world leaders and campaign groups are exaggerated and based on a misguided sense of triumphalism.

In the first place, the sum of all the Intended Nationally Determined Contributions (INDCs) pledged fall short of the emissions reductions required to keep temperature rise within 2°C, a pitfall of the very architecture of voluntary commitments adopted since the Copenhagen COP and enshrined in the PA. While the Agreement text itself "notes with concern that ... emission levels ... resulting from the INDCs do not fall within least-cost 2°C scenarios," and stresses the need to address "this significant gap" of close to 15 gigatons (Gt) or billion tons at some later stage (UNFCCC 2015: 2–3) there was no mechanism at the Paris Summit to address this critical shortfall.

This gap could have been closed if the developed countries had taken on the deep emission cuts called for by the IPCC (2007: 90). But the precise problem stems from the refusal by the global North to step up emission cuts and their attempt to shift the burden to developing countries. It is noteworthy that the latter have already committed to substantial voluntary emissions, by some estimations more than those of developed countries.

As seen earlier, this trend of the developed countries, particularly the US, pushing developing countries, especially the large "emerging" economies of China, India and Brazil to take on an increasing share of emission reduction, has been evident ever since the Bali conference and the events leading up to Copenhagen, when the seeds of the present PA framework were sown, ultimately leading to the architecture enshrined in the PA.

Two key features of the PA architecture are germane here, which facilitate the transfer by developed countries of a greater share of the emissions reduction burden on to developing countries, with the rather frightening prospect of even greater transfers in the future.

One, the complete disregard of historical emissions and the adoption of a purely "forward looking" perspective means that the enormous impact of past emissions mostly by the industrialised nations has been ignored. This undercuts the very foundational principle of the UNFCCC based on international law, namely the 'polluter pays', in this case implying that since developed countries have caused most of the problem, they should shoulder the most responsibility for ameliorating it. Two, and even more importantly, since emission levels in most developed countries are flattening out or declining, but developing country emissions are increasing and are likely to do so for some time, development of the latter will be seriously hampered by constraints on economic growth as would be required for cutting emissions.

This becomes clearer with the idea of carbon budgets, which were put forward by several researchers and think tanks around the world and forcefully articulated in the Fifth Assessment Report (AR5) of the IPCC. Put simply, the atmosphere can hold only a finite amount of carbon dioxide if temperature rise is to be limited to under 2°C. IPCC/AR5 estimates that of the roughly 3,000 Gt (billion tons) budget since the industrial era, about 2,000 Gt has already been used up, around 75% having been contributed by the US and other developed countries. The UNFCCC equity principle would require the remaining carbon budget to be fairly apportioned between developed and developing countries taking into account their respective historical emissions but, pushed by the developed countries led by the US, the PA ignores all historical emissions and deals only with the remaining carbon budget.

Going forward, the balance of carbon is only 1,000 Gt, of which 750 Gt would have been used up by the NDCs by 2030, leaving only a small 250 Gt to be shared by around 200 countries, both developed and developing. In effect, this squeezes developing countries, such as India, and severely restricts their ability to overcome their poverty burden and development deficit. Thus, it perpetuates the vast inequality in living standards and per capita energy use between developed and developing countries (Kanitkar 2015).

There have been many claims that the PA is highly ambitious, notably because it aims to keep global average surface temperature rise to "*well below* 2°C above pre-industrial levels and pursuing efforts to limit the temperature increase to *1.5°C*" (italics added). All studies show this is highly unlikely. With a 1.5°C goal, the remaining global budget would be an impossible 500 Gt of CO_2, with roughly

750 Gt *already committed by 2030* as per the present INDCs (ibid.)! The carbon budget metric, so explicitly stated in IPCC/AR5 in order to aid clarity with regard to goals and pathways toward them, seems to have been ignored in the Paris text. However, the tightening numbers will only further increase the pressure on developing countries in the years to come.

10.4 India's NDC

As required, India submitted its INDCs to the UNFCCC before the Paris Summit. These became India's NDC once the Agreement was reached and signed (UNFCCC 2015). While a bland statement indicating its commitment toward a mitigation target would have met the formal requirement, India, like several other countries, took the opportunity to spell out a fairly detailed account of proposed domestic climate actions, mostly relating to mitigation. Rationale for such a submission, as suggested during discussions on the INDCs at different COPs and special expert group meetings, is that this kind of submission provides a good foundation for governments to conceptualise, seek opinion on and plan the more detailed policies and programmes that would be required at a national level.

The headline announcement in India's NDC is that it would reduce its Emissions Intensity of GDP by 33–35% by 2030 compared to 2005 levels. It should be noted that this target has been broadly welcomed across the board in India, with few voices arguing that India has committed more than it should have. This shows the acceptance of the paradigm shift in India's pre-Copenhagen position by most policy actors in India, including by two governments belonging to different political dispensations, which changed from a rejection of mitigation commitments to the post-Copenhagen position that despite not having been historically part of the problem, India was stepping forward to be part of the global effort toward a solution.

India's NDC does not discuss the global scenario of emissions reduction targets relating to the 2°C goal or the more ambitious wishful goal of 1.5°C, particularly the implications for India of the pledges by developed countries and the consequent shrinking of atmospheric carbon space left for India's development needs. The broad discussion of inequity between developed and developing nations leading up to Paris is not adequate to clarify these issues. It would have been useful if India's NDC had laid out a view of these carbon constraints as setting the context for the various sectoral and sub-sectoral targets and programmes contained in the NDC. Such a framing would also have been useful for preparing future UNFCCC discussions on the global stocktake for reviewing the adequacy of mitigation measures by other nations, and taking steps to raise global ambition, during which India and other countries may again be required, one way or another, to spell out their future mitigation commitments.

In itself, India's headline NDC target has been widely deemed to be reasonable, if not particularly ambitious (Climate Tracker 2019). It represents a rough extrapolation from the pre-existing Cancun pledge of reducing the emissions intensity of GDP by 20–25% by 2020, representing a decline of this indicator by a little under 1.5% CAGR (Planning Commission 2014). This is a moderate target considering that the NDC itself states that India's energy intensity showed a decline from 2005 to 2012 by around 2.5% per year (UNFCCC 2015).

The NDC relies on two main policy instruments to realise this headline target. First, the NDC promises an ambitious ramping up of electricity generation capacity from non-fossil fuel sources to reach 40% of total capacity by 2030 which would be several times greater than baseline ratios. The targets set include 175,000 MW of solar and wind energy by 2022, of which 100 GW would be solar, 60 GW wind, 10 GW from biomass and 5 GW from small hydro, apart from conventional hydro and a huge 63,000 MW of nuclear power subject to India being able to obtain requisite nuclear fuel from abroad, given conditionalities of the Nuclear Suppliers Group (UNFCCC 2015).

Space limitations preclude a comprehensive analysis of this and other electricity generation targets of India's NDC, but two specific observations may be made.

This renewable energy (RE) goal, originally announced by the new BJP-led Government in 2015 with a target date of 2019, is a notable and significant increase over the earlier target of 20,000 MW of solar power by 2020 announced in the Solar Mission under the National Action Plan on Climate Change unveiled by the then Congress-led government before the Copenhagen Summit (NAPCC 2009, UNFCCC 2015). There has been considerable debate in India on the RE targets in the NDC. The solar and wind projections initially appeared to be ambitious, especially considering that the installed capacity was around 5.8 GW at the end of the fiscal year 2016 and only 8.6 GW the following year (MNRE 2017). However, the rapid scaling up of solar power thereafter, spurred on by incentives and falling solar panel prices, seems to have belied the early apprehensions and vindicated the level of ambition in the NDC targets.

Assessments of performance of the new targets present a somewhat mixed picture. The early years showed a rapid increase of solar power capacity, mainly due to a sharp drop in solar panel prices worldwide and due to various government initiatives, such as the new auction process. More recently, the growth rate in the uptake of grid-connected solar photovoltaic (SPV) shows clear signs of plateauing out, raising some concerns about India achieving its ambitious target. A Parliamentary report noted that, in order to achieve the 100 GW target by 2022, India should have had an installed capacity of 32,000 MW by 2017–2018 but had achieved only 18,455 MW by early 2018, leaving a requirement of over 20,000 MW annually over the next 4 years, a much higher rate than achieved so far (Lok Sabha 2018).

Problems envisaged even by government bodies are less to do with resource availability, as there appears to be ample solar, wind and micro-hydro potential for many times the installed capacity projected in the NDC, but more to do with grid capability, evacuation and distribution network, investments, transmission and distribution losses, and structural weaknesses of utilities (Niti Aayog 2015). One of the major problems envisaged is likely to be the requirement for high levels of foreign investment since experience suggests that requisite levels of domestic investment are unlikely to fructify. While investment inflows during 2015 and

2016 have been promising, it remains to be seen whether these investment levels can be sustained (IEEFA 2015). Other constraints arise from the capability of the already weak grid to cope with the fluctuations that will inevitably come with high percentages of solar and wind power, and the possible need for large storage systems when a certain threshold is crossed, especially in solar power where large capacities are envisaged.

The NDC does speak of smart grids and the creation of green energy corridors, but there appears to be less action on these fronts than on others. It should be noted that the Solar Mission under the NAPCC, given the co-benefits thrust of this earlier action plan, included several other objectives, such as development of manufacturing capability, research on storage, etc. (NAPCC 2009), all of which have been relegated to the background in the NDC's almost exclusive focus on power generation even through imports if necessary.

Nevertheless, it has been noted that if India does achieve this RE target by 2022 and continues to expand its RE capacity, even if at a slower rate, India may well exceed its NDC emissions intensity target by a fairly wide margin, perhaps taking it to around 41–42% below 2005 levels (Climate Tracker 2019).

Another issue of concern pertains to access to electricity, which remains a big worry in India despite much recent progress in rural electrification (see also Chapter 7 in this volume). It is estimated that at present around one-third of the population, mostly in rural areas, do not receive electricity supply in their homes (UNFCCC 2015, p. 5). Even among those who do, the quality of power supplied and the regularity of supply are notoriously poor (IEA 2015). The NDC does underline the government's policy of "electricity for all" by 2020, but such promises have been *de rigeur* for many successive governments, with end dates being extended repeatedly citing various constraints. The current focus is on the electrification of villages, which could show high rates of penetration, but connectivity to households is still quite poor. Power utilities face considerable difficulty even in providing "lifeline" supply of 1kWhr per household per day (Niti Aayog 2015). It is important to note that an exclusive focus on electricity supply, as in the NDC, without adequate attention to ensuring universal access, especially for rural and poorer segments of the population, will continue to hamper domestic energy equity and quality of life of citizens, especially in rural areas.

A curious, if relatively, minor issue is the large target of 63,000 MW of nuclear power included in the NDC, whereas India has only about 10 GW installed nuclear power at present including projects in the pipeline. It is questionable if such a projection for nuclear energy is realistic, given the high costs, enormous risks, fuel supply constraints and considerable local opposition wherever plants are envisaged. The attempt in the NDC to link the completion of 100% electrification of households to the availability of nuclear fuel from other countries (UNFCCC 2015, p. 10) is a somewhat disingenuous attempt to bring in an official political agenda regarding arrangements involving the Nuclear Suppliers Group for which India has long been lobbying.

The NDC discussion on a push to large hydropower with mention of 100 GW potential is also questionable. Most current scenarios and projections suggest far lower realistic possibilities, with most large hydropower sources outside the North-East having already been tapped, and with high associated physical, social and environmental costs in most sites. Hydel power's share of India's total capacity has come down to just 13% [Press Information Bureau (PIB) 2019] from its one time high of around 50%. The government has recently initiated several measures to revive the hydel sector, even though barely 10,000 MW of hydel power have been added over the past decade due to the above difficulties, including reversal of an earlier decision not to consider large hydel projects above 25 MW as RE.

The second major quantified mitigation target in the NDC is a reiteration of earlier forestry targets, including under the NAPCC's National Mission for a Green India (NAPCC 2008 p. 5) of increasing forest/tree cover to 33% from the 2005 level of 23.4%, along with a specific target of increase area under forest/tree cover by 5 m ha, along with improving the quality of forest/tree cover in another 5 mha (UNFCCC 2015). Together these measures are expected to increase carbon sequestration by 100 million tonnes of CO_2 per year. The NDC also mentions the Green Highways Policy and programme that had earlier and separately been initiated by the government (MORTH 2015) under which trees are to be planted along 140,000 km of highways with a target of sequestering 1.2 million tonnes of carbon (UNFCCC 2015).

The conflating of "tree cover" with "forest cover" (see also Chapter 5 in this volume) and the importance given in the NDC to $6 billion worth of compensatory afforestation for various infrastructure or industrial projects are both problematic assertions, especially in the light of previous and on-going experience in the forestry and plantation sectors.

Experts have long voiced concerns regarding the methodologies for determining forest and tree cover, often resulting in overestimating forest cover (Ravindranath *et al.* 2014). Obviously, such errors in assessing forest cover not only err in estimating carbon sequestration potential, since monoculture forest plantations or plantations outside forests have considerably less potential than natural mixed forests, but they also lead to mistaken assessments of other social and ecological services provided (Dhanapal 2019). Indeed, a recent report of an official expert panel, therefore, recommended distinct and separate methodologies for assessing non-forest green cover (MOEF&CC 2018). This aspect assumes significance in view of notable trends under the BJP-led government, which has jeopardised integrity of forest areas by relaxing earlier restrictions on development activities in forest areas and permitted diversion of forest lands for irrigation, mining, highways, "linear projects" and other infrastructure projects, as discussed further below (Raghunandan 2014). Again, it may be noted that, in contrast with the NDC's almost exclusive focus on carbon sequestration, the NAPCC Green India Mission dealt not only with carbon sequestration, but also with biodiversity, ecological services, and social and livelihood benefits for forest dwellers, etc. (MORTH 2015), whereas the NDC is almost exclusively concerned with carbon sequestration.

There are many other measures included in the NDCs but with few or minor quantitative deliverables. A few notes on some of these follow.

Transport is the second highest sector in terms of total emissions in India (MOEF 2012 NATCOM2, p. viii). Road transport comprises 87% of these emissions which are rising fast with rapid increase in numbers of vehicles on the road (INCCA 2010: 14–15). Clearly, substantial efforts are required to tackle these emissions and the NDC devotes considerable attention to some proposals. An integrated view of the transport sector as a whole, with a holistic perspective on mitigation measures and co-benefits, would have been useful, but the NDC contains only several disjointed suggestions.

An inter-modal shift from road to rail is envisaged, amounting to an increase of rail share in transportation from 36 to 45%, presumably till 2030 (UNFCCC 2015a, p. 14). While no break-up between passenger and freight shares is specified, an implicit emphasis on freight transportation may be assumed since the NDC specifically discussed the two dedicated rail-based freight corridors under construction connecting the four major metropolitan cities and areas of industrial concentration in the north, west and east of the country. These freight corridors are expected to reduce emissions by 457 million tonnes of CO_2 over 30 years (UNFCCC 2015a, p. 14). However, there is little discussion of any inter-modal shift of passenger movement from road to rail which would also have assisted in reducing emissions while also providing better long-distance transportation for poorer passengers.

The only mention of mass public transportation is, in fact, with reference to metro rail projects which are expected to come up only in a few metropolitan or large cities. There are also no proposals regarding public bus or surface rail transport systems in major towns and cities. Such measures for mass public transportation could have had major mitigation benefits through avoidance of personal vehicle use, and could also have reduced the prevalent sharp inequity in access to transportation, with share of buses in total vehicles having come down from around 11% in 1951 to around 1% in 2011, with the rate of decline being the fastest in the last decade of this period (Planning Commission 2014, p. 6). There are also no measures pertaining to the rapidly rising emissions from domestic aviation, with estimated growth double digit growth rates for many years and 15–20% annual growth over the past 3–4 years (IATA 2018, p. 1), and virtually no policy directions to enable prioritisation of different transportation modes, routes and infrastructure.

The sub-section on biofuels essentially repeats an earlier "aspirational" target goal of 20% blending of both bioethanol and biodiesel with gasoline and diesel, respectively (UNFCCC 2015b, p. 18). In India, bioethanol based on sugarcane faces major constraints of raw material availability due to a marginal gap between domestic demand and production of sugar, shortage of land and water resources for cultivation of additional sugar cane, and competing demands on the finite amount of cane juice or molasses from the sugar, potable alcohol and industrial alcohol industries. India has therefore struggled to reach even the present 2% bioethanol and 1% biodiesel blending in 2018. The caution of the Food and Agriculture Organisation (FAO) against use of land for fuel rather than food is also germane (FAO, 2008).

Similarly, biodiesel based on *jatropha* also poses competitive demand for land, and experience has belied the earlier assumed promise of good oilseed yields even from non-irrigated degraded lands, sharply raising the cost of biodiesel and the suppositions about ease of availability. The use of degraded lands often on the outskirts of forests has seen opposition from local tribal and forest-dwelling communities over the competitive use of land resources for fuelwood, medicinal plants and other usufructs. Once again, while the projected mitigation benefits have been privileged, the possible disadvantages regarding the impact on the food basket, the competitive uses of resources especially by the poor, costs and other local environmental factors do not appear to have been taken into account (Raghunandan 2013, Dubash et al. 2013). It is not surprising therefore that the National Biofuels Policy 2018 has revised the biodiesel target down from the NDC goal of 20% to 5% (Ministry of Petroleum & Natural Gas, 2018).

It is also a pity that the introduction of new technologies for reducing energy consumption for cooling residential buildings has not been tackled in the NDC. Although India has already embarked on a graded approach to introduce energy-saving materials and techniques to large commercial and office buildings, residential buildings have not been considered, perhaps under a mistaken notion that this will have a negative impact on the real estate sector and economic growth. With rapid urbanisation in India and contemporary rural housing leaving much to be desired, a sizeable percentage of the necessary housing stock is still to be built (IDFC 2018). If this opportunity is missed, then as the Council for Energy Environment and Water (CEEW) states, India may lock-in huge amounts of carbon for the foreseeable future, which is a matter of concern considering also the rapid expansion of air conditioning in the country at annual rates of around 20% in the past decade (CEEW et al. 2013).

The NDC is supposed to incorporate all other climate-related programmes adopted by the government, so a detailed discussion of these is not undertaken here. However, since some on-going programmes are quite major initiatives, a brief examination of current status of some of these may be useful here.

In the run-up to Copenhagen, possibly as an indicator of India's seriousness with respect to its emission reduction pledges and also not wanting to be seen to be lagging behind China, which had declared a similar initiative, India announced a National Action Plan on Climate Change (NAPCC) with eight Missions under it (NAPCC op. cit.). Most of the Missions on solar power, energy efficiency and carbon sequestration in forests deal with mitigation. The Missions on sustainable agriculture, water, sustainable habitat and Himalayan ecosystems are primarily oriented to adaptation, while the others deal with knowledge generation and capacity building.

Although the Missions themselves were announced in 2009, there was a considerable lack of clarity especially as regards implementation; for many of them, the allocation of funds and institutional mechanisms were only set in place around 2013 (Rattani 2018). The then Congress-led government completed its term in 2014, having made little progress, and the new BJP-led government took over with somewhat different priorities as regards environment and climate change. It should not be a surprise that the Missions have somewhat languished since then, with poor progress visible in most Missions (ibid.).

One indicator of the low priority accorded to these climate Missions is the funds allocated to them under successive Central Government budgets. In some cases, there seems to have been an implicit assumption that concerned government Ministries would cover much of the costs using their own funds, such as in urban development, agriculture and perhaps water as well. The Mission on Sustainable Habitat in fact did not seek any special funds and has not earmarked any funds of its own (ibid.), so Mission activities if any are subsumed under mainstream urban development programmes such as on solid waste disposal. In the National Water Mission, a sector of serious anticipated climate impacts, against a budget of Rs. 200 billion initially proposed in 2007, only Rs. 150 billion was approved in the 12th Five-Year Plan period of 2012–2017, but actual allocations were only Rs. 3.5 billion during 2012–2015 of which only Rs. 21.6 million was spent till 2015 (ibid.). This pattern of low allocations and even lower spending is visible in most other Missions as well (Lok Sabha 2018).

The knowledge Mission has thrown up a substantial body of research projects in universities and research institutions, but these appear to be somewhat disparate and without a clear sense of direction or purpose (Rattani 2018). In agriculture too, where major impacts are anticipated, the Mission has so far consisted of a few research and pilot projects, with achievements mainly shown in terms of fund utilisation of 40–50% of allocation as reflected in its website (NMSA), but there is little evidence on the ground in terms of research output, new packages of practices, new climate-resilient cultivars etc. By and large, therefore, the evidence points to a marked dwindling of government interest in the NAPCC Missions and, where there is interest, there remains an absence or shortage of climate-specific programmes.

A set of State Action Plans on Climate Change (SAPCC) have also been formulated, with multilateral and bilateral international agencies playing important roles in assisting the States with this exercise. The SAPCCs were, however, characterised by considerable confusion as to whether their main focus should be on mitigation or adaptation and as regards funding for any programmes undertaken. Although no comprehensive review has been carried out, important research suggests that the SAPCCs, rather than being concrete programmes of climate-specific action, are best regarded as the beginning of a more systematic examination of potential state-level programmes, particularly as regards adaptation (Dubash and Jogesh 2014).

Two other recent significant initiatives will be worth watching in the years to come. The Government has initiated a programme to promote electric vehicles, under which various incentives and promotional schemes have been enumerated (Department of Heavy Industry 2019). While the government has periodically announced various targets for the percentage of electric vehicles on India's roads, these have been modified several times due to the current headwinds being faced by the automobile industry. Second, the government's Ujjwala Scheme aims to deliver liquified petroleum gas to rural households in cylinders, just as they have been available to urban consumers for a long time. While this will undoubtedly push up emissions, it will also promote the adoption of modern energy for cooking in rural areas and vastly improve quality of life.

10.5 Recent trends in environment regulation

The above brief review of various domestic actions related to climate change testifies to the hypothesis advanced at the outset of this chapter that India's climate policy has been focused mainly on international negotiations and has mostly been driven by foreign relations concerns. It has been noted that India's negotiating stance has largely disregarded the substantial climate impacts India and its neighbourhood are expected to experience. It has also been seen that this marginalisation of domestic climate concerns manifests in a benign neglect of actions to ameliorate these climate impacts and build climate resilience in different aspects of the economy.

Perhaps the relatively low priority given to tackling climate impacts is not a surprise when one considers recent trends in environment regulation, particularly since the advent of the BJP-led government in 2014 and its re-election with an even larger mandate in 2019. It should be made clear that the dilution of environment regulations was also pursued by the previous Congress-led government in the pursuit of economic growth, but there were countervailing trends within the government itself that acted to maintain environment protection. Nevertheless, although this is not directly related to the subject of climate change, a very brief discussion of recent trends in environment regulation may assist in throwing some light on what has been described as the "development-first" perspective of the present governing dispensation, and also point to a prevailing government attitude on domestic aspects of climate change (see Chapter 8, Fernandes, Jörgensen and Narayanan, this volume).

An early clue to the viewpoint of the BJP, which evidently saw environment regulations as obstructions to economic development, both in terms of content and procedural delays to development projects, lay in their election manifesto for the 2014 elections to the Lok Sabha. This proclaimed that, while a BJP government would put "sustainability at the centre of our thoughts and actions," it would "frame the environment laws in a manner that provides no scope for confusion and will lead to speedy clearance of proposals without delay" (BJP Election Manifesto 2014).

The new government took early steps to implement this vision by seeking changes in concerned legislation as well as through administrative actions. A Committee was appointed to review and rationalize all environmental laws and, although its controversial report (MOEF 2014) was rejected by a Parliamentary Committee, many of its recommendations were introduced into processes and procedures, such that project approvals became routine, and proposal scrutiny and review became rare exceptions. Clearances were rapidly given to hundreds of industrial and mining projects, which invoked new project appraisal guidelines, including inside forests and wildlife conservation areas with barely any due diligence, and by reconstituted environment clearance committees (CSE 2016, Raghunandan 2014). Committees to consider environment appraisals were constituted with hand-picked members, few experts and virtually no non-governmental representatives. Even the Supreme Court had to intervene in one instance and order proper constitution of the National Board for Wildlife (The Hindu 2014).

Since questions about procedures can always be parried on the grounds of subjectivity or exercise of discretionary powers, a few specific executive actions or notifications may be discussed briefly.

Environmental regulations relating to large construction projects were sought to be eased so as to facilitate the real estate business. A Notification by the Ministry of Environment and Forests & Climate Change in December 2016 allowed construction projects of under 50,000 m^2 area to self-certify environmental compliance and for local authorities to permit construction based on this, rather than await scrutiny of state environment assessment bodies (PIB 2016). The new procedure was struck down by the National Green Tribunal (NGT) in November 2017 on the grounds that environmental impact had not been taken into account. Two further attempts were made in November 2018 to pass similar rules but were again struck down this time by the Delhi High Court (Huffington Post 2019).

Another example is the amendments notified in 2018 to the Coastal Regulatory Zones (CRZ) which regulate various construction, infrastructure and other such commercial or industrial activities along India's long coastline. The original CRZ Notification of 2011 had unfortunately already been amended 11 times, diluting its provisions considerably. The government's latest notification reduces the "No Development Zone" from 100 m for highly populated areas and 200 m for less densely populated areas to a mere 50 m for all categories of activities, including those for which special studies were recommended. The notification also shifts decision-making powers for coastal waters, inter-tidal regions and ecologically sensitive regions from the States to the Centre, and also set up a special body at the Centre to delineate high tide and low tide lines, reversing a trend to shift such powers from the Centre to the States (PIB 2018).

10.6 Conclusions

As seen in this chapter, the architecture of the global emissions control regime now enshrined in the PA represents a major departure from the architecture of the KKP. The PA is now concerned only with future emissions and completely ignores historical emissions with their in-built causality of the climate crisis by the industrialised countries of the global North. The PA also calls only for voluntary emission reduction pledges by all countries, leaving considerable uncertainty about outcomes, particularly adequacy to meet the agreed 2°C goal. As many anticipated after the Paris Summit, this has precipitated a "race to the bottom," with one country after another lowering its emissions reduction commitments, led by the US which under President trump simply walked out of PA altogether. Australia, Japan and Canada have significantly rolled back earlier pledges and even the EU pledges are considerable lower than once promised.

India, too, shifted from its traditional position, where it had championed the cause for developing countries and placed responsibility for the problem, and hence for the solution, on the shoulders of developed countries. India has committed to its own emission reduction pledge in its NDC, generously proclaiming, as many in India wanted it to, that India wants to contribute to the solution despite not having caused this global problem. However, it did so in order to be a member of the "big boys' club" along with the major global powers, and without leveraging its commitment to extract the required higher emission reductions by developed countries. Instead, India used its new position only as a hedge against further developed country pressure, in that sense continuing with its earlier defensive posture despite the paradigm shift in its own position. An iniquitous system thus prevails under the PA, wherein powerful developed countries, especially the US, perpetuate their dominance over the global atmospheric carbon space, with tacit if apprehensive support of large developing nations such as India for the sake of their own slice of the cake.

Given this reading of India's negotiating position and strategy, these are unlikely to change in the coming years, despite the rapid escalation of the climate crisis. The overall global situation too is unlikely to change much, although there may be some minor upward revisions in pledges after the global stocktake in 2023 of efforts under the PA. Going by their record, and by the motivations of the major global and regional powers both developed and developing, neither is likely to be interested in upsetting the prevailing modus vivendi built around voluntary commitments. Unfortunately, this may result in the inexorable movement towards 2°C global average temperature rise or more.

This worsening climate crisis would lead to intensification of impacts across the world as already witnessed, such as heat waves, increased frequency and intensity of cyclones and storms, rising sea levels. Although all countries will be affected, the vulnerable around the world will suffer the most. It seems almost incredible that governments are not more concerned. This applies to India as well which, as this chapter has shown, is among the most vulnerable regions in the world but where this vulnerability has not been among the drivers of its negotiating position, and where adaptation and building climate resilience do not figure among national priorities either in India's NDC or in other development programmes. One can only hope that this will change in the years to come, although current policy trends do not provide grounds for optimism.

Ever since India embarked in the mid-1990s on the path of economic liberalisation and globalisation, it has increasingly adopted the *mantras* of privatisation and de-regulation. Environmental regulation has been a major casualty, with the exception of rare periods and instances. The present government appears determined to press on in the same vein putting economic growth first. It has a commanding majority in Parliament and, with its allies in most States, and has demonstrated its willingness to push through its agenda through legislation where possible and executive action where necessary. While it is likely to ensure that India meets its moderate NDC obligations under the PA, conditions in the local environment are likely to worsen, with adverse impact on livelihoods and well-being of vulnerable populations, and on sustainability.

We have seen in this chapter that some think tanks, civil society organisations and academics in India have developed considerable capability to study, understand and arrive at policy recommendations in important areas of climate change and related social, technological and economic sectors. This rich capability and a desire to make positive contributions to the policy environment in the country have served India well, often making up for a shortage of comparable capabilities within the government. However, the ability to influence policy choices has always been subject to the willingness of the government and its agencies to be receptive to ideas and voices from outside. Current trends do not lead to much optimism on this count, and time will tell if this situation changes.

References

Agarwal, A. and Narain, S. 2012. "Global warming in an unequal world: a case of environmental colonialism (selected excerpts)." In: N.K. Dubash (Ed.) "Handbook of climate change and India," New Delhi, Oxford University Press, 81–88. Originally published by Centre for Science and Environment, New Delhi, 1991.

Bharatiya Janata Party. (2014). "Election manifesto," (online) www.bjp.org/en/manifesto?archives=1

Black, R. 2012. "Climate change talks end with late deal," 11 December 2011, BBC, www.bbc.co.uk/news/science-environment-16124670

Dasgupta C. 2012. "Present at the creation: the making of the UN Framework Convention on climate change." In: N.K. Dubash (Ed.) "Handbook of climate change and India," New Delhi, Oxford University Press, 89–98.

Department of Heavy Industry, Govt of India 2019. "Notification: scheme for faster adoption and manufacturing of electric vehicles in India Phase-II," 8 March 2019 (online) https://dhi.nic.in/writereaddata/UploadFile/publicationNotificationFAME%20II%208March2019.pdf

Campaign for Progressive Climate Action and Policy (2009). "India's position on climate change: statement submitted to PM," (online) http://progressiveclimatepolicycampaign-ind.blogspot.in, accessed 28 August 2019.

Centre for Science & Environment (CSE) 2016. "Environmental governance: two years of NDA," (online) www.indiaenvironmentportal.org.in/files/file/nda_env-governance-20160614.pdf, accessed 28 August 2019.

Climate Tracker (updated June 2019), (online) https://climateactiontracker.org/countries/india/, accessed 29 August 2019.

Clinton H.R. 2009. "The US is on board," International Herald Tribune, 15 December 2009. (online) www.nytimes.com/2009/12/15/opinion/15iht-edclinton.html?_r=0 accessed 24 June 2013.

Council for Energy Environment & Water (CEEW) et al. 2013. "Cooling India without warming," Issue Paper June 2013 (online) www.ceew.in/sites/all/themes/ceew/images/CEEW-IGSD-NRDC-TERI-Cooling-India-With-Less-Warming-Jun13.pdf

Dhanapal 2019. "Correspondence," Current Science, Vol. 116, No. 2, 25 January 2019 (online) www.currentscience.ac.in/Volumes/116/02/0158.pdf

Dubash N.D., Jogesh A. 2014. "From margins to mainstream? State climate change planning in India," Economic & Political Weekly, Nov. 29, Vol. xlix, No. 48.

Dubash N.D. et al. 2013. "Indian climate change policy: exploring a co-benefits based approach," Economic & Political Weekly, June 1, 2013.

Food & Agriculture Organization 2008. "State of food & agriculture," (online) www.fao.org/tempref/docrep/fao/011/i0100e/i0290e.pdf, accessed 30 August 2019.

Ghosh P. 2012. "Climate change debate: the rationale of India's position." In: N.K. Dubash (ed.) "Handbook of climate change and India," New Delhi, Oxford University Press, 157–169.

Huffington Post 2019. Deshmane A., "Documents reveal Javadekar and Modi's war on India's environment," 25 March 2019 (online) www.huffingtonpost.in/entry/documents-reveal-modi-and-javadekars-war-on-indias-environment_in_5c97cba3e4b0a6329e180367, accessed 30 August 2019.

IDFC Institute 2018. "India Infrastructure Report 2018: making housing affordable," Mumbai, June 2018 (online) http://idfcinstitute.org/site/assets/files/14428/idfc_institute_housing_report.pdf, accessed 30 August 2019.

IEA 2015. International Energy Agency, World Energy Outlook, Electricity Access Database, 2015.

IEEFA 2015. "Report of institute for energy economics and financial analysis," (online) http://ieefa.org/wp-content/uploads/2015/08/IEEFA-Indian-Electricity-Sector-Transformation-11-August-2015.pdf

INCCA 2010. "Indian National Climate Change Assessment, Ministry for Environment and Forests," pp. 14–15. (online) www.indiaenvironmentportal.org.in/files/fin-rpt-incca.pdf

International Air Transport Association (IATA) 2018. "India's air transport sector," (online) www.iata.org/publications/economics/Reports/India-aviation-summit-Aug18.pdf

IPCC 2007. "Mitigation of Climate Change": Contribution of Working Group III to the Fourth Assessment Report of the Intergovernmental Panel on Climate Change. In: B. Metz, O.R. Davidson, P.R. Bosch, R. Dave & L.A. Meyer (Eds) Cambridge University Press, Cambridge and New York, NY.

IPCC 2007a. "Impacts, adaptation and vulnerability": Contribution of Working Group II to the Fourth Assessment Report of the Intergovernmental Panel on Climate Change, 2007. In: M.L. Parry, O.F. Canziani, J.P. Palutikof, P.J. van der Linden and C.E. Hanson (Eds) Cambridge University Press, Cambridge and New York, NY.

Kanitkar T. 2015. "What should the climate goal be, 1.5°C or 2°C," Review of Agrarian Studies, Vol. 5, No. 2, July–Dec 2015 (online) http://ras.org.in/what_should_the_climate_goal_be, accessed 29 August 2019.

Lok Sabha 2018. 39th Report, Standing Committee on Energy, Ministry of New & Renewable Energy (2017–18), Lok Sabha Secretariat 2018 (online) http://164.100.47.193/lsscommittee/Energy/16_Energy_39.pdf

Ministry of Petroleum & Natural Gas 2018. "Gazette notification, National Policy on biofuels 2018," 4 June 2018 (online) http://petroleum.nic.in/sites/default/files/biofuelpolicy2018_1.pdf, accessed 30 August 2019.

MNRE. 2017. Ministry of New & Renewable Energy, "Commissioning Status of Grid Connected Solar Projects as on 31-10-2017," (online) http://mnre.gov.in/file-manager/UserFiles/grid-connected-solar-power-project-installed-capacity.pdf

MOEF 2012. "India's Second National communication to UNFCCC," or NATCOM2, Ministry for Environment & Forests, 2012 (online) https://UNFCCC.int/resource/docs/natc/indnc2.pdf, accessed 29 August 2019.

MOEF. 2014. "Report of High level Committee to review various Acts administered by MoEF," Ministry for Environment & Forests, November 2014 (online) www.naredco.in/notification/pdfs/Final_Report_of_HLC.pdf

MOEF&CC 2018. "Report of Expert Committee on strategy for increasing green cover outside recorded forest areas," (online) http://moef.gov.in/wp-content/uploads/2019/04/EXPERT-COMMITTEE-REPORT-ON-TOF-18112018_0.pdf

MORTH (Ministry of Road Transport & Highways), Green India Policy 2015 (online) www.morth.gov.in/sites/default/files/Green%20Highways%20Policy.pdf

National Action Plan on Climate Change (NAPCC) 2008. (online) https://archive.india.gov.in/innerwin20.php?id=15651, accessed 30 August 2019.

National Action Plan on Climate Change 2009. National Solar Mission under the NAPCC, Government of India, 2009 (online) http://pmindia.gov.in/climate_change_english.pdf

NITI Aayog 2015. "Report of the Expert Group on 175 GW RE by 2022," December 2015 (online) http://niti.gov.in/writereaddata/files/writereaddata/files/document_publication/report-175-GW-RE.pdf

NMSA 2019. National Mission on Sustainable Agriculture (website) (online). https://nmsa.dac.gov.in/RptActivityAchievement.aspx

Parashar, D.C. et al. 1996. "Methane Budget from Paddy Fields in India", Chemosphere, 33(4): 737–757.

Press Information Bureau (PIB) 2016. "Amendment in EIA Notification, 2006 on integration of environmental conditions with building permissions," Press Information Bureau, Govt of India, 16 December 2016 (online) https://pib.gov.in/newsite/PrintRelease.aspx?relid=155550

PIB 2018. "Cabinet approves Coastal Regulation Zone (CRZ) notification 2018," Press Information Bureau, Govt of India, 28 December 2018 (online) https://pib.gov.in/newsite/PrintRelease.aspx?relid=186875, accessed 29 August 2019.

PIB 2019. "Cabinet approves measures to promote hydro-power sector," Press Information Bureau, Government of India, 7 March 2019 (online) https://pib.gov.in/PressReleaseIframePage.aspx?PRID=1567817, accessed 30 August 2019.

Planning Commission 2014. "Final Report of Expert Group on low carbon inclusive growth," April 2014, New Delhi (online) http://planningcommission.nic.in/reports/genrep/rep_carbon2005.pdf

Raghunandan D. 2002. "Flop-8: Climate Conference in Delhi," (online) https://delhiscienceforum.net/flop-8-climate-conference-in-delhi-by-raghu/, accessed 10 June 2019.

Raghunandan D. 2008. "G8+5: numbers don't add up for climate change," (online) https://delhiscienceforum.net/g85-numbers-dont-add-up-for-climate-change/, accessed 28 August 2019.

Raghunandan D. 2009. "Hokkaido G8 summit and climate change," (online) https://delhiscienceforum.net/hokkaido-g8-summit-a-climate-changeg8-o5-mem16-0/

Raghunandan D. 2009a. "G8 Climate Declaration: cart before the horse," (online) https://delhiscienceforum.net/g85-numbers-dont-add-up-for-climate-change/

Raghunandan D. 2012. "India's official position: a critical view based on science." In: N.D. Dubash (Ed.), op. cit., 170–179.

Raghunandan D. 2012a. "India's climate policy: squaring the circle," IDS Bulletin, 8 July 2012

Raghunandan D. 2013. "Rethinking India's policy and the global negotiations," Oxfam India, New Delhi (online) www.oxfamindia.org/sites/default/files/Raghu%27s%20paper.pdf, accessed 29 August 2019.

Raghunandan D. 2014. "Ministry against environment and forests?" (online) https://delhiscienceforum.net/ministry-against-environment-a-forests/, accessed 20 August 2019.

Raghunandan D. et al. 2007. "Climate crisis: challenges and options," All-India Peoples Science Network & Tata Institute of Social Sciences, Delhi.

Rajamani L. 2011. "Deconstructing Durban," Indian Express, New Delhi, 15 December 2011.

Rattani V. 2018. "Coping with climate change: An analysis of India's National Action Plan on climate change," Centre for Science and Environment, New Delhi.

Ravindranath N.H. 2014. "Forest area estimation and reporting: implications for conservation, management and REDD+," Current Science, Vol. 106, No. 9, 10 May 2014.

Sengupta S. 2012. "International climate negotiations and India's role." In: S.K. Dubash (ed.) op. cit., 101–117.

The Hindu 2014. Meena Menon, "National Board for Wildlife reconstituted," The Hindu, New Delhi, 14 September 2014 (online) www.thehindu.com/sci-tech/energy-and-environment/national-board-for-wildlife-reconstituted/article6410349.ece, accessed 30 August 2019.

UNFCCC 2015a. "Adoption of the Paris Agreement," FCCC/CP/2015/L.9/Rev1 (online) https://UNFCCC.int/resource/docs/2015/cop21/eng/l09r01.pdf

UNFCCC 2015b. "India INDC to UNFCCC" (online) www4.UNFCCC.int/sites/submissions/INDC/Published%20Documents/India/1/INDIA%20INDC%20TO%20UNFCCC.pdf

11 India's relations with the European Union on environmental policy

Diarmuid Torney

11.1 Introduction

India and the European Union (EU) have had a long-standing diplomatic relationship. Indeed, India was one of the first countries to establish diplomatic relations with the then European Economic Community (EEC) in 1963. Over the period since the mid-2000s, environmental issues, including climate change, have occupied a growing place on the agenda of this bilateral relationship, including joint declarations on climate change and related themes issued at the India–EU summits of 2005, 2008, 2016 and 2017.

In recent decades, the EU sought to make environment and climate change an increasingly central part of its external relations. Indeed, as far back as 1990, European leaders identified climate change as an area around which the EU could develop a distinctive presence in the world (European Council 1990, see also Torney 2015, chapter 3). Since the mid-2000s in particular, the EU sought to develop and strengthen relations with other major players on environmental issues and, particularly, climate change. As part of a broader strategy of bilateral outreach to so-called "major emitters" of greenhouse gases (GHGs), the EU sought to develop dialogue and cooperation with the Indian government. This occurred in a context of growing concern globally over the rising contribution of emerging powers to global environmental degradation, particularly from the mid-2000s onwards (see, e.g., International Energy Agency 2004, 2007).

Scholars, policy analysts and practitioners have identified various areas of environment, climate and energy policy where India and the EU could fruitfully collaborate (see, e.g., Action for a Global Climate Community 2009, Sinha 2012, Upadhyay 2012). Their bilateral relationship has, however, to a large extent failed to deliver. This chapter traces the development of India–EU cooperation on environment and climate.

The chapter argues that cooperation between India and the EU on environment and climate has been constrained by a problematic development of the broader India–EU relationship, which was characterised by significant tensions and conflicting priorities on a range of issues. It also argues that conflicting climate and environmental policy paradigms between India and the EU constrained fruitful cooperation. However, recent years have seen a gradual convergence of policy paradigms. It is too early to judge the impact of this convergence, but indications from the 2016 and 2017 India–EU summits suggest a more fruitful era of cooperation may be underway.

India–EU relations on environmental issues have an important multilevel dimension (Jörgensen and Wagner 2017). On the Indian side, states play an important role in environmental policymaking alongside the Union government (see Chapters 3, Jörgensen, and 4, Ganguly, this volume). On the EU side, not only the EU (through the EU Delegation in India) but also its member states play important roles. Indeed, those EU member states with a larger and better-resourced presence in India, such as Germany, France and the UK, have often been more effective in their engagement with India on environmental policy (Torney 2015, chapter 6). This, in turn, raises the question of the impact of the UK's decision to leave the EU on the future of India–EU relations on climate and environment, and also more generally. However, due to space constraints, this chapter focuses specifically on EU-level engagement with the Union Government of India.

This chapter is structured as follows. The next section identifies how the respective policy paradigms of India and the EU differ with respect to climate change and environmental policy. The following section then sets this in the context of the broader India–EU relationship, arguing that it has acted as a further constraint on the potential for India–EU cooperation in this area. This sets the scene for a subsequent discussion of the development of India–EU relations on environment and climate change over time.

11.2 Indian and European environmental policy paradigms

Indian and European approaches to environmental politics have, historically, frequently been characterised by significantly divergent policy paradigms. Nowhere has this been more clearly evident than in the case of international climate change policy. In this respect, one controversial issue in international negotiations concerns the extent to which policies and actions should focus on climate change mitigation or adaptation. Historically, the UN climate negotiations have focused more on mitigation than adaptation, partly out of fear that an emphasis on adaptation would lessen the urgency attached to mitigation. Indeed, according to Pielke, adaptation was a "taboo" subject in the early years of the negotiations (Pielke, 1998). This balance has shifted over the past decade.[1] India argued strongly for greater priority to be devoted to adaptation, which was particularly evident at COP-8 in New Delhi in 2002. However, some of the most significant divergences between the EU and India relate to the issues of equity and differentiation.

11.2.1 The European policy paradigm

The EU has generally supported the principle of "common but differentiated responsibilities" set out in the United Nations Framework Convention on Climate Change (UNFCCC) of 1992, but has argued that the differentiation between

Annex I (industrialised) and non-Annex I (developing) countries should evolve over time. Over much of the period since the first negotiations on climate change in the early 1990s, the EU generally took the view that industrialised countries should undertake domestic GHG gas emissions reductions. From the start, the European interpretation differentiation involved strong action by developed countries to reduce their emissions in the short term, along with commitments on the part of developing countries once their emissions and economic development reached a certain level. In other words, the European position supported the concept of evolution of the responsibilities of non-Annex I countries, under certain conditions. The EU sought to bring up the question of developing country participation as early as 1995, but this was strongly resisted by India, China and other developing countries.

Around 2005, the EU became increasingly concerned with the growth of emissions from large developing countries, driven partly by broader international concern with the projected contribution of the developing world to future emissions growth (see, e.g., International Energy Agency 2004, 2007). This was reflected in the European Commission's January 2005 communication, *Winning the Battle Against Climate Change* which flagged "broadening international participation" – including large developing countries – as a key EU goal for the international climate negotiations. It argued that

> [t]he importance of broadening international participation in efforts to tackle climate change cannot be overestimated. In the coming decades, the share of EU-25 emissions in world greenhouse gas emissions is expected to decline to less than 10%, while those of developing countries will expand to more than half of the total.
>
> (European Commission 2005, p. 4)

The March 2007 European Council, which agreed the EU's headline climate and energy targets for 2020, highlighted the increasing share of global emissions from developing countries and "the need for these countries to address the increase in these emissions by reducing the emission intensity of their economic development, in line with the general principle of common but differentiated responsibilities and respective capabilities" (European Council 2007, p. 13). In October 2008, the Environment Council called on developing countries, "in particular the most advanced among them", to "reduce their emissions by 15 to 30% below business as usual" (Council of the European Union 2008, p. 6). From that point on, the EU position remained that developing countries should be required to shoulder some of the burden of climate mitigation. Increasingly, the EU pushed for universal coverage – including developing countries – of a binding global climate agreement. The Copenhagen Accord of 2009 did not fulfil the EU's desires in this regard due to its non-binding character. In the negotiations that led to the Paris Agreement in 2015, the EU once again pushed for a legally binding global agreement with universal applicability, that is, that would cover both developed and developing countries.

Differing perspectives on responsibility and differentiation have been underpinned, in turn, by different ways of accounting for global GHG emissions. This is due to the fact that the distribution of shares of cumulative historical emissions between countries and regions contrasts markedly with the distribution of shares of current emissions. While the 28 member states of the EU accounted for 23.5% of cumulative total CO_2 emissions (excluding land-use change and forestry) from 1850 to 2014, they accounted for just 9.4% of total emissions in 2014 (World Resources Institute, 2017). The EU has tended to favour the status quo emissions accounting rules, which focus on aggregate emissions at the national level, current day rather than accumulated historical emissions, and emissions associated with production rather than consumption. Furthermore, the base year for emissions limitation targets under the Kyoto Protocol – 1990 – is very favourable to EU emissions levels, since EU emissions declined significantly over the course of the 1990s for reasons that had little or nothing to do with climate change policy.[2]

11.2.2 The Indian policy paradigm

As discussed by Raghunandan (see Chapter 10, this volume), global environmental politics – and particularly climate change – have traditionally been viewed by the Indian Government through a North–South lens. India's approach to climate change – and to global environmental governance more generally – can be traced back to Indira Gandhi's speech to the UN Conference on the Human Environment in Stockholm in 1972 in which she defended the right of developing countries to pursue economic development, describing poverty as "the greatest polluter". She also challenged the emerging discourse in industrialised countries that the root of environmental degradation was excessive industrialisation, overpopulation and economic growth (Gandhi 1972).

The Indian Government historically placed very strong emphasis on equity considerations in its approach to global environmental politics. With respect to climate change, this position is underpinned by India's comparatively low level of cumulative emissions and low per-capita emissions. In contrast to the EU-28 which, as noted above, was responsible for 23.5% of cumulative total CO_2 emissions (excluding land-use change and forestry) from 1850 to 2014, India was responsible for just 2.8% of emissions over the same period (World Resources Institute 2017).

With respect to per-capita CO2 emissions, although India's per-capita emissions increased by nearly 70% between 1990 and 2017 – rising from 1.59 tonnes in 1990 to 2.68 tonnes in 2017 – they are still very significantly lower compared with China (9.55 tonnes), the EU-28 (8.95 tonnes) and the US (20.47 tonnes) (Olivier and Peters 2018). Moreover, based on India's low emissions profile, the Indian Government maintained for many years that it bore no obligation to reduce or limit its GHG emissions. The long-standing framing of responsibility for climate change by the Indian Government has held that industrialised countries bear historical responsibility for climate change and therefore have a responsibility to reduce their emissions, while developing countries should be granted an equitable share of "carbon space" in order to pursue their development objectives.

Second and related, the Indian Government insisted historically on the primacy of development and the eradication of poverty. It has argued forcefully that tackling climate change should not come at the expense of its right to work to eliminate poverty and develop its economy and society. According to World Bank data, India accounts for one-third of all those in the world living below the poverty line of USD 1.90 per day, with 21.2% of the Indian population falling within this category (World Bank 2016, pp. 40, 49). India is rapidly urbanising and, according to United Nations projections, is expected to add 404 urban dwellers between 2014 and 2050 (United Nations 2014). This rapid urbanisation will require very significant development of infrastructure, which in turn will lead to higher GHG emissions.

There is, moreover, a close connection between the poverty, development, urbanisation, and access to energy. Sixty-three percent of the Indian population rely on traditional use of biomass for cooking, while 19% do not have access to electricity (International Energy Agency 2016). For this reason, energy demand is likely to continue to grow rapidly. Thus, eradicating poverty and tackling development challenges in India over the coming decades will lead to an unavoidable rise in energy consumption and, therefore, GHG emissions.

Underpinned by these factors, the Indian Government for many years defended a strict interpretation of "common but differentiated responsibility" and resisted climate change commitments for developing countries. The Indian Government often framed attempts by industrialised countries to persuade developing countries to accept emission limitation commitments as "environmental colonialism".[3] India also strongly defended the binary differentiation between Annex I and non-Annex I Parties, thereby opposing the concept of "evolution" which would allow a country to "graduate" from non-Annex I to Annex I status. It also demanded compensation from developed countries for the full incremental costs of domestic mitigation and adaptation actions (Fujiwara 2010, p. 11). This framing of the distribution of responsibility for climate change increasingly came into conflict with the predominant European framing of responsibility for climate change, discussed above.

However, the period since 2007 has seen an evolution in the Indian climate policy paradigm. This shift can be characterised as a move from outright rejection of climate imperatives towards a "co-benefits" approach – under which India is prepared to take actions that limit the rise in greenhouse emissions as long as these are consistent with other policy goals (Dubash, 2013). For example, although the 2008 National Action Plan on Climate change reaffirmed some of the core tenets of India's position on climate change, including "common but differentiated responsibilities" and the equity principle, the Action Plan's eight National Missions were shaped broadly around India's domestic development needs, providing evidence of a co-benefits approach (Atteridge et al. 2012).

This change was driven by concerns over energy security as well as emphasis on newer policy issues such as vulnerability to climate change and international leadership aspirations, and has led to a plurality of discourses around climate change in India rather than one singular perspective (Thaker and Leiserowitz 2014). Similarly, Isaksen and Stokke argue that, since 2007, Indian discourses around climate change have shifted from a "Third World" discourse to a "Win-Win" discourse that emphasises the co-benefits of climate action and broadly in line with the dominant international climate discourse of ecological modernisation, though they note that this has not translated into a substantial change in India's international negotiating positions (Isaksen and Stokke 2014). The advent of the Modi era reinforced and entrenched this evolution. Prime Minister Modi has been arguably more proactive on the international stage with respect to climate change, for example, at the COP-21 summit and through the International Solar Alliance initiative launched in conjunction with France at the summit (see below).

11.2.3 Contrasting, but converging, European and Indian policy paradigms

Contrasting the Indian and European policy paradigms, it is clear that the two perspectives differed historically in striking ways, but it is also true that there has been a gradual convergence over time. Over the 1990s and much of the 2000s, a "normative gap" characterised India–EU climate relations (Torney 2015, chapter 4). Their respective positions on key issues in global climate governance have differed markedly, including emissions accounting, the conceptualisation of India as a "major emitter", differentiation between developing and developed countries, the relative importance attached to environmental protection and economic development. This clash of policy paradigms significantly constrained the development of India–EU relations on climate change. Not only did these differences constrain cooperation at the level of the international climate negotiations, but they also significantly impeded cooperation on mutually beneficial activities at the bilateral level.

However, the gradual but significant evolution in the Indian approach to climate change from the late 2000s onwards has led to a gradual convergence in the Indian and EU perspectives. To be sure, there are still significant differences, including whether climate change should be characterised as a central policy goal or a co-benefit. Nonetheless, the extent of the normative gap has clearly narrowed over time.

11.3 A relationship of mutual neglect

The broader India–EU bilateral relationship has also served to constrain the development of India–EU cooperation on environmental issues. Rather than providing an enabling institutional environment within which the EU could progressively develop engagement with India on climate change, this broader relationship has acted instead strongly as an inhibiting factor in the development of such engagement. Although India was one of the first countries to establish diplomatic relations with the then EEC in 1963, the India–EU relationship has been characterised by mutual neglect. The EU has historically concentrated much more on its relationship with China than India, while India has concentrated first and foremost on its relations with the US, then China, Russia and countries in its neighborhood, and only then Europe.

The mutual neglect that has characterised the India–EU relationship has its origins in a number of related factors. First, the EU and India approach many global issues in strikingly different ways. With regard to two dominant themes in Indian foreign policy – the nuclear control regime and terrorism emanating from Pakistan – India has been disappointed by the response of the EU which has not, in Indian eyes, adequately appreciated India's concerns about its external security environment. Furthermore, the two sides conceive of multilateralism in quite different ways: while the EU views it in terms of strengthening international institutions, India views the concept of multilateralism through a great power lens, with a strong emphasis on national sovereignty and a desire to refashion some of the rules of international order according to its own preferences (Wagner 2008).

Second, these differences of approach to world politics are compounded by the fact that, on many of the issues that matter most to India, the EU is divided. Nowhere is this more evident than on the issue of United Nations Security Council reform. For these reasons, the Indian Government has tended to treat the EU as a primarily economic rather than political actor, and to deal bilaterally with EU member states on matters of political or strategic concern. For this reason, India was described by EU officials as a "Eurosceptic" third country in the sense that it fails to see the added value of dealing with the EU on political issues, and prefers to deal with member states on a bilateral basis on matters other than trade. As noted by Jain, Indian officials have perhaps been influenced by the Eurosceptic Anglo-Saxon media (Jain 2009). It remains to be seen how the UK's vote to leave the EU in June 2016 will impact on the future of India–EU relations.

This mutual neglect and strategic disconnect provided the context for the development of the India–EU relationship in the 21st century. The EU and India agreed in 2000 to institutionalise annual summits at head of state or government level. The establishment of a so-called "strategic partnership" in 2004 created a false illusion of a deepening of the institutional basis of the relationship. This "strategic partnership" provided the context within which the EU attempted to launch more sustained engagement with India on climate change. However, underlying this optimistic rhetoric was continued mutual neglect. In fact, although India–EU summits were supposed to be held annually, there was a gap of four years between the 2012 and 2016 summits.

Thus, the India–EU strategic partnership was arguably neither strategic nor a partnership, and the problematic nature of the broader relationship has acted as a constraint on the India–EU relationship in the area of climate change. Indeed, painting a pessimistic picture Kavalski argues that "the India–EU relationship is likely to remain one of non-strategic unpartnership for the foreseeable future" (Kavalski 2016, emphasis in original).

11.4 Evolution of India–EU cooperation on environment and climate change

India–EU relations on environment and climate change have developed slowly. Initially there was very strong resistance on the Indian side to any cooperation with the EU in this area, but this has moderated to some extent over recent years.

11.4.1 Climate dialogue on paper

EU engagement with India has developed in the framework of the "India–EU Initiative on Clean Development and Climate Change", agreed at the 2005 India–EU summit, under which the two sides agreed to focus on "voluntary practical measures". Areas identified for cooperation included: (i) eliminating barriers to dissemination of technologies; (ii) increasing funding for research and development; (iii) climate change adaptation, including research and development and integration of adaptation into sustainable development strategies; (iv) reducing the cost of cleaner technologies by achieving economies of scale; and (v) strengthening implementation of the Clean Development Mechanism. Compared with the formulaic statements on climate change of earlier summit joint declarations, this was a detailed and reasonably specific statement of priorities, though there were few if any targets to be achieved. However, follow-up on these points of agreed cooperation was very limited.

The two sides agreed that the "Joint Working Group on Environment", which had been established in 1999 but had met infrequently, would meet on a yearly basis. The Joint Working Group on Environment at senior official level was envisaged as a forum in which policy objectives would be exchanged, upcoming bilateral political meetings would be discussed and other matters – such as the topic for the Environment Forum – could be agreed. An "EU–India Environment Forum" was intended to bring together governments, business and civil society from each side. A number of one-off workshops and conferences were held in the period 2006–2007, including on adaptation, the Clean Development Mechanism, and climate change research needs. However, in general there was little substantive activity before 2008 (Boldt and Das 2008, Action for a Global Climate Community 2009).

An EU–India Energy Panel was also established in 2005, involving DG Energy on the EU side and the Ministry of Power on the Indian side. It met for the first time in June 2005 and established three sub-working groups: (i) coal and clean coal technology, (ii) renewable energy and energy efficiency, and (iii) fusion energy and international thermonuclear experimental reactor (ITER). A fourth Working Group on Petroleum and Natural Gas was established in 2006. However, although there were periodic meetings of the Energy Panel and at least some of its working groups, progress was very limited. Moreover, by mid-2010, the Energy Efficiency & Renewable Energy Working Group had not met for some time, and the Working Group on Coal was the only one which continued to make progress (Torney 2015, chapter 6).

11.4.2 Another false start

India–EU cooperation received fresh impetus in 2008 in the context of a broader reconsideration of the India–EU relationship that year. At the 2008 India–EU summit, the overall EU–India Joint Action Plan was revised following recognition that the Joint Action Plan agreed in 2005 was too ambitious, and it was scaled back in terms of action so that it was more focused on a smaller range of issues (European Union and Government of India 2008a). As part of this process, the French EU Presidency secured agreement on a "Joint Work Programme, EU–India Cooperation on Energy, Clean Development and Climate Change" (European Union and Government of India 2008b).

Under the heading "cooperation on energy", this Joint Work Programme identified coal, energy efficiency, fusion energy and renewables as areas for cooperation, with a strong emphasis on joint research and development. Proposed cooperation under the heading of "climate change" was more limited. The two areas identified were (i) the organisation of workshops on modeling mitigation options, deployment of climate-friendly technology and the future of the Clean Development Mechanism, and (ii) the establishment of a pool of expertise to support capacity building in India.

Under the heading "private sector cooperation", it was proposed that European Investment Bank funding would be provided for mitigation and adaptation projects in India,[4] and that a proposed "European Business Technology Centre" (EBTC) would advance private sector and research cooperation. Following on from this, the EBTC was established in New Delhi with the support of the European Commission in January 2009. It was established with funding primarily from the European Commission.[5] Implemented by the Association of European Chambers of Commerce and Industry (EuroChambres), it aimed to provide support and advice to European businesses seeking entry into the Indian market in four sectors: energy, environment, biotechnology and transport. Its focus was primarily on small and medium size enterprises, particularly from those EU member states without existing trade-promotion offices in India.

While the 2008 Joint Work Programme was reasonably specific in identifying particular areas for cooperation, it was in large part a re-statement of the priorities that had been identified under the 2005 Initiative on Clean Development and Climate Change. This reflected the fact that the activities set out in 2005 had, by and large, not yet taken place. As such, the activities proposed under the 2008 Joint Work Programme represented a continuation of the means by which the EU had sought to engage India from 2005 onwards. As von Muenchow-Pohl has argued, the 2008 Joint Work Programme

> reveals the same shortcomings as the original version and almost all other documents that have hailed from India–EU summits so far. They are long on shared fundamentals and abstract political objectives but short on specifics and deliverables, and devoid of timelines ... In most instances, 'action' translates into some form of dialogue.
>
> (von Muenchow-Pohl 2012, p. 13)

234 Diarmuid Torney

The period from 2008 onward saw a gradual increase in the level of cooperation on issues of energy and environmental policy. It is noteworthy, however, that this cooperation did not take place under the heading of "climate change". The EU provided development cooperation support for India in a number of areas, including through the State Partnership Programme in Rajasthan and Chhattisgarh, projects on sustainable cities and water and waste management, energy projects, and support for the SWITCH Asia programme which aims to encourage sustainable production and consumption.

The February 2012 India–EU summit agreed a "Joint Declaration for Enhanced Cooperation on Energy". This outlined a range of areas for cooperation, including: clean energy, particularly clean coal and advanced coal mining; energy efficiency of products and buildings; smart grids; renewable energy innovation and deployment; energy safety, particularly nuclear safety and offshore drilling safety; and fusion energy (EU Delegation to India 2012b). In November 2012, the 6th EU–India Environment Forum was held in focused on the themes of sustainable forestry and biodiversity (EU Delegation to India 2012a).

However, the relationship continued to be characterised by tensions. After 16 rounds of talks, Free Trade Agreement negotiations were suspended in 2013 (Mohan and Sandhu 2016). In the climate and environment arena, perhaps the most visible tension was over the decision by the EU to include international aviation from the beginning of 2012 in the EU Emissions Trading Scheme (EU ETS). In February 2012, India and 22 other countries agreed the "Declaration of the Moscow Meeting on Inclusion of International Civil Aviation in the EU-ETS" rejecting the EU's move as unilateral and called on it to reverse its decision (IISD 2012). In November 2012, EU Climate Commissioner Connie Hedegaard announced that the EU would "stop the clock" on the inclusion of aviation in the EU ETS for one year to allow for multilateral negotiations in the framework of the International Civil Aviation Organisation (DG Climate Action 2012).

11.4.3 A new impetus?

The process leading to the Twenty-first Conference of the Parties to the UNFCCC (COP-21) in Paris in December 2015 gave greater profile and urgency to climate change both at global level and also within India and the EU. The International Solar Alliance was launched at COP-21 by Prime Minister Modi and French President Francois Hollande, though notably without the participation of the EU. The ISA aims to mobilise more than USD 1 trillion of investments in solar by 2030, and approximately 80 countries signed the declaration at COP-21.

There was no India–EU summit between 2012 and 2016, but the 2016 summit saw an attempt to reinvigorate the relationship. The two sides agreed a "Joint Declaration on a Clean Energy and Climate Partnership" This partnership was framed in terms of the CBDR-RC principle, but with the additional "in light of different national circumstances", a qualifier that first emerged from the US–China join statement on climate change in November 2014 and ended up incorporated in the text of the Paris Agreement. The Joint Declaration included many of the commitments included in the 2005 and 2008 iterations, including exchanging views, strengthening joint initiatives including on energy efficiency in buildings, smart grids and phasing out hydrofluorocarbons. This suggests that, as was the case with the 2008 Joint Work Programme, the 2016 iteration was merely a re-statement of previously announced objectives that failed to materialise. One noteworthy development in the 2016 Joint Declaration is a new focus on implementation of the two sides' respective (Intended) Nationally Determined Contributions, the climate action pledges made in advance of the Paris climate change conference within the UNFCCC framework.

In terms of concrete cooperation, the context of EU support for India changed in 2014, when the EU categorised India as a "graduated" country. As a result, the EU phased out bilateral development cooperation support to India. Accordingly, in the 2014–2020 funding period, no development cooperation funding was allocated to bilateral projects in India, though thematic and regional cooperation continued. However, a number of bilateral cooperation projects are ongoing on energy and climate change, including within the framework of the Clean Energy and Climate Partnership. These include "FOWIND", a study of offshore wind energy potential, and "FOWPI", which is providing the design for a 200 MW offshore wind farm off the coast of Gujarat or Tamil Nadu. The EU has also provided assistance to India's solar park programme to facilitate integration of solar power into the electricity grid (EEAS 2017).

The European Investment Bank (EIB) has also increased its support. Having previously committed more than EUR 1.2 billion principally in the areas of energy and climate mitigation projects, at the 2016 India–EU summit the EIB agreed a loan of EUR 450 million with the Indian Government for a metro project in Lucknow city (European Council 2016). A year later, in March 2017, the EIB opened a regional office in Delhi, and announced EUR 200 million in support for solar power generation in India over 20 years, in partnership with the State Bank of India (European Investment Bank 2017).

India–EU cooperation has also developed in some other aspects of environmental policy. In the area of water policy, the first "Indo-European Water Forum" was held in in New Delhi on 23–24 November 2015. Following on from this, an EU–India Water Partnership was agreed at the 2016 India–EU summit. Building on this, EU Commissioner for Environment Karmenu Vella and India's Minister for Water Resources Uma Bharti signed, in November 2016, a Memorandum of Understanding. This partnership foresees cooperation in a range of areas, including water law and governance, research and innovation and joint initiatives to rejuvenate the Ganga river as well as India's other water bodies. The Water Partnership aims to bring together a range of stakeholders including EU Member States, Indian States, European and Indian institutions, industry, and civil society (EEAS 2017).

The 2017 India–EU summit, held in New Delhi, agreed a new Joint Statement on Clean Energy and Climate Change (European Union and Government of India 2017a). This was agreed against the backdrop of US President Donald Trump's announcement in June 2017 that he intended to withdraw the US from the Paris Agreement on climate change. The EU–India Joint Statement included a section on "Climate Action and the Paris Agreement" and several pointed statements seemingly aimed at Trump, including "call[ing] on all Parties to uphold the Paris Agreement, to implement their NDCs and to strengthen efforts over time" (European Union and Government of India 2017a, p. 1). The summit also endorsed a Joint Declaration on a partnership for Smart and Sustainable Urbanisation (European Union and Government of India 2017b).

In November 2018, the European Commission and the EU High Representative for Foreign and Security Policy published a joint communication entitled "Elements for an EU strategy on India" (European Commission 2018). Climate change and environmental issues featured prominently in this European vision of the future of India–EU relations, both in terms of bilateral cooperation and their relations at the global level. However, it is too early to judge the success of this most recent wave of initiatives, and to evaluate whether the 2016–2019 period represents an inflection point in the India–EU relationship on environment climate change and energy.

11.5 Conclusion and outlook

Despite many optimistic statements set out in successive India–EU declarations, India's relations with the EU have not yet delivered on their potential. In earlier years in particular, the relationship was characterised by neglect and often conflict. This was despite the existence of common interests in areas such as the development of non-fossil energy sources and the promotion of energy efficiency. By contrast, recent years have seen an upswing in the breadth and depth of cooperation between the two sides on climate, environment and clean energy. This chapter has sought to trace and understand this pattern limited but growing cooperation as a function of the broader India–EU relationship as well as a gradual convergence of environmental policy paradigms.

The India–EU relationship on environment and climate change has been constrained by mutual neglect in the broader India–EU relationship. Neither side is the other's main external priority or point of reference in world politics, and there has been a wide disconnect across a broad range of policy issues, including security and terrorism, nuclear proliferation, UN Security Council reform and conceptions of multilateralism and sovereignty. Disagreement across this range of issues, and the inability of the EU to deliver on matters of such central importance to India, has led the Indian Government to treat the EU as primarily an economic actor and to deal with individual member states rather than the EU as an entity in itself. Indeed, between 2012 and 2016 there was no India–EU summit – an event that would ordinarily be held annually. Since 2016, the practice of annual summits has resumed.

These broader difficulties in the India–EU relationship were compounded by clashing environmental policy paradigms. On the paradigmatic issue of climate change, the EU became increasingly concerned with securing the participation of large developing countries in global climate governance, including India.

The Indian Government, by contrast, in the 1990s and much of the 2000s framed the climate issue as one which India has no significant responsibility to address in global terms. Initially, the "normative gap" between the policy paradigms of India and the EU grew over time as European policy-makers increasingly moved to conceptualise India as a "major emitter" of GHGs. Over time, however, India's move from a development-first to a co-benefits framing of climate change altered this.

After a four-year period in which no India–EU summits were held, the 2016 and 2017 India–EU summits both agreed joint statements on climate change and clean energy. This coincides with the gradual convergence in the Indian and European environmental policy paradigms, and suggests that the future of the relationship may be more positive. Nonetheless, the future of the relationship remains uncertain, particularly in the aftermath of the UK vote to leave the EU in June 2016. For historical and cultural reasons, the UK has among the broadest and deepest relationship with India. Although coordination and sharing of information among EU member states on the ground in India, as elsewhere, has been patchy, the EU's loss of this interlocutor with India is likely to harm the broader India–EU relationship.

At the level of societal relations, it is unclear to what extent civil society actors and academics in India and the EU have established or deepened networks of cooperation. Certainly, there are sporadic instances of cooperation, such as collaboration that has brought this volume to fruition. However, to a large extent the patterns that characterise the India–EU relationship at the government-to-government level appear to characterise societal relations as well. Within Indian academia, the US is often the first port of call, while in the EU academics remain fixated by the rise of China and the opportunities and challenges that this presents.

The future is uncertain for global environmental governance, with Donald Trump's election as US president and his announcement that he intends to withdraw the US from the Paris Agreement on climate change as well as his commitment to rolling back US domestic climate and environmental policies. On the other hand, however, there are many signs of other countries maintaining their commitment to environmental protection and even boosting their international cooperation in the face of Trump's policies, not least the Joint Statement on climate change and clean energy issued by the 2017 India–EU summit. Time will tell whether the India–EU relationship can contribute to bolstering global environmental protection in the face of such uncertainty.

Notes

1 COP-12, held in Nairobi in 2006, was dubbed the Africa adaptation COP (IISD 2006).
2 Principally, these were (i) the collapse of heavy industry in East Germany and the countries of Central Europe that would later join the EU, as a result of the fall of Communism; and (ii) the "dash to gas" in the UK in the aftermath of the closure of coal mines by then Prime Minister Margaret Thatcher, which resulted in a significant fall in UK emissions due to the fact that gas is a less carbon-intensive fuel than coal.

3 This way of framing the debate about global climate change governance can be traced to a report published in 1991 by the Indian NGO Centre for Science and Environment, which had a strong influence on the Indian approach to the INC negotiations in 1991–1992 (Agarwal and Narain, 1991).
4 Following on from the Summit, in December 2008, the European Investment Bank agreed to provide a loan of EUR 150 million to the Export–Import Bank of India, two thirds of which was earmarked for projects to mitigate climate change in the renewable energy and energy efficiency sectors (European Investment Bank 2008).
5 The project was funded for five years initially. It transitioned to an independent organisation in March 2016.

References

Action for a Global Climate Community, 2009. *Enhancing Cooperation: Report of the High-Level India-EU Dialogue*. London: Action for a Global Climate Community.

Agarwal, A. and Narain, D., 1991. *Global Warming in an Unequal World: A Case of Environmental Colonialism*. New Delhi: Centre for Science and Environment.

Atteridge, A., et al. 2012. Climate policy in India: What shapes International, National and State Policy? *Ambio*, 41(S1), 68–77.

Boldt, J. and Das, A., 2008. *Study on Environment and Energy in India—Consolidated Report*. Hemel Hempstead: HTPSE Ltd.

Council of the European Union, 2008. *Preparations for the 14th Session of the Conference of the Parties (COP 14) to the United Nations Framework Convention on Climate Change (UNFCCC) and the 4th Session of the Meeting of the Parties to the Kyoto Protocol (CMP 4)—Council Conclusions*. Brussels, 14562/08, 21 October 2008.

DG Climate Action, 2012. *Stopping the Clock of ETS and Aviation Emissions following Last Week's International Civil Aviation Organisation (ICAO) Council* [online]. Available at: http://europa.eu/rapid/press-release_MEMO-12-854_en.htm.

Dubash, N. K., 2013. The politics of climate change in India: Narratives of equity and co-benefits. *WIREs Climate Change*, 4(3), 191–201.

EEAS, 2017. *EU Environment, Energy, Climate Change and Urbanization* [online]. Available at: https://eeas.europa.eu/delegations/india/33612/eu-environment-energy-climate-change-and-urbanization_en.

EU Delegation to India, 2012a. *6th EU–India Environment Forum: Sustainable Forestry and Biodiversity—Programme* [online]. Available at: http://eeas.europa.eu/delegations/india/documents/eu_india/2012_eu_india_environment_forum/programme_6th_eu_india_environment_forum_on_sustainable_forestry_and_biodiversity_new_delhi_21_november_2012.pdf.

EU Delegation to India, 2012b. *Joint Declaration for Enhanced Cooperation on Energy between the European Union and the Government of India* [online]. Available at: http://eeas.europa.eu/india/sum02_12/docs/20120210_jdenergy_en.pdf.

European Commission, 2005. *Communication from the Commission to the European Parliament, the Council, the Economic and Social Committee and the Committee of the Regions: Winning the Battle Against Global Climate Change*. COM(2005) 35 final. Brussels: European Commission.

European Commission, 2018. *Joint Communication to the European Parliament and the Council: Elements for an EU strategy on India*. JOIN(2018) 28 final. Brussels: European Commission and High Representative of the Union for Foreign Affairs and Security Policy.

European Council, 1990. *Presidency Conclusions: Dublin European Council, 25 and 26 June 1990*. SN 60/1/90. Brussels: Council of the European Union.

European Council, 2007. *Brussels European Council, 8–9 March 2007: Presidency Conclusions*. 7224/1/07. Brussels: Council of the European Union.

European Council, 2016. *EU–India summit, Brussels, 30/03/2016* [online]. Available at: www.consilium.europa.eu/en/meetings/international-summit/2016/03/30/.

European Investment Bank, 2008. *EIB Loan to Mitigate Climate Change and Support EU Presence in India* [online]. Available at: http://europa.eu/rapid/press-release_BEI-08-126_en.htm.

European Investment Bank, 2017. *European Investment Bank Confirms EUR 200 miooion Long-term, Loan to State Bank of India to Support Indian Large Scale Solar Projects* [online]. Available at: www.eib.org/infocentre/press/releases/all/2017/2017-093-eib-confirms-eur-200-million-long-term-loan-to-state-bank-of-india-to-support-indian-large-scale-solar-projects.htm.

European Union and Government of India, 2008a. *Global Partners for Global Challenges: The EU-India Joint Action Plan* [online]. Available at: www.eeas.europa.eu/india/sum09_08/joint_action_plan_2008_en.pdf.

European Union and Government of India, 2008b. *EU–India Summit, Marseille, 29 September 2008* [online]. European Commission website. Available at: https://europa.eu/rapid/press-release_PRES-08-277_en.htm.

European Union and Government of India, 2017a. *EU–India Joint Statement on Clean Energy and Climate Change* [online]. European Council website. Available at: www.consilium.europa.eu/media/23515/eu-india-joint-statement.pdf.

European Union and Government of India, 2017b. *Joint Declaration between the European Uniona and the Republic of India on a Partnership for Smart & Sustainable Urbanisation* [online]. European Council website. Available at: www.consilium.europa.eu/media/23518/eu-india-joint-declaration-partnership-smart-and-sustainable-urbanisation.pdf.

Fujiwara, N., 2010. *The Political Economy of India's Climate Agenda*. Brussels: Centre for European Policy Studies.

Gandhi, I., 1972. *Man and Environment*. Plenary Session of United Nations Conference on Human Environment, Stockholm, 14th June, 1972.

IISD, 2006. *Summary of the Twelfth Conference of the Parties to the UN Framework Convention on Climate Change and Second Meeting of the Parties to the Kyoto Protocol: 6–17 November 2006, 12(318)* [online]. Available at: http://enb.iisd.org/vol12/enb12318e.html.

IISD, 2012. *Moscow Meeting Adopts Declaration on Inclusion of International Civil Aviation in the EU-ETS* [online]. Available at: http://climate-l.iisd.org/news/moscow-meeting-adopts-declaration-on-inclusion-of-international-civil-aviation-in-the-eu-ets/.

International Energy Agency, 2004. *World Energy Outlook 2004*. Paris: International Energy Agency.

International Energy Agency, 2007. *World Energy Outlook 2007: China and India Insights*. Paris: International Energy Agency.

International Energy Agency, 2016. *World Energy Outlook 2016*. Paris: International Energy Agency.

Isaksen, K.A. and Stokke, K., 2014. Changing climate discourses and politics in India: Climate change as challenge and opportunity for diplomacy and development. *Geoforum*, 57, 110–119.

Jain, R.K., 2009. Engaging the European Superpower: India and the European Union. In B. Gaens, J. Jokela, and E. Limnell, Eds. *The Role of the European Union in Asia: China and India as Strategic Partners*. Farnham: Ashgate.

Jörgensen, K. and Wagner, C., 2017. Low carbon governance in multi-level structures: EU–India relations on energy and climate. *Environmental Policy and Governance*, 27, 137–148.

Kavalski, E., 2016. The EU–India strategic partnership: Neither very strategic, nor much of a partnership. *Cambridge Review of International Affairs*, 29(1), 192–208.

Mohan, G. and Sandhu, J., 2016. Can EU–India Summit Revive Flagging Partnership? [online]. EU Observer, 29 March. Available at: https://euobserver.com/opinion/132810.

von Muenchow-Pohl, B., 2012. *India and Europe in a Multipolar World*. Washington: Carnegie Endowment for International Peace.

Olivier, J.G.J. and Peters, J.A.H.W., 2018. *Trends in Global CO_2 and Total Greenhouse Gas Emissions: 2018 Report*. The Hague: PBL Netherlands Environmental Assessment Agency.

Pielke, R.A., 1998. Rethinking the role of adaptation in climate policy. *Global Environmental Change*, 8(2), 159–170.

Sinha, U.K., 2012. Interlocking Challenges: EU–India convergence on climate change. *In* L. Peral and V. Sakhuja, Eds.. *The EU–India Partnership: Time to go strategic?* Paris: EU Institute for Security Studies.

Thaker, J. and Leiserowitz, A., 2014. Shifting discourses of climate change in India. *Climatic Change*, 123, 107–119.

Torney, D., 2015. *European Climate Leadership in Question: Policies toward China and India*. Cambridge, MA: MIT Press.

United Nations, 2014. *World Urbanization Prospects: The 2014 Revision, Highlights*. New York: UN Department of Economic and Social Affairs, Population Division.

Upadhyay, D.K., 2012. EU–India energy cooperation: Promoting renewable sources and widening commitments. *In*: L. Peral and V. Sakhuja, Eds. *The EU–India Partnership: Time to go Strategic?* Paris: EU Institute for Security Studies.

Wagner, C., 2008. The EU and India: A Deepening Partnership. *In*: G. Grevi, and A. de Vasconcelos, Eds. *Partnerships for Effective Multilateralism: EU Relations with Brazil, China, India and Russia*. Paris: EU Institute for Security Studies.

World Bank, 2016. *Poverty and Shared Prosperity 2016: Taking on Inequality*. Washington, DC: World Bank.

World Resources Institute, 2017. *CAIT Climate Data Explorer* [online]. Available at: http://cait.wri.org/.

12 Environmental politics in India

Institutions, actors and
environmental governance

Natalia Ciecierska-Holmes and Kirsten Jörgensen

12.1 Introduction

In the second half of the 20th century, the focus which had been placed on processes of democratization, economic progress and security modernisation shifted. Driven by major industrial pollution disasters and global environmental problems, not least the worsening climate crisis, environmental protection became another important function of state action. This is reflected in the emergence of global environmental governance and the global diffusion of national environmental policies.

Safeguarding the environment has become a major responsibility of the state, a phenomenon which is reflected in debates about ecological modernisation, greening of the state and sustainable development (Meadowcroft 2012). With the emergence of comparative environmental politics literature in the 1980s (Steinberg and VanDeveer 2012), literature about the political system's capacity for environmental policy initially focused on developed Organisation for Economic Cooperation and Development (OECD) countries, but the concept "capacity" was naturally also considered useful for developing countries (Jänicke 1997). Drawing from their comparative research of 36 countries, which includes India as a case study, Jänicke and Weidner (2002) show that at the start of the 2000s, OECD countries had developed significant environmental policy capacities and that spread of environmental policy globally had "strengthened environmental proponents and capacities for action" (Weidner et al. 2002, p. 439). However, much less was known about the trajectories of environmental capacity-building in developing and newly industrialising countries, and to what extent this differed from industrialised countries in the global North.

As one of the few stable non-Western democracies and multi-ethnic societies, India does not fit easily into comparative politics debates and its success in maintaining democratic rule has taken democracy scholars by surprise (Lijphart 1996). Thus, India's environmental politics is complex and it is not easy to classify the country in the debate about the greening of the state. India is a large developing country with a rapidly growing population and expanding middle class. It has shown strong economic growth over the last two decades, yet still has high poverty rates. India has a democratic system, which at the same time is prone to corruption and patronage. The federal system features centralized top-down policy structures on the one hand, and a broad variation of federal states with rising economic and political importance. A vibrant civil society with numerous non-governmental organisations (NGOs), think tanks and grass root movements is influential at different stages of the policy cycles, especially in perceiving problems, agenda-setting, formulating demands and contributing to implementation.

The aim of this chapter is to craft conclusions about factors which have shaped the trajectories of environmental and climate policy in India since the 1970s until today. Drawing on Indian politics literature, the impact of federalism and decentralisation, and the changes in the party system on environmental policy-making will be discussed against the background of book chapters. Moreover, this concluding chapter also engages with comparative environmental politics literature about the linkages between democracy, civil society, political parties, the judiciary and environmental performance. Broadly following the structure of this book, this chapter is split into three sections. First, we draw on aspects of India's political institutions and actor constellations from across federal decision-making structures, India's states and civil society. Second, we highlight important features, ideas and strategies from specific policy subsystems, focusing on policy change and paradigmatic change, while also shedding light on more recent developments. The third section connects Indian environmental policy with the international context of environmental policy-making.

12.2 Institutions and actors

12.2.1 Centralisation and decentralisation in India's federal system

Since independence, India has had a strongly centralised federal system, which is "asymmetrical in favor of the central government" (Lijphart 1996, p. 260). Asymmetric power sharing concerns the relation between India's central government and the subnational states, but even more so the local level – India's rural and urban areas – which have for many decades lacked constitutional opportunities for local self-government and representation. The constitution grants the national government the possibility to make laws with respect to items enumerated in the State List, to override state legislation, to proclaim emergency and the "assumption of all state government powers by the President in case of emergency" (Sáez 2002a, p. 39). Not considered in the early debates of India's constitution was a certain degree of economic self-rule, which would provide lower levels with resources needed for independent action (Parikh and Weingast 1997, p. 1609). Mainly controlled by national institutions, such as the erstwhile Planning Commission and the Finance Commission, the financial transfers system placed the "states at the mercy of the central government" (Parikh and Weingast 1997, p. 1607). In the 1940s, the high degree of centralisation and lacking consideration of local representation were debated and contested in India's Constituent Assembly (Sáez 2002b, p. 34).

With the institutionalisation of environmental policy in the 1970s, centralised environmental policy-making has in India, like in other countries, proven successful in establishing this new policy field. However, long-term environmental policy capacity-building and the implementation of environmental policy have suffered due to political, legislative and fiscal centralisation. "Excessive centralisation" has not only hindered decentral policy innovation, but also has affected the cooperation between the governmental levels in areas such as climate policy (see Chapter 2, Swenden and Saxena, this volume). Different waves of federalism shaped India's environmental politics: centralisation in the 1970s and 1980s which was triggered by the one-party dominant system; modest decentralisation driven by India's economic liberalisation in 1991, the decentralising constitutional amendments in 1992 and the fading dominance of the Congress party which still retained regulatory control of the central state; and, finally, significant recentralisation under the Bharatiya Janata Party (BJP)-led NDA government since 2014 (Sharma and Swenden 2018).

12.2.2 Lacking empowerment of the local level

Jänicke and Weidner's international comparative study shows that decentralisation is a necessary condition for "socially rooted environmental policy" but not a sufficient condition for effective environmental protection when implementation capacity is lacking (Weidner et al. 2002, p. 421). In 1993, the 73rd and 74th amendments to India's constitution radically changed the legal basis of federalism in India, which set the scene for the long expected decentralising local government reform. The constitutional provisions strengthened "voice" and "accountability" and reduced "hierarchy", thus introducing local representation via required direct elections to the rural local panchayats and the urban local governments (Rao and Singh 2007, p. 386). While rights were partly shifted from the erstwhile dominant subnational states to the local level, this was insufficient as "state or non-elected officials have often been the key government decision-makers" in the local context (Rao and Singh 2007, p. 386).

In fact, the reality is that decentralisation and empowerment of the local level has proceeded extremely slowly. It did not materialise substantively in the development of institutions and capacities and is a key factor behind poor monitoring, implementation and enforcement of existing regulations and the enactment of regionally appropriate laws. Decentralisation was hindered by both national actors as well as various subnational states, and the most outstanding deficit concerns the revenue stream to the local level (Kapur et al. 2018). The "local governments were kept under administrative tutelage of the state governments" (see Chapter 2, Swenden and Saxena, this volume). Across the explored policy subsystems of forests, water, energy, climate and urban development in India's environmental policy domain, lacking decentralisation has affected environmental performance and socially inclusive development. The potentials of a "socially rooted environmental policy" were demonstrated by the decentralising and participative approaches of India's Joint Forest Management Programme (1990) and the Forest

Rights Act (2006) – a policy innovation which made progress regarding social inclusiveness and forest protection (see Chapter 5, Das, this volume) and diffused to other developing countries (Kashwan, 2013).

12.2.3 Political stability and the transition of the party system

Two phenomena have had a lasting impact on the economic role of India's state: the decline of the one-party dominance system and the process of liberalisation India embarked on in 1991 (Sharma and Swenden 2018). In the first decades after India's independence, political stability rested on the one-party dominance of the Congress party (Lijphart 1996). During the 1950s and 1960s the Congress party, which had emerged from the national movement that led India into independence, occupied the position of a central actor in India's policy processes (Sil 2014). The party was in power at the level of the national and state governments. Due to the pronounced political integration capacity of the party organisation, the centralisation of India's politics was effective. The party played a dominating role in shaping India's development narratives and policies and in coordinating policies across the federal system (Kapur and Mehta 2007). This central role of the Congress party and the one-party dominant system began to weaken in 1967 after non-Congress governments formed in several states. Moreover, the Congress central government was defeated after the Emergency in 1977, and then disappeared altogether after 1989 when governments were formed as minority coalition governments (Sharma and Swenden 2018). From 1996 to 2014, governments were formed with either the Congress or the ultra-nationalist BJP involving regional parties, which had been emerging in large numbers since the 1980s. Thirty-seven parties had seats in India's lower house, the Lok Sabha, in 2014 (Kapur et al. 2018, p. 7).

India's pendulum of federalism swung back in India's national elections in 2014 which reset the one-party dominant system. The BJP, which had led the government coalition from 1999 to 2004, emerged as the new leader and side-lined the Congress Party. The BJP earned the first single-party majority in three decades with a sweeping election victory (Kapur et al. 2018), a victory, which was even more substantial in the 2019 election. In 2019, the BJP increased its control of state governments and participation in coalition governments in the states. Although the BJP had propagated a cooperative federalism it has since 2014 reactivated political, and administrative centralisation and practiced "'partisan federalism' rather than genuinely 'competitive federalism'" (Sharma and Swenden 2018, p. 54).

Since the 1970s, green parties have diffused worldwide and since the end of 1979 have also transitioned from social movements to parliamentarian parties (O'Neill, 2012b). Two green parties exist in India, the regional Uttarakhand Transformation Party (UKPP) founded in 2009 and The India Greens founded in 2018.

In the policy subsystems explored in the chapters of this volume, parties do not matter significantly in varying environmental policy outcomes. Policy continuity and incremental change predominantly marks environmental policy trajectories in the urban context, regarding water and forests. Regional communist coalition parties in the United Progressive Alliance (UPA), led by Congress, took influence in safeguarding the rights of the tribal communities over natural resources (Kashwan 2017). In accordance with a more pronounced neo-liberal economic development approach, the BJP appears to pursue a slightly more aggressive growth-first strategy, regardless of negative environmental and social impacts (see chapters by Swenden and Saxena, Gupta and Tiagy, Singhal and Jain, and Jörgensen, this volume).

12.2.4 Democracy and environmental governance

Whether "political institutions are democratic or authoritarian affects how well the environment is protected" (Hochstetler 2012, p. 199). This relates to the opportunity structures offered by democratic systems to environmental protagonists, through freer media and access to information. In some contexts, decentralisation and participatory approaches even "give better results than either authoritarian or liberal arrangements" (Hochstetler 2012, p. 222). Despite this, the effectiveness of environmental performance in liberal democracies might be affected by instances of corruption (Hochstetler 2012). In India, corruption has been significant since the 1970s, when "briefcases full of cash filled the coffers of the Congress Party" (Jaffrelot et al. 2019, p. 8).

Agrawal and Yokozuka (2002) argue that in contrast to institutional contexts in other developing countries, India's democratic political system provides an opportunity structure for environmental policy. The mixture of "bureaucratic organization and participatory politics with indigenous practices and institutions" allows different interests and environmental actors to influence outcomes and direct action and mass mobilisation are significant in India (Agrawal and Yokozuka 2002, p. 243).

India has been able to maintain a democratic system despite weak government output and various destabilising factors, such as high poverty rates, increasing social and economic inequality, religious and ethnic conflicts and increasing political instability since the 1980s (Kapur 2007). The rule of law has been upheld with an independent judiciary since independence, except for the time of the Emergency in 1975–1977 under Indira Gandhi (Sil 2014). However, in different political phases, India has seen a concentration of power at the national level vis-à-vis the states (see Chapter 2, Swenden and Saxena, this volume) or a concentration of power in India's states, restricting decision-making space at the local level (Manor, 2016). The centralisation of power is quite often related to personalised one-leader political structures (Manor 2016).

As the chapters depict policy processes and outcomes in different times, under different governments and in different environmental issue areas, general conclusions on how democratic institutions matter in India's environmental performance cannot be drawn. However, it is still possible to carve out a few features. Democratic achievements and drawbacks have affected environmental performance with diverse affects at different junctures, and there is no linear trajectory. The most critical drawback was the imposition of the Emergency by Indira Gandhi from 1975 to 1977 which curtailed democratic institutions, including the power of the judiciary, democratic rights and the press. Surprisingly though, as Ganguly shows (see Chapter 4, this volume), environmental protection of all things "was a crucial area of concern and interest for Indira Gandhi" as she was taking action to protect tigers, parks and forests. Gandhi's authoritarian approach to conservation was ecologically effective but lacked social justice – it "came at the cost of displacement and enclosure". After India's emergency, the revival of environmental movements, environmental advocates and media were influential and triggered institutionalisation of environmental policy, and amongst others, the introduction of India's Ministry of Environment and Forests (MOEF) in the 1980s (Ganguly). The first non-Congress government (Janata government) strengthened civil society capacities between 1977 and 1980.

In the 1980s and 1990s, civil society actors were significantly involved in the implementation of government policies and international projects, however less so in the design of policies. Ganguly's chapter gives ample evidence of environmental policies being catalysed by civil society, such as in forests, hazardous and polluting industries, and environmental regulations during this period (see Chapter 4, this volume).

Since this time, the influence of the corporate sector on the state, on India's sub-national state legislatures, and regulatory agencies has grown considerably (Jaffrelot et al. 2019). Business is also very well represented in the BJP-dominated Lok Sabha (Sinha 2019). The corporate sector had become more influential in the shaping of economic policy; "a slow but definite transformation of India from a socialist political economy to one that sharply prioritizes economic growth and business interests" had started in the 1980s (Jaffrelot et al. 2019, p. 8). India's Congress Party partly eased restrictions on conducting private business. In the 2000s, rapid industrial growth entailed increasing conflicts surrounding electricity infrastructures, nuclear power plants, mining, genetically modified organisms, hydroelectric dams, and extractive industries, and land acquisition for industrial purposes (Ganguly, this volume). In response, democratic institutions, the voice of NGOs and legislative procedures have been trimmed under the Congress-led UPA and much more so under the BJP-led NDA coalition government led by Prime Minister Modi. Modi's power-concentrating policy style was known from his time as Chief Minister of the Gujarat, which he seems to have transposed in the context of the national government (Sharma and Swenden 2018, and Chapters 2, Swenden and Saxena, and 4, Ganguly, this volume). Moreover, state-business relations in Gujarat involved environmental corruption (see Chapter 3, Jörgensen, this volume).

Since the watershed election in 2014, which brought the BJP into power with an absolute majority in the Parliament, decision-making is concentrated in the Prime Minister's Office. The dismissal of non-BJP governors in nine Indian states and the unilateral decision to demonetise in November 2016 are just two examples indicating centralisation (Sharma and Swenden 2018). The introduction of the NITI Aayog which replaced the Planning Commission and which was meant to innovate inter-governmental processes and increase influence of the states rather serves as an instrument for the national decision-makers (Sharma and Swenden 2018). Another facet of the new one-party dominant system is the reinforcement of populist politics and authoritarian components. The scholarly debate states a "personalistic, centralised, technocratic style of leadership that bypasses representative institutions and uses the media and symbolism in populist ways" (Chacko, 2018, p. 542). In 2014, the BJP-led government under Prime Minister Modi restricted the political voice of ENGOs with international ties for "anti-national activities" as they were involved in environmental controversies (Chacko 2018, p. 557). The populist political argument of the national government drew on data produced by India's Intelligence Bureau according to which ENGOs had negatively impacted economic growth by 2%–3% of gross domestic product per annum (Chacko 2018, p. 557).

Caused by lacking decentralisation, democratic representation is particularly missing in the context of urban development politics (see Chapter 9, Singhal and Jain, this volume). Actor networks focused on city development are rather missing "city-based political and economic elites collude instead to share land rents" (Jaffrelot et al. 2019, p. 16).

12.2.5 Judiciary

In India, the judiciary has emerged as an important environmental actor since the late 1970s, due to the weakening of India's legislative and executive institutions (Jasanoff 1986). The role of judges in environmental protection depends on a country's legal and administrative systems (Carnwath 2011). In countries with relatively less developed administrative systems, the role of the court has become one of a "gap-filler" through the creative interpretation of constitutional guarantees (Desai and Sidhu 2010). The Indian Supreme Court has both a legal role as a court of law with constitutional powers as well as a public institution tasked with negotiating political and social pressures. Moreover, coupled with procedural developments through "public interest litigation" (PIL) in the 1970s and 1980s, the accessibility of different stakeholders to the Supreme Court has increased (Khosla and Padmanabhan 2018).

Evidence from the chapters depicts the ambiguous role of India's courts, both in promoting and constraining environmental protection at different junctures. The "activist" role of the Supreme Court and judges saw the development of PIL, which has become an important regulatory tool for pro-environment legislation (Desai and Sidhu 2010). The Forest Rights Act (2006) is one such piece of legislation. Das' chapter shows how the courts have also played a role in promoting environmental protection and capacity-building, for example, the strengthening of the rights of the *Gram Sabha* by the Supreme Court under the Panchayat Extension to Scheduled Areas (PESA). She also highlights the resulting conflicts between the judiciary and other institutions, such as the MOEF, whereby the judiciary has been perceived as encroaching on executive and legislative roles (see Chapter 5, this volume). In Gupta and Tyagi's chapter on water policy, however, there is also evidence of the courts counteracting the goals of resource protection, as the issue regarding the handling of river-linking shows (see Chapter 6, this volume).

12.2.6 Political-administrative capacity

Governing quality in India is mixed and predominantly not effective at the state and local level (Kohli and Singh 2013). As the chapters of the book dealing with the subsystems of forests, water, urban development, energy and climate change show, this is not different in environmental policy. Political and legislative centralisation of environmental governance and India's fiscal federalism have hindered environmental capacity-building at lower levels, both in India's states and at the local level (see Chapters 2, Swenden and Saxena, and 3, Jörgensen, this volume). In particular, capacity-building of resources for self-government at the local level, including expertise, administration and technical infrastructures, was severely hampered by lacking authority, financial transfers and financial revenues (Rao and Singh 2007). Lacking local capacity-building has "to some extent, been a self-fulfilling expectation, since decision-makers at that level have not been given the opportunity to learn by doing" (Rao and Singh 2007, p. 395).

According to the literature, the following conditions contribute significantly to weak environmental policy performance: low administrative capacity, a high degree of fragmentation, ineffective policy coordination, weak accountability, lack of knowledge and violations of the rule of law including patronage and corruption.

An administrative "capacity gap" marks India's institutional development which is insufficient in relation to population and economic growth and materialises, amongst others, in lower public sector employment (Kapur et al. 2018). Bandyopadhyay, Joshi and Quitzow point to the lack of personnel working on climate issues (see Chapter 7, this volume), and Jörgensen addresses the weak capacities of the State Pollution Control Boards (see Chapter 3, this volume). Administrative capacity in India to carry out policies is generally low; this includes the capability to cope with assigned tasks, to spend budgetary allocations and to mobilise knowledge (Kapur and Mehta 2007, p. 18). This is, in turn, caused by lacking resources, skills, ineffective recruitment structures and patronage. Patronage also diminishes accountability (Kapur and Mehta 2007).

Despite the centralised character of top-down governing, India's institutional landscape is caught in a high degree of fragmentation, which constrains not only implementation but also policy formulation and decision-making (Agrawal and Yokozuka 2002). Kapur et al. (2018) point to the horizontal fragmentation of energy, a policy field which belongs to the core priorities of India's development strategy. In 2017, energy policy involved the coordination between seven ministries, not to mention various public agencies involved. Policy failure in the water sector is related to fragmentation, as Gupta and Tyagi show. In many policy areas, the institutional landscape is quite dispersed and lacks interplay. Public and private institutions that "weave a 'thick' institutional web" are not highly effective in dealing with present and future long-term problems, environmental issues included (Kapur 2007, p. 31). Old institutions are sticky and path dependencies are being maintained. The institutional polity shields against pluralistic influence on public policy-making and leads to path dependence (Kapur 2007).

Lacking accountability is an Achilles' heel in India's political-administrative system, eminently at the local level, where locally elected officials are underrepresented (Rao and Singh 2007). Moreover, politicians and public service officials are barely held accountable. This is related to internal procedures in the public service, the practice of the judiciary, corruption and lacking information at the local level (Kapur and Mehta 2007, p. 19). Cognitive-informational capacities, the knowledge base and how it is used in policy processes (Jänicke 1997) are an important governance resource in the policy systems of climate, energy, forests, water and urban development. However, India's institutions struggle to provide access to information. Public action is still affected by the struggle between secrecy of information and an approach of open access to information in the public sector. Old modes of hierarchical governing which had previously relied on bureaucratic secrecy of information even towards lower levels of government of information are becoming less important while civil society and the science sector are producing and disseminating large amounts of knowledge (Kapur et al. 2018).

Despite this gloomy assessment of India's governance capacity, the ability to pursue public policies at the national level and in the subnational states vary and both levels can sometimes "manage highly complex tasks, but fail in executing simple ones" (Kapur et al. 2018, p. 5).

12.2.7 Economic liberalisation and the growth-first paradigm

In 1991, responding to economic and financial pressures, India's Congress-led government started the economic liberalisation process, which removed constraints on private sector activity and opened up the economy to the rest of the world. This raised questions regarding the government's role in the economy, where trade-offs exist between the market's promotion of economic growth and employment and the well-being of its citizens (Singh 2018). Although this process of economic liberalisation did not proceed as fast as, for example, as in Eastern European countries and was quite consensual among the large parties (Sil 2014), it fundamentally changed India's development strategy (Bhaduri and Nayyar 1996, p. 48). It also affected the environmental policy subsystems explored in this book. The Washington Consensus and the neo-liberal policy paradigm of the World Bank and the International Monetary Fund (IMF) at that time were not considerate of the implications economic liberalisation had for development, social inclusiveness, industrialisation and the environment in developing countries (Bhaduri and Nayyar 1996).

Economic liberalisation was a double edged sword. New regulatory frameworks in India's energy policy, which were set into place in the context of economic liberalisation, paved the way for the development and production of sustainable energy technologies in India as Bandyopadhyay, Joshi and Quitzow show in the energy chapter and they also spurred renewable energy policy in India's states as Jörgensen shows in her chapter.

Some features of India's political system posed particular challenges, which were not considered in the transition process in India. This included insufficient decentralisation, lacking accountability and transparency and weak knowledge transfer within the political-administrative system (Bhaduri and Nayyar 1996).

Neo-liberal ideas were on the other hand not commensurable with the ideas of participatory democracy and social justice which had developed as new policy paradigms in India's approaches to Joint Forest Governance (see Chapter 5, Das, this volume) and they were also not able to contribute significantly to problem-solving in the water sector (see Chapter 6, Gupta and Tyagi, this volume), let alone equity. Implemented in the context of urban politics and smart city policy and in the absence of democratic city governance they ran into danger to pave the way for "corporate" and elite city development (see Chapter 9, Singhal and Jain, this volume).

The neo-liberal policy paradigm fuelled India's growth-first paradigm, which had emerged in the 1980s triggered by India's economic crises. Previously, in the 1970s, Prime Minister Indira Gandhi had criticised "undivided attention to the maximisation of GNP" and called it "Growthmanship", concerned by the problematic social implications growth processes might cause in spurring social inequality and political unrest (Pilling 2018, p. 153). At the start of the 1980s, the development paradigm changed from "garibi hatao" to the growth-first model of development (Jaffrelot et al. 2019, p. 9). The chapters reveal the significance of India's growth strategies, particularly since economic liberalisation in 1991. In many of India's environmental policy subsystems, priorities of economic growth, the eradication of poverty and environmental protection came into conflict.

12.2.8 Civil society

Scholarship on environmental movements explores the ideas, strategies and political contexts that shape the actions and outcomes of such movements (O'Neill 2012a). In India, environmental movements are inextricably linked with democratic politics and environmental capacity-building, where there is need for politically conscious citizens and institutional arrangements for participation so that actors have a voice to secure environmental protection (Agrawal and Yokozuka 2002). Moreover, NGOs have had a positive influence on monitoring, data access and capacities.

India has the Gandhian tradition and collective experience of "nonviolent non-cooperation" which helped to undermine British colonial economic and political structures in the past and still presents a collective experience of successful social mass mobilisation (Sil 2014, p. 345). Ganguly's chapter gives prominence to India's various environmentalisms, whereby civil society organisations emerged around the idea of "environmentalism of the poor" (Guha and Martínez-Alier 1997) to highlight the livelihoods of poor communities and social justice in opposition to the elite interests of the state.

Ganguly's chapter looks at how civil society organisations in India have pursued various strategies of contestation, by putting pressure on the state, shining a light on ideas regarding livelihoods and justice, and forming new ideas regarding environmental protection. For example, improved enforcement came about under the Environmental Protection Act of 1986 (EPA), which was instrumental in giving citizens the ability to prosecute offenders under Indian environmental laws. Moreover, Fernandes, Jörgensen and Narayanan highlight the role of non-state experts, research organisations, NGOs and the corporate sector in producing climate-related knowledge and driving policy learning (see Chapter 8, this volume).

Additionally, such institutions and organisations can form a bridge with international actors, whereby transnational factors have shaped environmental movements around the world through transboundary knowledge transfer, transnational communication and networking (O'Neill 2012a). India's NGOs, including the Centre for Science and Environment and The Energy and Resources Institute (TERI) were, for example, instrumental in embedding the "common but differentiated responsibilities" approach in international climate policy (Fernandes, Jörgensen and Narayanan).

12.3 Features of environmental policy in India

Having outlined environmental institutions in India in the first section of this chapter, we now highlight three important features of environmental policymaking. The first is social inclusiveness, which emerges as one of the most important topics in India's development trajectory. Second, we look at environmental leapfrogging and the high potential of technological development to bring about environmental solutions. Third, we look at the role of ideas and knowledge in paradigmatic shifts. The final subsection of this chapter will then deal with the role of international factors in India's environmental politics and how India, in turn, influenced the global system.

12.3.1 Livelihoods and social inclusiveness

Lacking social inclusiveness is a major topic in India's environmental politics. The concept is laced throughout the sustainable development goals (SDGs), which aim to foster socially inclusive and environmentally sound development on a global scale. In India's environmental subsystems, social inclusiveness is often employed as a strategy by both state and non-state actors through decentralisation and participation, albeit to varying degrees. India's forest policy, for example, demonstrates the Indian state's capacity to "address environmental issues by becoming more inclusive" (Agrawal and Yokozuka 2002, p. 252).

Inclusiveness in environmental policy raises questions regarding rights, ownership of and access to resources (Ganguly; Das). India's forest and urban development policy subsystems provide examples of the use of social inclusiveness as a declaratory ideal, despite de facto exclusion of certain sections of society that depend on forests for their livelihoods. As Das shows in India's forest policy, the gradual paradigmatic policy shift over the last 30 years has headed towards more democratic and inclusive forest management. The reality, however, is that insufficient policy implementation has hampered the participation of forest communities. A departure from state control over forest land, which had dominated forest policy since Independence, is indicated in the National Forest Policy of 1988 and the inclusive approach brought about through the Joint Forest Management (JFM) scheme in 1990. While the JFM shared responsibility for protecting the forests with local communities, decision-making for resource management remained under the control of the Forest Department. With liberalisation, state land acquisition for commercial use led to the displacement of forest communities and conflicts regarding land use and rights. The recognition of the community forest rights lies at the core of paradigmatic change indicated by the Forest Rights Act (FRA) 2006, which gave a voice to marginalised communities, despite implementation shortcomings.

Lacking inclusiveness can also be seen in India's urban development policy, where inclusive participation is poised as an ideal in the push for higher living standards in India's smart cities. Evidence from Singhal and Jain shows, however, the creation of smart enclaves for the urban elite, while slum development has largely been neglected in state planning. In addition to gentrification, the use of information and communications technology (ICTs) is a double-edged sword, providing a tool to solve urban problems, but also potentially excluding those not digitally literate.

In the face of insufficient access to safe drinking water, India's Supreme Court holds that the right to water is a "Right to Life" under Article 21 of the Constitution, as amended in 1993. Gupta and Tyagi's chapter shows how the right to water has stimulated self-governance approaches on urban and rural local levels, and led to amendments in state laws, which have demanded the reconciliation between the fundamental right to water and water resources (see Chapter 6, this volume). In energy policy, Bandyopadhyay, Quitzow and Joshi highlight the Modi government's rural electrification scheme, announced in 2015, aims to connect 100% of village households. Electrification, however, does not tell us much about the affordability or quality of electricity, which is of relevance for poorer households. Looking at technology diffusion, programmes to increase cooking stove capacities have been relatively successful in urban areas, but barriers remain for the rural population, many of whom are largely still dependent on traditional fuels (see Chapter 7, this volume).

The exclusion of certain communities has often been contested by non-state and mobilised community actors. For example, Das' chapter on forests reveals how new actor networks of forest communities have developed in opposition to state actors; the former have made claims to India's forest on the basis of subsistence and livelihoods and the latter have tended to push development and national needs. Non-state actors, with the community-based Chipko movement often brought forward as a prime example, have been influential in helping rights-based discourse to gain salience, resulting in policy change, such as the FRA in

2006. Similarly, in India's water policy (Gupta and Tyagi), the privatisation of water since the 1990s has been contested by movements, such as the *Pani Panchayats* of Maharashtra which have aimed to encourage collective management and distribution of water. They include landless people by delinking water use from land ownership to ensure more progressive water governance (see Chapter 6, this volume).

12.3.2 Leapfrogging and carbon lock-in

India's energy and climate policy is torn between the growth-first development paradigm and approaches to green growth (Jörgensen 2017). The two conflicting directions are reflected in India's carbon lock-in, on the one hand, and policies approaching environmental leapfrogging, on the other. Examining the targets in the coal and renewables sector, the energy chapter by Bandyopadhyay, Quitzow and Joshi points to the coal dependence of India's energy sector and the need for rethinking India's energy narrative. India's political and administrative fragmentation, both horizontally and vertically, and lacking political will perpetuate the energy sector's carbon lock-in. Important constraints include a "multiplicity of actors with poor inter-ministerial and inter-governmental coordination, multiple targets with a focus on distribution instead of usage and inadequate institutional reviews of past policies" (see Chapter 7, Bandyopadhyay, Quitzow and Joshi, this volume).

The benefits of environmental leapfrogging is that it can "bypass the 'dirty' stages of economic growth through the use of modern technologies that use fewer resources and/or generate less pollution" (Perkins 2003, p. 187). Environmental leapfrogging to cleaner and greener technologies is an important option for developing countries to balance economic development with the protection of natural resources. Leapfrogging policies need to be adjusted to development priorities, technological capabilities, and be pursued as a long-term process, which is driven by national policy frameworks, political will and financial and technological assistance by developed countries (Perkins 2003, p. 186).

As the chapters about sustainable cities (see Chapter 9, Singhal and Jain, this volume), energy policy (Bandyopadhyay, Joshi and Quitzow) and climate policy (Fernandes, Jörgensen and Nayaranan) in this book show, India has a considerable policy output targeted at the development and dissemination of cleaner and greener technologies. This concerns policies and measures to provide decentralised electricity and cooking tools in rural areas, renewable energy in the farming sector and India's national and state-based renewable energy policies, as well as the ever more ambitious national renewable energy targets. Meanwhile, renewable energy has grid parity, as the authors of the energy chapter argue. Environmental leapfrogging initiatives are not only unleashed by the national level, but also in India's states, such as Gujarat (solar), Rajasthan (renewables) and Sikkim (organic farming) (see Chapter 3, Jörgensen, this volume). However, despite an array of ambitious goals and policies, leapfrogging is hardly pursued as a long-term process; future challenges are not taken into adequate consideration and the vast potential lying in the energy sector and urban development are not systematically addressed. India's programme to promote improved cookstoves based on traditional biomass (known in national vernacular Hindi as *Unnat Chula Abhiyan*) is just one example of an insufficient leapfrogging strategy, as the energy chapter shows.

Domestic think tanks and research organizations in India have produced impressive amounts of knowledge to address the potentials for environmental leapfrogging and low carbon development. The chapters about sustainable energy policy (Bandyopadhyay et al.) and sustainable city development (Singhal and Jain) show that policies triggering environmental leapfrogging could help to cope with the three vast challenges presented by demographic and urban development and the need for infrastructure, and could help to govern towards the sustainable development goals. Such approaches would involve large-scale infrastructure investments in renewable energy technology and cities. The policy proposals floating in India's policy streams of ideas seemingly lack policy advocacy among India's decision-makers and have difficulties to spread across India's fragmented political-administrative structures.

12.3.3 Paradigmatic change

Of the many factors that contribute to policy change and stasis, the concept of "policy paradigm" provides a lens to explore the role ideas and knowledge play in policy processes. Sets of ideas which are significant in policy processes can be called policy paradigms if they are widely shared by a group of involved actors in the policy subsystem (Baumgartner 2013). As environmental and climate policy are knowledge-intense policy fields and rely on continuously developing knowledge, this is a useful avenue of analysis to potentially identify shifts in the dominant policy paradigms. Two significant cases of shifts in policy paradigms were identified in the chapters of this book. In interaction with other factors, they took influence on the policy processes triggering policy change. The first concerns India's forest policy subsystem and the long-term struggle surrounding ownership, forest rights, use and management of India's forests. Smriti Das describes the shift in the forest policy paradigm towards democratic and inclusive forest governance, a process which spanned three decades and was triggered by changing actor constellations, including forest dwellers, activists, think tanks, scientists and the public administration. This paradigmatic policy shift gave rise to policy change and resulted in the introduction of India's JFM, which strengthened the rights of forest dwellers. Despite this, the social and democratic achievements of the forest law have been contested in the 2000s and under the BJP-led government under Prime Minister Modi.

The second case concerns the shift in India's climate policy paradigm, which occurred in the 2000s and is described by Fernandes, Jörgensen and Nayaranan in the climate policy chapter. Since the 1990s, Indian governmental actors, activists and think tanks widely shared the global "climate equity" paradigm, which implies that the problem of climate change was created by industrialised countries. Consequently, India's first priority as a developing country should be development and poverty reduction and these aims should not be hampered by emission reduction goals. Since 2007, knowledge, climate science insights disseminated by the Inter-governmental Panel Climate Change (IPCC), and a new domestic actor constellation spurred change in India's climate policy paradigm, thus raising the ideas of the co-benefits of climate action. This shift mattered in India's climate policy and opened a window of opportunity for explicit climate mitigation goals without giving up on the idea of climate equity.

A third example points to a different phenomenon observed in India's urban politics. Singhal and Jain highlight not just what there is but also what is missing: caused by lacking decentralisation and democratic representation, mature policy subsystems, including actor constellation which could shape new policy paradigms for India's city politics are missing.

12.4 India as a global environmental policy actor

India's interplay with global environmental and climate governance regimes is multi-faceted. It ranges from India acting as a naysayer in the international climate process to becoming a global leader in renewable energy. India has exerted cognitive leadership and aligned developing countries strategically around the climate justice approach. It has also adopted ideas from the global water, forest, and climate debates, fed in ideas, and India's rights based forest policy innovations have diffused internationally.

The first UN Conference on the Human Environment in Stockholm in 1972 was the starting point for the development of international environmental governance. Since then, various factors have triggered the diffusion of environmental institutions across the globe. The salience of environmental issues on the global agenda also spilled over to India's political agenda in the 1970s. Since economic liberalisation in 1991, problems and ideas discussed in international contexts resonated significantly with India's domestic debates, as the chapters of the book show. Serious concerns emerged related to the burdens which international obligations could impose on India's economic development and resources (see Chapter 4, Ganguly, this volume).

India has influenced the climate negotiation process and, likewise, the international climate regime has shaped India's domestic policy. In the 1990s, climate policy was regarded solely as an international diplomatic issue, which should not meddle in the country's national development strategy. This is indicated in the leading role India played in introducing the development first approach, known as "Common But Differentiated Responsibility" (CBDR), into the international treaties. Despite this, the international climate process and, in particular, the concerning reports published by the IPCC have facilitated domestic policy processes towards climate mitigation since the 2000s (Fernandes, Jörgensen and Narayanan; Raghunandan; Torney).

Raghunandan addresses the emergence of the international climate justice debate, which unfolded around the issue of historical emissions of developed countries and related responsibilities and obligations towards developing, and the burden-sharing between developed and developing countries (see Chapter 10, this volume). Since the 1990s, India has been an important global player in the international climate negotiations, with its influence ranging from cognitive and strategic leadership to defensive foot-dragging and obstruction.

Raghunandan explains that India "correctly grounded the issue of burden-sharing on equity", insisting that the developed countries should shoulder the emission reduction burden in the first place erecting "a strict firewall between developed and developing countries". Yet as India transitioned from a least developing country to a fast emerging economy in the 2010s its insistence on "more leeway for development" temporarily isolated it in the context of the developing countries and particular the small Island states (Raghunandan). Raghunandan points to the achievements but also pitfalls of the Paris Agreement, the latter lying in an asymmetric distribution of emission reduction burdens disadvantaging developing countries based on "the complete disregard of historical emissions" not apportioning the carbon budget. India's Nationally Determined Contribution (NDC) reflects the paradigm shift in India's climate policy (Raghunandan; Fernandes, Jörgensen and Nayaranan). Looking to the global arena, it was surprising when India committed to quite ambitious climate policy objectives in its NDA and launched an "International Solar Alliance" in November 2015 at the UNCCC Conference in Paris. The latter aims to provide a platform for policy learning, technology transfer and diffusion among countries with solar energy potentials (Bandyopadhyay, Joshi, and Quitzow, Jörgensen, Torney, this volume).

Bilateral and multilateral relationships with industrialised countries and international economic and aid organisations are supportive for domestic environmental policy capacity-building in newly industrialising countries (Weidner et al. 2002, p. 423). India's smart cities policy relies on bilateral financial partnerships with other countries and involves development organisations from abroad (Singhal and Jain). The bilateral cooperation between India and the EU, which has huge cooperation potentials regarding low carbon development was characterised by weak results in the 2000s (see Chapter 11, Torney, this volume). Divergence and convergence in the climate policy paradigms of the EU and India constrained collaboration between the two partners until 2016. Torney shows that the bilateral strategic partnership itself was not particularly helpful in spurring political climate cooperation. One of the issues was the EU's oversight regarding the topic of climate adaptation at the start of the 2000s. Another discordance concerned the issues of equity and differentiation. Torney traces India's position back to Indira Gandhi's speech at the UN Conference on the Human Environment in Stockholm in 1972, in which she defended the right of developing countries to pursue economic development and described poverty as "the greatest polluter". She also challenged the emerging discourse in industrialised countries, which held that the root of environmental degradation was excessive industrialisation, overpopulation and economic growth. Another facet explaining the weakness of the bilateral cooperation in the past lies, according to Torney, in Euroscepticism on India's side.

More recently, there has been an upswing in the "breadth and depth" (Torney) of the bilateral cooperation between the EU and India since 2016. This has materialised in the areas of climate, environmental and clean energy, and is related to a "gradual convergence" in Indian and European environmental policy paradigms.

Overall, India's domestic environmental politics and its role as a global environmental actor are marked both by impressive strides, but more so by worrying inaction. It is high time for government, civil society and corporate sector to shift environmental protection higher up the political agenda and to push for more significant moves towards a socially inclusive low-carbon development.

References

Agrawal, A., and Yokozuka, N., 2002. Environmental Capacity-Building: India's democratic politics and environmental management. *In:* H. Weidner, M. Jänicke, and H. Jörgens, eds. *Capacity building in national environmental policy. A comparative study of 17 countries.* Berlin, New York: Springer.

Baumgartner, F.R. 2013. Ideas and Policy Change. *Governance*, 26 (2), 239–258. doi:10.1111/gove.12007.

Bhaduri, A., and Nayyar, D. (1996). *The Intelligent Person's Guide to Liberalization.* New Delhi, Toronto: Penguin.

Carnwath, R., 2011. Institutional innovation for environmental justice. *Pace Environmental Law Review*, 29, 555.

Chacko, P., 2018. The right turn in India: Authoritarianism, populism and neoliberalisation. *Journal of Contemporary Asia*, 48 (4), 541–565.

Desai, B.H., and Sidhu, B., 2010. On the quest for Green Courts in India. *Journal of Court Innovation*, 3, 79.

Guha, R. and Martínez-Alier, J. (1997) *Varieties of Environmentalism: Essays North and South.* London: Earthscan. doi:10.4324/9781315070766

Hochstetler, K., 2012. Democracy and the environmental in Latin America and Eastern Europe. *In:* P.F. Steinberg and S.D. VanDeveer, eds. *Comparative environmental politics.* Cambridge, MA: MIT Press, 199–229.

Jaffrelot, C., Kohli, A., and Murali, K., Eds., 2019. *Business and politics in India.* New York: Oxford University Press.

Jänicke, M., 1997. The political system's capacity for environmental policy. *In:* M. Jänicke and H. Weidner, eds. *National environmental policies. A comparative study of capacity-building.* Berlin: Springer Verlag, 1–24.Jasanoff, S., 1986. Managing India's Environment: New Opportunities, New Perspectives. *Environment*, 28 (8), 12–16, 31–38.

Jörgensen, K., 2017. India: The global climate power torn between 'growth-first' and 'green growth'. *In:* R.K.W. Wurzel, J. Connelly, and D. Liefferink, eds. *The European Union in International Climate Change Politics. Still Taking a Lead?* London, New York: Routledge, Taylor & Francis Group, 270–283.

Kapur, D., 2007. Explaining democratic durability and economic performance. The role of India's institutions. *In:* D. Kapur and P.B. Mehta, eds. *Public institutions in India. Performance and design.* New Delhi: Oxford University Press, 28–64.

Kapur, D., and Mehta, P.B., Eds., 2007). *Public institutions in India. Performance and design.* New Delhi: Oxford University Press.

Kapur, D., Mehta, P.B., and Vaishnav, M., Eds., 2018. *Rethinking public institutions in India.* New Delhi: Oxford University Press.

Kashwan, P., 2013. The politics of rights-based approaches in conservation. *Land Use Policy*, 31, 613–626. doi:10.1016/j.landusepol.2012.09.009.

Kashwan, P., 2017. *Democracy in the woods. Environmental conservation and social justice in India, Tanzania, and Mexico.* New York, NY: Oxford University Press.

Khosla, M., and Padmanabhan, A., 2018. The Supreme Court. In: D. Kapur, P.B. Mehta, and M. Vaishnav, eds. *Rethinking public institutions in India.* New Delhi: Oxford University Press, 104–138.

Kohli, A., and Singh, P., 2013. Introduction: Politics in India – an overview. In: A. Kohli and P. Singh, eds. *Routledge handbook of Indian politics.* Milton Park, Abingdon, Oxon, New York: Routledge, 1–18.

Lijphart, A., 1996. The puzzle of Indian democracy. A consociational interpretation. *American Political Science Review*, 90 (2), 258.

Manor, J., 2016. India's States: The struggle to govern. *Studies in Indian Politics*, 4 (1), 8–21. doi:10.1177/2321023016634909.

Meadowcroft, J., 2012. Greening the state? In: P.F. Steinberg and S.D. VanDeveer, eds. *Comparative environmental politics.* Cambridge, MA: MIT Press, 63–89.

O'Neill, K., 2012a. The comparative study of environmental movements. In: P.F. Steinberg and S.D. VanDeveer, eds. *Comparative environmental politics.* Cambridge, MA: MIT Press, 115–142.

O'Neill, M., 2012b. Political parties and the "meaning of greening" in European politics. In: P.F. Steinberg and S.D. VanDeveer, eds. *Comparative environmental politics.* Cambridge, MA: MIT Press, 171–195.

Parikh, S., and Weingast, B.R., 1997. A comparative theory of federalism: India. *Virginia Law Review*, 83, 1593–1615.

Perkins, R., 2003. Environmental leapfrogging in developing countries. A critical assessment and reconstruction. *Natural Resources Forum*, 27 (3), 177–188. doi:10.1111/1477-8947.00053.

Pilling, D., 2018. *The growth delusion. The wealth and well-being of nations.* London: Bloomsbury Publishing.

Rao, M.G., and Singh, N., 2007. India's Federal Institutions and Economic Reform. In: D. Kapur and P.B. Mehta, eds. *Public institutions in India. Performance and design.* New Delhi: Oxford University Press, 351–405.

Sáez, L., 2002a. *Federalism without a centre. The impact of political and economic reform on India's federal system.* 1st ed. New Delhi [u.a.]: Sage.

Sáez, L., 2002b. *Federalism without a centre. The impact of political and economic reform on India's federal system.* Thousand Oaks, CA: Sage Publications.

Sharma, C.K., and Swenden, W., 2018. Modi-fying Indian federalism? Center-State relations under Modi's tenure as Prime Minister. *Indian Politics & Policy*, 1 (1). doi:10.18278/inpp.1.1.4.

Sil, R., 2014. India. In: J. Kopstein, M. Lichbach, and S.E. Hanson, eds. *Comparative Politics.* Cambridge, UK: Cambridge University Press, 339–390.

Singh, N., 2018. Reforming India's institutions of public expenditure governance. In: D. Kapur, P.B. Mehta, and M. Vaishnav, eds. *Rethinking public institutions in India.* New Delhi: Oxford University Press.

Sinha, A., 2019. India's porous state: Blurred boundaries and the evolving business-state relationship. In: C. Jaffrelot, A. Kohli, and K. Murali, eds. *Business and politics in India.* New York: Oxford University Press, 50–94.

Steinberg, P.F., and VanDeveer, S.D., Eds., 2012. *Comparative environmental politics.* Cambridge, MA: MIT Press.

Weidner, H., Jänicke, M., and Jörgens, H., Eds., 2002. *Capacity building in National environmental policy. A comparative study of 17 countries.* Berlin, New York: Springer.

Index

Note: **Bold** page numbers refer to tables; *italic* page numbers refer to figures and page numbers followed by "b" and "n" denote boxes and endnotes respectively.

Aamodt, S. 169
actors and ideas 6–7
adaptive water governance **112**
aggregate technical and commercial (AT&C) 149
Agrawal, A. 245
Agriculture Demand Side Management (AgDSM) 140
Air Act 68
Albino, V. 180
All India Services 24
animal husbandry programmes 65
anthropocentrism 61
area-based development (ABD) 186, *186*, **188**
Ashoka Trust for Research in Ecology (ATREE) 74
Asian Institute of Transport Development (AITD) 141
Atal Mission for Rejuvenation and Urban Transformation (AMRUT) 180

Bandyopadhyay, K.R. 12
Bawa, K.S. 104
Bharatiya Janata Party (BJP) 14, 205
big boys' club 220
Billion Units (BU) 140
Biological Diversity Act (2002) 70
bluewater **112**
Bombay Natural History Society (BNHS) 65
build, own, operate, transfer (BOOT) agreement 119
bureaucratic organisation 63
Bureau of Energy Efficiency (BEE) 138
bus rapid transit system (BRTS) 190–191

carbon lock-in 4–5, 10, 159, 160–161, 165, 169, 253–254
Ciecierska-Holmes, N. 14
central coalition government 35
Central Electricity Authority (CEA) 145
Central Electricity Regulatory Commission (CERC) 148
Central Empowerment Committee (CEC) 96
Central Ground Water Authority (CGWA) 116
Central Ground Water Board (CGWB) 116
Centrally Sponsored Schemes 22, 23
Central Pollution Control Board 42, 45
Central Social Welfare Board (CSWB) 64
Central Water Commission (CWC) 121
Centre for Development and Environment Policy (CDEP) 74
Centre for Science and Environment (CSE) 74
centre-state conflict on land acquisition 30–31b
Chipko movement 65, 94, 252
civil society 6, 48, 61–62, 169, 192, 242, 250–251; actors 91, 246; emergency and return of (1970–1980) 66–69; *see also* state and civil society
civil society organisations (CSOs) 11, 60; campaign organisations 76, **78**; CBOs 73–74, **78**; conservation organisations 76–77, **78**; SMO 75–76, **78**; Think tanks 74–75, **78**
Clean Development Mechanisms (CDMs) 161

260 Index

Climate Action and the Paris Agreement 236
climate change, ministries (2014) **147**
climate equity paradigm 254
climate policy process 50–52, 253, 256; advocacy coalition 168–169; biofuels 215–216; climate-denier countries 206; climate negotiations, Paris 205–209; co-benefit principle 170; developing domestic (2007–2013) 163–164; domestic factors 159–160; electric vehicles 217–218; emergence (1990–2006) 162–163; environmental regulation 220; environment regulation, trends in 218–219; FCCC negotiations 208; forward looking perspective 210; geo-political realm 207; impacts in India 204–205b; INDCs 211–218; influential factors 160–162; investment 212–213; knowledge, agency and policy 166–167; knowledge agencies 167–168; linear projects 214, 215; PA context 209–211; phases 170–171; policy change (2014–2018) 164–166; policy stability/change 170; polluter pays 210; significant initiatives 217–218; third-world critique 168; UNFCCC process 161–162
climate proofing **112**
coal-based energy mix 5
Coal of India (CIL) 149
Coal Regulatory Authority (CRA) 149
Coastal Regulatory Zones (CRZ) 219
co-benefit principle 164, 170
coca-cola case 119b
common but differentiated responsibility (CBDR) 162, 206, 55
common property resource (CPR) 97
community-based organisations (CBOs) 73–74, 180
Compensatory Afforestation Management and Planning Authority (CAMPA) 96
competitive federalism 244
Copenhagen Summit 208
compressed natural gas (CNG) 48
Confederation of Indian Industries (CII) 169
Conference of Parties (CoP) 104, 162–163
Constitutional Amendment Act (CAA) 178
Council of Scientific and Industrial Research (CSIR) 167
Council on Energy, Environment and Water (CEEW) 74, 216

Das, S. 12
decentralisation 14, 54, 89, 97, 126–127, 242–243
Deep Ecology approaches 61
demand *vs.* supply 145
democracy 102, 241, 245–246
Department of Environment (DOE) 67
designated consumers (DCs) 138
Domestic Efficient Lighting Programme (DELP) 139
Draft National Energy Policy (2017) 165

Earth Summit 70
economic liberalisation 3, 11, 47, 95–97, 178, 249–250, 255
ecosystem people 90
Electricity Act (2003) 137, 148
Electricity Regulatory Commissions Act (1998) 148
emergence 4
empowerment local level 94, 103, 192, 193, 243–244
Energy Conservation Act (2001) 50, 141
energy conservation building codes (ECBC) 139
energy governance, SDG7: electricity sector 149–150; institutional capacity, policy-making 146, 148–149; PNGRB 148; supply and demand 144–145
energy-saving certificates (ESCerts) 139
environmental capacity-building 241
Environmental Impact Assessment (EIA) 71, 116
environmental innovations: agriculture 47; clean air 48; climate policy 50–52; low-carbon development 49–50; planning processes 51; water policy 48–49
environmentalism 62
environmental leapfrogging 7–8
environmental policy-making: global, actor 255–257; leapfrogging/carbon lock-in 253–254; livelihoods and social inclusiveness 251–253; paradigmatic change 254–255
Environmental Protection Act of 1986 (EPA) 251
environmental regulations 4
Environment Protection Act (EPA) 19, 68, 116
EU Emissions Trading Scheme (EU ETS) 234
European Economic Community (EEC) 225

European vs. Indian policy paradigms 230; mutual neglect 231
European Investment Bank (EIB) 235
European policy paradigm 226–228

Factories Act (1948) 20, 65
federal system: central hierarchy 35–36; centre-state relations, coordination on environmental issues by legislative actors 28–29; centre-state relations, executive coordination on environmental issues 24–28; environmental competencies 18–19; intergovernmental coordination, need for 21–23; intergovernmental coordination, practice of 23–24; legislative competencies 20; paradigm shift 19
Fernandes, D. 13
Finance Commission report 35
Forest Act (1927) 20, 65, 90
Forest Conservation Act (1980) 25, 97, 121
forest cover 90, 214
forest governance: carbon sink 105; civil society actors 91; climate change 104–105; colonial period 89; colonial/post-colonial development phase 92–94; complexity of 91–92; economic liberalisation, (post-1980) 95–97; forest rights 97–99; locals/indigenous communities 93; NDA 102–103; participatory management 94; policy subsystem 105–107; scientific definitions 90; tribal/non-tribal communities 91; tribals/forest dwellers 93
Forest Policy of India 89
Forest Rights Act (FRA) 12, 70, 76, 247, 252; implementation of 100, *100*, **101**; objectives 99b; uncertainties 102
fossil fuel-based energy systems 5

Ganguly, S. 11
German federal politics 50
Gesellschaft für Internationale Zusammenarbeit (GIZ) 193
global environmental governance 8
Godavarman case 96b
government institutions 4
Government of Gujarat (GoG) 49
Government of India (GoI) 134
grade pricing system 122
greenhouse gas (GHG) 47, 205
greenhouse gas emissions (GHGE) 158

Greenhouse Gas Inventories (GGIs) 52
Green India Mission 104
Green Rating for Integrated Habitat Assessment (GRIHA) 75, 139, 179
green water **112**
grey/black water **112**
groundwater law 118–120
Grow More Food campaign 93
growth first paradigm 6, 13, 46, 96, 249–250
Growthmanship 250
Gupta, J. 12

Harvey, D. 183
Haydock, K. 61
Heritage City Development and Augmentation Yojana (HRIDAY) 180
Hollands, R.G. 180
Housing and Lands Rights Network (HLRN) 193
Human Development Index (HDI) 3, 175

inclusive development **112**, 114
inclusive growth **112**, 114, 164
India–EU relations on environment and climate change: another false start 233–234; climate dialogue on paper 232; difficulties 236–237; major emitter 237
Indian Administrative Services (IAS) 24
Indian Climate Research Programme (ICRP) 167
Indian Council for Research on International Economic Relation (ICRIER) 193
Indian Easement Act (1882) 118
Indian Forest Services (IFS) 24
Indian Institute of Science (IISc) 74
Indian Institutes of Technology (IITs) 167
Indian policy paradigm 228–230
Indian National Congress (INC) 102
Indian water governance 12
India's National Ambient Air Quality Standards (NAAQS) 42
India's Smart Cities Mission 13
Indira Gandhi National Forest Academy (IGNFA) 74
Indo-European Water Forum 235
information and communication technology (ICT) 180, 252
institutions and actors 5–6; capacity gap 248; centralisation and decentralisation, India's federal system 242–243; civil society 250–251; civil society actors 246;

Index

democracy/environmental governance 245–247; economic liberalisation, growth-first paradigm 249–250; inter-governmental processes 247; judiciary 247–248; lacking empowerment of the local level 243–244; political-administrative capacity 248–249; political stability, transition 244–245; transition process 250
Integrated Power Development Scheme (IPDS) 149
integrated river basin development and management (IRBDM) 122
integrated water resource management **112**
Intended Nationally Determined Contributions (INDCs) 51, 133, 161, 209
Inter-governmental Panel on Climate Change (IPCC) 158, 206, 255
international context 13–14
International Monetary Fund (IMF) 249
international thermonuclear experimental reactor (ITER) 232
inter-state river water disputes 31–32, 32–34b

Jain, S. 13
Jänicke, M. 241, 243
Jasanoff, S. 63
Jawaharlal Nehru National Solar Mission (JNNSM) 51
Jawaharlal Nehru National Urban Renewal Mission (JNNURM) 179
Joint Declaration on a Clean Energy and Climate Partnership 234
Joint Forest Management Committee (JEMC) 103
Joint Forest Management Programme (JFM) 95, 252
Joint Parliamentary Committee (JPC) 99
Jörgensen, K. 11, 13, 14, 137, 140
Joshi, M. 12
judiciary 14, 66, 96, 242, 245, 247–248

Kapur, D. 248
Kerala Groundwater Act (2002) 119b
Kisan Urja Suraksha evam Utthaan Mahabhiyan (KUSUM) 140
Kyoto Protocol (KP) 206

Land Acquisition Rehabilitation and Resettlement (LARR) Act 30–31b
land-related water rights 126
Leadership in Energy and Environmental Design (LEED) 139

leapfrogging 5, 7–8, 52–53, 150, 191–193, 253–254
least developed countries (LDCs) 206
legacies of colonial rule 5
Light Emitting Diode (LED) 50
liquefied petroleum gas (LPG) 134, 136
livelihoods 5, 251–253; and social inclusiveness 7
local community associations (LCAs) 192
low-carbon development 141
low-carbon development, SDG7: energy efficiency, benefits 143; issues 150–151; multiple benefits 143–144; renewable energy, benefits 142–143

McCarthy, J.D. 75
metropolitan planning committees (MPCs) 178
Millennium Development Goals (MDGs) 133
Minister of Environment and Forests (MoEF) 67, 116, 168, 246
Ministry of Drinking Water 23
Ministry of Tribal Affairs (MoTA) 99
Ministry of Urban Development (MoUD) 23, 189
monoculture forest plantations 214
Mundari khuntkatti 94

Narayanan, N.C. 13
Narmada Bachao Andolan (NDA) 76
National Action Plan on Climate Change (NAPCC) 50, 116, 137, 163, 178
National Advisory Council (NAC) 103
National Alliance of People's Movements (NAPM) 76
National Ambient Air Quality Monitoring Programme (NAMP) 45
National Biogas and Manure Management Programme (NBMMP) 136
National Board for Wildlife (NBWL) 72
National Committee on Environmental Planning and Coordination (NCEPC) 67
National Forest Policy (1988) 12
National Green Tribunal (NGT) 72, 219
National Institute of Urban Affairs (NIUA) 193
Nationally Determined Contributions (NDC) 14, 137, 203, 256
National Mission for Enhanced Energy Efficiency (NMEEE) 138
National Mission for Strategic Knowledge of Climate Change (NMSKCC) 167

National Solar Mission (NSM) 137
National Thermal Power Corporation (NTPC) 71
National Urban Transport Policy (2006) 178
National Water Board (NWB) 116
National Water Commission (NWC) 121
National Water Framework (NWF) Bill 121
National Water Mission 51, 217
National Water Resources Council (NWRC) 116
neo-colonial mode 5
neoliberal 6; economic rules 6
neo-liberal policy paradigm 250
Nexus approach 112
non-governmental organisations (NGOs) 160
Nuclear Suppliers Group 213

oiling and gluing 24
Organic Mission 47
Organization for Economic Co-operation and Development (OECD) 163, 241

Panchayat Extension to Scheduled Areas (PESA) 98
pani panchayats 120
Parikh, S. 48
Paris Agreement (PA) 203
partisan federalism 244
party system 244–245
path-dependencies 10, 112, 161
Perform, Achieve and Trade (PAT) 50, 138
Petroleum and Natural Gas Regulatory Board (PNGRB) 148
planetary boundaries 112
PM's Council on Climate Change (PMCCC) 168
policy change 9–10, 164–166
policy paradigms 9, 162–163, 226–230, 254
policy subsystems 7–10, 12–14, 40, 105–107, 169, 242–244, 254, 255; climate 160, 166, 170; environmental 249, 250
political administrative capacity 11, 14, 55, 248–249
Pradhan Mantri Sahaj Bijli Har Ghar Yojana 135
Press Information Bureau (PIB) 214
Prevention of Cruelty of Animals Act (1960) 66

Prime Minister's Office (PMO) 168
public good 112
public interest litigation (PIL) 70, 247
public-private partnership (PPP) 103

Quitzow, R. 12

Raghunandan, D. 13, 255, 256
Randeria, S. 63
redistributive welfarism 135
Reducing Emission from Deforestation and Forest Degradation (REDD) 104
riparians 112
River Basin Authority (RBA) 123
river basin management approach 124
River Boards Act (1956) 124
role play, India's states: bottom-up approaches (see environmental innovations); constitutional responsibilities 55; economic and political role 40; economic stagnation 39; environmental innovations (see environmental innovations); environmental leapfrogging 52–53; environmental policy 41; federal competencies 41; governmental/nongovernmental proponents 45; health risks 44; laboratories for experimentation 55; legislators 41; liberalisation 43; national and subnational agencies 42; Policy learning, emulation and diffusion 53–54; policy subsystems 40; race-to-the-bottom 43–46; significant decentralized traits 39; thematic focuses 43

Save Mon Region Federation and Anr. v. Union of India and Ors., Appeal No. 39/2012 127n1
Saxena, R. 11
Schmid, G. 137
Seidler, R. 104
seventh Goal of the 2030 Agenda (SDG7) 133; access to power 135–136; clean cooking 135–136; energy efficiency, agriculture 140; energy efficiency, buildings 139; energy efficiency, industry 138–139; energy efficiency, transport sector 140–141; energy governance (see energy governance, SDG7); low-carbon development (see low-carbon development, SDG7); renewable energy 137–138; targets 133

264 Index

Singhal, S. 13
Smart Cities Mission (SCM) 176; three cities, comparison of **188**
smart sustainable cities 180–181; environmental sustainability 184–185; social inclusiveness 185–186; urbanisation 174 (*see also* urban development policy)
social inclusiveness 7, 185–187, 251–252
social movement organisation (SMO) 75
Solar Energy Corporation of India Ltd. (SECI) 137
solar parks 137–138
solar photovoltaic (SPV) 212
Srivastava, H. 61
Standards and Labelling (S&L) programme 139
State Action Plans on Climate Change (SAPCC) 50, 217
state and civil society: complexity of 64; CSO's, interaction with state 72–73; CSO typology, relationship with state; emergence of societal forces 60; emergency and return of civil society (1970–1980) 66–69; environmental philosophies 61; environmental space 60; fences and fines 63, 79; global environmental agenda 69; Institutionalizing environmentalism (1950–1960) 64–66; Liberalizing environmentalism (1990–2000) 69–71; strategies for contestation 64; Subverting environmentalism (2000–2019) 71–72; technocratic approaches 80
State Environment Impact Assessment Authority (SEIAA) 72
State Pollution Control Boards (SPCBs) 42
State Regulatory Electricity Commission (SERC) 148
Stensdal, I. 169
Sterlite Industries (India) (SIIL) 72
subnational states 11, 40, 43, 47, 49, 50, 243, 249
supply targets, key energy 145b
surface *vs.* groundwater 124
sustainable development **112**
Sustainable Development Goals (SDGs) 113, 251
Swachh Bharat Mission – Urban (SBM-U) 180
Swenden, W. 11, 39

The Energy and Resource Institute (TERI) 74, 167, 179, 251
theoretical concepts: path dependencies 10; policy change 9–10; policy paradigms 9; policy subsystems 8–9, 12
transboundary rivers 124
Twenty-first Conference of the Parties to the UNFCCC (COP-21) 234, 237n1
Tyagi, R. 12

Ujjwala Scheme 217–218
United Nations Conference on Environment and Development (UNCED) 70
United Nations Framework Convention on Climate Change (UNFCCC) 51, 161, 205
United Progressive Alliance (UPA) 245
Unnat Chula Abhiyan 254
Unruh, G.C. 159
urban development policy: ABD 186; capital investments, scarcity 183–184; civic actors 192–193; environmental leapfrogging 191–193; Five-Year Plans **177**; Government change (2014) 179–180; ICTs 184; implementation processes 194; inequitable distribution of government support 185; land management and green infrastructure 185; local urban governance 182–183; long-term climate change risks 184–185; not-for-profit groups 193; post-economic liberalisation (1991) 176, 178–179; post-independence era 176; potential gentrification 186; scalability for megacities 190–191; similarities and differences **181**; three cities, SCM 187–189; urban service delivery mechanism 186–187
urban local bodies (ULBs) 117, 178
Urban Services Environmental Rating System (USERS) 179
Uttarakhand Transformation Party (UKPP) 244

voluntary organisations(VOs) 64

watch-dog functions 76
Water Act (1988) 68
Water Disputes Act (1956) 117
Water for Life 122
water governance: adaptive **112**; administrative scale 125–126;

aspects 113; challenges 111, 123–126; climate change 111, 125; crises of water 112; decentralisation of water policy 126–127; ecosystem services **112**; environmental clearance 120–121; evolution of water law/policy, India since (1970) 115–116; Goal 6 114; groundwater law 118–120; irrigation 118; land-related water rights 126; new water regime 121–123; ownership issues 125; pollution 125; post-independence development 115; surface *vs.* groundwater 124; water-related bills 126

Water Ministry's Groundwater Bill (2016) 122
Water (Prevention and Control of Pollution) Act (1974) 119
water-related bills 126
Water Users Associations (WUAs) 118
Weidner, H. 241, 243
Weingast, B.R. 48
Wild Life Protection Act (1972) 25

Yokozuka, N. 245

Zald, M.N. 75

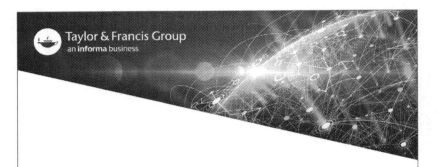

Printed in the United States
By Bookmasters